T0305317

New Directions in Productivity
Measurement and Efficiency Analysis

New Directions in Productivity Measurement and Efficiency Analysis

Counting the Environment and Natural Resources

Edited by

Tihomir Ancev

School of Economics, University of Sydney, Australia

M.A. Samad Azad

Tasmanian School of Business and Economics, University of Tasmania and School of Economics, University of Sydney, Australia

Francesc Hernández-Sancho
University of Valencia, Spain

Cheltenham, UK • Northampton, MA, USA

Published by
Edward Elgar Publishing Limited
The Lypiatts
15 Lansdown Road
Cheltenham
Glos GL50 2JA
UK

Edward Elgar Publishing, Inc.
William Pratt House
9 Dewey Court
Northampton
Massachusetts 01060
USA

A catalogue record for this book
is available from the British Library

Library of Congress Control Number: 2016962581

This book is available electronically in the **Elgar**online
Economics subject collection
DOI 10.4337/9781786432421

ISBN 978 1 78643 241 4 (cased)
ISBN 978 1 78643 242 1 (eBook)

Typeset by Servis Filmsetting Ltd, Stockport, Cheshire
Printed and bound by CPI Group (UK) Ltd, Croydon, CR0 4YY

Contents

Contributors

Mahmuda Akter is a PhD candidate at the Tasmanian School of Business and Economics of the University of Tasmania. Her research focuses on valuing and accounting for natural capital on Australian farms, and interests include environmental and resource economics; measurement of productivity and efficiency in agriculture sector; and sustainable development of agriculture. From 2007 to 2015, she worked as an agricultural economist at the Bangladesh Agricultural Research Institute, successfully completing a number of projects, including: the adoption of new agricultural technologies at farm level; efficiency and productivity analysis of cereal crops; and the impacts of modern agricultural technologies on rural livelihoods. Akter received her undergraduate degree in agricultural economics from the Bangladesh Agricultural University and her masters from the Bangabandhu Sheikh Mujibur Rahman Agricultural University, Bangladesh.

Tiho Ancev is an Associate Professor in environmental and resource economics at the School of Economics, University of Sydney, where he teaches and researches in the areas of environmental economics, natural resource economics and water economics and policy. He has published widely on topics related to economics of water use and its environmental consequences (for example salinity, water depletion), and on economics of air and water pollution. He has co-authored several articles in the area of environmentally adjusted productivity and efficiency measurement.

M.A. Samad Azad is a postdoctoral research fellow at the Tasmanian School of Business and Economics of the University of Tasmania (UTAS), having earlier worked as a research associate in the Department of Agricultural and Resource Economics and the School of Economics of the University of Sydney. As an agricultural economist he also worked at the Bangladesh Rice Research Institute and the Department of Agricultural Extension within the Bangladesh Ministry of Agriculture. Samad earned his PhD in agricultural resource economics from the University of Sydney in 2012. His primary research focuses on developing methods for environmentally adjusted productivity and efficiency measurement. Samad is currently involved in a project that aims to develop a conceptual framework for measuring natural capital accounting at farm level. His papers have appeared in wide range of peer-reviewed journals, including *Ecological Economics, Journal of Environmental Management, Water Resources Management, Journal of Developing Areas* and *Water Economics and Policy.*

Águeda Bellver-Domingo has a degree in environmental science from the University of Valencia. She completed a masters in water resources management and is currently a PhD student in water economics. She has been a member of the University of Valencia's Water Economics Group since 2011. Her research is focused on the economic valuation of environmental goods and services and their integration into decision-making processes through various methodologies.

H. K. Edmonds has completed a PhD in environmental science through the Australian Rivers Institute at Griffith University, Queensland. Her research focuses on spatial analysis of urban freshwater ecosystems, and she has also worked extensively in biodiversity assessment.

Mark Eigenraam is a Senior Environmental Accounting Specialist with the Victorian Department of Environment, Land, Water and Planning (DELWP) and director at the Institute for the Development of Environmental-Economic Accounting (IDEEA). Since the mid-1990s, he has played a leading role in the development and application of environmental markets and ecosystem accounting. His work has ranged from training landholders (farmers) to participate in environmental markets, to contributing to global initiatives in environmental-economic accounting. Mark has applied his insights and experience to establishing environmental markets to inform Australia's approach to environmental-economic accounting, and produced a world first set of experimental ecosystem accounts for Victoria. He continues to develop new systems and processes to produce and publish environmental-economic accounts.

Rolf G. Färe has been a Professor of Economics and Applied Economics at Oregon State University since 1998. As a former student of Ronald W. Shephard, his main research interest is in production theory. In particular, he models multi-output technologies in both static and dynamic settings. These have proven to be especially useful in the development of tools to measure performance, especially in an activity analysis or DEA framework. Rolf has honorary doctorates from Lund University and Gothenburg University, and his other awards include Web of Science most highly cited in economics and finance and an entry in *Who's Who in Economics.*

Kevin J. Fox works primarily in the field of economic measurement, with a focus on productivity and prices. He is a Fellow of the Academy of the Social Sciences in Australia, Fellow of the Society for Economic Measurement, and a Member of the NBER-affiliated US Conference on Research on Income and Wealth. He is an elected member of the Australasian Standing Committee of the Econometric Society; elected council member of the International Association for Research on Income and Wealth; an associate editor of the Journal of Productivity Analysis; director of the UNSW Centre for Applied Economic Research; and leads the UNSW Business School's Real Estate Initiative. In 2016 he was appointed as an advisor to the Australian Treasury, and in 2015 he was elected as a member of the Policy and Advocacy Committee of the Academy of the Social Sciences in Australia, continuing a career-long commitment to research-led public policy engagement. He chaired the Australian Bureau of Statistics (ABS) 16th Series Consumer Price Index Review Advisory Group in 2009–10, and is a member of the ABS Methodology Advisory Committee and Productivity Measurement Reference Group. He was a member and subgroup leader of the Expert Working Group of the Australian Council of Learned Academies on productivity 2012–14 that reported to the Prime Minister's Science, Engineering and Innovation Council.

Shawna Grosskopf is Professor Emerita in the economics department at Oregon State University (OSU). She received her PhD from Syracuse University in 1977 and joined OSU in 1998 after 21 years at Southern Illinois University. Her research interests include public economics, performance measurement, environmental economics and health economics. Recent research has included work on the relative performance of charter schools using directional distance functions to model and measure productivity in the presence of environmental byproducts, assessing performance in the health sector. She is an associate editor of the *Journal of Productivity Analysis* and the *Data Envelopment Analysis Journal*, and is on the editorial board of *Health Care Management Science*. She has published nine books and over 190 peer-reviewed journal articles. She has featured in the ISI Web of Knowledge 250 most cited scholars in economics and finance since 2005 and in *Who's Who in Economics* since 2002. Other awards include Kerstin Hesselgren Chair awarded in honour of the first woman in the Swedish parliament and an honorary doctorate from the University of Gothenburg. She has received grants from USEPA, USDA, the New Zealand Foundation for Research, Science and Technology, and the Ford Foundation.

Atakelty Hailu is currently an Associate Professor at the University of Western Australia. Prior to joining UWA, he worked at the University of

Alberta (Canada) and Alemaya University (Ethiopia). His primary areas of research include productivity and efficiency analysis in the presence of undesirable outputs, agricultural economics, environmental policy, economics of recreational fishing, and bioeconomic and agent-based modelling.

Francesc Hernández-Sancho has a PhD in environmental economics and is a professor at the University of Valencia, where he is head of the Water Economics Research Group and director of the Water Management masters programme. He is also a member of the Management Committee of the International Water Association (IWA) Specialist Group on Statistics and Economics, and leader of the IWA Water Economics Working Group. His research focuses on water tariffs and the economic efficiency of water utilities. He has also worked on economic feasibility studies of wastewater treatment and water reuse projects including the economic valuation of externalities. Francesc has taken part in more than 25 research projects related to water management and water economics financed by the Spanish Government and the European Commission. He is associate editor of *Water Science and Technology*, *Water Science and Technology: Water Supply* and *Water Economics and Policy Journal*.

Viet-Ngu (Vincent) Hoang is Senior Lecturer in Economics at the School of Economics and Finance (Queensland University of Technology). His research areas include applied economics, environmental and ecological economics, agricultural economics, efficiency and productivity analysis, development economics, and health economics. His work has been published in leading journals, including *Journal of Environmental Economics and Management*, *Journal of Environmental and Resources Economics*, *Ecological Economics*, *Agricultural Economics*, *Agricultural Systems*, *Journal of Environmental Management* and *Environment and Development Economics*.

Neal Hughes is a senior economist with the Australian Bureau of Agricultural and Resource Economics and Sciences (ABARES). Since joining ABARES in 2006, he has undertaken research on a range of water, climate and agricultural productivity issues, with an emphasis on applied economic modelling and data analysis. In 2011 Neal was awarded an Australian Government Sir Roland Wilson Foundation PhD Scholarship. He holds an honours degree in economics from the University of Melbourne and a PhD in economics from the Australian National University.

William Ingram is at the start of a career in the environmental arena. After studying chemistry, he pursued research on heavy metal water pollution in the Indian city of Mumbai, where he worked with scholars from the Indian Institute of Technology to assess concentrations of certain heavy metals throughout Mumbai's wastewater. He also conducted research on the effectiveness of constructed wetland technology on heavy metal removal from wastewater, which further inspired him to focus on solutions to environmental problems. Will gained experience with the London-based NGO Forum for the Future before spending time under the tutelage of Birguy Lamizana-Diallo at UNEP, Nairobi. Here, he assisted with the work of the Global Programme of Action for the Protection of the Marine Environment from Land-Based Activities (GPA). He is currently working on assisting developing countries with the UN climate change negotiations and outlining the case for a zero-emissions world by providing policy research and support with the NGO Track 0. Alongside an interest in science communication, Will has a particular interest in water security, especially in vulnerable countries. He endeavours to research the interaction between science and policy, and how effective data collection can aid good governance of natural resources.

Hasneen Jahan is a professor in the Department of Agricultural Economics at the Bangladesh Agricultural University (BAU), Mymensingh. Hasneen's areas of specialization are environmental economics, agricultural economics, fisheries economics and rural livelihood. Hasneen completed her BSc Ag. Econ. (Hons) degree from BAU with a 1st, and in 1st position with gold medal. She has two masters degrees: in agricultural economics from BAU and in development economics from Ritsumeikan Asia Pacific University, Japan. Hasneen gained her PhD in the field of environmental economics from the University of Sydney, Australia, where she has also worked as a research fellow in the Department of Economics. She has a number of research papers in reputed journals and is also engaged in several national and international projects related to her research areas, including running the Shayaan Foundation charity organization which mainly works for the betterment of the education sector in Bangladesh.

Birguy Lamizana-Diallo is a development professional with broad interests and more than 20 years' work experience, including extensive knowledge of ecosystem and water resource management, environmental impact assessment, community involvement and capacity-building skills. She participated in the Training of Trainers (ToT) for decision makers on Integrated Water Resource Management (IWRM). She possesses a strong record of accomplishments in developing actions plans in IWRM for West and East African countries and coordinating partnerships. Birguy holds an engineering degree in water resources management and a doctorate in freshwater ecology in relation to environmental flows requirements. She has extensive working experience with river basin organizations, NGOs and community involvement in managing national parks and protected areas in West and Central Africa. Prior to joining the United Nations Office for Project Services (UNOPS) in 2009 and UNEP in 2012, she served as coordinator of the IUCN West Africa regional wetlands and water resources programme. Birguy has also worked with the Global Water Partnership (GWP) as regional coordinator for Africa water development and with the African Development Bank (AfDB) as technical advisor for their Water Partnership Programme Trust fund. Birguy is currently a programme officer in charge of wastewater management within the UNEP-Global Programme of Action for the Protection of the Marine Environment from Land-Based Activities (GPA). She has also coordinated UNEP's flagship project on the restoration of Lake Faguibine ecosystems in northern Mali, which attracted the interest of many development partners as well as substantial funding from donors. Birguy is also currently vice chair of the IUCN Commission of Ecosystem Management (CEM) in charge of Africa, drylands and wetlands thematic groups.

Kenton Lawson is a senior economist with the Australian Bureau of Agricultural and Resource Economics and Sciences (ABARES). Since joining ABARES in 1987, he has undertaken mathematical programming, economic modelling, numerical programming and spatial and statistical analyses across a broad range of agricultural and natural resource issues. Kenton holds an honours degree in mathematics and a masters in economics from the Australian National University.

Lisa Y.T. Lee is an environmental economist with interests in the fields of water and energy economics. Her PhD from the University of Sydney analysed the cost of environmental targets on irrigation industries in the Murray-Darling Basin in Australia and how water markets and irrigation technologies could help smooth structural adjustment in the industry. She has since conducted postdoctoral research at the University of New South Wales and the United Nations University in Japan in a variety of topic areas, including in salinity, biofuels, energy and wildlife trading. She currently works at the Productivity Commission – the Australian Government's independent research and advisory body.

C. A. K. Lovell is Honorary Professor in the School of Economics at the University of Queensland and a former editor of *Journal of Productivity Analysis*.

J. E. Lovell is a freelance researcher who holds a research masters degree from the School of Economics at the University of Queensland.

Chunbo Ma is currently an Associate Professor of Economics at the University of Western Australia (UWA). He was also an Australian Research Council DECRA Fellow (2013–15) and, prior to joining UWA, was a research fellow in the University of Michigan (2007–09). His primary research interests lie in energy, environmental, agricultural economics and policies. His recent work has focused on the adoption of green electricity and rooftop solar PVs in Australia and energy/climate policies in China.

Carl Obst is a director of the Institute for the Development of Environmental-Economic Accounting (IDEEA) and an Honorary Fellow of the University of Melbourne. From 2010 to 2013, he was the lead author and editor of the *System of Environmental-Economic Accounting* (SEEA), building on a long career working in national accounts, including five years as head of the Australian national accounts. His current work involves projects on environmental-economic accounting with the World Bank, the Food and Agriculture Organization of the UN (FAO), the UN Environment Programme (UNEP), the UN World Tourism Organization and several projects extending SEEA approaches to the corporate sector.

Carl A. Pasurka, Jr. is an economist with the National Center for Environmental Economics at the US Environmental Protection Agency, and an Adjunct Professor with the Schar School of Policy and Government at George Mason University. His current research focuses on cost and pro-ductivity issues associated with environmental regulations. In addition, he was an associate editor for the *Journal of Environmental Economics and Management* (1994–96) and has been an associate editor for *Energy Economics* since 2013.

Clevo Wilson is a Professor of Economics at Queensland University of Technology (QUT). He specializes in environmental, ecological, agricul-tural, energy, tourism and development economics with a special interest in using environmental valuation techniques, both revealed and stated, for policy decision-making. He has published widely in diverse topics includ-ing energy and water conservation, agriculture, aquaculture, eco-tourism and environmental sustainability. Clevo has a PhD in environmental and resource economics from St Andrews, Scotland; an MSc in econom-ics from Glasgow University; an MPhil in environment and develop-ment from Cambridge; and a BA in economics from the University of Peradeniya, Sri Lanka.

1. Introduction

**Tiho Ancev, M.A. Samad Azad and
Francesc Hernández-Sancho**

Measurement of productivity and efficiency of companies, institutions and various other enterprises is a well-defined area of economics. This area of research and practice, which started around the mid-1950s, is now a standard tool in national accounting and in various assessments of economic sectors or individual enterprises (Fried et al., 2008; Peacock et al., 2001).

The development of productivity and efficiency theory and practice has coincided with a period in human history that has perhaps witnessed the largest ever extent of anthropogenic environmental change. Consequently, environmental conditions and the effects that various human economic activities impose on the environment have become of key concern to society. Standard methods of productivity and efficiency analysis are, in general, not designed to consider these environmental considerations.

In response, the concept of environmentally adjusted productivity analysis and efficiency measurement has been rapidly developing since the early 1990s. This approach is addressing the need to account for environmental impacts from various economic activities in human society. This is becoming increasingly important as the environment and the ecosystem services it provides are significantly threatened by air pollution, land degradation, deterioration of water quality and biodiversity losses. In this light, a fundamental question is how to accommodate environmental effects into the standard practices for measuring productivity and efficiency. This book explores some new ways of addressing that question.

Over the recent years, there has been a growing debate in the literature about how to most effectively incorporate the environmental effects from production activities in economic models designed to measure productivity and efficiency (Färe et al., 2013; Kumar and Khanna, 2009; Zhou et al., 2008; Coelli et al., 2007; Ball et al., 2004). A variety of existing methodological approaches – including those based on index number theory, stochastic production frontier, and non-parametric approaches – have been adapted to serve the purpose of measuring environmentally adjusted efficiency of various units of observation (e.g. firms, industries, or countries). A number of recent papers have identified some drawbacks of the existing models and proposed alternative approaches to measure environmentally adjusted production efficiency (e.g. Abad, 2015; Azad and Ancev, 2014; Hoang and Thanh, 2013).

In addition, the UN Statistical Commission has recently adopted an international standard accounting approach – the System for Environmental-Economic Accounts (SEEA) – for incorporating environmental and natural capital into national accounting practices (European Commission et al., 2013). This has been followed by many national statistical offices that have started to incorporate environmental indicators in some components of national accounts.

This book offers a collection of chapters that address various conceptual, methodological and empirical aspects relevant to environmentally adjusted productivity and efficiency measurement. It provides a wide-ranging survey of the work on the intersection of environmental/natural resource economics and productivity analysis, which emphasizes the connection between the theory of economic efficiency and the measurement of environmental effects. The purpose of the book is to:

- take stock of the current state of environmentally adjusted productivity and efficiency literature;
- present some new approaches/methods that have been recently developed to estimate environmentally adjusted productivity and efficiency;
- present empirical studies that conduct environmentally adjusted productivity and efficiency measurements in a wide range of contexts.

The advances that this book is making are relevant to a broad array of applications, including air and water pollution, climate change, natural capital accounting, environmental regulation and the use of natural resources.

The book has a truly global appeal as it covers a range of empirical studies conducted in various countries across the globe – including Bangladesh, China, the US, Australia, Spain and Iceland – as well as comparisons across 32 Organisation for Economic Co-operation and Development (OECD) countries. This showcases the substantial international significance of the problems that this volume is addressing.

The book does not follow any particular structure, but the chapters are grouped in a logical sequence. At the outset, Chapter 2 provides an exhaustive overview of the environmentally adjusted productivity and efficiency models that have been reported in the economics literature. This is followed by a group of three chapters that address specific methodological issues. A significant amount of work in environmentally adjusted productivity and efficiency measurement has been done in the agricultural sector, which is reflected in this book, with Chapters 6, 7 and 8 focusing on measures of agricultural total factor productivity and on accounting for natural capital in agriculture. The municipal water supply and wastewater sector has also been subject to numerous efficiency analyses, and Chapters 9 and 10 focus on this sector. Chapters 11 and 12 present important international applications of environmentally adjusted productivity and efficiency methods.

This book is making a contribution to knowledge by pointing out various ways of articulating the environmental issues in productivity and efficiency models. In this way, it enhances conceptual and applied knowledge by improving our understanding of how to couple standard economic models and frameworks with indicators for environmental effects and natural resource use.

In addition, several chapters of the book have strong policy implications that will help policymakers around the world in addressing environmental problems in an efficient way. The models presented in this book are applicable to a wide range of economic sectors where the reduction of environmental pressures from economic activities is needed, desired or implemented by different policy strategies. In the context of natural resource management, the ultimate aim of the authorities is to sustainably manage environmental resources at local or regional levels, and to attain the best possible economic and environmental outcomes. Environmental goals in many countries around the globe are concerned with ensuring that natural and environmental resources are managed efficiently, both in terms of quantity and quality. To achieve these objectives, many countries are currently adopting ambitious regulations whose design could benefit from improved understanding of the interactions between environmental and economic performance, which is the focus of this volume.

Several types of audience were kept in mind when preparing this book. Researchers and scholars working in the area of productivity and efficiency analysis are obviously a key audience who will benefit from reading this book. This includes postgraduate students and, to a certain degree, upper-level undergraduate students. Another important audience is practising statisticians and national accountants, who will find some of the chapters highly relevant for their work. This book will also appeal to quantitatively minded policy professionals working in government departments and international institutions who are interested in productivity and efficiency measurement and in accounting for environmental effects. Some members of the wider economics, ecological and environmental professions will also find this book appealing as it articulates together two notions that are often seemingly irreconcilable: economic efficiency and environmental efficiency.

In what follows, we briefly introduce each of the remaining 11 chapters. Chapter 2 by Ancev, Azad and Akter provides a comprehensive review of the literature on environmentally adjusted productivity and efficiency since its inception in the early 1990s. This chapter also provides an overview of the key conceptual and methodological approaches that have been used in this literature. For those readers who are not familiar with the concepts of frontiers, distance or directional distance functions, or with the various productivity and efficiency indicators, this chapter will provide an excellent introduction that will make the rest of the book a much easier read.

Chapter 3 is authored by Färe, Grosskopf and Pasurka, and proposes a modification of the existing approaches to modelling joint production of good (desirable) and bad (undesirable) outputs in the context of pollution abatement. The chapter is motivated by the argument that traditional joint production models treat the process of transforming inputs into good and bad outputs as a black box, thereby clouding the crux of the problem. In order to investigate the consequences of this approach that ignores the transformation process, this chapter introduces a model of network technology that effectively looks inside the black box. It finds that the transformation process consists of a set of sub-technologies or sub-processes. After specifying both network and non-network models, the authors use a panel dataset of coal-fired power plants in the US to compare empirical results generated by the two specifications of the production technology. They find that the network models produce superior results.

This is followed by Chapter 4, authored by Fox and Lee, which focuses on the methodological problem of outliers in the data. In particular, the case where some firms may achieve relatively high/low levels of output due to environmental effects that are unrelated to their efficiency is examined. These firms may be treated as outliers. The chapter implements an innovative approach to outlier detection in two separate case studies, using data for a fishery and an irrigated agriculture industry. The detection of outliers allows either for an explicit adjustment of the scores for environmental factors or the exclusion of the outliers, and hence an implicit adjustment of the scores that would have otherwise resulted. This is very important for the quality assurance of sample data that forms the basis from which many agencies undertake productivity comparisons.

Chapter 5, authored by Edmonds, Lovell and Lovell, makes a methodological contribution by presenting procedures for creating ecological indexes that are invaluable as a representation of environmental conditions in environmentally adjusted efficiency studies. The specific indexes considered in this chapter measure the health of water streams using macroinvertebrate and fish diversity and abundance indicators. The authors specify three influences on stream health: an ecological connectivity index created by aggregating two indicators of in-stream longitudinal connectivity; a land cover index created by aggregating two indicators of land cover; and an upstream sub-catchment drainage area. Data envelopment analysis is used to create the indexes, and stochastic frontier analysis is used to explain variation in the two stream health indicators. The chapter relies also on dominance analysis, which is independent of the concept of a frontier and which provides the foundation for the evaluation of the ability to translate ecological connectivity, land cover and upstream drainage area to stream health.

The first in a series of three chapters that discuss the interface between environmental factors and agricultural productivity is Chapter 6, authored by Hoang and Wilson. This chapter describes a method based on the concept of material balance to derive environmentally adjusted efficiency measures in the context of agricultural production, where excess nutrients (nitrogen and phosphorus) and the emission of greenhouse gases are two notable environmental pressures. Malmquist total factor productivity indexes are used to derive environmentally adjusted efficiency measures. The empirical application is for the case of agricultural production in 32 OECD economies over the period 1992–2008. The findings show that the agricultural sectors of the OECD countries should have been able to produce the same output levels with significantly less nutrient input and emissions of CO_2. By improving materials-based efficiency, these countries could have reduced potential damage in the air, water and land systems.

This is followed by Chapter 7, by Obst and Eigenraam. The chapter articulates a conceptual approach to the integration of ecosystem services and ecosystem assets into standard national accounting practices. This is explored through an analysis of possible measures of environmentally adjusted agricultural productivity. The conceptual approach is explained through description of the treatment of soil degradation and the treatment of particular ecosystem services of relevance to agriculture, including pollination, water supply and nutrient absorption. The chapter also discusses the many conceptual and measurement issues that remain to be further explored.

Chapter 8 is authored by Hughes and Lawson and deals with measures of agricultural total factor productivity adjusted for climate change. This chapter makes a point that a significant part of the observed stagnant total factor productivity (TFP) measures of the agricultural sector in Australia can be attributed to the systematic worsening of the climatic conditions since the mid-1960s. The approach makes use of advanced quantitative methods based on machine learning to derive climate-adjusted estimates of TFP in agriculture. The results show that, after adjustments are made for persistently worsening climate that can be attributed to climate change, the agricultural productivity in Australia has in fact experienced a good productivity growth. This highlights the importance of considering exogenous factors, like changing climate, in undertaking productivity analyses.

A pair of chapters that focus on efficiency of the urban water and wastewater treatment sectors starts with Chapter 9, authored by Hernández-Sancho and Bellver-Domingo. This chapter provides a comprehensive literature review of the productivity and efficiency studies in the urban water and wastewater treatment sectors. It then specifically focuses on the literature on environmentally adjusted productivity and efficiency measurement in these sectors. In this direction, a specific interest is in the extent of water leaks in the supply network. From an environmental point of view, leakages cause inefficient energy use in the water supply network and may also affect water quality by increasing susceptibility to contamination under low pressure conditions. The chapter evaluates the efficiency of municipal water suppliers in terms of water leakages, and demonstrates how inefficiency in the supply process can negatively affect urban water users.

This is followed by Chapter 10, by Hernández-Sancho, Lamizana-Diallo and Ingram, which demonstrates that the accurate assessment of the environmental and health costs of not taking action to improve wastewater treatment quality is necessary when evaluating suitable investment policies for an efficient wastewater treatment. Estimation of the environmental costs of no action can be based on the traditional approach, on the premise that economic value arises from the interaction between an individual and an environmental asset as an expression of an individual's preferences. An alternative approach is to estimate shadow prices of pollutants that are to be removed by an efficient wastewater treatment. This alternative method is derived from a 'cost of production perspective' and uses the concept of distance function to estimate shadow prices. These shadow prices represent the value of external effects that could damage the environment if wastewater is inefficiently treated. Several empirical applications verify the reliability and usefulness of estimating shadow prices of wastewater pollutants as a proxy to estimate the environmental costs of no action.

The discourse on shadow prices is continued in Chapter 11, authored by Hailu and Ma, but this time in the context of abatement cost of carbon dioxide emissions in China. China is now the leading source of carbon emissions, and has become the subject of a growing number of studies attempting to estimate marginal carbon abatement costs using distance functions. Provincial-level data for China are used to estimate the functions using mathematical programming (deterministic frontier) and

Bayesian methods (stochastic frontiers). Carbon abatement cost estimates in the form of shadow prices are compared to the values reported in the literature and to market prices for carbon. The Bayesian results are found to produce lower shadow prices that are closer to the observed market prices, compared to the estimates obtained through the use of mathematical programming.

The final chapter in the book, Chapter 12, is authored by Jahan and Ancev, and provides an application of the environmentally adjusted productivity and efficiency methods in the context of shrimp farming in Bangladesh. The chapter uses those methods to evaluate the economic and environmental efficiency of shrimp farms, which have become more numerous and more important for the economy of Bangladesh since the mid-1990s. At the same time, shrimp farming has been blamed for the serious environmental degradation in the areas where it has expanded. A directional output distance function approach is used to measure the efficiency of shrimp farms in the presence of desirable and undesirable outputs. The study covers the major shrimp-farming regions in Bangladesh and evaluates their performance at two time points, the years 2000 and 2010. An environmental efficiency index is estimated using alternative assumptions of weak and strong disposability of outputs. The results help identify areas where shrimp farming has been economically beneficial and has not caused large environmental damage, as well as areas where the opposite is true.

Overall, the 12 chapters of this book provide, in our view, a comprehensive coverage of theories, methods and empirical applications relevant to environmentally adjusted productivity and efficiency measurements. They also open up new horizons in terms of directions for future research in this rapidly growing area of knowledge. We believe that readers will find the volume informative, instructional and inspirational, and that they will find the investment in the time devoted to reading this book worthwhile.

REFERENCES

Abad, A. (2015), 'An environmental generalised Luenberger-Hicks-Moorsteen productivity indicator and an environmental generalised Hicks-Moorsteen productivity index', *Journal of Environmental Management*, **161**, 325–334.

Azad, M.A.S. and T. Ancev (2014), 'Measuring environmental efficiency of agricultural water use: a Luenberger environmental indicator', *Journal of Environmental Management*, **145**, 314–320.

Ball V.E., C.A.K. Lovell, H. Luu and R. Nehring (2004), 'Incorporating environmental impacts in the measurement of agricultural productivity growth', *Journal of Agricultural Resource Economics*, **29**, 436–60.

Coelli, T., L. Lauwers and G. Van Huylenbroeck (2007), 'Environmental efficiency measurement and the materials balance condition', *Journal of Productivity Analysis*, **28**, 3–12.

European Commission, Organisation for Economic Co-operation and Development, United Nations and World Bank System of Environmental-Economic Accounting (SEEA) 2012, 'Experimental ecosystem accounting', White cover publication. UN Statistics Division, 2013. http://unstats.un.org/unsd/envaccounting/eea_white_cover.pdf.

Färe, R., S. Grosskopf and C. Pasurka (2013), 'Joint production of good and bad outputs with a network application', in J. Shogren (ed.), *Encyclopedia of Energy, Natural Resources and Environmental Economics*, Elsevier, Amsterdam.

Fried, H.O., C.A.K. Lovell and S.S. Schmidt (2008), *The Measurement of Productive Efficiency and Productivity Growth*, Oxford University Press, New York.

Hoang, V.N and Thanh, T. (2013), 'Analysis of environmental efficiency variation: a materials balance approach', *Ecological Economics*, **86** (1), 37–46.

Kumar, S. and M. Khanna (2009), 'Measurement of environmental efficiency and productivity: a cross-country analysis', *Environment and Development Economics*, **14**, 473–495.

Peacock, S., C. Chan, M. Mangolini and D. Johansen (2001), 'Techniques for measuring efficiency in health services', Productivity Commission staff working paper, July.

Zhou, P., B.W. Ang and K. Poh (2008), 'Measuring environmental performance under different environmental DEA technologies', *Energy Economics*, **30** (1), 1–14.

2. Environmentally adjusted productivity and efficiency: a review of concepts, methods and empirical work

Tiho Ancev, M.A. Samad Azad and Mahmuda Akter

2.1 INTRODUCTION

The necessity of accounting for environmental impacts from production activities is increasingly important as the environment and the ecosystem services it provides are significantly threatened by various forms of environmental degradation, including air pollution, deterioration of water quality, land degradation and biodiversity losses. Since the early 1990s, environmental impacts from economic activities have been incorporated in the productivity and efficiency modelling framework. We refer to the productivity and efficiency measurement that includes environmental effects as 'environmentally adjusted productivity and efficiency' (*EAPE*). A wide range of conceptual and modelling frameworks – including those based on index number theory, distance and directional distance function approaches, parametric and non-parametric models – have been developed for the purpose of measuring environmentally adjusted productivity and efficiency of a given unit of observation (e.g. farm, firm, industry, country). These efficiency measurements allow us to identify productive activities that create high economic value and have relatively little environmental effects, as well as productive activities that create substantial environmental pressure but only create modest economic value. In this chapter, we critically overview the concepts and methods developed and applied to measure environmentally adjusted productivity and efficiency in various contexts. We also overview some recently developed efficiency models that can be applied to measure environmentally adjusted efficiency of various sectors within the economy.

This chapter proceeds as follows. Next section presents some background on the development of environmentally adjusted productivity and efficiency measurement, followed by a section that discusses the tradeoffs between economic and environmental performance of a unit of observation. The concept of environmentally adjusted productivity and efficiency is discussed in section 2.4, while section 2.5 describes the main functional forms that are used in constructing the environmentally adjusted efficiency models. Section 2.6 presents some of the recently developed and widely used models of environmentally adjusted productivity and efficiency measurement. Section 2.7 describes parametric and non-parametric approaches that are frequently used in efficiency estimation. Some empirical applications of environmentally adjusted efficiency models are also briefly discussed in section 2.8. The final section draws conclusions.

2.2   BACKGROUND

The economic performance of a production unit is generally represented by two key indicators: 'productivity' and 'efficiency'. By measuring productivity and efficiency, economic performance can be evaluated and compared among production units within an industry or across industries. The pioneering work on the efficiency modelling by Farrell (1957) has inspired many empirical studies on efficiency measures. In this highly influential work, Farrell showed that the efficiency of a firm consists of two components: (i) technical efficiency, which reflects the ability of a firm to obtain maximum output from a given set of inputs; and (ii) allocative efficiency, which reflects the ability of a firm to use the inputs in optimal proportions, given their respective prices. The combination of these two components provides a measure of total economic (or productive) efficiency. A number of studies (i.e. Farrell and Fieldhouse, 1962; Seitz, 1970; Afriat, 1972; Meller, 1976) adopted and extended this approach to measure economic efficiency. Later on, Banker et al. (1984) and Färe et al. (1985, 1994, 1989) demonstrated, by constructing a 'production frontier', that Farrell's measure of technical efficiency can be further decomposed, and that inefficiency can be identified by the failure to achieve best possible output levels and/or usage of excessive amount of inputs. This production frontier is a fundamental element of measuring economic efficiency.

The analysis of economic efficiency in the traditional productivity and efficiency measurement literature only focuses on accounting for the usual, or desirable outputs (i.e. volume of production, or gross revenue) of firms relative to paid factors of production (Chung et al., 1997; Yang and Pollitt, 2009). But in many sectors of the economy an agent (e.g. a firm, a farm) frequently produces other, undesirable outputs, in addition to the desirable outputs. These are the negative environmental externalities that are the unintended consequences of a production process (i.e. any type of emission of harmful substances in the air, water and on the soil). Since undesirable outputs have harmful effects on the environment, and by extension on human society and its wellbeing, both desirable and undesirable outputs should be treated simultaneously when measuring productivity and economic performance. However, this joint production of desirable and undesirable outputs has been typically ignored in traditional productivity and efficiency studies, predominantly because prices for these undesirable outputs are not observable (Färe et al., 1989; Chung et. al., 1997).

In response to this, Pittman (1983) authored one of the earliest studies that incorporate undesirable outputs (environmental effects) into efficiency analysis. This study was the first to extend the multilateral productivity measurement technique of Caves et al. (1982) for comparing the performance among units of observation while explicitly considering both desirable and undesirable outputs. Since undesirable outputs are not marketable goods and are not typically priced, this approach is feasible only if undesirable outputs can be valued by their shadow prices (Reinhard et al., 1999; Graham, 2004). The assigning of shadow prices to undesirable outputs is a challenging task. Pittman (1983) first attempted to estimate shadow prices of undesirable outputs. But his estimates of the value of shadow prices appeared somewhat arbitrary, since they were estimated at an aggregate level (i.e. state level) rather than at an individual level (i.e. plant, firm), and may not have reflected the actual operating conditions (Tyteca, 1996). In addition, under Pittman's framework, inefficiency of undesirable outputs was not properly penalized, since both the desirable and undesirable outputs were allowed to increase (Färe et al., 2007).

Since Pittman's work, a number of other studies have incorporated undesirable outputs into productivity and efficiency analysis (e.g. Färe et al., 1989, 1993, 1996; Yaisawarng and Klein 1994, and many others). Färe et al. (1989) considered environmental impacts as undesirable outputs, and developed a non-parametric hyperbolic efficiency measure to evaluate a farm's performance in the presence of undesirable outputs. This approach modified Farrell's (1957) measure of technical efficiency, which allows an asymmetric treatment of desirable and undesirable outputs to determine environmental performance in terms of the ability to expand desirable outputs and reduce undesirable outputs. The efficiency measure that Färe et al. (1989) developed is an alternative to the enhanced multilateral productivity index introduced by Pittman (1983), which requires only data on the quantity of undesirable outputs rather than their shadow prices.

In estimating the shadow price of undesirable output, Färe et al. (1993) also used a parametric specification of a distance function defined by

Shephard (1970), which enabled them to calculate plant-specific shadow prices for undesirable outputs. A number of studies (e.g. Coggins and Swinton, 1996; Kwon and Yun, 1999; Huang and Leung, 2007) followed this approach to estimate shadow prices of undesirable outputs. Inspired by these studies, a debate has developed in the literature on how shadow prices of undesirable outputs should be treated in productivity analysis. Although shadow prices of undesirable outputs under the approach of Färe et al. (1993) were imposed to be non-positive (weak disposability), Hetemäki (1993) used a stochastic distance function without requiring non-positive shadow prices, and subsequently obtained positive values for the shadow prices. Like Färe et al. (1993), most other studies, with the notable exceptions of Hetemäki (1996) and Reinhard et al. (1999), constrain the shadow price of undesirable outputs to be negative. Another study by Ha et al. (2008) argued that it may be inappropriate to restrict the shadow prices of undesirable outputs to be non-positive.

While determining shadow prices of undesirable outputs remains an active area of research, another possible way of incorporating environmental impacts in productivity measurement is to use a productivity index proposed by Malmquist (1953), which does not require price information, and only requires quantity information in its construction. Environmental impacts cannot be incorporated into the Fisher or Törnqvist productivity indexes without price information, but this is possible with a Malmquist productivity index (Ball et al., 2004a). However, Chung et al. (1997) argued that a Malmquist index may not be computable in the presence of undesirable outputs. To overcome this problem, they introduced a directional distance function and used it as a component in a new productivity index defined as a Malmquist-Luenberger productivity index. Both Malmquist and Malmquist-Luenberger productivity indexes are discussed in some detail in section 2.6.

In recent years, a number of environmentally adjusted productivity and efficiency models have been developed and applied in various economic sectors to identify potential economic performance relating to environmental resource use (e.g., Azad, 2012; Azad et al., 2015; Azad and Ancev, 2010, 2014, 2016; Färe et al., 2013; Kumar and Khanna, 2009; Zhou et al., 2008; Coelli et al., 2007; Ball et al., 2004a). These studies point to a growing debate on how to effectively incorporate the environmental impacts from production activities in the models for measuring productivity and efficiency. Several studies attempted to integrate technical and economic efficiency with the environmental performance measures by making adjustments to standard parametric and non-parametric efficiency analysis techniques (Coelli et al., 2005). In other words, the environmentally adjusted efficiency indicators can be categorized in those that are measured using techniques (parametric or non-parametric) that are suitable for analysing deterministic processes, and those that are measured using techniques (exclusively parametric) suitable for analysing stochastic processes. Findings of our extensive literature survey (more than 150 articles were reviewed) show that data envelopment analysis (a non-parametric technique) is the most commonly used method in an environmentally adjusted productivity and efficiency analysis (see Table 2.1).

Measurement of environmentally adjusted productivity and efficiency analysis can also be categorized on the basis of whether the model treats the environmental effects as inputs into, or as outputs from the production process. There has been mixed evidence in the literature related to considering environmental impacts as either input or output in efficiency models. While some studies have treated the undesirable impacts as input (e.g. Cropper and Oates, 1992; Pittman, 1981; Haynes et al., 1993, 1994; Boggs, 1997; Kopp, 1998; Reinhard et al., 1999; Murty and Kumar, 2004), others have treated them as output (e.g. Gollop and Roberts, 1983; Azad and Ancev, 2014).

A summary of previous published work on environmentally adjusted productivity and efficiency is presented in Table 2.1 (further below).[1] Most of the reviewed studies have used either distance functions or directional distance functions while constructing an environmentally adjusted efficiency model. This is because these functional approaches appear to be most promising, particularly for those analyses based on non-parametric approaches. A detailed discussion on the importance and usefulness of the distance function and directional distance function in building environmentally adjusted efficiency models is presented in section 2.5.

2.3   TRADEOFFS BETWEEN ECONOMIC AND ENVIRONMENTAL PERFORMANCE

The use of methods for environmentally adjusted productivity and efficiency analysis allows us to jointly investigate the economic and environmental performance of individual production units, and to evaluate the tradeoffs between them. For example, the tradeoff between economic and environmental efficiency in the context of water industries can be represented by Figure 2.1. The figure shows that water resources can be either withdrawn from the environment for economic use (i.e. irrigation or municipal use) or left to support ecological and environmental needs of water-dependent systems (i.e. a river or a wetland). Both economic and environmental uses are beneficial to our society through the production of man-made goods and services (which can be defined as desirable outputs)

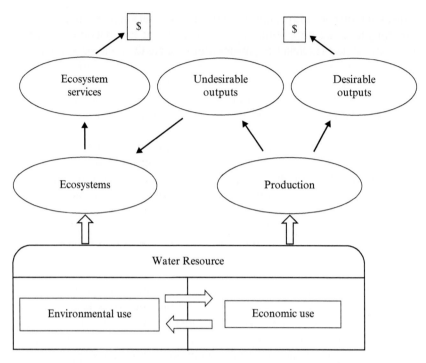

Figure 2.1   Tradeoffs between economic and environmental water use

and the provision of ecosystem services. However, as discussed earlier, the production of man-made goods and services often creates negative impacts on environmental and natural resources. For instance, excessive water withdrawal for irrigation purposes results in deterioration of river health and wetland degradation, and thus threatens the freshwater eco-logical system (Azad and Ancev, 2010). While evaluating performance of an irrigated enterprise within a production efficiency measurement frame-work, this type of environmental pressure can be exemplified by the term 'undesirable outputs' (Figure 2.1).

These apparent tradeoffs between withdrawing water and leaving it for the environment suggest that a rational approach to allocating water is not only to compare the values created in economic and environmental uses, but also to account for the undesirable outputs generated from economic use. Withdrawing water may be justified as long as the value of that water to society (net of the negative environmental effects associated with the production process to which water is an input) is greater than the value of that water in environmental use. Environmentally adjusted efficiency measurements allow us to evaluate these tradeoffs and identify productive activities that create high economic value and have relatively small environmental impacts, as well as productive activities that create large environmental impact but only create modest economic value.

2.4 CONCEPTS OF ENVIRONMENTALLY ADJUSTED PRODUCTIVITY AND EFFICIENCY

This section first describes the fundamental notions of measuring productivity and efficiency of a production unit, and then illustrates the main ideas behind environmentally adjusted productivity and efficiency measurement. An in-depth exposition on productivity and efficiency measurement and their environmental adjustment can be found in Färe and Grosskopf (2004) and Fried et al. (2008). For the purposes of an empirical study, the efficiency of a production unit can be conceptualized in a straightforward way by presenting input and output data on a scatter plot and creating an outer envelope (frontier) based on these data points. The observations that are on the frontier are deemed to be efficient production units (Figure 2.2). An efficient production unit produces the maximum possible output using a given level of inputs; or, vice versa, it uses the minimum level of input to produce a given level of output. For instance, the input and output data on the production unit B in Figure 2.2 indicates that it is an efficient production unit, whereas the data on unit A indicates that this unit is inefficient as it uses the same amount of input as unit B but produces substantially less output. The inefficiency of production unit A

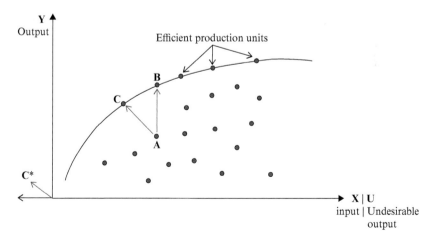

Figure 2.2   Environmentally adjusted efficiency of production units

can be measured by estimating the Euclidean distance between production unit A and the frontier. This distance can be measured by a distance function, as introduced by Farrell (1957).[2]

The general efficiency approach described above has been extensively used in many studies and within a number of methodological frameworks (Emrouznejad et al., 2008). However, this standard approach focuses exclusively on the economic efficiency and does not take into account any environmental and natural resource use implications from a productive activity. Since environmental concerns have grown throughout the world, the concept of efficiency measurement described above needs to be adjusted by taking into account the environmental performance of individual production units. This is approached by noting that many production processes use environmentally sensitive inputs (e.g. water, energy) and produce undesirable outputs (e.g. emission of pollutants) together with desirable outputs (Färe et al., 2004; Chung et al., 1997). If these 'environmental' inputs and outputs and their effects can be quantified, the standard efficiency measurements can be adjusted to reflect not only economic but also environmental efficiency (Färe et al., 1989).

This concept can be explained using Figure 2.2. The quantity of undesirable output can be presented on the horizontal axis along with the inputs. It may be assumed that the levels of inputs are unchanged, and we are interested to increase the level of desirable outputs but to reduce the level of undesirable outputs. In this case, production unit A is inefficient because it creates the same amount of environmental effects (undesirable outputs) as unit B while producing considerably less desirable outputs. This implies that production unit A damages the environment without providing a commensurate economic benefit. Therefore, from society's point of view, it will be beneficial for unit A to improve its performance, and either increase its desirable output to the level of unit B or indeed increase its desirable output and simultaneously decrease its undesirable output by moving to point C on the frontier. In this way, the economic performance will be improved (even though not to the maximum possible extent), and at the same time environmental performance will be considerably improved by reducing environmental effects.

This is a move in a specific direction, and in this case productive efficiency can be measured using a special type of function, called directional distance function (Chambers et al., 1996).[3] This function allows researchers to choose a direction in which the efficiency of a production unit is to be evaluated. For example, it can be in a straight vertical direction (towards point B in Figure 2.2), which will be a measure of pure economic inefficiency, or in a radial direction (towards point C), which measures both economic and environmental inefficiency, or even in a straight horizontal direction that measures only environmental inefficiency. The direction of this movement can be defined as a directional vector in the functional form.

A key requirement for this environmentally adjusted efficiency measurement is to have data on the quantity of environmental effects caused by individual production units. This can sometimes be obtained in a fairly straightforward way. For instance, data are often available for such environmental effects as greenhouse gas emissions or energy use in municipal wastewater treatment plants, use of water in irrigation activities or the quantity of remaining pollutants in the treated wastewater. But at other times gathering data can be very difficult, and specifically when the aim is to quantify the effects of environmental impacts from productive activities on ecological assets. For example, withdrawing water from rivers and streams can have very different environmental impacts depending on the location and the associated climate as well as the type of ecosystem that is affected (Azad and Ancev, 2010).

2.5   FUNCTIONAL FORM OF EAPE MODELS

Under the general framework of production functions, the aggregation of multiple outputs that are produced from a production process is quite difficult. Hence, some commonly used functional forms such as 'distance function' and 'directional distance function' can be adapted in modelling production technologies with multiple inputs and outputs. Consequently, many productivity and efficiency models are constructed based on these functional forms. We introduce below the distance and the directional distance functions.[4]

2.5.1   Distance Functions

Distance functions were first introduced by Debreu (1951) and later developed by Malmquist (1953) and Shephard (1953, 1970), and are now the cornerstone of primal analysis of performance measurement (Cuesta et al., 2009). Distance functions can be input and output oriented. Although until the 1990s very few studies used input and/or output-oriented distance functions in empirical analysis, they have been widely employed in a number of environmentally adjusted productivity and efficiency analyses in recent years (see Table 2.1). In most cases, the distance function approach was followed to derive shadow prices of undesirable outputs. The key advantage of the distance function approach is that it allows production modelling of a multi-input and multi-output technology when the prices of some outputs or inputs are not available (Färe and Primont, 1995).

A distance function is multiplicative in structure and is used in constructing a number of environmentally adjusted productivity and efficiency models, as further described in section 6. This function can be defined in terms of production technology using the following notation. Let $x \in \Re_+^N$ denote the input vector: $x = (x_1, ..., x_N) \in \Re_+^N$ and $y \in \Re_+^M$ the output vector: $y = (y_1, ..., y_M) \in \Re_+^M$ then the production technology, T, can be written as:

$$T = \{((x, y): x \ can \ produce \ y)\} \qquad (2.1)$$

This production technology can be represented by its input set as: $L(y) = \{x: (x, y) \in T\}$ which is assumed to be closed and nonempty for each $y \in \Re_+^M$, and to satisfy strong disposability with respect to inputs and outputs (Färe and Primont, 1995). Consequently, the input distance function (Shephard, 1953) can be defined as:

$$D_i(x, y) = \sup\{\lambda: (x/\lambda) \in L(y)\} \qquad (2.2)$$

which is a complete characterization of the technology in the sense that $D_i(x, y) \geq 1$ if and only if $x \in L(y)$. If the value of input distance function $D_i(x, y)$ equals one, it means that the production unit lies on the production frontier and that it is technically efficient. Any production unit above the frontier must have a distance value greater than one, indicating the degree of inefficiency. Similarly, the production technology can be also represented by its output requirement set (production possibility set) as: $P(x) = \{y: (x, y) \in T\}$. The output distance function relative to the output set can be defined as:[5]

$$D_0(x, y) = \inf\{\theta: (y/\theta) \in P(x)\} \qquad (2.3)$$

The output distance function generalizes the concept of the conventional production function, and is defined as the maximum output that can be produced from an exogenously given input vector.

The distance function approaches appear to be most promising for a number of reasons (Hailu and Veeman, 2001), including:

- Distance function approaches require only quantity data.
- When flexible functional forms are employed, input and output distance functions can provide good representations of the underlying technology.
- Using this functional approach, one can readily obtain estimates of the cost of pollution abatement.

- Different components of productivity growth (change in the degree of technical efficiency, technical change and scale effects) can be readily identified from estimated distance functions.

Using the distance function approach a number of studies have developed various models of measuring environmentally adjusted efficiency, and applied these efficiency models in evaluating performance of individual firms, industries or countries. A detailed list of those productivity and efficiency studies is presented in Table 2.1.

2.5.2   Directional Distance Function

Since the mid-1990s, the directional distance function has grown in importance in production theory. It has been recognized as a useful functional approach to modelling production processes, particularly where the undesirable outputs are present (Chung et al., 1997; Ball et al., 1994). The directional distance function allows simultaneous expansion of desirable outputs and contraction of undesirable outputs. It is additive in nature, and it is the basic building block of some productivity and efficiency measurement models such as the Luenberger productivity indicator and Luenberger environmental indicator, which are discussed in the following section.

   To derive a representation of a directional distance function, assume a sample of K production units each of which uses a vector of inputs $x = (x_1, ..., x_N) \in \Re_+^N$ to produce a vector of desirable outputs $d = (d_1, ..., d_M) \in \Re_+^M$, but as a consequence of the production process some undesirable outputs $u = (u_1, ..., u_J) \in \Re_+^J$ are also produced. This production technology can be represented by the directional output distance function as follows:

$$\vec{D}_o(x,d,u;g_d,-g_u) = \sup\{\beta:(d+\beta g_d, u-\beta g_u) \in P(x)\} \qquad (2.4)$$

The directional vector is defined by (g_d, g_u). The directional output distance function seeks to achieve the maximum feasible expansion of desirable outputs in the g_d direction, but at the same time the largest possible contraction of undesirable outputs in the g_u direction.

   Several studies have been conducted using directional distance function to measure environmentally adjusted productivity and efficiency in various sectors (see Table 2.1). The advantage of using a directional distance function in an environmentally adjusted efficiency model is that it enables researchers to estimate efficiency of a productive unit taking into account simultaneously desirable and undesirable outputs of a production technology. Put differently, it allows us to analyse

Table 2.1a Studies of measuring environmentally adjusted productivity and efficiency

Author and year	Country	Method	Functional form	EAPE model
Färe et al.1989	USA	DEA	Hyperbolic efficiency measure	Multilateral productivity index
Färe et al.1994	USA	DEA	Output distance function	Malmquist productivity index
Yaisawarng and Klein 1994	USA	DEA	Input based	Malmquist productivity index
Färe et al. 1996	USA	DEA	Input distance function	Environmental performance indicator
Chambers et al. 1996		DEA	Directional distance function	Luenberger productivity indicator
Tyteca 1996		DEA	Various functional forms	Environmental performance indicator
Chung et al. 1997	Sweden	DEA	Directional distance function	Malmquist-Luenberger productivity index
Reinhard et al. 2000	Denmark	DEA, SFA	Distance function	Environmental efficiency
Hailu and Veeman 2000	Canada	DEA	Parametric input distance function	Malmquist productivity index
Zaim and Taskin 2000	OECD countries	DEA	Hyperbolic graph measure	Environmental productivity index
Färe et al. 2001	USA	DEA	Directional distance function	Malmquist-Luenberger productivity index
Hailu and Veeman 2001	Canada	DEA	Distance function	Malmquist productivity Index
Reinhard et al. 2002	Denmark	SFA		Conditional environmental efficiency
Färe and Grosskopf 2004	USA	DEA	Directional distance function	Luenberger productivity indicator
Chambers 2002	USA	SFA, DEA		Stochastic productivity indicator, Luenberger productivity indicator
Färe et al. 2004	OECD countries	DEA	Distance function	Environmental performance index
Kwon and Lee 2004	Korea	SFA, DEA	Directional distance function	Malmquist index, Luenberger indicator
Lansink and Reinhard 2004	Netherlands	DEA		DEA-based linear programming
Weber and Weber 2004	USA	DEA	Directional distance function	Luenberger productivity indicator
Kuosmanen and Kortelainen 2005	Finland	DEA		Eco-efficiency
Coelli and Walding 2005	Australia	DEA		DEA total factor productivity
Kumar 2006	41 countries	DEA	Directional distance function	Luenberger productivity indicator

Note: DEA = data envelopment analysis, SFA = stochastic frontier analysis.

Table 2.1b   Studies of measuring environmentally adjusted productivity and efficiency

Authors and year	Country	Method	Functional form	EAPE model
Zhou et al. 2006	OECD countries	DEA	Slacks-based	Slacks-based efficiency index
Nanere et al. 2007	Australia	DEA		Environmental TFP
Managi and Jena 2008	India	DEA	Directional distance function	Environmental TFP
Honma and Hu 2009	Japan	DEA		Total factor energy productivity index
Zhou and Ang 2008	OECD countries	DEA		Energy efficiency performance index
Zhou et al. 2008	Eight world regions	DEA	Radial DEA	Environmental performance index
Kumar and Khanna 2009	Major developed countries	DEA	Directional distance function	Environmental efficiency
Cuesta et al. 2009		SFA	Distance function	Hyperbolic environmental efficiency
Koutsomanoli-Filippaki et al. 2009	Central and Eastern Europe	SFA	Directional distance function	Luenberger productivity indicator
Briec and Kerstens 2009		DEA	Directional distance function	Luenberger productivity indicator
Williams et al. 2011	10 EU countries	DEA	Directional distance function	Luenberger productivity indicator
Coelli and Rao 2010	93 countries	DEA	Shephard distance function	Malmquist productivity index
Azad and Ancev 2010	Australia	DEA	Input and output distance function	Environmental performance index
Hoang and Coelli 2011	OECD countries	DEA	Input distance function	Nutrient total factor productivity
Zhang et al. 2011	China	DEA	Directional distance function	Malmquist-Luenberger productivity index
Picazo-Tadeo et al. 2011	Spain	DEA	Non-radial distance function	Eco-efficiency
Epure et al. 2011	Spain	DEA	Distance function	Luenberger productivity indicator
Murty et al. 2012	USA	DEA	Hyperbolic and directional distance function	Hyperbolic and directional distance function index
Färe et al. 2012	Sweden	DEA	Directional distance function	Luenberger total factor productivity indicator
Tamini et al. 2012	Canada	SFA	Input distance function	Malmquist input-based productivity index
Hoang and Alauddin 2012	OECD countries	DEA	Frontier based approach	Input oriented eco-efficiency

Note: DEA = data envelopment analysis, SFA = stochastic frontier analysis.

Table 2.1c Studies of measuring environmentally adjusted productivity and efficiency

Author and year	Country	Method	Functional form	EAPE model
Hoang and Nguyen 2013	South Korea	DEA SFA		Nutrient stochastic model, Nutrient inefficiency model
Picazo-Tadeo et al. 2012	Spain	DEA	Directional distance function	Eco-efficiency
Zhou et al. 2012	OECD countries	DEA	Non-radial directional distance function	Energy carbon performance index
Feng et al. 2013	China	DEA	Distance function	Malmquist-Luenberger productivity index
Chang et al. 2013	China	DEA	Non-radial distance function	Environmental efficiency, Carbon efficiency
Molinos-Senante et al. 2014	England and Wales	DEA	Directional distance function, Shephard distance function	Luenberger productivity indicator, Malmquist productivity index
Diewert and Fox 2014		DEA	Output distance function	Malmquist productivity index
Azad and Ancev 2014	Australia	DEA	Directional distance function	Luenberger environmental indicator
Hampf and Krüger 2014	62 countries	DEA	Directional distance function	Malmquist-Luenberger index
Picazo-Tadeo et al. 2014	European Union	DEA	Directional distance function	Luenberger productivity indicator
Whittaker et al. 2015	Mexico	DEA	Distance function	Malmquist water quality index
Abad 2015		DEA	Directional distance function	Luenberger-Hicks-Moorsteen index
Azad et al. 2015	Australia	DEA	Non-radial distance function	Water use efficiency index
Li et al. 2015	Airlines	DEA	Directional distance function	Malmquist-Luenberger productivity index
Zhou et al. 2015	China	SFA	Non-radial distance function	Cobb-Douglas translog production function
Woo et al. 2015	OECD countries	DEA	Output distance function	Malmquist productivity index
Wang et al. 2015	China	Metafrontier DEA		Total environmental efficiency
Zhang et al. 2015	China	DEA	Slacks-based	Metafrontier environmental efficiency
Yang et al. 2015	China	DEA		Super-efficiency DEA
Song et al. 2015	China	DEA	Slacks-based	Efficiency slack-based measurement
Arabi et al. 2016	Iran	DEA	Slacks-based	Malmquist-Luenberger productivity index

Note: DEA = data envelopment analysis, SFA = stochastic frontier analysis.

Table 2.1d Studies of measuring environmentally adjusted productivity and efficiency

Author and year	Country	Method	Functional form	EAPE model
Alfredsson et al. 2016	Sweden	DEA	Directional distance function	Scale of directional distance function model
Balezentis et al. 2016	Lithuania	DEA	Output distance function	Environmental performance index
Dakpo et al. 2016	France	DEA		Pollution adjusted efficiency
Du et al. 2016	China	SFA	Metafrontier directional output distance function	Environmental technical efficiency
Fujii et al. 2016	Japan	Bayesian SFA		Tobit model
Jiang et al. 2016	China	DEA	Structural equation model	Structural equation model
Li and Lin 2016	China	DEA	Directional distance function	Malmquist-Luenberger productivity index
Liu et al. 2016	China	DEA		Range-adjusted measurement
Huang et al. 2016	China	SFA	Input distance function	Environmental performance index
Mamardashvili et al. 2016	Switzerland	SFA	Hyperbolic distance function	Hyperbolic efficiency, enhanced hyperbolic efficiency
Njuki et al. 2016	USA	SFA	Directional output distance function	
Song and Zheng 2016	China	DEA	Slacks-based	Super-efficiency slack-based measurement
Sueyoshi and Yuan 2016	Europe and North America	DEA	Distance function	Marginal rate of transformation, rate of substitution
Molinos-Senante et al. 2016	Spain	DEA	Directional distance function	Malmquist-Luenberger productivity index
Wang and Zhao 2016	China	DEA	Non-radial	Eco-efficiency
Valadkhani et al. 2016	46 countries	DEA	Directional distance function	Environmental and energy efficiency index
Wang et al. 2016	China	DEA	Non-radial	Unified efficiency under natural and marginal disposability
Wang and Wei 2016	China	DEA	Slacks-based	Luenberger aggregated energy productivity indicator
Yu et al. 2016	China	DEA	Slacks-based	Eco-efficiency, Malmquist-Luenberger index
Zhang and Chen 2016	China	DEA	Non-radial Directional distance function	Environmental efficiency indicator
Zhang et al. 2016	China	DEA	Non-radial Directional distance function	Metafrontier carbon emission performance index

Note: DEA = data envelopment analysis, SFA = stochastic frontier analysis.

production units while considering their ability to increase desirable outputs and to reduce undesirable outputs in a multi-output production process.

2.6   METHODS OF ENVIRONMENTALLY ADJUSTED EFFICIENCY MEASUREMENT

Throughout this section, we briefly describe a number of productivity and efficiency models that can be used in evaluating environmentally adjusted performance of production units. In recent years, various types of methods and approaches have been used in estimating environmentally adjusted productivity and efficiency. However, our discussion will be confined in particular to those efficiency models constructed based on the non-parametric approach that is widely used in measuring environmentally adjusted productivity and efficiency (*EAPE*).[6] Since the non-parametric efficiency measures can be readily and usefully adopted for the derivation of environmentally adjusted performance indicators, this approach is prevalent among productivity and efficiency studies. Some of the popular and frequently used methods and approaches of *EAPE* are briefly overviewed in the following section.

2.6.1   Environmental Performance Index

The environmental performance index (*EPI*) is a modelling framework for measuring tradeoffs between economic and environmental efficiency. It measures the relative potential of a production unit to proportionally increase desirable outputs and reduce undesirable outputs. Färe et al. (2004) first proposed a formal index number for evaluating environmental performance of 17 OECD countries. Later on, Azad and Ancev (2010, 2016) adapted this *EPI* to measure the tradeoffs between economic and environmental performance of irrigated agricultural enterprises. The *EPI* is the ratio of a quantity index of desirable output and a quantity index of undesirable output, which can be expressed as:

$$E^{k,l}(x^o,d^o,u^o,d^k,d^l,u^k,u^l) = \frac{Q_d(x^o,d^o,d^k,d^l)}{Q_u(x^o,d^o,u^k,u^l)} \tag{2.5}$$

where x^o, d^o and u^o are vectors of inputs, desirable outputs and undesirable outputs, respectively; d^k and d^l are two observations of desirable output vectors; and u^k and u^l are two undesirable output vectors for representative production units k and l.

The components of the *EPI*, the index of desirable output $Q_d(.)$ and the index of undesirable output Q_u (.) are constructed based on two distance functions as follows:

$$Q_d(x^o, d^o, d^k, d^l) = \frac{D_d(x^o, d^k, u^o)}{D_d(x^o, d^l, u^o)} \qquad (2.6)$$

$$Q_u(x^o, d^o, u^k, u^l) = \frac{D_d(x^o, d^o, u^k)}{D_d(x^o, d^o, u^l)} \qquad (2.7)$$

$D_d(x, d, u)$ is a Shephard output distance function (Shephard, 1970) which can be written as:

$$D_d(x, d, u) = inf\left\{\theta : \left(x, \frac{d}{\theta}, u\right) \in T\right\} \qquad (2.8)$$

This function expands desirable outputs (*d*) as much as feasible, while keeping inputs (*x*) and undesirable outputs (*u*) constant.

Similarly, $D_d(x, d, u)$ is an input distance function for the undesirable outputs that can be written as:

$$D_u(x, d, u) = sup\left\{\lambda : \left(x, d, \frac{u}{\lambda}\right) \in T\right\} \qquad (2.9)$$

This function holds the inputs (*x*) and desirable outputs (*d*) fixed, and contracts the undesirable output (*u*) as much as possible. In an empirical study, the resulting *EPI* scores indicate the tradeoff between the economic and environmental performance of production units. A farm or an industrial unit with a low *EPI* score creates relatively greater environmental pressure and/or experiences relatively low economic return. Conversely, a production unit with a high *EPI* score creates relatively modest environmental pressure, but generates relatively high economic value-added. Using this efficiency approach, Azad and Ancev (2016) evaluated the tradeoffs between the benefits derived from irrigated cotton enterprises and their associated environmental damage using a sample of 53 observations in Australia.

The environmental performance index described above is a ratio-based efficiency measure, and thus the efficiency of production activities depends on the estimated value of the numerator (economic performance) and the denominator (environmental pressure/damage) of the index. Therefore, this index does not explicitly take into account the absolute magnitude of environmental damage created in a production process, but only considers the environmental damage relative to the economic value added. Consequently, a unit that creates very large environmental pressure may appear to be very efficient as long as it efficiently produces the desirable output. This is an issue that we address further below with the review of the Luenberger indicator (section 2.6.3).

2.6.2 Malmquist Productivity Index

The Malmquist productivity index (*MPI*) initially defined by Caves et al. (1982) can be used to evaluate dynamic productivity changes of a production unit.[7] In other words, this productivity index examines the change in efficiency between periods *t* and *t+1*. The *MPI* can be expressed as a geometric mean of a product of two distance functions ratios as follows:

$$M_t^{t+1} = \left[\frac{D_o^t(x_o^{t+1}, d_o^{t+1})}{D_o^t(x_o^t, d_o^t)} \times \frac{D_o^{t+1}(x_o^{t+1}, d_o^{t+1})}{D_o^{t+1}(x_o^t, d_o^t)} \right]^{1/2} \tag{2.10}$$

where, M_t^{t+1} denotes the Malmquist index, while $D_o^t(x_o^t, d_o^t)$ and $D_o^{t+1}(x_o^t, d_o^t)$ are the output-oriented distance functions for periods *t* and *t* + 1, respectively. If $M_t^{t+1} > 1$, productivity improves; if $M_t^{t+1} < 1$ productivity declines, and productivity remains constant when $M_t^{t+1} = 0$.

The *MPI* can be geometrically decomposed into two components, namely Malmquist technical change (*MTCH*) and Malmquist efficiency change (*MECH*) as follows:

$$MTCH = \left[\frac{D_o^t(x_o^{t+1}, d_o^{t+1})}{D_o^{t+1}(x_o^{t+1}, d_o^{t+1})} \times \frac{D_o^t(x_o^t, d_o^t)}{D_o^{t+1}(x_o^t, d_o^t)} \right]^{1/2} \tag{2.11}$$

$$MECH = \frac{D_o^{t+1}(x_o^{t+1}, d_o^{t+1})}{D_o^t(x_o^t, d_o^t)} \tag{2.12}$$

The *MPI* has a number of important features, including that it is a total factor productivity index and that, since it is based on data on input and output quantities, it can be applicable in any efficiency study when price information is unavailable. Many studies adopt this index to estimate dynamic environmentally adjusted efficiency (see Table 2.1). This productivity index also has several limitations. One of the limitations of the index is that it does not properly credit reduction of undesirable outputs, since both desirable and undesirable outputs expand at the same rate. It also does not explain the impact of environmental regulation on productivity (Oh and Heshmati, 2010).

2.6.3 Luenberger Productivity Indicator

The Luenberger productivity indicator (*LPI*) was introduced by Chambers (1996). In contrast to the Malmquist productivity index, the *LPI* is constructed based on the directional output distance functions, and can be defined as:

$$\overrightarrow{D}_0^{t+1}(x^t,d^t,u^t;g_d,-g_u) = \sup[\beta:(d^t+\beta g_d,u^t-\beta g_u) \in P^{t+1}(x^t)] \quad (2.13)$$

where g is the directional vector by which desirable and undesirable outputs are scaled, and β is the maximum feasible expansion of desirable outputs and contraction of undesirable outputs when expansion and contraction are in identical proportions for a given level of inputs. The Luenberger productivity indicator can be expressed as follows:

$$LPI_t^{t+1}(x^t,d^t,u^t,x^{t+1},d^{t+1},u^{t+1})$$
$$= \frac{1}{2}[\overrightarrow{D}_0^t(x^t,d^t,u^t;g) - \overrightarrow{D}_0^t(x^{t+1},d^{t+1},u^{t+1};g) + \overrightarrow{D}_0^{t+1}(x^t,d^t,u^t;g)$$
$$- \overrightarrow{D}_0^{t+1}(x^{t+1},d^{t+1},u^{t+1};g)] \quad (2.14)$$

This productivity indicator can be used to estimate productivity and efficiency changes of production units over a period of time. Its value can be interpreted as follows: if $LPI = 0$, the productivity remains constant, $LPI > 0$ indicates an improvement in the productivity and $LPI < 0$ means that productivity is declining over time.

While the *MPI* is a ratio-based approach, the *LPI* is a difference-based efficiency measure, which can be additively decomposed into two components: Luenberger efficiency change (*LECH*) and Luenberger technical change (*LTCH*) as follows:

$$LPI_t^{t+1}(x^t,d^t,u^t,x^{t+1},d^{t+1},u^{t+1}) = [\overrightarrow{D}_0^t(x^t,d^t,u^t;g) - \overrightarrow{D}_0^{t+1}(x^{t+1},d^{t+1},u^{t+1};g)] +$$
$$\frac{1}{2}[\overrightarrow{D}_0^{t+1}(x^{t+1},d^{t+1},u^{t+1};g) - \overrightarrow{D}_0^t(x^{t+1},d^{t+1},u^{t+1};g) + \overrightarrow{D}_0^{t+1}(x^t,d^t,u^t;g)$$
$$- \overrightarrow{D}_0^t(x^t,d^t,u^t;g)] \quad (2.15)$$
$$= LECH + LTCH$$

The *LPI* has been applied in various types of productivity and efficiency studies to estimate the change in productivity and efficiency for various economic units (e.g. Picazo-Tadeo et al., 2014; Epure et al., 2011; Weber and Weber, 2004). In most cases it has been applied to estimate the productivity growth of a country, or to measure the efficiency change of enterprises over a period of time (a detailed list of such types of studies can be found in Table 2.1).

2.6.4 Malmquist-Luenberger Index

The Malmquist-Luenberger productivity index (*MLPI*), developed by Chung et al. (1997), is similar to the Luenberger productivity index. While the traditional Malmquist productivity index expands the desirable and undesirable outputs proportionally as much as it is possible, it does not credit the reduction of undesirable outputs. To overcome this shortcoming, Chung et al. (1997) developed the *MLPI* using directional output distance functions. The *MLPI* readily models joint production of desirable and undesirable outputs, while enabling that production units be credited for reduction of undesirable and increase in desirable outputs.

Based on the directional distance function expressed in Equation 2.13 that considers observation at time *t* based on technology at time *t+1*, the *MLPI* between period *t* and *t+1* can be expressed as follows:

$$ML_t^{t+1} = \left[\frac{\{1 + \vec{D}_o^{t+1}(x^t,d^t,u^t;d^t,-u^t)\}}{\{1 + \vec{D}_o^{t+1}(x^{t+1},d^{t+1},u^{t+1};d^{t+1},-u^{t+1})\}} \times \frac{\{1 + \vec{D}_o^t(x^t,d^t,u^t;d^t,-u^t)\}}{\{1 + \vec{D}_o^t(x^{t+1},d^{t+1},u^{t+1};d^{t+1},-u^{t+1})\}} \right]^{1/2} \quad (2.16)$$

If the value of *MLPI* is greater than one, it implies productivity improvement, and, conversely, productivity declines if the value is less than one.

Like the Malmquist productivity index, the *MLPI* can be decomposed in two parts – technical change (*MLTCH*) and efficiency change (*MLECH*) – which can be expressed as follows:

$MLTCH_t^{t+1}$

$$= \left[\frac{\{1+\vec{D}_o^{t+1}(x^t,d^t,u^t;d^t,-u^t)\}}{\{1+\vec{D}_o^t(x^t,d^t,u^t;d^t,-u^t)\}} \times \frac{\{1+\vec{D}_o^t(x^{t+1},d^{t+1},u^{t+1};d^{t+1},-u^{t+1})\}}{\{1+\vec{D}_o^t(x^{t+1},d^{t+1},u^{t+1};d^{t+1},-u^{t+1})\}} \right]^{1/2} \quad (2.17)$$

$$MLECH_t^{t+1} = \left[\frac{\{1+\vec{D}_o^t(x^t,d^t,u^t;d^t,-u^t)\}}{\{1+\vec{D}_o^{t+1}(x^{t+1},d^{t+1},u^{t+1};d^{t+1},-u^{t+1})\}} \right] \quad (2.18)$$

This productivity index has been widely used in resource and environmental economics, in particular to measure performance of a range of decision making units (see Table 2.1). Some recent studies (e.g. Falavigna et al., 2013; Wu et al., 2012; Zhang et al., 2011; Kumar and Khanna, 2009) applied this efficiency approach to measure environmentally adjusted productivity growth in various industries or countries. Although this model does not require shadow prices of undesirable outputs, finding an appropriate directional vector of the directional distance functions is a critical task in order to obtain acceptable estimates of efficiency and productivity (Lee et al., 2002). While the Malmquist-Luenberger productivity index is certainly an improvement over the traditional measures of productivity growth, it has some limitations, as it fails to establish a link between pollution intensities (pollution emission per unit of desirable output) and productivity growth (Zaim, 2004).

2.6.5 Luenberger Environmental Index

Following the conceptual framework of the *LPI*, Azad and Ancev (2014) developed a new environmentally adjusted productivity and efficiency measurement approach, defined as the Luenberger environmental indicator (*LEI*). Although both *LPI* and *LEI* are constructed using the directional distance functions, the *LPI* is a time-variant efficiency approach that requires time series data to estimate the productivity growth of a country, or to measure the efficiency change of production units over a period of time. In contrast, the *LEI* is a spatially referenced efficiency model that enables researchers to compare the efficiency of production units across space rather than across time.

While many studies use the time-variant directional distance functions to estimate productivity growth and efficiency change of production units, the *LEI* is constructed based on the area-specific directional output distance function as the aim of this indictor is to compare environmental performance of a production unit between two areas (say, region *a* and region *b*). For instance, the area-specific directional output distance function (for region *a*) can be written as:

$$\vec{D}_0^a (x^a, d^a, u^a; g_{d_i} - g_u) = \sup[\beta : (d^a + \beta g_{d_i}, u^a - \beta g_u) \in P^a(x^a)] \quad (2.19)$$

where x is a vector of inputs, $x = (x_1,...,x_N) \in \Re_+^N$, d is a vector of desirable outputs, $d = (d_1,...,d_M) \in \Re_+^M$, and u is a vector of undesirable outputs, $u = (u_1,...,u_J) \in \Re_+^J$. Following Azad and Ancev (2014), the output-oriented Luenberger environmental indicator (*LEI*) can be formulated as:

$$
\begin{aligned}
LEI_a^b = \frac{1}{2} [&\vec{D}_0^b(x^a, d^a, u^a; g_{d_i} - g_u) - \vec{D}_0^b(x^b, d^b, u^b; g_{d_i} - g_u) \\
+ &\vec{D}_0^a(x^a, d^a, u^a; g_{d_i} - g_u) - \vec{D}_0^a(x^b, d^b, u^b; g_{d_i} - g_u)]
\end{aligned}
\quad (2.20)
$$

The output-oriented directional distance function for region *b* can be symbolized as $\vec{D}_o^b$, representing the reference technology constructed from data collected in region *b*. Equation 2.20 can be used to compare the environmentally adjusted performance of a production unit between regions *a* and *b*. If the value of LE_a^b is greater than zero, it indicates that the environmentally adjusted efficiency of a production technology in region *a* is greater than that of region *b*. Put differently, a production activity of region *a* is more economically and environmentally efficient than that of region *b*.

The *LEI* can be additively decomposed (Chambers et al., 1996) as follows:

$$LPI_a^b = [\vec{D}_0^a(x^a,d^a,u^a;g_d,-g_u) - \vec{D}_0^b(x^b,d^b,u^b;g_d,-g_u)] +$$

$$\frac{1}{2}[\vec{D}_0^b(x^b,d^b,u^b;g_d,-g_u) - \vec{D}_0^a(x^b,d^b,u^b;g_d,-g_u) +$$

$$\vec{D}_0^b(x^a,d^a,u^a;g_d,-g_u) - \vec{D}_0^a(x^a,d^a,u^a;g_d,-g_u)] \qquad (2.21)$$

The expression in the first set of brackets of Equation 2.21 represents the efficiency variation between regions *a* and *b,* while the arithmetic mean of the difference between the two terms inside the second set of brackets expresses the technological variation between the two regions.

The quality and abundance of environmental assets, or the significance of ambient environmental quality in the local area or a region where a production unit operates, can be very different compared to another area where another production unit operates. Likewise, the availability of environmentally sensitive resources often used as inputs in productive activities (e.g. water, soil, fish and forests) can vary significantly across regions where different units of observation operate. For example, taking water from the environment for irrigation purposes can be very harmful if it occurs in regions with important but fragile water-dependent ecosystems where water is scarce, as opposed to occurring in regions with relatively plentiful water resources where there are no unique water-dependent ecosystems. When other *EAPE* models have largely overlooked this regional distribution of environmental effects, the *LEI* may be applied to illustrate this regional variability while estimating the efficiency of production units.

2.6.6   Efficiency Models Adjusted Using the Material Balance Principle

Using the material balance principle (*MBP*) to adjust efficiency models provides an alternative view on evaluating environmental and economic outcomes from production processes. This efficiency model is based on the traditional economic model that provides an explicit link between the production technology and the environmental outcome. Lauwers et al. (1999) and Coelli et al. (2007) introduce these approaches in a production process for modelling environmental efficiency measurement. Adjusting based on material balance in a production technology is useful for analysing possible tradeoffs between costs and environmental performance. This model helps in decision making by identifying potential material flow (e.g. nutrients) which can simultaneously increase output and improve environmental quality. Hoang and Coelli (2011) describe this model in agricultural production activity as a part of ecosystems that are invariably subject to the laws of thermodynamics.≠

The *MBP* is mostly applicable in the agricultural and other bio-production sectors, where production activities are considered to be a part of an ecosystem. The concept of the *MBP* postulates that materials used as inputs (e.g. nutrients) in a production process can be transformed not only into desirable outputs but also into pollutants that have the potential to cause emissions (Ayres, 1995). Recent literature provides many examples of the environmental efficiency measurement based on the material balance principle, particularly in the agricultural sector (e.g. Coelli et al., 2007; Lauwers, 2009; Hoang and Coelli, 2011; Hoang and Alauddin, 2012; Hoang and Nguyen, 2013).

2.6.7 Eco-Efficiency Model

Eco-efficiency is one of the environmentally adjusted efficiency models that measures the capability of a production unit to produce goods and services while maintaining minimal environmental degradation. Based on the standard approach in the eco-efficiency literature (e.g. Schmidheiny and Zorraquín, 1996; Helminen, 2000), the formal definition of eco-efficiency is proposed by Kuosmanen and Kortelainen (2005), expressed as a ratio of economic value added to the environmental damage as follows:

Eco-efficiency = Economic value added/Environmental pressure (damage) (2.22)

This definition emphasizes the tradeoffs between economic and environmental characteristics of a production unit. Data envelopment analysis is an effective way to assess eco-efficiency, by estimating relative performance of adopted technologies in relation to the best practice. Eco-efficiency can be improved either by reducing environmental damage while maintaining economic value added, or by improving economic value added but maintaining the environmental damage at the same level. However, the improvement of eco-efficiency through reduction of environmental pressure is often the most cost effective (Urdiales et al., 2016). Furthermore, policies targeted at efficiency improvement tend to be easier to adopt than policies that restrict the level of economic activity. Thus, measurement of eco-efficiency is critical for finding ways of reducing environmental pressure. Several studies have been conducted to measure eco-efficiency in different sectors to provide information about potential improvement based on economic and ecological performance (e.g. Tahara et al., 2005; Kuosmanen and Kortelainen, 2005; Cha et al., 2008). One of the limitations of this method is that it requires extensive data while measuring relative efficiency compared to its general framework. In addition, the sample size must be sufficiently large.

2.6.8 Slack-Based Efficiency Index

Slacks in inputs and outputs are not explicitly accounted in most of the environmental performance measurements that are based on the distance function approach. In particular, a radial model does not account for any slack of undesirable outputs while measuring efficiency. To address this, Tone (2001) proposed a slack-based measure of efficiency that is non-radial and non-oriented and that can utilize inputs and outputs slacks directly in the process of estimating an efficiency measure. Following this approach, Zhou et al. (2006) were the first to construct a composite index that measures both environmental and economic inefficiency. The conceptual framework of the slack-based efficiency model is consistent with the environmental measurement index proposed by Färe et al. (1996). Recent studies that use a slack-based approach include Zhang et al. (2015), Song et al. (2015), Arabi et al. (2016), Peng et al. (2015) and Wang and Wei (2016).

2.6.9 Non-Radial DEA Approach

While many empirical studies (e.g. Veettil et al., 2013; Ali and Klein, 2014) used *DEA* based radial efficiency measures as proposed by Debreu (1951) and Farrell (1957), a non-radial *DEA* approach has been proposed successively by Färe (1975), Färe and Lovell (1978) and Zieschang (1984). Using a radial *DEA* approach one can measure the efficiency of a productive unit by estimating the maximum possible proportional reduction in inputs that is attainable at a given output level. However, the limitation of this approach is that the reduction needs to be the same for all inputs. In contrast, a non-radial approach allows us to reduce inputs in different proportions.

Using a non-radial *DEA* type approach, an environmentally adjusted efficiency index, a global efficiency index (*GEI*) for a production unit (*k*) can be expressed as (Azad et al., 2015):

$$GEI^k(y,x) = \min\left\{\sum_{n=1}^{N} \frac{\lambda_n}{N} : (\lambda_1 x_1, \lambda_2 x_2, ..., \lambda_N x_N) \in L(y), 0 \le \lambda_n \le 1\right\} \tag{2.23}$$

where *GEI* refers to the global efficiency index for a representative production unit that uses a vector of inputs $x = (x_1, ..., x_N) \in \mathfrak{R}_+^N$ to produce a vector of outputs $y = (y_1, ..., y_M) \in \mathfrak{R}_+^M$.

This index implies that various inputs employed in the production process could be minimized by different proportions. In contrast to the radial measure, all inputs are reduced by the same proportion. This degree of flexibility guarantees that the *GEI* measure always uses the subset of efficient points as a reference.

Using the non-radial efficiency measures one can produce fairly robust empirical results (Borger and Kerstens, 1996). However, a review of the theoretical intuition and empirical analysis conducted by Ferrier et al. (1994) found that the radial efficiency measure is not a good empirical substitute for the non-radial alternatives, since it scales inefficient observations down to projection points far removed from the efficient subset. In addition, using radial efficiency measures often leads to a situation where a number of production units have the same efficiency score of unity, and hence creates difficulty in ranking the efficiency level of these units based only on their efficiency scores (Zhou et al., 2007).

Non-radial efficiency measures have a higher discriminating power in evaluating the efficiencies of the production units, and these types of model seem to be more effective in measuring economic and environmental performance. Therefore, in recent years, a number of efficiency studies (e.g. Azad et al., 2015; Meng et al., 2012; Hernández-Sancho et al., 2011; Zhou et al., 2007) used the non-radial DEA approach.

2.6.10 Environmentally Adjusted Total Factor Productivity

The term 'total factor productivity' (*TFP*) accounts for total output growth relative to the growth of inputs. *TFP* can be used to measure efficient use of inputs to produce output in a production process over a period of time. It can measure the productivity growth of individual firms, industries or countries in a variety of ways. An advantage of using *TFP* is that it can address both efficiency change and technical change. The efficiency change index measures the intensity of the utilization of production factors, whereas the technical change index reflects technical improvements. When environmental factors are included in an efficiency model for measuring *TFP*, we have an environmentally adjusted total factor productivity. This model can examine the impact of various environmental factors on the production efficiency. The analysis of environmentally adjusted *TFP* provides information on sustainable use and management of environmental resources for policy making. Many studies proposed different models to construct environmentally adjusted total factor productivity in order to make effective environmental management decisions (e.g. Yaisawarng and Klein, 1994; Hailu and Veeman, 2001; Ball et al., 2004b; Nanere et al., 2007; Hoang and Coelli, 2011).

2.6.11   Metafrontier Malmquist-Luenberger Productivity Index

The Malmquist-Luenberger productivity index (*MLPI*) discussed above is considered to be a powerful tool for estimation of environmentally sensitive productivity growth. However, it does not consider heterogeneity among the observations (i.e. firms) when estimating production efficiency. If heterogeneity exists across firms, then the *MLPI* may lead to biased estimation. To address this issue, O'Donnell et al. (2008) first developed an analytical framework to construct separately two types of frontiers, group frontiers and a metafrontier. While the group frontiers are defined as the boundaries of restricted technology sets (derived from different production characteristics and environments), the metafrontier is constructed as the boundary of an unrestricted technology set. Most importantly, the metafrontier evolves from the group frontiers. This metafrontier production technology can also be decomposed into two components: technological change and efficiency change. This efficiency estimation method can be adapted while considering different technologies in the environmentally adjusted efficiency analysis. It can also be applied to the computation of changes in the technology gap between regional and global frontiers. Recently, several studies have incorporated this metafrontier approach into the *MLPI* measure environmentally adjusted productivity growth of various industry sectors and countries (e.g. O'Donnell et al., 2008; Oh, 2010; Zhang et al., 2013; Du et al., 2016).

2.6.12   Sequential Malmquist-Luenberger Productivity Index

While the traditional Malmquist-Luenberger productivity index integrates the features of technology appropriately, it cannot distinguish between the shift of frontier induced by random shocks from those induced by innovations in technology. In order to overcome this weakness, Oh and Heshmati (2010) developed a sequential Malmquist-Luenberger productivity index (*SMLPI*) for calculating environmentally sensitive productivity growth. They introduced this method by combining the concepts of successive sequential reference production sets (Tulkens and Van den Eeckaut, 1995) and the directional distance function (Luenberger, 1992). The *SMLPI* is an expansion of the *MLPI*, by accumulating the technological knowledge over time. This methodology can be used to estimate technical change and efficiency change indices by eliminating the possibility of contraction of the production sets.

2.7 DISCUSSION ON THE RATIO- AND DIFFERENCE-BASED EFFICIENCY APPROACHES

The discussion in section 2.6 reveals that there are two general types of primal productivity indexes that are used in environmentally adjusted productivity and efficiency analysis: ratio-based indexes and difference-based indexes. A difference-based index measures productivity and efficiency of an economic activity in terms of differences of distance, or directional distance functions, rather than ratios, as is the case with ratio-based indexes. For example, *LPI* and *LEI* are difference-based approaches, while *EPI*, *MPI* and *MLPI* are ratio-based efficiency models. While the ratio-based indexes have been employed in a large number of empirical applications, few studies have applied the difference-based indexes (see Table 2.1). However, the very nature of the ratio-based indexes creates a problem with evaluation of the actual environmental impacts. Ratio-based indexes can only indicate a relative difference in environmental performance. For instance, based on using a ratio-based index, two production units might be found to have the same environmentally adjusted efficiency score even though one of them causes many times greater environmental damage than the other.

When it comes to evaluating environmental effects, the extent of the environmental impact is often more important than the relative tradeoff between economic and environmental efficiency. When we want to measure the economic contribution made by an individual production unit net of the environmental degradation caused by making that contribution, difference-based indexes lend themselves well to this purpose. In addition, there are several known limitations of using ratio-based indexes. For instance, one source of nuisance with a ratio-based index obviously occurs when the denominator of the index has a zero value. Another limitation, as some empirical studies have shown (Boussemart et al., 2003; Briec and Kerstens, 2004; Managi, 2003), is that ratio-based productivity indexes overestimate productivity change compared to other productivity indicators.

In contrast, there are strong justifications for applying the difference-based approach in the productivity and efficiency analysis, in general, and in environmentally adjusted analysis in particular. For instance, while the *MPI* (a ratio-based approach) focuses on either cost minimization or revenue maximization, the *LPI* (a difference-based approach) is the dual to the profit function, and implies profit maximization (Boussemart et al., 2003; Chambers et al., 1996). In addition, using the *MPI* requires a choice to be made between an input and an output perspective (Färe et al., 1985; Chambers et al., 1996), whereas the *LPI* can address simultaneously input contraction and output expansion (Boussemart et al., 2003; Managi, 2003). Therefore, the ratio-based efficiency approaches like the *LPI* require less restrictive assumptions than the other standard productivity indexes (Williams et al., 2011).

2.8 MEASUREMENT TECHNIQUES OF *EAPE* MODELS

This section describes the most frequently used estimation techniques for *EAPE* models in the literature. Within the literature on environmentally adjusted productivity and efficiency measurement, there are two broad classes of methods available to compute efficiency performance of production units. These are: (a) parametric, or econometric methods; and (b) non-parametric, or mathematical programming methods. There are two essential differences between these approaches in the calculation of a production frontier function (Lovell, 1993). The econometric approach (e.g. the stochastic frontier approach) requires specification of technology (i.e. production function), which is likely to be restrictive in many cases (Azad et al., 2015). This approach attempts to distinguish the effects of statistical noise from the effects of productive inefficiency. On the other hand, non-parametric methods (such as data envelopment analysis) use linear programming to construct a non-parametric piece-wise surface over the data so as to be able to estimate production efficiencies without parametrizing the production technology. It combines statistical noise (measurement error) and inefficiency. Both of these efficiency measurement techniques are briefly described in the following sections.

2.8.1 Stochastic Frontier Approach

The stochastic frontier approach (*SFA*) was first introduced independently by Aigner et al. (1977) and Meeusen and Van den Broeck (1977) to measure efficiency of a unit of observation.[8] The strength of the *SFA* is that it considers stochastic noise in data, and also allows for the statistical testing of hypotheses concerning production structure and degree of inefficiency. Two types of error components appear in stochastic frontier specification. One accounts for the existence of technical inefficiency, and the other accounts for random disturbances. This model offers a comprehensive efficiency analysis based on the econometric estimation of the production frontier. Thus, stochastic frontier yields technical, allocative and economic efficiency which are free from distortions stemming from statistical noise. The limitation of the *SFA* is the restrictive assumption of the functional form of the production function and distribution of one-sided error (Førsund et al., 1980).

A number of studies used the *SFA* in the *EAPE* efficiency models (see Table 2.1). In an early study, Reinhard et al. (1999) used a stochastic translog production frontier to investigate the environmental impacts of dairy farms, in which nitrogen surplus was treated as an environmental detrimental input. Reinhard et al. (2000) extended their approach to multiple environmentally detrimental inputs, and implemented this approach using both stochastic frontier analysis and data envelopment analysis. Cuesta and Zofío (2005) introduced the parametric hyperbolic distance function specification in conventional input-output space to estimate technical efficiency with the stochastic frontier approach. Cuesta et al. (2009) extended this approach to accommodate undesirable outputs and to estimate environmental efficiency. In recent years, Tamini et al. (2012), Hoang and Nguyen (2013), Zhou et al. (2015); Du et al. (2016), Huang et al. (2016), Mamardashvili et al. (2016) and others used the *SFA* to estimate environmentally adjusted efficiency of various decision-making units (see Table 2.1).

2.8.2   Data Envelopment Analysis

The body of literature on data envelopment analysis (*DEA*) is very large and growing rapidly (see Table 2.1). *DEA*, originally proposed by Farrell (1957) and further developed by Charnes et al. (1978), is now a popular non-parametric approach to measuring productivity and efficiency. One of the great advantages of *DEA* is that there is no requirement to specify a particular functional form on the technology, which enables it to accommodate multiple inputs and outputs (Färe et al., 1996).

Detailed descriptions of *DEA* are available in a number of studies, including Färe et al. (1985), Seiford and Thrall (1990), Charnes et al. (1995), Lovell (1993, 1994), Ali and Seiford (1993), Färe et al. (1994), Seiford (1996), Cooper et al. (2000) and Thanassoulis (2001). Färe et al. (1989) was one of the earliest studies in which *DEA* was proposed to calculate an environmental efficiency measure. Since that work, a number of studies have been devoted to modeling undesirable outputs in the traditional *DEA* framework, as *DEA* can be successfully used in aggregating ecological and environmental pressures in measuring the performance of a productive unit. Using *DEA*, Färe et al. (1996) developed an environmental performance indicator, and argued that there are various reasons for choosing *DEA* as an alternative method for quantifying environmental performance. Some of the specific reasons are:

- a clear and obvious standardization since all productive units are ranked using a score;
- an important flexibility since various versions of the model can be formulated easily by stressing important aspects in different ways;
- the robustness of the non-linear programming methods used to compute the indicators;
- one does not need to define factors to weight the various environmental impacts (i.e. pollution) of a firm, since the weights are self-defined by the activity analysis model applied during the computation of the efficiency scores;
- the explicit reference to best practice, which is indeed the essence of the activity analysis models.

Based on a comprehensive survey of the literature, Tyteca (1996) recommended the use of *DEA* for environmentally adjusted productivity and efficiency measurement. The application of *DEA* to estimate environmental performance is mainly focused on comparing two types of units: various countries (e.g. Lovell et al., 1995; Taskin and Zaim, 2001; Zofío and Prieto, 2001; Färe et al., 2004; Zhou et al., 2008) or various sectors in an economy (e.g. Golany et al., 1994; Ball et al., 1994; Färe et al., 1996; Tyteca, 1997; Reinhard et al., 1999, 2000; Hailu and Veeman, 2001; Sarkis and Cordeiro, 2001; Jung et al., 2001; Bevilacqua and Braglia, 2002). These examples from the literature have shown that *DEA* is a lucrative approach for measurement of environmental performance for any type of productive activity. In addition, Hoang and Nguyen (2013) conducted a comparative study between the stochastic frontier analysis and data envelopment analysis, and concluded that both methods have some strengths and weaknesses, and therefore researchers should exercise caution when choosing between models for measuring environmentally adjusted productivity and efficiency so as to best address the research questions posed and make best use of the available data.

2.9   EMPIRICAL APPLICATIONS OF ENVIRONMENTALLY ADJUSTED EFFICIENCY MEASUREMENTS

In the early 1990s, few studies attempted to develop the *EAPE* models, while an increasing trend of developing *EAPE* methods has been observed since 2006 (Figure 2.3). With the increase in environmental awareness, the number of *EAPE* studies has also increased. There are a large number of studies within the efficiency literature that applied environmentally

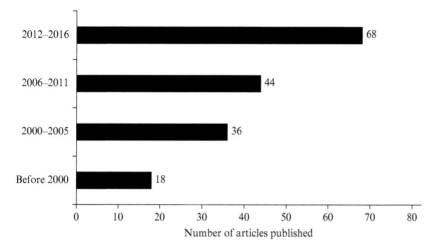

Figure 2.3 Number of articles related to EAPE published over the last 25 years

adjusted efficiency measurement techniques in various sectors of the economy, including agricultural production, the power plant/generation industry, the manufacturing industry, the transport sector and others. In addition, a large number of studies have investigated environmentally adjusted efficiency across countries or various regions within a country (Table 2.2). As can be observed from Figure 2.4, the *EAPE* methods have been often used in the agricultural sector, the fuel/energy industries and the manufacturing industry. On the other hand, a significant number of studies evaluated the performance of OECD countries using the *EAPE* methods.

Several agricultural and resource economic studies have focused on the assessment of environmental–economic performance in the agricultural sector. This is due to the fact that environmental impacts of agricultural production have recently become key concerns for sustainable agriculture. Agricultural production activities significantly affect the environment in the form of pollution or degradation of soil, water and air through excessive use of pesticides, fertilizers and other agro-chemicals (OECD, 2008). Efficient use of natural and environmental resources in agricultural activities can reduce the environmental impacts. Therefore, several methods and models have been developed and applied to measure economic–environmental efficiency of the agricultural sector (Table 2.2 and Figure 2.4). Ball et al. (1994b) provided an empirical application for the US agricultural production based on the model proposed by Färe et al. (1989). Nitrogen surplus was considered an undesirable output in this study.

Table 2.2a   Empirical application of EAPE analysis

Analysis	Areas of application
Färe et al. 1989	Paper mills
Färe et al. 1994	Country level
Ball et al. 1994	US agricultural farms
Yaisawarng and Klein 1994	US electric power industry
Fare et al.1996	Fossil fuel-fired electric utilities
Chung et al.1997	Pulp and paper mills
Tyteca 1997	US fossil fuel-fired electric utilities
Courcelle et al. 1998	Municipal solid waste
Reinhard et al. 1999	Dutch dairy farms
Kumar 2006	Country level
Reinhard et al. 2000	Dutch dairy farms
Reinhard and Thijssen 2000	Dutch dairy farms
Färe et al. 2001	Manufacturing sector
Sueyoshi and Goto 2001	Coal-fired power plant
Hailu and Veeman 2001	Canadian paper and pulp industry
Weber and Domazlicky 2001	Manufacturing industry
Arocena and Waddams Price 2002	Coal-fired power plant
Lee et al. 2002	Fossil-fuelled power plants
Bevilacqua and Braglia 2002	Oil refineries
Koeijer et al. 2002	Sugar beet farms
Ball et al. 2004b	US farms
Chambers 2002	Agricultural production
Weber and Weber 2004	Transport industry
Kwon and Lee 2004	Rice farms
Lansink and Reinhard 2004	Pig farms
Gang and Felmingham 2004	Australian irrigation industry
Färe et al. 2004	OECD countries
Zaim 2004	Manufacturing firms
Coelli and Walding 2005	Urban water supply
Kuosmanen and Kortelainen 2005	Road transportation
Färe et al. 2005	Electric utilities
Zhang and Xue 2005	Vegetable farms
Picazo-Tadeo et al. 2005	Manufacturing industry
Färe et al. 2006	US agriculture industry
Zhou et al. 2006	OECD countries
Färe et al. 2007	Coal-fired power plants, fisheries
Nanere et al. 2007	Australian agriculture
Murty et al. 2007	Thermal power plant
Piot-Lepetit and Moing 2007	Pig farms
Managi and Jena 2008	India
Zhou and Ang 2008	OECD countries
Zhou et al. 2008	Country

Table 2.2b   Empirical application of EAPE analysis

Analysis	Areas of application
Yang and Pollitt 2009	Chinese coal-fired power plants
Kumar and Khanna 2009	Country
Sueyoshi and Goto 2009	Electricity utilities
Azad and Ancev 2010	Irrigated agriculture
Oh 2010	OECD countries
Sueyoshi et al. 2010	Coal-fired power plants
Oh and Heshmati 2010	OECD countries
Coelli and Rao 2010	Agriculture
Hoang and Alauddin 2010	Agriculture
Kumar and Managi 2010	Electric utility
Mandal and Madheswaran 2010	Cement industry
Hoang 2011	Agriculture
Oggioni et al. 2011	Cement industry
Zhang et al. 2011	Regional level
Hoang and Alauddin 2011	Agricultural production
Picazo-Tadeo et al. 2011	Rain-fed agriculture
Sueyoshi and Goto 2011	Fossil-fuel power plants
Hoang and Coelli 2011	Crops and livestock
Tamini et al. 2012	Agricultural production
Hoang and Alauddin 2012	Agricultural production
Färe et al. 2012	Coal-fired power plants
Heng et al. 2012	Trucking industry
Picazo-Tadeo et al. 2012	Olive farms
Wu et al. 2012	Regional industrial sector
Sueyoshi and Goto 2012	Coal-fired power plants
Zhang et al. 2012	China province
Zhou et al. 2012	Electric power industry
Chang et al. 2013	Transportation system
Falavigna et al. 2013	Agriculture
Hoang and Nguyen 2013	Rice farms
Guesmi 2013	Crop farms
Zhang et al. 2013	Fossil-fuel electricity generation
Martini et al. 2013	Airports
Feng et al. 2013	Iron and steel industry
Halkos and Tzeremes 2013	Regional-level efficiency
Azad and Ancev 2014	Irrigated agriculture
Xie et al. 2014	Electric power industry
Azad et al. 2015	Irrigated enterprises
Chang et al. 2014	Airlines
Jin et al. 2014	APEC countries
Molinos-Senante et al. 2014	Water industry
Sueyoshi and Goto 2014	Chemical and pharmaceutical firms
Picazo-Tadeo et al. 2014	GHG emissions in European Union

Table 2.2c   Empirical application of EAPE analysis

Analysis	Areas of application
Bi et al. 2015	Industrial sector
Liu et al. 2016	Industrial sector
Song et al. 2015	Transportation
Mohammadi et al. 2015	Paddy farms
Tsionas et al. 2015	Dairy farms
Wang et al. 2015	Chinese cities
Woo et al. 2015	Renewable energy
Yang et al. 2015	Province level
Lee et al. 2015	Airlines industry
Oh and Shin 2015	Manufacturing industry
Zhang et al. 2015	Fossil energy industry
Zhou et al. 2015	Hog production
Azad and Ancev 2016	Cotton enterprises
Arabi et al. 2016	Power industry
Balezentis et al. 2016	Country level
Duan et al. 2016	Thermal power industry
Dakpo et al. 2016	Sheep meat farming
Du et al. 2016	Electric power plant
Fujii et al. 2016	Manufacturing industry
Huang et al. 2016	Livestock
Liu et al. 2016	Coal-fired power plant
Li and Lin 2016	Manufacturing industry
Mamardashvili et al. 2016	Dairy farms
Jiang et al. 2016	Textile industry
Njuki et al. 2016	Dairy farms
Song and Zheng 2016	Thermoelectric power plant
Yaqubi et al. 2016	Rice farms
Valadkhani et al. 2016	Cross-country analysis
Wang et al. 2016	Industrial sector
Wang and Wei 2016	Country level
Wang and Zhao 2016	Metals industry
Yu et al. 2016	Pulp and paper industry
Zhang and Chen 2016	Country level
Zhang et al. 2016	Manufacturing industry
Alfredsson et al. 2016	Pulp and paper industry
Sueyoshi and Yuan 2016	Country level

Considering nitrogen surplus as an environmentally determinant input, Reinhard et al. (1999) conducted a similar type of study, but the application was to Dutch dairy farms. Recent studies of *EAPI* models that focused on agriculture are Färe et al. (2006, 2007), Piot-Lepetit and Moing

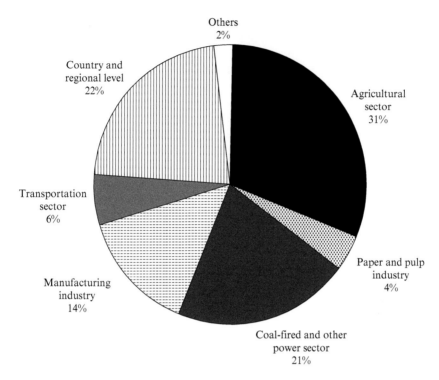

Figure 2.4 Application of EAPE models in various areas

(2007), Azad and Ancev (2010, 2014, 2016), Hoang and Alauddin (2010), Azad et al. (2015), Njuki et al. (2016) and Huang et al. (2016). Some other contributions are also listed in Table 2.2. The applications of *EAPE* in the agricultural sector used a wide range of approaches, including input and output distance function and directional distance function (e.g., Zhang and Xue, 2005; Picazo-Tadeo et al., 2011; Mohammadi et al., 2015; Tsionas et al., 2015; Njuki et al., 2016). Some other studies used the material balance principle to derive environmental efficiency measures in agriculture (e.g. Reinhard and Thijssen, 2000; Coelli et al., 2007; Lauwers, 2009).

Economic growth is often linked to a rapid development of an industrial sector. However, the development of the industrial sector often results in various forms of pollution of air and water, and other contamination of the environment. This kind of environmental degradation is associated with climate change and health problems that threaten future generations. It is thus necessary to look for a balance between economic development and industrialization on one hand, and pollution mitigation on the other, in order to move towards sustainable development. Therefore, there are a number of studies in the productivity measurement and efficiency analysis literature that have applied environmentally adjusted efficiency techniques to various industrial sectors, including the coal-fired power industry, various types of manufacturing and other industries (Table 2.2 and Figure 2.4). Some studies focused on estimating the environmentally adjusted efficiency of the paper, solid waste, water management and transport sectors. Other studies have focused on measuring country or regional level environmental efficiency in relation to carbon dioxide (CO_2) emissions. Woo et al. (2015) offer an extensive summary of this literature.

Since greenhouse gases are a common industrial pollutant, carbon emissions have been of considerable interest. Since 2006 there have been a large number of studies that evaluated the environmental and economic performance of CO_2 emission allocation at firm, regional and country level (Zhou and Wang, 2016). Many of these studies deal with regional or country level environmentally adjusted efficiency analysis (e.g., Zhang et al., 2011; Zhou et al., 2012; Wang et al., 2013; Huang et al., 2013; Zhou et al., 2012; Yang et al., 2015; Valadkhani et al., 2016). For instance, Zhou et al. (2012) constructed an energy efficiency performance index (as the ratio of actual energy efficiency to potential energy efficiency) and a carbon emission performance index (as the ratio of potential carbon intensity to actual carbon intensity) to evaluate the comparative efficiency of OECD and non-OECD countries in relation to energy and CO_2 emission performance in electricity generation. This type of analysis can provide information about the potential amount of energy savings. Some other papers include Lee et al. (2002), Färe et al. (2012) and Xie et al. (2014), which focused on measuring efficiency of firms in relation to their carbon emissions.

2.10   CONCLUSIONS

The necessity for effective measurement of environmentally adjusted productivity and efficiency of production units becomes an essential element of environmental policy development and analysis. This chapter aimed to present as complete a list as possible of the literature on environmentally adjusted productivity measurement and efficiency analysis models developed and applied in various economic sectors since the 1990s. An extensive literature survey on the development of such measurement techniques reveals that *EAPE* methods have been gaining popularity. This can be linked to a particular period in time when public concern about the environmental impacts of production activities started to grow substantially. We briefly discussed some of the widely used *EAPE* approaches and models applied in various sectors of the economy.

Our extensive literature survey shows that most of the *EAPE* models are based on either distance functions or directional distance functions approaches. These *EAPE* models are constructed based on non-parametric approaches or data envelopment analysis (*DEA*) as these methods enable researchers to adequately incorporate environmental variables in any type of productivity measurement and efficiency analysis. The *DEA* method has been extensively used in many empirical studies as the most popular technique for the computation of the components of *EAPE* models.

The analysis of empirical applications shows that *EAPE* models have been widely used to evaluate environmental adjusted productivity growth and efficiency/performance across countries or regions. In contrast, a sector-wise analysis reveals that the coal-fired power sector and the electricity sector more generally have drawn a lot of attention in the environmentally adjusted productivity measurement and efficiency analysis. This may be justified with the argument that the environmental impacts generated from the power generation sector are significant, and perhaps more significant than those of other sectors of the economy.

As discussed in this chapter, each *EAPE* model has some strengths and drawbacks; therefore, researchers should be cautious when choosing appropriate methods to measure environmentally adjusted productivity and efficiency of decision-making units. Appropriate use of such methods for measuring tradeoffs between economic and environmental efficiency enables researchers to identify efficient production technologies and practices that can deliver good economic outcomes at the least cost to the environment and natural resources.

NOTES

1. We do not provide here an exhaustive list of the literature that reports research on general productivity and efficiency. Exhaustive list of studies reporting on efficiency and productivity in various economic sectors can be found in Fried et al. (2008) and Abbott and Cohen (2009).
2. A detailed discussion on the distance function is provided in Section 2.5.
3. Directional distance function is discussed in Section 2.5.
4. Detailed comparison of Shephard's distance function and directional distance function can be found in Färe and Primont 1990 and Chung et al. 1997, respectively.
5. This output distance function is known as a Shephard distance function.
6. Some discussion on non-parametric methods is presented in Section 2.7.
7. Since the theoretical framework behind the Malmquist productivity index is lengthy, we do not discuss this index in this chapter in great detail. Readers can be directed to Färe et al. (2001) or Fried et al. (2008) for a detailed discussion of this index.
8. Due to space limits we exclude basic descriptions of the *SFA*, but interested readers are directed to Green (2008) for detailed discussion of this method.

REFERENCES

Abbott, M. and B. Cohen (2009), 'Productivity and efficiency in water industry', *Utilities Policies*, **17**, 233–244.

Abad, A. (2015), 'An environmental generalised Luenberger-Hicks-Moorsteen productivity indicator and an environmental generalised Hicks-Moorsteen productivity index,' *Journal of Environmental Management*, **161**, 325–334.

Afriat, S.N. (1972), 'Efficiency estimation of production function', *International Economic Review*, **13**, 568–598.

Aigner, D., C.A.K. Lovell and P. Schmidt (1977), 'Formulation and estimation of stochastic frontier production function models', *Journal of Econometrics*, **6**, 21–37.

Alfredsson, E., J. Mansson and P. Vikstrom (2016), 'Internalizing external environmental effects in efficiency analysis the Swedish pulp and paper industry 2000–2007', *Economic Analysis and Policy*, **51**, 22–31.

Ali, A.I. and L.M. Seiford (1993), 'The mathematical programming approach to efficiency analysis', in H.O. Fried, C.A.K. Lovell and S.S. Schmidt (eds), *The Measurement of Productive Efficiency: Techniques and Applications*, Oxford University Press, New York.

Ali, M.K. and K.K. Klein (2014), 'Water use efficiency and productivity of the irrigation districts in Southern Alberta', *Water Resources Management*, **28**, 2751–2766.

Arabi, B., S. Munisamy, A. Emrouznejad, M. Toloo and M.S. Ghazizades (2016), 'Eco-efficiency considering the issue of heterogeneity among power plants', *Energy*, **111**, 722–732.

Arocena, P. and C.W. Price (2002), 'Generating efficiency: economic and environmental regulation of public and private electricity generators in Spain', *International Journal of Industrial Organization*, 20(1), 41–69.

Ayres, R.U. (1995), 'Thermodynamics and process analysis for future economic scenarios', *Environmental and Resource Economics*, **6**, 207–230.

Azad, M.A.S. (2012), 'Economic and environmental efficiency of irrigated agriculture in the Murray-Darling Basin' Doctor of Philosophy (Ph.D) dissertation, Faculty of Agriculture and Environment, the University of Sydney, New South Wales.

Azad, M.A.S. and T. Ancev (2016), 'Economics of salinity effects from irrigated cotton: an efficiency analysis', *Water Economics and Policy*, **2**(1). DOI: 10.1142/S2382624X16500028.

Azad M.A.S. and T. Ancev (2014), 'Measuring environmental efficiency of agricultural water use: a Luenberger environmental indicator', *Journal of Environmental Management*, **145**, 314–320.

Azad, M.A.S. and T. Ancev (2010), 'Using ecological indexes to measure economic and environmental performance of irrigated agriculture', *Ecological Economics*, **69**, 1731–1739.

Azad, M.A.S., T. Ancev and F. Hernández-Sancho (2015), 'Efficient water use for sustainable irrigation industry', *Water Resources Management*, **29**(5), 1683–1696.

Balezentis, T., T.B. Li, D. Streimikiene and A. Balezentis (2016), 'Is the Lithuanian economy approaching the goals of sustainable energy and climate change mitigation? Evidence from DEA-based environmental performance index', *Journal of Cleaner Production*, **116**, 23–31.

Ball, V.E., C.A.K. Lovell, H. Luu and R. Nehring (2004a), 'Incorporating environmental impacts in the measurement of agricultural productivity growth', *Journal of Agricultural Resource Economics*, **29**, 436–60.

Ball V.E., R. Färe, S. Grosskopf and R. Nehring (2004b), 'Productivity of the U.S. agricultural sector: the case of undesirable outputs', in C. Hulten, E. Dean and M. Harper (eds), *New Development in Productivity Analysis*, University of Chicago Press, Chicago, pp. 541–585.

Ball, V.E., C.A.K. Lovell, R.F. Nehring and A. Somwaru (1994), 'Incorporating undesirable outputs into models of production: an application to U.S. agriculture', *Cahiers d'Economie et Sociologie Rurales*, **31**, 59–73.

Banker, R.D., A. Charnes, and W. Copper (1984), 'Some models for estimation of technical and scale inefficiencies in data envelopment analysis', *Management Science*, **30**, 1078–1092.

Bevilacqua, M. and M. Braglia (2002), 'Environmental efficiency analysis for ENI oil refineries', *Journal of Cleaner Production*, **10** (1), 85–92.

Bi, G., Y. Luo, J. Ding and L. Liang (2015), 'Environmental performance analysis of Chinese industry from a slacks-based perspective', *Annual Operational Research*, **228**, 65–80.

Boggs, R.L. (1997), 'Hazardous waste treatment facilities: modelling production with pollution as both an input and an output', unpublished PhD dissertation, University of North Carolina, Chapel Hill.

Borger, B.D. and K. Kerstens (1996), 'Radial and nonradial measures of technical efficiency: an empirical illustration for Belgian local governments using an FDH reference technology', *Journal of Productivity Analysis*, **7**, 4–62.

Boussemart, J.P., W. Briec, K. Kerstens and J.C. Poutineau (2003), 'Luenberger and Malmquist productivity indexes: theoretical comparisons and empirical illustration', *Bulletin of Economic Research*, **55**(4), 391–405.

Briec, W. and K. Kerstens (2004), 'A Luenberger–Hicks–Moorsteen productivity indicator: its relation to the Hicks–Moorsteen productivity index and the Luenberger productivity indicator', *Economic Theory*, **23**, 925–934.

Briec, W. and K. Kerstens (2009), "The Luenberger productivity indicator: an economic specification leading to infeasibilities', *Economic Model*, **25**(3), 597–600.

Caves, D.W., L.R. Christensen and W.E. Diewert (1982), 'Multilateral comparisons of output, input, and productivity using superlative index numbers', *Economic Journal*, **92**, 73–86.

Cha, K., S. Lim and T. Hur (2008), 'Eco-efficiency approach for global warming in the context of Kyoto mechanism', *Ecological Economics*, **67**, 274–280.

Chambers, R.G. (1996), 'A new look at exact input, output, productivity and technical change measurement, Working paper 96-05, Department of Agricultural and Resource Economics, University of Maryland, College Park.

Chambers, R.G. (2002), 'Exact nonradial input, output, and productivity measurement, *Economic Theory*', **20**(4), 751–765.

Chambers, R.G., R. Färe and S. Grosskopf (1996), 'Productivity growth in APEC countries', *Pacific Economic Review*, **1** (3), 181–190.

Chang Y.T., N. Zhang, D. Danao and N. Zhang (2013), 'Environmental efficiency analysis of transportation system in China: a non-radial DEA approach', *Energy Policy*, **58**, 277–283.

Chang, Y.T., H.S. Park, J.B. Jeong and J.W. Lee (2014), 'Evaluating economic and environmental efficiency of global airlines: a SBM-DEA approach', *Transportation Research Development*, **27**, 46–50.

Charnes, A., W.W. Cooper and E. Rhodes (1978), 'Measuring efficiency of decision-making units', *European Journal of Operational Research*, **2**(6), 429–444.

Charnes, A., W.W. Cooper, A.Y. Lewin and L.M. Seiford (1995), *Data Envelopment Analysis: Theory Methodology and Application*, Kluwer Academic Publishers, Boston.

Chung, Y., R. Färe and S. Grosskopf (1997), 'Productivity and undesirable outputs: a directional distance function approach', *Journal of Environmental Management*, **51**, 229–240.

Coelli, T. and S. Walding (2005), 'Performance measurement in the Australian water supply industry', Working paper series no 1/2005, Centre for Efficiency and Productivity Analysis, School of Economics, University of Queensland, Brisbane.

Coelli, T.J. and D.S.P. Rao (2010), 'Total factor productivity growth in agriculture: a Malmquist index analysis of 93 countries, 1980–2000', Centre for Efficiency and Productivity Analysis, School of Economics, Brisbane.

Coelli, T., L. Lauwers and G. Van Huylenbroeck (2007), 'Environmental efficiency measurement and the materials balance condition', *Journal of Productivity Analysis*, **28**, 3–12.

Coelli, T.J., D.S.P. Rao, C.J. O'Donnell and G.E. Battese (2005), *An Introduction to Efficiency and Productivity Analysis* (2nd edition), Springer, New York.

Coggins, J.S. and J. R. Swinton (1996), 'The price of pollution: a dual approach to valuing SO2 allowances', *Journal of Environmental Economics and Management*, **30**, 58–72.

Cooper, W.W., L.M. Seiford and K. Tone (2000), *Data Envelopment Analysis: A Comprehensive Text with Models, Applications, References and DEA-Solver Software*, Kluwer Academic Publishers, Boston.

Courcelle, C., M.P. Kestemount, D. Tyteca and M. Istalle (1998), 'Assessing the economic and environmental performance of municipal soil waste collection and sorting programmers', *Waste Management and Research*, **16**(3), 253–263.

Cropper, M.L. and W.E. Oates (1992), 'Environmental economics: a survey', *Journal of Economic Literature*, **30**(2), 675–740.

Cuesta, R.A. and J.L. Zofío (2005), 'Hyperbolic efficiency and parametric distance functions with application to Spanish saving banks', *Journal of Productivity Analysis*, **24**, 31–48.

Cuesta, R.A., Lovell. C.A.K. and Zofío, J.L. (2009). Environmental efficiency measurement with translog distance function: a parametric approach, *Ecological Economics*, **68**(8–9), 2232–2242.

Dakpo, K.H., P. Jeanneaux and L. Latruffe (2016), 'Greenhouse gas emission and efficiency in French sheep meat farming: a non-parametric framework of pollution-adjusted technology', *European Review of Agricultural Economics*, **44**(1), 33–65.

Debreu, G. (1951), 'The coefficient of resource utilization', *Econometrica*, **19**, 273–292.

Diewert, W.E. and K. Fox. (2014), 'Reference technology sets, free disposal hulls and productivity decompositions,' *Economics Letters*, **122**, 238–242.

Du, L., A. Hanley and N. Zhang (2016), 'Environmental technical efficiency, technology gap and shadow price of coal fuelled power plants in China: a parametric metafrontier analysis', *Resource and Energy Economics*, **43**, 14–32.

Duan, N., J.P. Guo and B.C. Xie (2016), 'Is there a difference between the energy and CO2 emission performance for China's thermal power industry?

A bootstrapped directional distance function approach', *Applied Energy*, **162**, 1552–1563.

Emrouznejad, A., B. Parker and G. Tavares (2008), 'Evaluation of research in efficiency and productivity: a survey and analysis of the first 30 years of scholarly literature in DEA', *Socio-Economic Planning Sciences*, **42**(3), 151–157.

Epure, M., K. Kerstens and D. Prior (2011), 'Bank productivity and performance groups: a decomposition approach based upon the Luenberger productivity indicator', *European Journal of Operational Research*, **211**, 630–641.

Falavigna, G., A. Manello and S. Pavone (2013), 'Environmental efficiency, productivity and public funds: the case of the Italian agricultural industry', *Agricultural System*, **121**, 73–80.

Färe, R. (1975), 'Efficiency and the production function', *Zeitschrift für Nationalökonomie*, **35**, 317–324.

Färe, R. and S. Grosskopf (2004), *New Directions: Efficiency and Productivity*, Boston: Kluwer Academic.

Färe, R. and C.A.K. Lovell (1978), 'Measuring the technical efficiency of production', *Journal of Economic Theory*, **19**, 150–162.

Färe, R. and D. Primont (1995), *Multi-Output Production and Duality: Theory and Applications*, Boston: Kluwer Academic.

Färe, R. and D. Primont (1990), 'A distance function approach to multioutput technologies', *Southern Economic Journal*, **56**(4), 879–891.

Färe, R., Grosskopf, S. and W. Weber (2006), 'Shadow prices and pollution costs in U.S. agriculture', *Ecological Economics*, **56**, 89–103.

Färe, R., J.E. Kirkley and J.B. Walden (2007), 'Estimating capacity and efficiency in fisheries with undesirable outputs', VIMS Marine research report no. 2007-06.

Färe, R., R. Grabowski and S. Grosskopf (1985), 'Technical efficiency in Philippine agriculture', *Applied Economics*, **17**, 205–214.

Färe, R., S. Grosskopf and C. Pasurka (2013), 'Joint production of good and bad outputs with a network application', in J. Shogren (ed.), *Encyclopedia of Energy, Natural Resources and Environmental Economics*, Amsterdam: Elsevier.

Färe, R., S. Grosskopf and C.A. Pasurka (2001), 'Accounting for air pollution emissions in measures of state manufacturing productivity growth', *Journal of Regional Science*, **41**(3), 381–409.

Färe, R., S. Grosskopf and C.A.K. Lovell (1994), *Production Frontiers*, Cambridge University Press, Cambridge.

Färe, R., S. Grosskopf and F. Hernández-Sancho (2004), 'Environmental performance: an index number approach', *Resource and Energy Economics*, **26**(4), 343–352.

Färe, R., S. Grosskopf and P. Roos (1996), 'On two definitions of productivity', *Economics Letters*, **53**(3), 269–274.

Färe, R., S. Grosskopf and P. Roos (1998), 'Malmquist productivity indexes: a survey of theory and practice', in R. Färe, S. Grosskopf and R. Russell (eds), *Index Numbers: Essays in Honour of Sten Malmquist*, Kluwer, Boston.

Färe, R., S. Grosskopf and W. Weber (2006), 'Shadow price and pollution costs in U.S. agriculture', *Ecological Economics*, **56**, 89–103.

Färe, R., S. Grosskopf, C.A.K. Lovell and C. Pasurka (1989), 'Multilateral productivity comparisons when some outputs are undesirable: a non-parametric approach', *Review of Economics and Statistics*, **71**, 90–98.

Färe, R., S. Grosskopf, C.A.K. Lovell and S. Yaisawarng (1993), 'Derivation of shadow prices for undesirable outputs: a distance function approach', *The Review of Economics and Statistics*, **75**(2), 374–380.

Färe, R., S. Grosskopf, C.A.K. Lovell, D. Noh and W. Weber (2005), 'Characteristics of a polluting technology: theory and practice', *Journal of Economics*, **126**, 469–92.
Färe, R., S. Grosskopf, T. Lundgren, P. Marklund and W. Zhou (2012), 'Productivity: should we include bad'? CERE working paper, 2012:13, Centre for Environmental and Resource Economics (CERE), Sweden.
Farrell, M.J. (1957), 'The measurement of productive efficiency', *Journal of the Royal Statistical Society, Series A*, **120** (3), 253–281.
Farrell, M.J. and N. Fieldhouse (1962), 'Estimating efficient production function under non-increasing return to scale', *Journal of Royal Statistics Society, Series A*, **125**, 252–267.
Feng, H., Q. Zhang., J. Lei., W. Fu and X. Xu. (2013), 'Energy efficiency and productivity change of China's iron and steel industry: accounting for undesirable output', *Energy Policy*, **54**, 204–213.
Ferrier, G.D., K. Kerstens and P.V. Eeckaut (1994), 'Radial and nonradial technical efficiency measures on a DEA reference technology: a comparison using US banking data', Core discussion paper 9423, Centre for Operations Research and Econometrics, Université catholique de Louvain.
Førsund, F.R., C.A.K. Lovell and P. Schmidt (1980), 'A survey of frontier production functions and their relationship to efficiency measurement', *Journal of Econometrics*, **13**, 5–25.
Fried, H.O., C.A.K. Lovell and S.S. Schmidt (eds) (2008), *The Measurement of Productive Efficiency and Productivity Growth*, Oxford University Press, New York.
Fujii, H., A.G. Assaf, S. Managi and R. Matousek (2016), 'Did the financial crisis affect environmental efficiency? Evidence from the Japanese manufacturing sector', *Environmental Economic Policy Study*, **18**, 159–168.
Gang, L. and B. Felmingham (2004), 'Environmental efficiency of the Australian irrigation industry in treating salt emissions', *Australian Economic Papers*, **43**(4), 475–490.
Golany, B., Y. Roll and D. Rybak (1994), 'Measuring efficiency of power plants in Israel by data envelopment analysis', *IEEE Transactions on Engineering Management*, **41**(3), 291–301.
Gollop, F.M. and M.J. Roberts (1983), 'Environmental regulations and productivity growth: the case of fossil-fuelled electric power generation', *Journal of Political Economy*, **91**(4), 654–674.
Graham, M. (2004), 'Environmental efficiency: meaning and measurement and application to Australian dairy farms', Paper presented at the 48th Annual AARES conference, 11–13 February, Melbourne.
Green, W.H. (2008), 'The econometric approach to efficiency analysis', in H.O. Fried, C.A.K. Lovell and S.S. Schmidt (eds), *The Measurement of Productive Efficiency and Productivity Growth*, New York: Oxford University Press.
Guesmi, B. and T. Serra (2013), Technical and environmental efficiency of Catalan arable crop farms, Paper presented at XIII European Workshop on Efficiency and Productivity Analysis, Helsinki.
Ha, N.V., S. Kant and V. Maclaren (2008), 'Shadow prices of environmental outputs and production efficiency of household-level paper recycling units in Vietnam', *Ecological Economics*, **65**(1), 98–110.
Hailu, A. and T.S. Veeman (2000), 'Environmentally sensitive productivity analysis of the Canadian pulp and paper industry, 1959–1994: an input distance function approach', *Journal of Environmental Economics and Management*, **40**(3), 251–274.

Hailu, A. and T.S. Veeman (2001), 'Alternative methods for environmentally adjusted productivity analysis', *Agricultural Economics*, **25**(2–3), 211–218.

Halkos, G. and N. Tzeremes (2012), 'Measuring German regions' environmental efficiency: a directional distance function approach', *Letters in Spatial and Resource Science*, **5**, 7–16.

Halkos, G.E. and N.G. Tzeremes (2013), 'A conditional directional distance function approach for measuring regional environmental efficiency: evidence from UK regions', *European Journal of Operational Research*, **227**(1), 182–189.

Hampf, B. and J.J. Krüger (2014), 'Optimal directions for directional distance functions: an exploration of potential reductions of greenhouse gases,' *American Journal of Agricultural Economics*, **97**(3), 920–938.

Haynes, K.E., S. Ratick, W.M. Bowen and J. Cummings-Saxton (1993), 'Environmental decision models: U.S. experience and a new approach to pollution management', *Environment International*, **19**(3), 261–275.

Haynes, K.E., S. Ratick and J. Cummings-Saxton (1994), 'Towards a pollution abetment monitoring policy: measurements, model mechanics and data requirements', *Environmental Professional*, **16**, 292–303.

Helminen, R.R. (2000), 'Developing tangible measures for eco-efficiency: the case of Finnish and Swedish pulp and paper industry', *Business Strategy and the Environment*, **9**(3), 196–210.

Heng, Y., S.H. Lim, and J. Chi (2012), 'Toxic air pollutants and trucking productivity in the US', *Transport and Environment*, **17**(4), 309–316.

Hernández-Sancho, F., M. Molinos-Senante and R. Sala-Garrido (2011), 'Energy efficiency in Spanish wastewater treatment plants: a non-radial DEA approach', *Science of the Total Environment*, **409**, 2693–2699.

Hetemäki, l. (1996), 'Essays on the impact of pollution control on a firm: a distance function approach' Finnish Forest Research Institute research papers 609, Helsinki Research Centre.

Hetemäki, L. (1993), 'The impact of pollution control on farm production technology and efficiency: a stochastic distance function approach', Paper presented at the European Association of Environmental and Resource Economists 4th annual conference, 30 June–3 July, Fontainebleau.

Hoang, V.-N. (2011), 'Measuring and decomposing changes in agricultural productivity, nitrogen use efficiency and cumulative exergy efficiency: application to OECD agriculture', *Ecological model*, **222**, 164–175.

Hoang, V.-N. and M. Alauddin (2010), 'Assessing the eco-environmental performance of agricultural production in OECD countries: the use of nitrogen flows and balance', *Nutrient Cycling in Agroecosystems*, **87**(3), 353–368.

Hoang V.-N. and M. Alauddin (2011), 'Analysis of agricultural sustainability: a review of exergy methodologies and their application in OECD', *International Journal of Energy Research*, **35**(6), 459–476.

Hoang, V.-N. and M. Alauddin, (2012), 'Input-oriented data envelopment analysis framework for measuring and decomposing economic, environmental and ecological efficiency: an application to OECD agriculture', *Environmental and Resource Economics*, **51**, 431–452.

Hoang, V.-N. and T. Coelli (2011), 'Measurement of agricultural total factor productivity growth incorporating environmental factors: a nutrients balance approach', *Journal of Environmental Economics and Management*, **62**(3), 462–474.

Hoang, V.-N. and T.T. Nguyen (2013), 'Analysis of environmental efficiency variations: a nutrient balance approach', *Ecological Economics*, **86**, 37–46.

Honma, S. and J.L. Hu (2009), 'Total-factor energy productivity growth of regions in Japan', *Energy Policy*, **37**, 3941–3950.

Huang, H. and P. Leung (2007), 'Modeling protected species as an undesirable output: the case of sea turtle interactions in Hawaii's longline fishery', *Journal of Environmental Management*, **84**, 523–533.

Huang, W., B. Bruemmer and L. Huntsinger (2016), Incorporating measures of grassland productivity into efficiency estimates for livestock grazing on the Qinghai-Tibetan plateau in China', *Ecological Economics*, **122**, 1–11.

Jiang, L., H. Folmer and M. Bu (2016), 'Interaction between output efficiency and environmental efficiency: evidence from the textile industry in Jiangsu province, China', *Journal of Cleaner Production*, **113**, 123–132,

Jin, J., D. Zhou and P. Zhou (2014), 'Measuring environmental performance with stochastic environmental DEA: the case of APEC economies' *Economic Model*, **38**, 80–86.

Jung, E.J., J.S. Kim and S.K. Rhee (2001), 'The measurement of corporate environmental performance and its application to the analysis of efficiency in oil industry', *Journal of Cleaner Production*, **9**(6), 551–563.

Koeijer, T.J., G.A.A. Wossink, P.C. Struik and J.A. Renkema (2002), 'Measuring agricultural sustainability in terms of efficiency: the case of Dutch sugar beet growers', *Journal of Environmental Management*, **66**, 9–17.

Kopp, G. (1998), 'Carbon dioxide emissions and economic growth: a structural approach', *Journal of Applied Statistics*, **25**(4), 489–515.

Koutsomanoli-Filippaki, A., D. Margaritis and C. Staikouras (2009), 'Efficiency and productivity growth in the banking industry of Central and Eastern Europe', *Journal of Banking and Finance*, **33**, 557–567.

Kumar, S. (2006), 'Environmentally sensitive productivity growth: a global analysis using Malmquist–Luenberger index', *Ecological Economics*, **56**, 280–93.

Kumar, S. and M. Khanna (2009), 'Measurement of environmental efficiency and productivity: a cross-country analysis', *Environment and Development Economics*, **14**, 473–495.

Kumar, S. and S. Managi (2010), 'Sulphur dioxide allowances: trading and technological progress', *Ecological Economics*, **69**, 623–31.

Kuosmanen, T. and M. Kortelainen (2005), 'Measuring eco-efficiency of production with data envelopment analysis', *Journal of Industrial Ecology*, **9**(4), 59–72.

Kwon, O. and H. Lee (2004), 'Productivity improvement in Korean rice farming: parametric and non-parametric analysis,' *Australian Journal of Agricultural and Resource Economics*, **48**(2), 323–346.

Kwon, O.S. and W.C. Yun (1999), 'Estimation of the marginal abatement costs of airborne pollutants in Korea's power generation sector', *Energy Economics*, **21**(6), 547–560.

Lansink, A.O. and S. Reinhard (2004), 'Investing technical efficiency and potential technological change in Dutch pig farming', *Agricultural Systems*, **79**, 353–367.

Lauwers, L. (2009), 'Justifying the incorporation of the materials balance principle into frontier-based eco-efficiency models', *Ecological Economics*, **68**, 1605–1614.

Lauwers, L., G. Van Huylenbroeck and G. Rogiers (1999), 'Technical, economic and environmental efficiency analysis of pig fattening farms', Poster presentation at the 9th European Congress of Agricultural Economists, Warsaw, Poland, 24–28 August.

Lee, J., J. Park and T. Kim (2002), 'Estimation of the shadow prices of pollutants with production/environment inefficiency taken in to account: a non-parametric directional distance function approach', *Journal of Environmental Management*, **64**, 365–375.

Li, K. and B. Lin (2016), 'Impact of energy conservation policies on the green productivity in China's manufacturing sector: evidence from a three stage DEA model', *Applied Energy*, **168**, 351–363.

Li, Y., Y. Wang, and Q. Cui (2015), Evaluating airline efficiency: an application of virtual frontier network SBM', *Transportation Research Part E*, **81**, 1–17.

Liu, J., H. Liu, X.L. Yao and Y. Liu, (2016), 'Evaluating the sustainability impact of consolidation policy in China's coal mining industry: a data envelopment analysis', *Journal of Cleaner Production*, **112**, 2969–2976.

Lovell, C.A.K. (1993), 'Production frontiers and productive efficiency', in H.O. Fried, C.A.K. Lovell and S.S. Schmidt (eds), *The Measurement of Productive Efficiency: Techniques and Applications*, Oxford University Press, New York, pp. 3–67.

Lovell, C.A.K. (1994), 'Linear programming approaches to the measurement and analysis of production efficiency', *TOP*, **2**(2), 175–224.

Lovell, C.A.K., J.T. Paster and J.A. Turner (1995), 'Measuring macroeconomic performance in the OECD: a comparison of European and non-European countries', *European Journal of Operational Research*, **87**(3), 507–518.

Luenberger, D.G. (1992), 'New optimality principles for economic efficiency and equilibrium', *Journal of Optimization Theory and Applications*, **75**(2), 221–264.

Malmquist, S. (1953), 'Index numbers and indifference surfaces', *Trabajos de Estadistica*, **4**, 209–242.

Mamardashvili, P., G. Emvalomatis and P. Jan (2016), 'Environmental performance and shadow value of polluting on Swiss dairy farms', *Journal of Agricultural and Resource Economics*, **41**(2), 225–246.

Managi, S. (2003), 'Luenberger and Malmquist productivity indexes in Japan, 1955–1995', *Applied Economics Letters*, **10**(9), 581–584.

Managi, S. and P.R. Jena (2008), 'Environmental productivity and Kuznets curve in India', *Ecological Economics*, **65**, 432–40.

Mandal, S.K. and S. Madheswaran (2010), 'Environmental efficiency of the Indian cement industry: an interstate analysis', *Energy Policy*, **38**, 1108–1118.

Martini, G., A. Manello and D. Scotti (2013), 'The influence of fleet mix, ownership and LCCs on airports' technical/environmental efficiency', *Transportation Research*, **50**, 37–52.

Mohammadi, A., S. Ratice, A. Jafari, A. Keyhani, T. Dalgard, M.T. Knudsen, T. Nguyen, R. Borek and J.E. Hermansen (2015), 'Joint life cycle assessment and data envelopment analysis for the benchmarking of environmental impact in rice paddy production', *Journal of Cleaner Production*, **106**, 521–532.

Meeusen, W. and J.V.D.B. Broeck (1977), 'Efficiency estimation from Cobb-Douglas production functions with composed error', *International Economic Review*, **18**, 435–44.

Meller, P. (1976), 'Efficiency frontiers for industrial establishments of different sizes', *Explorations in Economic Research*, **3**, 379–407.

Meng, F.Y., L.W. Fanb, P. Zhou and D.Q. Zhou (2012), 'Measuring environmental performance in China's industrial sectors with non-radial DEA', *Mathematical and Computer Modelling*, **58**(5–6), 1047–1056.

Molinos-Senante, M., F. Hernández-Sancho, M. Mocholí-Arce and R. Sala-Garrido (2016), 'Productivity growth of wastewater treatment plants – accounting for environmental impacts: a Malmquist-Luenberger index approach', *Urban Water Journal*, **13**(5), 476–485.

Molinos-Senante, M., F. Hernández-Sancho and R. Sala-Garrido (2014), 'Benchmarking in wastewater treatment plants: a tool to save operational costs', *Clean Technologies and Environmental Policy*, **16**, 149–161.

Murty, M.N. and S. Kumar (2004), *Environmental and Economic Accounting for Industry*, Oxford University Press, New Delhi.

Murty, M.N., S. Kumar and K. Dhavala (2007), 'Measuring environmental efficiency of industry: a case study of thermal power generation in India', *Environmental Resource Economics*, **38**, 31–50.

Murty, S., R.R. Russell and S.B. Levkoff (2012), 'On modeling pollution-generating technologies', *Journal of Environmental Economics and Management*, **64**, 117–135.

Nanere, M., I. Fraser, A. Quazi and C. D'Souza (2007), 'Environmentally adjusted productivity measurement: an Australian case study', *Journal of Environmental Management*, **85**, 350–362.

Njuki, E., B.E. Ureta and D. Mukherjee (2016), 'The good and the bad: environmental efficiency in northern U.S. dairy farming', *Agricultural and Resource Economics Review*, **45**, 22–43.

OECD (2008), 'Environmental performance of agriculture in OECD countries since 1990', Organisation for Economic Co-operation and Development, Paris.

O'Donnell, C.J., D.S.P. Rao and G.E. Battese (2008), 'Metafrontier frameworks for the study of a firm-level efficiencies and technology ratios', *Empirical Economics*, **34**, 231–255.

Oggioni, G., R. Riccardi and R. Toninelli (2011), 'Eco-efficiency of the world cement industry: a data envelopment analysis', *Energy Policy*, **39**(5), 2842–2854.

Oh, D. (2010), 'A metafrontier approach for measuring an environmentally sensitive productivity growth index', *Energy Economics*, **32**, 146–57.

Oh, D. and A. Heshmati (2010), 'A sequential Malmquist–Luenberger productivity index: environmentally sensitive productivity growth considering the progressive nature of technology', *Energy Economics*, **32**, 1345–55.

Oh, S.C. and Shin, J. (2015), 'The impact of mismeasurement in performance benchmarking: a Monte Carlo comparison of SFA and DEA with different multi-period budgeting strategies', *European Journal of Operational Research*, **240**, 518–227.

Peng, L. X. Zeng, Y. Wang and G.B. Hong (2015), 'Analysis of energy efficiency and carbon dioxide reduction in the Chinese pulp and paper industry', *Energy Policy*, **80**, 65–75.

Picazo-Tadeo, A., J. Castillo-Giménez and M. Beltrán-Esteve (2014), 'An intertemporal approach to measuring environmental performance with directional distance functions: greenhouse gas emissions in the European Union', *Ecological Economics*, **100**, 173–182.

Picazo-Tadeo, A., M. Beltrán-Esteve and J.A. Gómez-Limón (2012), 'Assessing eco-efficiency with directional distance functions', *European Journal of Operational Research*, **220**, 798–809.

Picazo-Tadeo, A., M. Beltrán-Esteve and J.A. Gómez-Limón (2011), 'Assessing eco-efficiency with directional distance functions', Working paper in Applied Economics 2011–10, Universitat de Valencia, Spain.

Picazo-Tadeo, A.J., E. Reig-Martínez and F. Hernández-Sancho (2005), 'Directional distance functions and environmental regulation', *Resource and Energy Economics*, 27, 131–42.

Piot-Lepetit, J. and M.L. Moing (2007), 'Productivity and environmental regulation:

the effect of the nitrates directive in the French pig sector', *Environmental Resources and Economics*, **38**, 433–446.

Pittman, R.W. (1981), 'Issues in pollution control: interplant cost differences and economies of scale', *Land Economics*, **57**(1), 1–17.

Pittman, R.W. (1983), 'Multilateral productivity comparisons with undesirable outputs', *Economic Journal*, **93**, 883–891.

Reinhard, S. and G. Thijssen (2000), 'Nitrogen efficiency of Dutch dairy farms: a shadow cost system approach', *European Review of Agricultural Economics*, **27**(2), 197–186.

Reinhard, S., C.A.K. Lovell and G. Thijssen (1999), 'Econometric estimation of technical and environmental efficiency: an application to Dutch dairy farms', *American Journal of Agricultural Economics*, **81**, 44–60.

Reinhard, S., C.A.K. Lovell and G. Thijssen (2000), 'Environmental efficiency with multiple environmentally detrimental variable: estimation with SFA and DEA', *European Journal of Operational Research*, **121**, 287–303.

Reinhard, S., C.A.K. Lovell and G. Thijssen (2002), 'Analysis of environmental efficiency variation', *American Journal of Agricultural Economics*, **84**, 1054–1065.

Sarkis, J. and J.J. Cordeiro (2001), 'An empirical evaluation of environmental efficiencies and firm performance: pollution prevention versus end-of pipe practice', *European Journal of Operational Research*, **135**(1), 102–113.

Schmidheiny, S. and F.J.L. Zorraquín (1996), *Financing Change: The Financial Community, Eco-Efficiency and Sustainable Development*, MIT Press, Cambridge, MA.

Seiford, L.M. (1996), 'Data envelopment analysis: the evolution of the state of the art (1978–1995)', *Journal of Productivity Analysis*, **7**(2–3), 99–137.

Seiford, L.M. and R.K. Thrall (1990), 'Recent developments in DEA: the mathematical approach to frontier analysis', *Journal of Econometrics*, **46**, 7–38.

Seitz, W.D. (1970), 'The measurement of efficiency relative to a frontier production function', *American Journal of Agricultural Economics*, **52**, 505–511.

Shephard, R.W. (1953), *Cost and Production Functions*, Princeton University Press, Princeton.

Shephard, R.W. (1970), *Theory of Cost and Production*, Princeton University Press, Princeton.

Song, M. and W. Zheng (2016), 'Computational analysis of thermoelectric enterprises environmental efficiency and Bayesian estimation of influence factors', *Social Science Journal*, **53**, 88–99.

Song, M., W. Zheng and Z. Wang (2015), 'Environmental efficiency and energy consumption of highway transportation system in China', *International Journal of Production Economics*, Online available at http://dx.doi.org/10.1016/jijpe.2015.09.030.

Sueyoshi, T. and M. Goto (2014), 'Environmental assessment for corporate sustainability by resource utilization and technology innovation: DEA radial measurement on Japanese industrial sectors', *Energy Econ*omics, **46**, 295–307.

Sueyoshi, T. and M. Goto (2012), 'Returns to scale and damages to scale on U.S. fossil fuel power plants: radial and non-radial approaches for DEA environmental assessment', *Energy Economics*, **34**, 2240–2259.

Sueyoshi, T. and M. Goto (2011), 'DEA approach for unified efficiency measurement: assessment of Japanese fossil fuel power generation', *Energy Economics*, **33**, 292–303.

Sueyoshi, T. and M. Goto (2009), 'Can environmental investment and expenditure enhance financial performance of US electric utility firms under the clean air act amendment of 1990'? *Energy Policy*, **37**, 4819–4826.

Sueyoshi, T. and M. Goto (2001), 'Slack-adjusted DEA for time series analysis: performance measurement of Japanese electric power generation industry in 1984–1993', *European Journal of Operational Research*, **133**, 232–259.

Sueyoshi, T. and Y. Yuan (2016), 'Marginal rate of transformation and rate of substitution measured by DEA environmental assessment: comparison among European and North American nations', *Energy Economics*, **56**, 270–287.

Sueyoshi, T., M. Goto and T. Ueno (2010), 'Performance analysis of U.S. coal-fired power plants by measuring three DEA efficiencies', *Energy Policy*, **38**, 1675–1688.

Tahara, K., M. Sagisaka, T. Ozawa, K. Yamaguchi, and A. Inaba (2005), 'Comparison of CO2 efficiency between company and industry', *Journal of Cleaner Production*, **13**(13), 1301–1308.

Tamini, L.D., B. Larue and G. West (2012), 'Technical and environmental efficiencies and best management practices in agriculture', *Applied Economics*, **44**, 1659–1672.

Taskin, F. and O. Zaim (2001), 'The role of international trade on environmental efficiency: a DEA approach', *Economic Modelling*, **18**(1), 1–17.

Thanassoulis, E. (2001), *Introduction to the Theory and Application of Data Envelopment Analysis: A Foundation Text with Integrated Software*, Kluwer Academic Publishers, Boston.

Tsionas, E.G., S.C. Kumbhakar and E. Malikov (2015), 'Estimation of input distance functions: a system approach', *American Journal of Agricultural Economics*, **97**(5), 1478–1493.

Tone, K. (2001), 'Variations on the theme of slack-based measure of efficiency in DEA', *European Journal of Operational Research*, **200**, 901–907.

Tulkens, H. and P. Vanden Eeckaut (1995), 'Non-parametric efficiency, progress and regress measures for panel data: methodological aspects', *European Journal of Operational Research*, **80**(3), 474–499.

Tyteca, D. (1996), 'On the measurement of the environmental performance of farms: a literature review and a productive efficiency perspective', *Journal of Environmental Management*, **46**(3), 281–308.

Tyteca, D. (1997), 'Linear programming models for the measurement of environmental performance of firms: concepts and empirical results', *Journal of Productivity Analysis*, **8**(2), 183–197.

Urdiales, M.P., A.O. Lansink and A. Wall (2016), 'Eco-efficiency among dairy farmers: the importance of socio-economic characteristics and farmer attitudes', *Environmental and Resource Economics*, **64**, 559–574.

Valadkhani, A., I. Roshdi and R. Smyth (2016), 'A multiplicative environmental DEA approach to measure efficiency change in the world's major polluters', *Energy Economics*, **54**, 363–375.

Veettil, P.C, S. Speelman and G.V. Huylenbroeck (2013), 'Estimating the impact of water pricing on water use efficiency in semi-arid cropping system: an application of probabilistically constrained nonparametric efficiency analysis', *Water Resources Management*, **27**, 55–73.

Wang, J. and T. Zhao (2016), 'Regional energy-environmental performance and investment strategy for China's non-ferrous metal industry: a non-radial DEA based analysis', *Journal of Cleaner Production*, available at http://dx.doi.org/10.1016.jclepro.2016.02.020.

Wang, J., T. Zhao and X. Zhang (2016), 'Environmental assessment and investment strategies of provincial industrial sector in China-analysis based on DEA model', *Environmental Impact Assessment Review*, **60**, 156–168.

Wang, K. and Y.M. Wei (2016), 'Source of energy productivity change in China during 1997–2012: a decomposition analysis based on Luenberger productivity indicator', *Energy Economics*, **54**, 50–59.

Wang, Q., Z. Zhao, N. Shen and T. Liu (2015), 'Have Chinese cities achieved the win-win between environmental protection and environmental development? From the perspective of environmental efficiency', *Ecological Indicator*, **51**, 151–158.

Wang, Q., Z. Zhao, P. Zhou and D. Zhou (2013), 'Energy efficiency and production technology heterogeneity in China: a meta-frontier DEA approach', *Economic Modelling*, **35**, 283–289.

Weber, M. and B. Domazlicky (2001), 'Productivity growth and pollution in state manufacturing', *Review of Economic Statistics*, **83**,195–199.

Weber, M.M. and W.L. Weber (2004), 'Productivity and efficiency in the trucking industry', *International Journal of Physical Distribution and Logistics Management*, **34**(1), 39–61.

Whittaker, G., B. Barnhart, R. Färe and S. Grosskopf (2015), 'Application of index number theory to the construction of a water quality index: aggregated nutrient loadings related to the areal extent of hypoxia in the northern Gulf of Mexico', *Ecological Indicators*, **49**,162–168.

Williams, J., N. Peypoch and C.P. Barrosc (2011), 'The Luenberger indicator and productivity growth: a note on the European savings banks sector', *Applied Economics*, **43**, 747–755.

Woo, C., Y., Chung, D. Chun, H. Seo and S. Hing (2015), 'The static and dynamic environmental efficiency of renewable energy: a Malmquist index analysis of OECD countries', *Renewable and Sustainable Energy Reviews*, **47**, 367–376.

Wu, F., L.W. Fan, P. Zhou and D.Q. Zhou (2012), 'Industrial energy efficiency with CO2 emission in China: a non-parametric analysis', *Energy Policy*, **44**, 140–152.

Xie, B.C., L.F. Shang, S.B. Yang and B.W. Yi (2014), 'Dynamic environmental efficiency evaluation of electric power industries: evidence from OECD (Organization for Economic Cooperation and Development) and BRIC (Brazil, Russia, India and China) countries', *Energy*, **74**, 147–157.

Yaisawarng, S. and J.D. Klein (1994), 'The effects of sulfur dioxide controls on productivity change in the U.S. electric power industry', *Review of Economics and Statistics*, **76**(3), 447–460.

Yang, H. and M. Pollitt (2009), 'Incorporating both undesirable outputs and uncontrollable variables into DEA: the performance of Chinese coal-fired power plants', *European Journal of Operational Research*, **197**(3), 1095–1105.

Yang, L., H. Ouyang, K. Fang, L. Ye and J. Zhang (2015), 'Evaluation of regional environmental efficiencies in China based on super-efficiency-DEA', *Ecological Indicator*, **51**, 13–19.

Yaqubi, M., J. Shaharaki and M.S Sabouni (2016), 'On dealing with the pollution costs in agriculture: a case study of paddy fields', *Science of the Total Environment*, **556**, 310–318.

Yu, C., L. Shi, Y. Wang, Y. Chang and B. Cheng (2016), 'The eco-efficiency of pulp and paper industry in China: an assessment based on slacks-based measure and Malmquist Luenberger index', *Journal of Cleaner Production*, **127**, 511–521.

Zaim, O. (2004), 'Measuring environmental performance of state manufacturing through changes in pollution intensities: a DEA framework', *Ecological Economics*, **48**(1), 37–47.

Zaim, O. and F. Taskin (2000), 'Environmental efficiency in carbon dioxide emissions in the OECD countries: a non-parametric approach', *Journal of Environmental Management*, **58**(2), 95–107.

Zhang, C., H. Liu, H.T.A. Bressers and K.S. Buchanan (2012), 'Productivity growth and environmental regulations – accounting for undesirable outputs: analysis of China's thirty provincial regions using the Malmquist–Luenberger index', *Ecological Economics*, **70**, 2369–2379.

Zhang, C.H., H.Y. Liu, H.T.A. Bressers and K.S. Buchanan (2011), 'Productivity growth and environmental regulations – accounting for undesirable outputs: Analysis of China's thirty provincial regions using the Malmquist–Luenberger index', *Ecological Economics*, **70**, 2369–2379.

Zhang, N. and Z. Chen (2016), 'Sustainability characteristics of China's Poyang lake eco-economic zone in the big data environment', *Journal of Cleaner Production*, Online available at http://dx.doi.org/10. 1016.jclepro.2016.02.052.

Zhang, N. and Y. Choi (2013), 'Total-factor carbon emission performance of fossil fuel power plants in China: a metafrontier non-radial Malmquist index analysis', *Energy Economics*, **40**, 549–59.

Zhang, N., B. Wang and Z. Chen (2016), 'Carbon emission reductions and technology gaps in the world's factory 1990–2012', *Energy Policy*, **91**, 28–37.

Zhang, N., F. Kong and Y. Yu, (2015), 'Measuring ecological total factor energy efficiency incorporating regional heterogeneities in China', *Ecological Indicator*, **51**,165–172.

Zhang, N., P. Zhou and Y. Choi (2013), 'Energy efficiency CO2 emission performance and technology gaps in fossil fuel electricity generation in Korea: a metafrontier non-radial directional distance function analysis', *Energy Policy*, **56**, 653–662.

Zhang, T. and B. Xue (2005), 'Environmental efficiency analysis of China's vegetable production', *Biomedical and Environmental Science*, **18**(1), 21–30.

Zhou P. and B.W. Ang (2008), 'Linear programming models for measuring economy-wide energy efficiency performance', *Energy Policy*, **36**, 11–29.

Zhou, P. and M. Wang (2016), 'Linear programming models for measuring economy-wide energy efficiency performance', *Energy Policy*, **36**(8), 2911–2916.

Zhou, P., B.W. Ang and K. Poh (2008), 'Measuring environmental performance under different environmental DEA technologies', *Energy Economics*, **30**(1), 1–14.

Zhou, P., B.W. Ang and K.L. Poh (2006), 'Slacks-based efficiency measures for modeling environmental performance', *Ecological Economics*, **60**, 111–118.

Zhou. P., B.W. Ang and H. Wang (2012), 'Energy and CO2 emission performance in electricity generation: a non-radial directional distance function approach', *European Journal of Operational Research*, **221**, 625–635.

Zhou, P., K.L. Poh and B.W. Ang (2007), 'A non-radial DEA approach to measuring environmental performance', *European Journal of Operational Research*, **178,** 1–9.

Zhou, Y., X. Zhang, X. Tian, X. Geng, P. Zhang and B. Yan (2015), 'Technical and environmental efficiency of hog production in China: a stochastic frontier production function analysis', *Journal of Integrative Agriculture*, **14**(6), 1069–1080.

Zieschang, K. (1984), 'An extended Farrell efficiency measure' *Journal of Economic Theory*, **33**, 387–396.

Zofio, J.L. and A.M. Prieto (2001), 'Environmental efficiency and regulatory standards: the case of CO2 emissions from OECD countries', *Resource and Energy Economics*, **23**(1), 63–83.

3. Modeling pollution abatement technologies as a network

Rolf G. Färe, Shawna Grosskopf and Carl A. Pasurka, Jr.*

3.1 INTRODUCTION

When society becomes concerned about the undesirable byproducts generated by its economic activity, it enacts regulations to reduce these byproducts with the goal of improving the quality of life for its citizens. When a
producer undertakes pollution abatement whose intent is to reduce bad
output production it reduces production of its marketed output (i.e., its
good output production) if inputs are held constant. The foregone good
output production is of interest not only to regulated entities but also to
society as a whole.

The reallocation of resources resulting from pollution abatement triggered
numerous theoretical and empirical studies. Aside from efforts to determine
the benefits of reducing bad outputs (e.g., reduced mortality associated with
reducing certain air pollutants), there is continuing interest in the resource
reallocation consequences of pollution abatement. These include the cost
of pollution abatement and the employment effects of pollution abatement,
along with the associated competitiveness effects (Pasurka, 2008). Interest in
more accurately modeling the effects of pollution abatement on an economy
also sparked efforts to integrate environmental data into the national income
accounting framework via satellite accounts.

The System of Environmental-Economic Accounting (SEEA) (United
Nations, 2003 pp. 188–189) classifies environmental protection activities
as either external activities, which occur when a producer hires an external
organization (e.g., a firm that removes solid waste), or as internal activities, which are ancillary (i.e., in-house) activities undertaken by the producer that generates the undesirable byproduct. Hence, current account
(or operating) expenditures for environmental protection are classified as
either external or internal expenditures. In this chapter, we concentrate on
modeling internal pollution abatement activities.

At least four options are available to producers that undertake internal pollution abatement activities. The first option consists of directly reducing bad output production via a simultaneous contraction of good and bad outputs. The second and third options represent variations of change-in-process (CIP) abatement techniques: fuel-switching is the second pollution abatement option available to producers; the third option involves reducing bad output production via techniques which integrate abatement into the technology used to produce the good output. The last option is installing an end-of-pipe (EOP) abatement process with a separate technology whose sole purpose is reducing the release of bad outputs after they are generated.

Assigned input models, which allocate inputs to either good output production or pollution abatement, and joint production (JP) models, which model the joint production of good and bad outputs, have been used to calculate the reduced good output production associated with pollution abatement. In this chapter, we employ a network of sub-technologies to identify the link between pollution abatement and good output production. The network model, which incorporates features of both the assigned input and joint production models, consists of two sub-technologies. The first is an electricity sub-technology that produces electricity and bad outputs (e.g., SO_2 emissions), which are byproducts of good output production. The bad output then serves as an intermediate input in the second sub-technology, which models EOP pollution abatement. In this chapter, the network model represents the "true" specification of the joint production technology, while the aforementioned joint production model is the simplified or reduced form specification of the production technology.

An activity analysis or data envelopment analysis (DEA) framework is used to compare the link between good output production and pollution abatement from the perspective of the network model and joint production model. We operationalize both models with a panel dataset of coal-fired electric power plants. Using observations from coal-fired electric power plants, we compare the joint production and network model estimates of maximum good output production for a given input vector and quantity of releases of bad outputs. Comparing the network model to the joint production model allows an examination of any biases of the joint production model. While there are challenges associated with identifying the quantities of exogenous inputs assigned to EOP abatement, a flue gas desulfurization (FGD) system represents a case where it is relatively easy to identify the inputs assigned to pollution abatement.

This chapter builds on the network model specified in Färe et al. (2013).[1] The remainder of the chapter is organized in the following manner. Section 3.2 introduces both a joint production model and a network technology with sub-technologies. In Section 3.3, we use a DEA framework to provide a theoretical comparison of the accuracy of the joint production model relative to the network model for different pollution abatement strategies. Section 3.4 discusses the data and empirical results, and Section 3.5 summarizes our findings.[2]

3.2 THE TECHNOLOGY

In this section we introduce the two technologies, the joint production model and the network model. We do this through Figure 3.1, which includes the "black box" joint technology as well as the sub-technologies inside the black box which constitute the network technology. However, before proceeding with our discussion some notation is required: $x \in \Re_{++}^{N}$, which denotes inputs; $y \in \Re_{+}^{M}$ denotes good or desirable outputs; and $b \in \Re_{+}^{J}$ denotes bad or undesirable outputs.

Processes shown inside the dashed box in Figure 3.1 are the sub-technologies of the network technology within the black box. In our example, electricity generation (the black box) at a coal-fired power plant is composed of two sub-technologies: (box B) electricity generation and (box C) EOP pollution abatement. The joint production model consists of the black box using inputs x (box A) to produce outputs $_{B}^{D}y$ (box D) and $_{C}^{E}b$ (box E).[3] In the case of the joint production model, we cannot identify which sub-technology generates the outputs because this model considers just the throughputs (black box) of inputs into outputs.

In the network model formulation, we identify which inputs are allocated

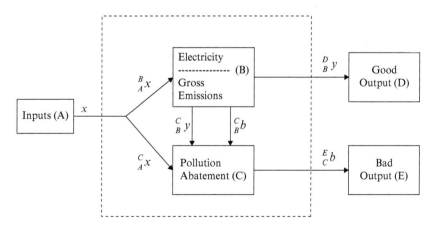

Figure 3.1   Network technology of sub-technologies

to each sub-technology, i.e., ${}_A^B x + {}_A^C x$. We also identify the following intermediate products:

> ${}_B^C y$ = electricity produced in box B and used in box C;
> ${}_B^C b$ = gross bad output produced in box B and sent to box C to be partially abated;
> ${}_B^D y$ and ${}_C^E b$ are the final outputs, which in the joint production model we think of as $y = {}_B^D y$ and $b = {}_C^E b$.

In other words, exogenous inputs—i.e., capital, labor and fuel—(box A) are employed by the two sub-technologies. The electricity (i.e., good output) sub-technology (box B) produces a good output, electricity (${}_B^C y + {}_B^D y$), and a bad output, gross SO_2 emissions (${}_B^C b$). A portion of the good output is used as an intermediate input (${}_B^C y$) by the EOP abatement sub-technology (box C), while the remainder is the final output of the plant, i.e., electricity sold on the market (${}_B^D y$). The difference between the power plant's gross production of electricity and electricity used by the EOP pollution abatement sub-technology (e.g., FGD system) is its net generation of electricity (box D).

Gross output of SO_2 (${}_B^C b$) reflects the level of bad output production after either no effort is made to reduce bad outputs or when any of the following pollution abatement strategies are employed: directly (i.e., proportionately) reducing good and bad output production, fuel-switching, or a CIP abatement strategy other than fuel-switching. In the network model, the gross output of SO_2 is sent to the EOP abatement sub-technology (box C) for additional processing. The exogenous inputs (${}_A^C x$) assigned to EOP abatement, the electricity (${}_B^C y$) used as an intermediate input by the FGD system, and SO_2 gross emissions (${}_B^C b$) are combined to reduce SO_2 emissions.[4] The output of the EOP abatement sub-technology is the quantity of SO_2 abated by the sub-technology. Net SO_2 emissions (${}_C^E b$)—i.e., gross SO_2 production minus the quantity of SO_2 abated—are released into the atmosphere (box E).[5] Net SO_2 production (${}_C^E b$) and the electricity sold to users outside the plant (${}_B^D y$) are the final outputs of the power plant.[6]

To operationalize these models we use activity analysis or data envelopment analysis (DEA). We assume there are $k = 1,\ldots,K$ observations of the inputs and outputs (x^k, y^k, b^k) for the joint production model and $(x^k, {}_A^B x^k, {}_A^C x^k, {}_B^C y^k, {}_B^C b^k, {}_B^D y^k, {}_C^E b^k)$ for the network model. We note that $x^k = {}_A^B x^k + {}_A^C x^k$ and that $y^k = {}_B^D y^k$ and $b^k = {}_C^E b^k$.

We propose to calculate the maximum good output for each observation by specifying the network and joint production technologies as activity analysis models. For both, we formulate linear programming (LP) representations of the production technology.

As previously mentioned, the joint production model treats the process of transforming inputs into good and bad outputs as a black box. Unlike the network technology model, which allows us to look inside the black box, the joint production model does not. As a consequence, the joint production model only requires information available outside the black box: the quantities and qualities of exogenous inputs (x); and the net quantities of good ($_B^D$y) and bad ($_C^E$b) outputs produced. In terms of Figure 3.1, the joint production technology requires information associated with boxes A, D, and E.

The joint production model associated with the data may be described by its output correspondence (JP), in particular for observation k' we have:

$$JP(x^k) = \{(y,b): \sum_{k=1}^{K} z_k y_{km} \geq y_m, m=1, ..., M \quad (3.1\text{i})$$

$$\sum_{k=1}^{K} z_k b_{kj} = b_j, j=1, ..., J \quad (\text{ii})$$

$$\sum_{k=1}^{K} z_k x_{kn} \leq x_{k'n}, n=1, ..., N \quad (\text{iii})$$

$$z_k \geq 0, k = 1, ..., K\} \quad (\text{iv})$$

where z_k (k = 1,..., K) are the intensity variables. These are weights assigned to each observation when constructing the production frontier. Recall that inputs are indexed by n = 1,...,N, good outputs by m = 1,...,M, and bad outputs by j = 1,...,J. The inequalities in (3.1i) model free or strong disposability of the good outputs [(y,b) ∈ JP(x) and y ≥ y′ imply (y′,b) ∈ JP(x)]. Expressions (3.1i) and (3.1ii) make good and bad outputs jointly weakly disposable [(y,b) ∈ JP(x) and 0 ≤ θ ≤ 1 imply (θy, θb) ∈ JP(x)].[7]

The equalities (3.1ii) prevent the bad outputs from being freely disposable. Expression (3.1iii) makes inputs freely disposable; and, finally, the nonnegativity constraints on the intensity variables z_k impose constant returns to scale on the technology [JP(λx) = λJP(x), λ>0]. In addition, we impose null-jointness of good and bad outputs [(y,b) ∈ JP(x) and b = 0 imply y = 0] by imposing the conditions:[8]

$$\sum_{k=1}^{K} b_{kj} > 0, \ j=1, ..., J, \text{ and } \sum_{j=1}^{J} b_{kj} > 0, \ k=1, ..., K.$$

The network model associated with the data is given by:

$$NP(x^k) = \{(_B^D y, _C^E b): \sum_{k=1}^{K} z_k^B (_B^C y_{km} + _B^D y_{km}) \geq (_B^C y_m + _B^D y_m), m=1, ..., M \ (3.2\text{i})$$

$$\sum_{k=1}^{K} z_k^B {}_B^C b_{kj} = {}_B^C b_j, j = 1, \ldots, J \tag{ii}$$

$$\sum_{k=1}^{K} z_k^B {}_A^B x_{kn} \leq {}_A^B x_n, n = 1, \ldots, N \tag{iii}$$

$$z_k^B \geq 0, k = 1, \ldots, K \tag{iv}$$

$$\sum_{k=1}^{K} z_k^C {}_C^E b_{kj} = {}_C^E b_j, j = 1, \ldots, J \tag{v}$$

$$\sum_{k=1}^{K} z_k^C {}_A^C x_{kn} \leq {}_A^C x_n, n = 1, \ldots, N \tag{vi}$$

$$\sum_{k=1}^{K} z_k^C {}_B^C y_{km} \leq {}_B^C y_m, m = 1, \ldots, M \tag{vii}$$

$$\sum_{k=1}^{K} z_k^C {}_B^C b_{kj} \leq {}_B^C b_j, j = 1, \ldots, J \tag{viii}$$

$$z_k^C \geq 0, k = 1, \ldots, K \tag{ix}$$

$$({}_A^B x_n + {}_A^C x_n) \leq x_{k'n}, n = 1, \ldots, N\} \tag{x}$$

The interpretation of the two sub-technologies B and C is similar to that of the joint production model. Within the network model, each sub-technology has its own set of intensity variables z_k^B and z_k^C, where $z_k^B (k = 1, \ldots, K)$ are the intensity variables for the electricity sub-technology and $z_k^C (k = 1, \ldots, K)$ are the intensity variables for the EOP abatement sub-technology.[9] The first set of constraints (3.2i–iv) constitutes the good output (electricity) sub-technology (box B) that produces electricity and SO_2 as an undesirable byproduct (i.e., the gross generation of the bad output). The second set of constraints (3.2v–ix) constitutes the EOP pollution abatement sub-technology (box C). In our example, this sub-technology combines gross output of SO_2 with inputs to produce net SO_2 emissions, while the last set of inequalities (3.2x)

$$ {}_A^B x + {}_A^C x \leq x_{k'n}, n = 1, \ldots, N $$

shows how the exogenous inputs ($x_{k'n}$) in box A are allocated between B and C.

In the electricity sub-technology (box B), constraint (3.2i) models gross good output production that is either consumed as a final good (box D) or as an intermediate (endogenous) input by the EOP abatement sub-technology (box C). Constraint (3.2ii) models gross bad output production. Constraint (3.2iii) models the exogenous inputs assigned to the electricity sub-technology. Finally, constraint (3.2iv) imposes constant returns to scale.

In the EOP abatement sub-technology (box C), constraint (3.2v) models the net bad output. Constraint (3.2vi) models exogenous inputs assigned to the EOP abatement sub-technology, while constraint (3.2vii) models the use of the good output as an intermediate input. Constraint (3.2viii) models gross bad output production from the electricity sub-technology as an input into the EOP abatement sub-technology. Finally, constraint (3.2ix) imposes constant returns to scale.

We compare the two technologies by calculating for each observation $k' = 1,...,K$ the maximal potential good output given the technologies $JP(x^{k'})$ and $NP(x^{k'})$ respectively:

$$y(k',J) = \max\{y: (y, b^{k'}) \in JP(x^{k'})\}$$

and

$$y(k',N) = \max\{{}^D_B y: ({}^D_B y, {}^E_C b^{k'}) \in NP(x^{k'})\}$$

where the technologies are the DEA formulations above given observed input $x^{k'}$ and observed net undesirable output $b^{k'}$.

To illustrate how the maximal output is computed, let $P(x^{k'})$ be a generic output set for observation k'—i.e., it could be $JP(x^{k'})$ or $NP(x^{k'})$. This output set has good and bad outputs weakly disposable and good outputs strongly disposable. In addition, the two outputs are null-joint. Let $b^{k'}$ be given, then the maximal feasible good output is at point f in Figure 3.2.

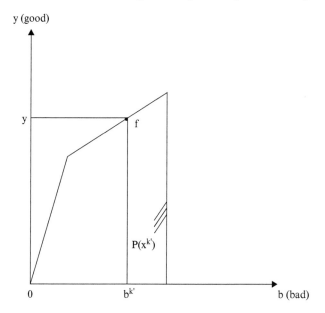

Figure 3.2   Estimation of maximal output

3.3   THEORETICAL COMPARISON OF THE JOINT PRODUCTION AND NETWORK MODELS

We can now compare the network model with the joint production model for each of the four internal pollution abatement options. If a producer pursues an abatement strategy by simply reducing its good output production (i.e., reducing the bad output via a proportional reduction in good output production), this activity occurs outside the black box. For example, if a producer is restricted to a single process (i.e., a Leontief fixed coefficient production technology), with a fixed input vector the only option to reduce bad output production is a proportional contraction of good and bad outputs. With constant returns to scale, this proportional reduction of good and bad outputs is achieved by an equivalent percentage reduction in the inputs. The excess inputs can then be employed by other producers. Because this pollution abatement activity occurs outside the black box, the network technology model collapses to the joint production model.

The opportunity cost of fuel switching is the reduced production of the good output associated with switching to a less polluting fuel—for example, reducing SO_2 emissions by switching from high-sulfur to low-sulfur coal (i.e., changing a fuel characteristic). Good output production declines because lower-sulfur coal has a lower heat (Btu) content. As a result, the opportunity cost of reducing the bad output is the decline in good output production resulting from the decline in the heat content of a given quantity of coal.[10] Because adopting fuel-switching abatement techniques occurs outside the black box, the network technology model collapses to the joint production model.

CIP abatement techniques—other than fuel-switching—modify the production processes used to produce a good output.[11] For example, a low-NO_x burner reduces nitrogen oxide emissions at the cost of reduced boiler efficiency. Because these abatement techniques involve activities outside the black box, the network technology model once more collapses to the joint production model.

We can explain why the network model collapses to the joint production model via the specification of the joint production model (3.1) and network model (3.2). If the EOP abatement sub-technology is not used, only constraints (3.2i) through (3.2iv) and (3.2x) in the network model (3.2) are relevant (i.e., $z_k^C = 0$). Because direct reductions in good output production, fuel switching, and CIP pollution abatement activities other than fuel switching occur outside the black box, they reduce gross and net bad output production equally because ${}_B^C b = {}_C^E b$. Combining input constraints (3.2iii), (3.2vi), and (3.2x) from the network technology model

(3.2) yields the input constraints (3.1iii) for the joint production model (3.1). Hence, the joint production and network models become identical. It follows that when no observations use EOP abatement sub-technologies, the network model collapses to the JP model.

Finally, we examine the relationship between the network model (3.2) and the joint production model (3.1) when the EOP abatement sub-technology is used. Because the joint production model implicitly assumes no factor reallocation between sub-technologies, the existence of the EOP abatement sub-technology results in the network frontier lying on or above the joint production frontier. Hence, the maximal good output of the network model equals or exceeds that of the joint production model. However, the extent of the difference in maximum good output production is not immediately obvious. In the next section, we use the activity analysis representations of the production technologies to calculate the maximum good output found for the joint production and network technologies.[12]

3.4   DATA AND RESULTS

For our example, the joint production and network models include one net good output, "net electrical generation"—kilowatt hours (kWh) $\binom{D}{B}y$), and one net bad output—sulfur dioxide (SO_2) emissions $\binom{E}{C}b$). The U.S. Department of Energy (DOE) "Steam-Electric Plant Operation and Design Report" (also known as the EIA-767 survey) provides information on net generation of electricity (kWh), while net SO_2 emission data are collected by the U.S. EPA Continuous Emissions Monitoring System (CEMS).

The exogenous inputs (x) consist of the capital stock;[13] the number of employees; the quantity (in physical units) of each type of fuel consumed (coal, oil and natural gas); the heat content per physical unit consumed of each of the three fuels; and the sulfur content per physical unit consumed of coal. The Federal Energy Regulatory Commission (FERC) is the source of labor and capital data for private electric power plants, while the U.S. DOE's "Annual Electric Industry Financial Report" (also known as the EIA-412 survey) is the source of labor and capital data for public power plants.[14] When the DOE halted the EIA-412 survey after 2003, the Tennessee Valley Authority (TVA) voluntarily reported 2004–06 data for its electric power plants.[15]

In this chapter, we offer a new approach to specifying fuel consumption by including the physical quantity of each fuel along with two fuel qualities—heat content and sulfur content. Previously, using total Btu would consider two plants to have identical fuel consumption even if they were using different quantities of fuels with different heat content. With our specification, the best practice frontier must match the fuel quantities and qualities of the observation being evaluated.

The EIA-767 survey is the source of information about fuel consumption (in physical units) and fuel quality. While plants may consume coal, oil, or natural gas, in order to model a homogeneous production technology coal must provide at least 95 percent of the Btu of fuels consumed by each plant.[16] The summary statistics in Table 3.1 below reveal that coal provides substantially more than 95 percent of the Btu consumed by most plants in the sample.

In addition to the data required for the joint production model, the network model requires three additional pieces of information. First, while all fuels are assigned to the electricity generation sub-technology, the network model requires information on how much capital and labor are assigned to each sub-technology. This is accomplished by identifying the amount of capital and labor assigned to the EOP pollution abatement sub-technology. Using a procedure similar to that employed to derive the total capital stock (see footnote 15), pre-1985 data on the installed cost of FGD systems from the *Cost and Quality of Fuels for Electric Utility Plants* (U.S. DOE, 1977–79, 1981–85) and the *Utility FGD (Flue Gas Desulfurization) Survey* (U.S. EPA, 1980) are combined with 1985–2005 data from the EIA-767 survey to estimate the pollution abatement capital stock.

The EIA-767 survey also collects data on the cost of labor employed to operate FGD systems. These data are combined with state-level data on the annual cost per employee to estimate the number of employees assigned to operate the FGD systems. The annual cost per employee is determined by dividing annual payroll costs by mid-March employment for state-level data found in various issues of the U.S. Census Bureau's *Country Business Patterns* for the following North American Industry Classification System (NAICS) codes based upon their availability: 221112 (Fossil Fuel Electric Power Generation); 22111 (Electric Power Generation); and 2211 (Electric Power Generation, Transmission, and Distribution).[17] Dividing the cost of labor employed to operate FGD systems by the derived annual cost per employee yields the number of employees assigned to operate the FGD systems. After calculating the values of the capital and labor assigned to the EOP pollution abatement sub-technology, the capital and labor assigned to the electricity sub-technology ($^B_A x$) is determined by taking the difference between the total capital and labor used by the power plant (x) and the capital and labor assigned to the EOP pollution abatement sub-technology ($^C_A x$). The second piece of information required by the network model—the amount of electricity consumed by FGD systems ($^C_B y$)—is also collected by the EIA-767 survey.

Finally, the network model requires information on gross SO_2 emissions. When an FGD system is not installed at a plant, we assume gross SO_2 emissions equal net SO_2 emissions. If a plant installs an FGD system, we estimate its gross SO_2 emissions by taking the product of the physical volume of fuel, the sulfur percentage of the fuel, and the emission factor of the fuel for each boiler and sum across all boilers.[18]

When assembling the data, our objective was to construct a balanced panel dataset of coal-fired power plants. While some capital stock and employment values were interpolated, we felt this was problematic for fuel consumption and net generation of electricity, both of which can exhibit greater year-to-year variation. As a result, of the approximately 148 plants with installed FGD systems in 2005, many are excluded due to missing data for one or more of the following inputs and outputs: capital, employment, fuel, and net generation. In addition, plants with installed FGD systems are excluded from the sample because they failed to provide information on the EIA-767 survey about the operation of the FGD system for one or more of the following categories: the installed cost of FGD systems, the cost of labor employed to operate the FGD system, or the amount of electricity consumed by the FGD system.

Table 3.1 shows summary statistics for the plants in 2001 and 2005 and Appendix A (not included here) contains additional information about the data. We then solve the LP problems using a balanced panel of 91 coal-fired power plants from 2001 to 2005, 15 of which had installed EOP pollution abatement equipment.

The maximal good output for each observation is calculated by both the joint production model and the network model. Because the network technology allows the labor and capital inputs to be allocated between the electricity sub-technology and the EOP abatement sub-technology, we model these inputs assigned to the sub-technologies, $_A^B x$ and $_A^C x$, as variables in constraints (iii), (vi), and (x) in (3.2). However, the total for each exogenous input ($x_{k'n}$) is fixed. In addition, we allow the plant to adjust its allocation of good output production between its use as an intermediate input by the EOP abatement sub-technology (Figure 3.1, box C) and its consumption as a final output (Figure 3.1, box D). Therefore, we model $_B^C y$ and $_B^D y$ as variables in constraints (i) and (vii). Finally, we allow the plant to adjust its gross bad output production that is used as an intermediate input by the EOP abatement sub-technology (Figure 3.1, box C). Therefore, we model $_B^C b$ as a variable in constraints (ii) and (viii). However, we model the net bad output released by the plant ($_C^E b$) as fixed in constraint (v). Appendix B (not included here) contains the formal specification of the LP models used to operationalize the joint production and network models.

Table 3.1   Summary statistics, 91 coal-fired power plants (2001 and 2005)

2001	Units	Mean	Sample std. dev.	Maximum	Minimum
Electricity	kWh (millions)	5,388	4,259	18,508	444
SO$_2$	Short tons	30	26	118	2
Capital stock	1973$ (millions)	279	208	918	40
Employees	Workers	166	102	427	31
Heat content of coal	Btu (billions)	55,629	42,785	188,581	5,302
Heat content of oil	Btu (billions)	89	122	716	0
Heat content of gas	Btu (billions)	106	318	2,557	0

2005	Units	Mean	Sample std. dev.	Maximum	Minimum
Electricity	kWh (millions)	5,575	4,435	21,326	176
SO$_2$	Short tons	29	24	110	2
Capital stock	1973$ (millions)	295	224	1,000	41
Employees	Workers	168	110	468	28
Heat content of coal	Btu (billions)	56,998	44,280	215,802	2,297
Heat content of oil	Btu (billions)	88	125	738	0
Heat content of gas	Btu (billions)	72	176	911	0

Table 3.2 reports the ratio of the maximal good output generated by these two models. The geometric mean of the ratio for all plants shows the maximum output of the network model is between 1.5 and 2.2 percent higher than the maximum good output of the joint production model, while for plants with FGD systems the maximum output of the network model is between 4.8 and 6.1 percent higher than the maximum good output of the joint production model. Except for 2005, the median value of the network model exceeds the maximum good output of the joint production model by less than 0.3 percent.

The number of plants with a ratio of unity ranged between 33 and 34 for each year in our sample. During 2001–05, 14 plants report a ratio value of unity for all five years. The plants with the highest ratios in each year were Johnsonville (ID 3406) in 2001, R.M. Heskett (ID 2790) in 2002, Mill Creek (ID 1364) in 2003, Cherokee (ID 469) in 2004, and Jim Bridger (ID

Table 3.2   *Ratio of maximal good output produced by the network model relative to the maximal good output produced by the joint production model, 2001–2005*

Plant name	Plant ID	2001	2002	2003	2004	2005
Barry	3	1.0000	1.0000	1.0000	1.0000	1.0000
Gorgas	8	1.0000	1.0000	1.0010	1.0009	1.0518
Colbert	47	1.0112	1.0015	1.0022	1.0266	1.0000
Widows Creek*	50	1.0368	1.0316	1.0253	1.0413	1.0852
Cholla*	113	1.0624	1.0453	1.0826	1.0943	1.0249
Cherokee*	469	1.0000	1.0815	1.1477	**1.1485**	1.0381
Comanche	470	1.0234	1.0029	1.0069	1.0166	1.0000
Crystal River	628	1.0000	1.0000	1.0000	1.0000	1.0000
Lansing Smith	643	1.0014	1.0000	1.0000	1.0000	1.0000
Harllee Branch	709	1.0000	1.0000	1.0068	1.0102	1.0105
Mitchell	727	1.0111	1.0195	1.0003	1.0379	1.0000
Joppa Steam	887	1.0000	1.0000	1.0365	1.0035	1.0006
Clifty Creek	983	1.0079	1.0000	1.0000	1.0024	1.0023
Tanners Creek	988	1.0220	1.0566	1.0109	1.0222	1.0333
Harding Street	990	1.0084	1.0520	1.0269	1.0000	1.0000
Eagle Valley	991	1.0210	1.0549	1.0129	1.0075	1.0440
AES Peterson*	994	1.0543	1.0438	1.0100	1.0555	1.0834
Cayuga	1001	1.0000	1.0150	1.0000	1.0000	1.0000
R. Gallagher	1008	1.1187	1.1191	1.0000	1.0000	1.0425
Lansing	1047	1.0381	1.0407	1.0481	1.0463	1.0072
Milton L. Kapp	1048	1.0051	1.0001	1.0007	1.0000	1.0000
Riverside	1081	1.1255	1.0088	1.0482	1.0364	1.0531
Burlington	1104	1.0000	1.0000	1.0005	1.0000	1.0000
La Cygne*	1241	1.0826	1.0824	1.0441	1.0260	1.0870
E.W. Brown	1355	1.0200	1.0574	1.0000	1.0000	1.0390
Ghent*	1356	1.0156	1.0469	1.0170	1.0040	1.0177
Cane Run*	1363	1.1210	1.0625	1.0730	1.0455	1.0234
Mill Creek*	1364	1.0548	1.0760	**1.1545**	1.0902	1.0573
Paradise*	1378	1.0033	1.0049	1.0226	1.0000	1.0136
Shawnee	1379	1.0501	1.0262	1.0060	1.0035	1.0394
Mount Tom	1606	1.0000	1.0184	1.0049	1.0000	1.0000
B C Cobb	1695	1.0766	1.0648	1.0116	1.0002	1.0126
J H Campbell	1710	1.0412	1.0292	1.0039	1.0002	1.0000
J R Whiting	1723	1.0526	1.0242	1.0032	1.0008	1.0008
Monroe	1733	1.0000	1.0025	1.0000	1.0000	1.0035
St. Clair	1743	1.0088	1.0031	1.0054	1.0219	1.0261
Trenton Channel	1745	1.0022	1.0002	1.0030	1.0000	1.0043
Presque Isle	1769	1.0027	1.0015	1.0016	1.0024	1.0217
High Bridge	1912	1.0378	1.0687	1.1230	1.1448	1.0540
Hoot Lake	1943	1.0000	1.0137	1.0000	1.0172	1.0110

Table 3.2   (continued)

Plant name	Plant ID	2001	2002	2003	2004	2005
Asbury	2076	1.0000	1.0000	1.0000	1.0016	1.0004
Sibley	2094	1.0003	1.0000	1.0000	1.0000	1.0000
Merrimack	2364	1.0000	1.0000	1.0000	1.0000	1.0000
Cape Fear	2708	1.0144	1.0195	1.0082	1.0289	1.0055
H.F. Lee	2709	1.0000	1.0000	1.0000	1.0015	1.0040
L.V. Sutton	2713	1.0016	1.0011	1.0000	1.0006	1.0076
Buck	2720	1.0011	1.0025	1.0188	1.0133	1.0568
Dan River	2723	1.0077	1.0236	1.0024	1.0132	1.0281
Riverbend	2732	1.0014	1.0164	1.0027	1.0042	1.0054
R M Heskett	2790	1.0590	**1.3142**	1.1049	1.0401	1.0887
Kyger Creek	2876	1.0219	1.0000	1.0000	1.0000	1.0000
H B Robinson	3251	1.0011	1.0039	1.0057	1.0000	1.0023
W S Lee	3264	1.0081	1.0002	1.0041	1.0134	1.0070
Canadys Stream	3280	1.0150	1.0170	1.0217	1.0621	1.0270
McMeekin	3287	1.0000	1.0000	1.0000	1.0000	1.0000
Urquhart	3295	1.0000	1.0000	1.0000	1.0129	1.0000
Watertree	3297	1.0043	1.0051	1.0006	1.0000	1.0166
Williams	3298	1.0000	1.0000	1.0000	1.0000	1.0000
Bull Run	3396	1.0000	1.0000	1.0000	1.0000	1.0000
Cumberland*	3399	1.0743	1.0799	1.0664	1.0281	1.1103
Gallatin	3403	1.0000	1.0000	1.0000	1.0000	1.0000
John Sevier	3405	1.0000	1.0000	1.0000	1.0000	1.0000
Johnsonville	3406	**1.1297**	1.0000	1.0000	1.0330	1.0104
Kingston	3407	1.0000	1.0000	1.0000	1.0066	1.0040
Carbon	3644	1.0000	1.0110	1.0043	1.0072	1.0108
Clinch River	3775	1.0000	1.0000	1.0000	1.0000	1.0016
Glen Lyn	3776	1.0007	1.0038	1.0226	1.0019	1.0076
Bremo Bluff	3796	1.0022	1.0000	1.0090	1.0021	1.0045
Chesterfield	3797	1.0006	1.0117	1.0143	1.0031	1.0000
Chesapeake	3803	1.0032	1.0001	1.0027	1.0000	1.0000
Kanawha River	3936	1.0016	1.0064	1.0052	1.0002	1.0068
Philip Sporn	3938	1.0050	1.0043	1.0019	1.0012	1.0108
Rivesville	3945	1.0021	1.0002	1.0029	1.0100	1.0098
South Oak Creek	4041	1.0000	1.0000	1.0000	1.0000	1.0000
Edgewater	4050	1.0007	1.0007	1.0081	1.0027	1.0000
Pulliam	4072	1.0000	1.0000	1.0026	1.0908	1.0070
Weston	4078	1.0000	1.0000	1.0000	1.0000	1.0000
Naughton*	4162	1.0753	1.0502	1.0140	1.0364	1.0407
James H. Miller Jr.	6002	1.0000	1.0000	1.0021	1.0000	1.0000
Belle River	6034	1.0079	1.0026	1.0000	1.0000	1.0358
R.M. Schaffer*	6085	1.0405	1.1245	1.0759	1.0604	1.0454
Sooner	6095	1.0000	1.0000	1.0000	1.0000	1.0000
Welsh	6139	1.0000	1.0000	1.0000	1.0000	1.0000

Table 3.2   (continued)

Plant name	Plant ID	2001	2002	2003	2004	2005
Pleasant Prairie	6170	1.0006	1.0000	1.0002	1.0000	1.0000
Harrington	6193	1.0000	1.0000	1.0000	1.0000	1.0000
Tolk Station	6194	1.0000	1.0000	1.0000	1.0000	1.0000
Pawnee	6248	1.0009	1.0009	1.0002	1.0003	1.0000
Ottumwa	6254	1.0040	1.0000	1.0064	1.0102	1.0000
Jim Bridger*	8066	1.0585	1.1016	1.0755	1.0691	**1.1125**
Huntington*	8069	1.0000	1.0544	1.0000	1.0027	1.0034
North Valmy*	8224	1.0000	1.0000	1.0000	1.0314	1.0711
Geometric means (all plants)		1.0178	1.0213	1.0152	1.0160	1.0176
Median (all plants)		1.0021	1.0025	1.0026	1.0021	1.0045
Maximum (all plants)		1.1297	1.3142	1.1545	1.1485	1.1125
Minimum (all plants)		1.0000	1.0000	1.0000	1.0000	1.0000
Geometric means (FGD plants)		1.0481	1.0604	1.0533	1.0484	1.0564
Geometric means (non-FGD plants)		1.0119	1.0138	1.0078	1.0098	1.0101

Notes:
Bold = *maximum* value.
Subtracting unity from the values in Table 3.2 and multiplying by 100 yield percent by which maximum good output generated by network model is greater than the maximum good output generated by the joint production model.
* A flue gas desulfurization (FGD) system was installed at the plant during 2001–05.

8066) in 2005. R.M. Heskett (ID 2790) had the highest average ratio during 2001–05.

Figure 3.3 allows us to visualize the results reported in Table 3.2 by showing the maximal good output calculated by the network (NP) and joint production (JP) models for each plant with an FGD system in 2005 after the plants are sorted in descending order according to the maximal good output calculated by the network model. If the maximal good output of the network model equals that of the joint production model, the ratio in Table 3.2 equals unity. For those observations, the two lines in Figure 3.3 merge. However, when the maximal good output of the network model exceeds that of the joint production model, the ratio in Table 3.2 exceeds unity. In that case, the network line lies above that of the joint production line.

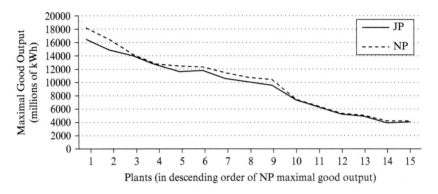

Figure 3.3   Maximal good output by plants with FGD (ordered by NP maximal good output)

As expected, many plants that did not install an EOP abatement sub-technology have identical maximal good output production for the network and joint production models. This confirms our conclusion in Section 3.3 that the network model collapses to the joint production model ($z_k^C = 0$) when the plants used to construct the frontier and the plants being evaluated have not installed EOP abatement sub-technology. However, the empirical results show that over one-half of the observations with no EOP abatement sub-technology (219 of 380 plant-year pairs) generated ratios greater than unity. We will now briefly examine potential sources of these discrepancies.

When evaluating plants without an EOP PA sub-technology, some plants used to construct the production frontier have EOP sub-technologies. For these cases, the network model may generate higher maximum good output production than the JP model. When constructing the frontier for an observation with no EOP abatement sub-technology, there is no need for inputs to be assigned to the EOP PA sub-technology. As a result, the network model allows inputs that were assigned to the EOP PA sub-technology to be assigned to the electricity sub-technology.

The JP and network models can also generate different results when no observation used to construct the frontier has installed an EOP abatement sub-technology. This can occur as a result of aggregating the consumption of bituminous and sub-bituminous coal, which for some boilers release different amounts of SO_2 from an identical quantity of coal with an identical sulfur content. If this results in different amounts of SO_2 emissions for a given sulfur content of fuel, this violates our assumption of a homogeneous production technology. As a result, a divergence between JP and network results emerges because our expectation that $_B^Cb = {}_C^Eb$ is violated. It follows that differences in the ratio of SO_2 emissions to the sulfur content of fuel due to errors in the estimated sulfur content of fuel and/ or errors in the measured SO_2 releases will also cause a divergence in the results generated by the JP and network models.

In Section 3.3, we mentioned that while the joint production model implicitly assumes no factor reallocations between sub-technologies, the network model allows factor reallocations between sub-technologies. As a result, for plants with installed FGD systems the network model yields good output levels that equal or exceed those found by the joint production model. In other words, the network frontier lies on or above the joint production frontier. For most plants with FGD systems in our sample, the maximal output of the network model exceeds the maximal output of the joint production model.

However, four plants with installed FGD systems—Cherokee (ID 469) in 2001, Paradise (ID 1378) in 2004, Huntington (ID 8069) in 2001 and 2003, and North Valmy (ID 8224) in 2001–03—have identical maximal output for the network and joint production models. With factor realloca- tion between sub-technologies allowed, the network and joint production models generate identical results only when reallocating inputs between the sub-technologies within the network model fails to generate an increase in good output production. Hence, for these observations the network model production frontier overlaps the joint production model frontier.

3.5   CONCLUSIONS

In this chapter, we compared two models when the production technology produces both good and bad outputs. While the joint production model looks solely outside the black box, the network technology looks inside the black box consisting of a set of sub-technologies or sub-processes. These sub- technologies are connected in a network that forms the joint production fron- tier or technology. By introducing a network technology of sub-technologies that models EOP pollution abatement as a sub-technology, we were able to investigate the consequences of generalizing the transformation process.[19]

The technologies specified by the network and joint production models differ in important aspects. While both incorporate information on bad output production, the network model explicitly models the EOP abate- ment sub-technology, whereas the joint production only models net bad output production. In addition, the exogenous input constraints in the two models differ because the network technology assigns inputs to either good output production or EOP abatement, while the joint production model only requires information on the total quantity of exogenous inputs involved in both activities.

An examination of the two models revealed that while the joint production model provides an exact specification of the production technology for certain cases, it only approximates the effect of an EOP abatement sub-technology. As a result, when an EOP abatement sub-technology is installed, only the network production technology provides a correct specification of the production technology.[20] Because the joint production model provides an approximation to the network production model when an EOP pollution abatement sub-technology is employed, we must weigh the trade-off between the reduced data requirements of the joint production model versus the inaccuracies introduced into an analysis when EOP processes are installed.

While the network model is the correct specification of the production technology when an EOP abatement sub-technology is installed, the joint production model possesses a key advantage—it does not require information about the EOP pollution abatement sub-technology. As a result, information about how exogenous inputs are allocated among the sub-technologies inside the black box, which is required by the network model, is not required to implement the joint production model. In addition, the joint production model does not require information about the gross bad output produced by the electricity sub-technology prior to being sent to the EOP abatement sub-technology. Because the joint production model introduces errors when calculating the maximal good output when an EOP abatement sub-technology is installed, we are left with a question: are these errors substantial enough to invalidate results produced by joint production models when producers use EOP abatement strategies? In this chapter, we addressed this question by comparing the joint production model and network model by calculating the maximal good output for a sample of 91 coal-fired electric power plants from 2001 to 2005.

In order to accommodate concerns about the manner in which fuel inputs were introduced in previous papers that modeled the production technology of electric power plants, we proposed a new strategy. We believe this specification allows a more accurate depiction of fuel consumed by electric power plants, and is a first step in addressing concerns about the failure to incorporate materials balance constraints into joint production models.

The network model developed in this chapter can be used to assess questions such as the opportunity costs and productivity consequences of pollution abatement. However, these applications require including the case when the producer is allowed to freely dispose of the bad output.

While our empirical results are interesting, empirical analyses using network models with good and bad outputs are hampered by the lack of available data. Unless there is a sustained effort to assemble the data required to operationalize these models, empirical applications of network models with EOP pollution abatement sub-technologies will remain rare events.

NOTES

* Earlier versions of this chapter were presented at a Western Economic Association conference, a Southern Economic Association conference, and a North American Productivity Workshop. We wish to thank David Evans for his assistance with data acquisition, and Curtis Carlson for providing his capital stock and employment data. Any errors, opinions, or conclusions are those of the authors and should not be attributed to the U.S. Environmental Protection Agency.

1. In addition to several papers cited in Kao (2014), Fukuyama and Weber (2014) and Zhu et al. (2014) incorporate bad output production into a network model. Hua and Bien (2008), Yang et al. (2008), Färe et al. (2013), and this chapter are unique due to their specification of a sub-technology dedicated to reducing the bad output.

2. All appendices, data, and GAMS programs are available from the authors upon request.

3. In this chapter, the subscript letter represents the source of the input or output, while the superscript letter represents its destination. For example, $\binom{C}{B}y$ represents the good output (y) produced by the electricity sub-technology (box B) that is an intermediate input for the EOP abatement sub-technology (box C).

4. EOP pollution abatement does not eliminate the undesirable byproduct of good output production. Instead, it transforms some of the byproduct from one medium (air) to another medium (solid waste), where it constitutes a reduced threat to human health and the environment, while the residual byproduct is released into the atmosphere (box E).

5. If a producer does not install an EOP pollution abatement sub-technology, no exogenous inputs are assigned to EOP abatement (i.e., $\binom{C}{A}x = 0$); nor is any electricity used as an intermediate input by EOP abatement ($\binom{C}{B}y = 0$). As a result, gross bad output production equals net bad output production ($\binom{C}{B}b = \binom{E}{C}b$).

6. A complete representation of the production technology requires accounting for the byproducts of the abatement process—e.g., the sludge and gypsum collected by the FGD system used to reduce releases of SO2 into the atmosphere.

7. Førsund (2009), Murty et al. (2012), and Rødseth (2011) investigated the implications of joint production models excluding material balance conditions.

8. Baumgärtner et al. (2001) discuss the relation between joint production and thermodynamics.

9. Except for the intensity variables (z_k^B and z_k^C), subscript or superscript k or k' indicates a fixed value or data. In NP(xk') and JP(xk'), the left-hand side of the constraints with summations include sample data on x, y, and b. Therefore, if only j, m, or n appear in the subscript, the input or output is a variable.

10. If a ton of high-sulfur coal and a ton of low-sulfur coal possess identical Btu content, there is no opportunity cost associated with reducing bad output production via fuel switching.

11. Modeling CIP abatement technologies in this manner eliminates the problem of calculating the input cost of CIP abatement technologies that requires knowing which inputs in an integrated production process are assigned to pollution abatement.

12. Since we do not allow for strong disposability of bad outputs, we sometimes think of the joint production and network models presented in this chapter as representing regulated technologies.

13. While the specification of the network technology employed in this chapter allows flexibility in the allocation of capital between the two sub-technologies, an alternative specification could treat the observed level of capital assigned to each sub-technology as fixed.

14. Data on the cost of plant and equipment for years prior to 1981 were published in *Steam-Electric Plant Construction Cost and Annual Production Expenses*, which was published annually by the Federal Power Commission and the U.S. DOE. The Utility Data Institute (1999) is the source of the cost of plant and equipment data for 1981–97. Finally, data for (1) the cost of plant and equipment and (2) employment collected by FERC for 1998–2005 and EIA-412 for 1998–2003 were downloaded from their respective websites.

15. While both surveys collect data on the historical cost of plant and equipment, they do not collect data on investment expenditures. Hence, changes in the value of plant and equipment reflect the value of additional plant and equipment plus the value of retired plant and equipment. For this study, we assume changes in cost of plant reflect net investment (NI), which is the same assumption employed by Yaisawarng and Klein (1994, p. 453, footnote 30) and Carlson et. al. (2000, p. 1322). We then convert the historical cost of plant data to constant dollar values using the Handy-Whitman Index (HWI) (see Whitman et al., 2012). The net constant dollar capital stock (CS) for year n is calculated in the following manner:

$$CS = \sum_{t=1}^{n} \frac{NI_t}{HWI_t}$$

In the first year of its operation, the net investment of a power plant is equivalent to the total value of its plant and equipment.

16. A number of plants consume fuels other than coal, oil, and natural gas (e.g., petroleum coke, blast furnace gas, coal-oil mixture, fuel oil #2, methanol, propane, wood and wood waste, and refuse, bagasse and other nonwood waste). In this study, any plant whose consumption of fuels other than coal, oil, and natural gas represented more than 0.0001 percent of its total fuel consumption (in Btu) is excluded. It follows that we ignore consumption of fuels other than coal, oil, and natural gas when they represent less than 0.0001 percent of a plant's fuel consumption.

17. Because data for these NAICS codes were not reported for Alabama, data from Tennessee are used for power plants in Alabama.

18. Fuel emission factors are from the *Electric Industry Power Annual 2004* (U.S. DOE, 2004, p. 74).

19. Førsund (2009), Murty et al. (2012), and Rødseth (2011) also model the production technology as a set of sub-technologies, although in a slightly different manner than we propose here.

20. The network technology provides a more adequate specification than the reduced form joint production model.

REFERENCES

Baumgärtner, S., H. Dyckhoff, M. Fabera, J. Proops and J. Schiller (2001), 'The concept of joint production and ecological economics' *Ecological Economics*, **36** (3), 365–371.

Carlson, C., D. Burtraw, M. Cropper and K. Palmer (2000), 'Sulfur dioxide control by electric utilities: what are the gains from trade?' *Journal of Political Economy*, **108** (6), 1292–1326.

Färe, R., S. Grosskopf and C. Pasurka (2013), 'Joint production of good and bad outputs with a network application', in Jason Shogren (ed.), *Encyclopedia of Energy, Natural Resource and Environmental Economics, Vol. 2: Resources*, San Diego: Elsevier Academic Press, pp. 109–118.

Federal Power Commission (various years), *Steam-Electric Plant Construction Cost and Annual Production Expenses*, Washington, D.C.

Førsund, F. (2009), 'Good modeling of bad outputs: pollution and multi-output production', *International Review of Environmental and Resource Economics*, **3** (1), 1–38.

Fukuyama, H. and W. L. Weber (2014), 'Two-stage network DEA with bad outputs', in W.D. Cook and J. Zhu (eds), *Data Envelopment Analysis*, New York: Springer, pp. 451–474.

Hua, Z. and Y. Bien (2008), 'Performance measurement for network DEA with undesirable factors', *International Journal of Management and Decision Making*, **9** (2), 141–152.

Kao, C. (2014), 'Network data envelopment analysis: a review', *European Journal of Operational Research*, **239** (1), 1–16.

Murty, S., R. R. Russell and B.S. Levkoff (2012), 'On modeling pollution-generating technologies', *Journal of Environmental Economics and Management*, **64** (1), 117–135.

Pasurka, C. (2008), 'Pollution abatement and competitiveness: a review of data and analyses' *Review of Environmental Economics and Policy*, **2** (2), 194–218.

Rødseth, K. L. (2011), Treatment of undesirable outputs in production analysis: desirable modelling strategies and applications, Unpublished PhD dissertation, Department of Economics and Resource Management, Norwegian University of Life Sciences.

United Nations (2003), *Handbook of National Accounting: Integrated Environmental and Economic Accounting 2003, Final Draft*, New York: United Nations.

U.S. Department of Commerce (various years), *County Business Patterns*.

U.S. Department of Energy, Energy Information Administration (2004), *Electric Industry Power Annual 2004*, Washington, DC. Available at www.eia.gov/electricity/annual.

U.S. Department of Energy, Energy Information Administration (various years), 'Annual electric industry financial report', Form EIA-412.

U.S. Department of Energy, Energy Information Administration (various years), *Steam-Electric Plant Construction Cost and Annual Production Expenses*, Washington, DC.

U.S. Department of Energy, Energy Information Administration (various years), 'Steam-electric plant operation and design report', Form EIA-767.

U.S. Environmental Protection Agency (1980), *Utility FGD Survey*.

U.S. Federal Energy Regulatory Commission (various years), 'Annual report of major electric utilities, licensees and others', FERC Form 1.

Utility Data Institute (1999), *North America Electric Power Data*, New York: McGraw-Hill.

Whitman, Requardt & Associates, LLP (2012), 'The Handy-Whitman index of public utility construction costs: trends of construction costs', Bulletin No. 175 (1912–January 1, 2012), Baltimore, MA.

Yaisawarng, S. and J. D. Klein (1994), 'The effects of sulfur dioxide controls on productivity change in the U.S. electric power industry', *Review of Economics and Statistics*, **76** (3), 447–460.

Yang, C., C. Hsiao and M. Yu (2008), 'Technical efficiency and impact of environmental regulations in farrow-to-finish swine production in Taiwan', *Agricultural Economics*, **39** (1), 51–61.

Zhu, Z., K. Wang and Bing Zhang (2014), 'Applying a network data envelopment analysis model to quantify the eco-efficiency of products: a case study of pesticides', *Journal of Cleaner Production*, **69**, 67–73.

4. Efficiency analysis in uncertain operating environments: the problem with outliers

Kevin J. Fox and Lisa Y.T. Lee*

4.1 INTRODUCTION

Firms may be unfairly labelled as inefficient using standard efficiency analysis techniques, due to random occurrences beyond their control. Cropping and fishing industries are especially subject to random events which may, for example, make the performance of growers and fishers appear poor. Sources of uncertainty include fish stock variability for fisheries, water availability for agriculture and weather conditions for both industries; individual fishers and growers generally have no influence on such environmental uncertainty. These are conditions which are difficult to incorporate into standard efficiency analysis methods. Hence, typically no adjustment, explicit or implicit, is made for environmental uncertainty that is beyond the control of firms.

In such cases it is important to identify possible outliers and the nature of these outliers. For example, are they outliers because of the scale they are operating at, or because of their mix of input utilization and output performance? It is the outliers of the 'mix' kind which we would expect to find when firms face uncertain environments – firms with the same technology and level of inputs may have quite different output levels due to particular environmental conditions. In practice, firms typically use different technologies and input mixes, which makes outlier detection considerably more difficult than just identifying firms with above or below average output performance. This is particularly relevant for natural resource managers who wish to make a comparison of performance across individual producers.

The method of outlier detection employed here is that introduced by Fox et al. (2004). Among other desirable properties, it allows for the possibility of multiple inputs and multiple outputs. This methodology is applied in a natural resource context to demonstrate its usefulness in identifying an outlier firm which displays unusual production activities relative to its peers, and the reasons for its dissimilarity. While the method is applicable to the general problem of outlier detection, the application of the method is also particularly attractive in the context of efficiency analysis. Nonparametric methods based on constructing a best-practice frontier using linear programming techniques such as data envelopment analysis (DEA) (Farrell, 1957; Charnes et al., 1978) do not yield the ordinary least squares (OLS) residuals or parameters which are typically used by outlier diagnostics. Moreover, the detection of outliers can be complicated by the existence of multiple outputs. The stochastic frontier approach to efficiency analysis (Aigner et al., 1977) does allow for some stochastic variation in estimating the frontier, but requires the specification of particular distributions for stochastic deviations from the frontier, and the fit can similarly be affected by outliers. The only substantial difference in this case is that the efficient frontier can be affected by outliers that are well inside the frontier.[1]

As it is frequently the outliers that define the frontier, it is not surprising that the results generated by frontier-based efficiency models are particularly sensitive to outliers. What is surprising is that the detection of outliers has not received more attention in the efficiency measurement literature; Wilson (1993) provides a useful survey.

A commonly suggested approach to outlier detection is sensitivity analysis – e.g., observations are deleted and the effect of their absence on average efficiency scores is used as a criterion. Using such an approach results in observations on the frontier having an asymmetric effect on the average efficiency scores as they can affect the efficiency scores of other observations, whereas observations on the interior cannot affect the scores of any other observation. The Fox et al. (2004) method used here does not draw a distinction between observations on the best-practice frontier and inside the frontier, allowing the effects of uncertainty, measurement and other errors in all observations to become apparent.

This chapter is organized as follows. Section 4.2 describes the details of the method of outlier detection that is employed. Section 4.3 notes some interesting properties of the method, while section 4.4 presents the results of applying the outlier detection method to Icelandic fishery data and section 4.5 applies the method to data from an Australian irrigated industry. Section 4.6 concludes.

4.2   MIX AND SCALE OUTLIER MEASURES

This section describes the mix and scale outlier measures of Fox et al. (2004). Suppose K firms use the same M inputs to produce N outputs. Let x_{ki} denote an input or output used by firm k. If $i = 1, \ldots, M$, then x_{ki} is an input, while if $i = M + 1, \ldots, M + N$ then x_{ki} is an output. Let $m(x_j, x_k)$ and $s(x_j, x_k)$ denote respectively the mix and scale distance between the input-output vectors of firms j and k. In the appendix we note some axioms that can be regarded as desirable properties for the mix and scale distance measures.

Consider the mix distance between firms j and k defined as the ordinary least squares residual sum of squares obtained by running the following regression:

$$\ln\left(\frac{x_{ki}}{x_{ji}}\right) = \alpha + \varepsilon_i, \ x_{ji}, x_{ki} > 0, i = 1, \ldots, M + N. \tag{4.1}$$

The coefficient α is essentially a measure of the relative scale of the vectors being compared (scale dissimilarity), whereas the sum squared residuals gives a measure of the variance of the difference in logs between corresponding elements of the vectors (mix dissimilarity).

The formula for the mix measure, $m(x_j, x_k)$, derived from (4.1) is as follows:[2]

$$m(x_j, x_k) = \frac{1}{M + N} \sum_{i=1}^{M+N} \hat{\varepsilon}_i^2$$

$$= \frac{1}{M + N} \sum_{i=1}^{M+N} \left\{ \ln\left(\frac{x_{kl}}{x_{jl}}\right) - \frac{1}{M + N} \sum_{i=1}^{M+N} \ln\left(\frac{x_{ki}}{x_{ji}}\right) \right\}^2 \tag{4.2}$$

It is easily verified that this mix measure satisfies axioms (M1)–(M6) of the appendix.

We define the scale distance between firms j and k to be equal to the squared ordinary least squares estimate of the parameter α in (4.1). The formula for the scale measure, $s(x_j, x_k)$, derived from (4.1) is then as follows:

$$s(x_j, x_k) = \left[\frac{1}{M+N} \sum_{i=1}^{M+N} \ln\left(\frac{x_{ki}}{x_{ji}}\right) \right]^2. \tag{4.3}$$

It is easily verified that this scale measure satisfies axioms (S1)–(S6) of the appendix.

Let K denote the full set of firms, $K = \{1, \ldots, K\}$. Also let K_n^c denote a subset of n firms. The possible combinations of n firms are indexed by $c = 1, \ldots, C$, where $C = \binom{K}{n}$ To construct a ranking of outliers based on the mix and scale distance measures, we need to construct a reference vector using $K - n$ firms not in the subset K_n^c, where C is the combination of n firms, n being the subset of outliers. The ith element of the reference input-output vector denoted by x_{Ri} is obtained by taking the geometric mean of the ith element of the input-output vectors of the $K - n$ firms, i.e.:

$$x_{Ri} = \left(\prod_{k \notin K_n^c} x_{ki} \right)^{1/(K-n)}. \tag{4.4}$$

The mix and scale measures from (4.2) and (4.3) are then measured relative to the reference input-output vector and are given in (4.5) and (4.6), respectively:

$$m(x_R, x_k) = \frac{1}{M+N} \sum_{l=1}^{M+N} \left\{ \ln\left(\frac{x_{kl}}{x_{Rl}} \right) - \frac{1}{M+N} \sum_{i=1}^{M+N} \ln\left(\frac{x_{ki}}{x_{Ri}} \right) \right\}^2 \tag{4.5}$$

$$s(x_R, x_k) = \left[\frac{1}{M+N} \sum_{i=1}^{M+N} \ln\left(\frac{x_{ki}}{x_{Ri}} \right) \right]^2. \tag{4.6}$$

By choosing different values of n we can identify the n mix and scale outliers up to an arbitrarily determined maximum number of possible outliers.

4.3   SOME INTERESTING PROPERTIES OF THE MEASURES

We note the following about the proposed mix and scale distance measures:[3]

- In relation to efficiency analysis, the measures are able to identify observations as outliers even if they are on the interior of the best-practice frontier. While these observations do not affect the efficiency scores of other observations when using DEA, their detection can alert researchers to their dissimilarity with other observations. They will affect the efficiency scores of other observations if a stochastic frontier approach is used. If the dissimilarity with other observations is due to, for example, environmental factors, measurement or other errors, then it is possible to avoid incorrect conclusions regarding their efficiency.
- Observations can be scale outliers because they are very small. The proposed method is based on a proportional concept of divergence rather than an arithmetic interpretation – for example, observations which are half as large as the mean are equal outliers to those which are twice as large as the mean.
- If all observations are along a ray in two dimensions, then mix scores will all be zero.

- One would expect the scale measure to select both the largest and smallest scale observations as outliers. This is what the scale measure does when $n = 1$ (i.e., when the possibility of a single outlier is considered). When there is more than one outlier, masking effects can arise; the extremeness of an outlier may be masked by other extreme observations. Groups of outliers are thus hard to detect without allowing n to vary. In this case, the scale measure will start to select observations only at one or other extreme, i.e. groups of either very large or very small observations (see Fox et al., 2004, p. 87). Because of this property, it is not clear that it is always desirable to control for masking. This point is equally applicable to the mix measure, and most other outlier detection methods. Of course, allowing n to vary has the additional disadvantage of dramatically increasing the number of computations.

4.4   APPLICATION TO THE ICELANDIC FISHERY DATA SET

The data set used was for Icelandic fisheries, taking outputs as to be 'total revenue' and 'other revenue', with 'expenditures' and 'depreciation' as inputs. These variables are labelled as total, other, expend and depre, respectively, in Figure 4.1.

The data set included 82 observations for 1990, 80 for 1991, 88 for 1992, 84 for 1993, 91 for 1994 and 90 for 1995. The data are measured in millions of Icelandic krona (US$1 $\approx$ 114 krona on 10 October 2016). For purposes of preserving confidentiality, the vessel numbers were transformed so that the numbers cited below do not correspond to the vessel numbers in the official data.

Pairwise plots of the data for one of the years, 1991, are presented in Figure 4.1 to allow a preliminary inspection of the data. It reveals that there seems to be close to constant returns to scale in the industry, if one considers only total revenue and expenditures; this is also found for the other years. This is perhaps rather surprising, especially as the data spans vessels using different technologies and fishing for different species. There is, however, some apparent variation between vessels, especially if other revenues and depreciation are considered. Over time, a major change in the pattern of the data is that vessels with other revenues have declined. Also, there appears to be more variance in the relationship between total revenue and expenditures in the later years.

As working with multiple dimensions can be confusing, we initially considered using only total revenues as the sole output and expenditures as the

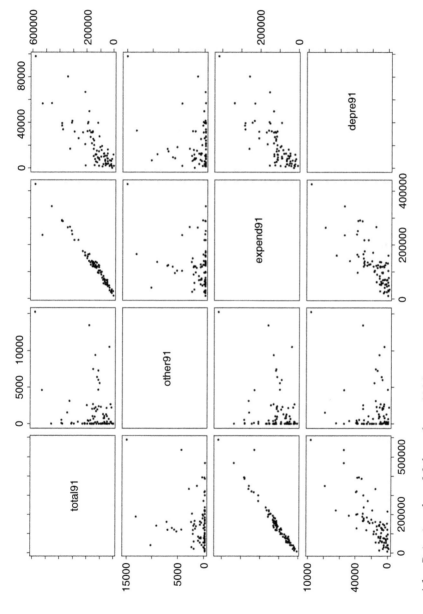

Figure 4.1   Pairwise plot of fishery data, 1991

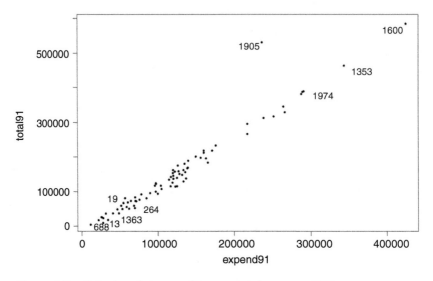

Figure 4.2   Pairwise plot expenditure vs total revenue, 1991

sole input for 1991. Figure 4.2 presents a pairwise plot of these data, with extreme observations (possible outliers) numbered. Figure 4.3a plots the mix scores for these data. By examining Figures 4.2 and 4.3a, we can see that in indentifying mix outliers our method does not discriminate between observations on the frontier and observations in the interior of the frontier. For example, looking at Figure 4.2, vessel 1905 would define the frontier technology in DEA (assuming constant returns to scale), whereas vessel 13 would not. However, looking at Figure 4.3a, vessel 13 is identified as an outlier, whereas 1905 is not. The sensitivity analysis approach to identifying outliers would not have suggested that there may be anything about vessel 13 worth examining further. Figure 4.3b plots the scale scores for these data. By comparing Figures 4.2 and 4.3b we see that it is not only the large observations which can be identified as outliers in terms of the scale of production, but also small observations; for example, compare the scale score of vessel 688 with that of vessel 1600 in Figure 4.3b.

Table 4.1 presents the top twelve outliers for each year for the mix and scale outliers respectively, using the full data set with two outputs and two inputs. From the pairwise plots of the data, there do not seem to be groups of outliers that might cause masking problems through mutually obscuring extremeness, so we consider only the case of there being one outlier at a time (i.e., $n = 1$).

As the mix and scale measures identify the observations that are different in some way from the other observations in the sample, the temptation

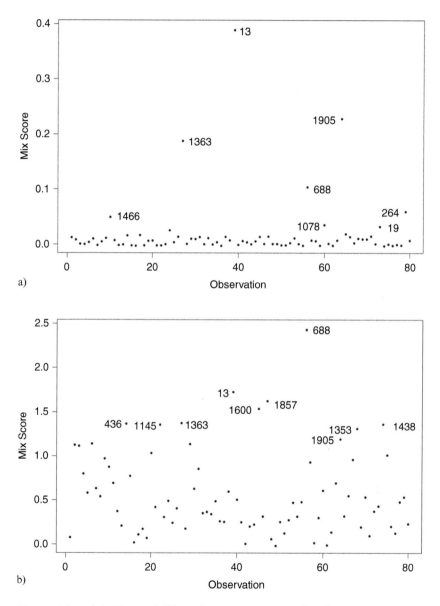

Figure 4.3 (a) *Mix and* (b) *scale scores using total and expend*

is to drop those observations from the sample. However, it is unclear how many should be dropped. It is also unclear if these are legitimate observations or are identified as outliers due to, e.g., measurement error. What is clear though, is that the mix and scale measures contain information about the observations compared with the rest of the sample, and this information can be used to more carefully examine the data for the corresponding environmental factors, as well as measurement and data entry errors. As uncertainty about fish catch may play a role in a vessel being identified as a mix outlier, it is useful to examine changes over time in the mix score rankings. This is because it is unlikely that, for example, a vessel gets lucky (unlucky) for two or more consecutive years and has a larger (lower) level of output than its inputs suggest it should have; that is, it is unlikely that it is systematically affected by random events such as rough seas or other environmental effects.[4]

As the data do not include the same sample of vessels for all six years, an examination of changes across time becomes difficult. However, we can note that, both for mix and scale rankings, there are some vessels which appear in the top twelve for two or more years. For example, vessel 1278 is in the top twelve mix outliers for all six years, suggesting that its difference from the rest of the fleet is not due to uncertainty, but to other factors that are worth investigating before drawing conclusions about efficiency. Similarly, vessel 2172 is noteworthy as it is in the sample for four years and appears in the top twelve mix outliers for all four years. Vessel 1353 is also notable as it appears in the top twelve mix outliers in four of the six years it is in the sample. On the other hand, many vessels make only brief appearances in the top twelve, indicating that they may have been subject to random occurrences that were beyond their control, and therefore non-replicable. Vessel 1105 is an interesting case as it is in the sample for each year, but appears as a scale outlier in only 1991, 1992 and 1993.

We can note that although vessels 1278 and 2172 feature as mix outliers, they do not appear in any year as a scale outlier. This highlights that the mix and scale measures are identifying different characteristics of the data, and are hence complementary and carry more information than aggregate outlier measures. Also, the benefits of being able to use multiple outputs and multiple inputs in outlier detection are highlighted by a comparison of the mix and scale rankings in Figure 4.3 with the rankings in Table 4.1. The figure presents the rankings using only one input and one output for 1991, while the table presents the rankings using two inputs and two outputs. A brief examination of these results reveals that there is very little relationship between them, suggesting that the use of an analysis based on only two dimensions can be misleading.

Table 4.1 Mix and scale outlier rankings, fishery (n=1)

Rank	1990	1991	1992	1993	1994	1995
1	1483	1363	2015	2172	1030	1904
2	1363	1353	1663	2015	122	2205
3	1388	2015	1278	1939	1353	2172
4	1466	1278	2175	1330	2172	1353
5	1014	1367	1478	1278	2063	1939
6	1353	1362	2172	1367	2199	1278
7	1560	1580	1461	2156	1278	1330
8	1278	1365	1397	1461	1580	2235
9	1536	1555	80	1362	228	1511
10	1397	1605	1614	1555	1558	1580
11	1414	1511	1266	1587	1367	1304
12	19	1507	252	1614	1511	2156

Rank	1990	1991	1992	1993	1994	1995
1	1014	688	1341	241	122	920
2	1388	1363	1466	2199	1107	95
3	1363	1105	436	1105	53	1631
4	1477	13	1105	743	1438	743
5	688	735	1438	147	1030	1086
6	1466	125	735	259	126	1362
7	1008	1426	1858	53	1266	1857
8	1857	264	1064	1858	1086	241
9	436	247	53	252	1295	1078
10	13	1536	1414	1437	1138	102
11	19	19	1857	1064	157	1328
12	1414	1078	1288	80	252	1130

4.5 APPLICATION TO AN AUSTRALIAN IRRIGATION INDUSTRY DATA SET

For this set of results, we use farm-level data from irrigation surveys conducted by the Australian Bureau of Agricultural and Resource Economics and Sciences (ABARES). The production data was for the 2008–09 season, and consists of 54 observations drawn from seven natural resource management regions with significant irrigation industry. For confidentiality reasons, we are unable to name the particular irrigated crop involved, but note that it is the same crop across all seven regions. The surveys were conducted in a controlled way to obtain a representative sample for a particular region. In addition, the population of farms to be sampled is rotated every five years so the data set is unbalanced. When the outlier detection method is applied to data collected via this sampling strategy, this case study can be akin to targeted monitoring. This refers to separating firms into a target group, which is more frequently sampled based on certain criteria such as its historical records (Cason and Gangadharan, 2006; Harrington, 1988), or randomly rotated into the group (Friesen, 2003).

The production data are comprehensive and include a large number of variables in terms of prices and quantities. A further area of investigation in this application is the type of data that is necessary in order to obtain the most reliable scores. While water applied is a strong indicator of yield, there may also be other factors of inputs that are correlated with output such that if these explanatory variables are not included then some observations may be inaccurately identified as more or less dissimilar than others. Following from this, our study also demonstrates the disadvantage of using partial productivity measures to make inferences regarding efficiency.

As with the fisheries example, we initially considered using only total yield as the sole output and water use as the sole input. Relating crop yield to the quantity of water applied is a common productivity measure by which resource managers judge an irrigator's productive performance. This can be misleading as partial-factor productivity measures do not account for improvements in or substitution among other categories of input (Fabricant, 1959). The farm's overall productivity may differ significantly when all factors of input and output are considered. To demonstrate, Figure 4.4 shows the pairwise plot of yield to water use with observations of interest numbered, and observations which are actual outliers using our approach are enclosed in a bold border. From the pairwise plot, there is an apparent diminishing return to irrigation water use, which is expected as excessive irrigation causes waterlogging and reduced crop yield. Two of the actual outliers (observations 51 and

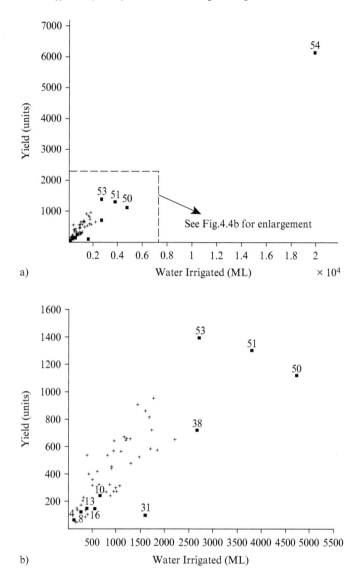

Figure 4.4   (a) Cross plot of water irrigated and yield, and (b) enlargement

54, in terms of mix and scale) are visually discernible as being dissimilar to the rest of the population. However, based on this pairwise plot, the apparently less efficient (observations 50 and 38) and more efficient irrigators (observation 53) may be identified as outliers, although these

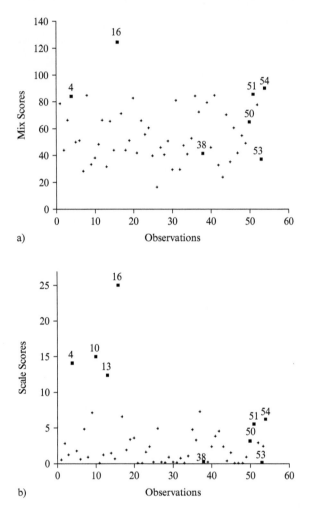

Figure 4.5   (a) Mix and (b) scale scores for irrigated industry

irrigators in fact rank below half of the observations in dissimilarity to the group average.

The results of scale and mix dissimilarity scores for the dataset using all available variables (both prices and quantities) are shown in Figure 4.5. Observation 16 stands out as both a mix and scale outlier, although this is difficult to discern in Figure 4.4 where only yield and water use is considered. Observations with the highest mix and scale dissimilarity scores are shown in Table 4.2. It can be seen that observations 16, 54, 51 and 4 appear

Table 4.2   Mix and scale scores, irrigated industry (all variables), n =1

Mix scores			Scale scores		
Rank	Observation	Mix score	Rank	Observation	Scale score
1	16	124.1	1	16	25.0
2	54	89.8	2	10	15.0
3	51	85.3	3	4	14.1
4	8	84.4	4	13	12.4
5	41	84.4	5	37	7.3
6	36	84.0	6	9	7.1
7	4	83.7	7	17	6.6
8	20	82.5	8	54	6.2
9	31	81.0	9	51	5.5
10	39	79.2	10	26	4.9
11	1	78.5	11	7	4.8
12	52	77.4	12	35	4.7

in both lists, which may suggest that these irrigators have different operational compositions relative to the rest of the industry. This may be due to something systematic in their production, or susceptibility to random events such as particularly adverse or favourable weather conditions affecting the regions where these growers are located. Again, these are factors that are worth investigating before drawing conclusions about efficiency.

Since the variables used are in terms of both quantity and price, it is possible for the different scales of measurement to affect the dissimilarity scores.[5] The objective of this supplementary analysis is to recalculate the indexes using only the quantity variables to determine if this would lead to significantly different results.[6]

The recalculated outlier scores using only quantity variables are shown in Table 4.3. The resulting mix and scale scores change considerably. For example, observation 16 drops its rank in terms of both mix and scale when only quantity variables are considered, to the extent that it does not appear in the top twelve ranked outliers using either criterion. There are a few observations which are in the top twelve ranks of both sets of results: namely, observations 37 and 10 remain highly ranked in terms of scale scores, while observations 20, 8, 39 and 36 remain highly ranked in terms of mix scores. Those that do appear in both sets of results may warrant further investigation to determine the reasons why these are dissimilar; there may be something unusual about their operations causing them to stand out in both results. While this may suggest possible instances of

*Table 4.3   Mix and scale scores, irrigated industry, quantity variables only,
n =1*

Mix scores			Scale scores		
Rank	Observation	Mix score	Rank	Observation	Scale score
1	20	90.9	1	44	36.0
2	8	85.0	2	37	33.1
3	11	81.2	3	11	31.5
4	15	78.6	4	20	29.8
5	22	77.8	5	29	28.2
6	37	77.4	6	22	27.6
7	44	76.4	7	15	22.9
8	29	72.2	8	8	22.4
9	39	49.9	9	10	13.1
10	36	48.2	10	36	8.3
11	10	43.7	11	39	7.0
12	54	8.3	12	2	4.4

misreporting, there may also be factors beyond their control. Analysis over time would help clarify the results.

The fisheries and irrigated cropping examples illustrate the usefulness of the proposed index methodology for efficiency analysis, particularly in natural resources settings which are subject to considerable uncertainty. The outlier-detection approach is also directly applicable in the context of water accounting, which is particularly relevant in discussions regarding 'sustainable diversion limits' in the Murray-Darling Basin Plan.

4.6   CONCLUSION

An innovative method is employed for detecting outliers in a natural resource context, using case studies of Icelandic fisheries and an Australian irrigated industry. The application to these industries is of interest as it is likely to be subject to random occurrences such as environmental effects beyond the control of firms. The method provides a natural interpretation of the division of outliers into mix and scale components, while other methods do not draw this distinction. The method is applicable to any outlier detection context, but it is particularly useful for detecting outliers in multiple-input, multiple-output data sets on firm production.

The method can be used as a straightforward framework for outlier detection, which can be important for the quality assurance of sample data that forms the basis from which many agencies undertake productivity comparisons. In terms of frontier-based efficiency analysis, the mix outlier measure has the advantage of detecting influential observations on the frontier while simultaneously detecting outliers in the interior.

The application of this method to the fisheries and irrigation industries highlights how uncertainty about weather, climate or natural resource abundance, as well as measurement errors, can influence whether a producer is being identified as either very efficient or inefficient. This allows the identification of firms, or groups of firms, that have particularly different production activities to the rest of the sample, either due to random events or systematic differences in their production practices. Using this method, firms which are different in some important aspect, such as the mix of inputs and outputs or the scale of production, can be further analysed before drawing conclusions about efficiency.

NOTES

* The authors would like to thank Tiho Ancev and participants at the Workshop on Environmentally Adjusted Productivity and Efficiency Measurement 2016, University of Sydney, for helpful comments. They also thank Tryggvi Thor Herbertson of the Institute of Economic Studies at the University of Iceland for making available the fisheries data set used in this chapter, and the Australian Bureau of Agricultural and Resource Economics and Sciences (ABARES) for making available the agricultural data. The financial support of the Australian Research Council (DP150100830) is gratefully acknowledged.
1. Useful reviews of frontier modelling for efficiency analysis include Førsund et al. (1980), Schmidt (1986), Bauer (1990), Seiford and Thrall (1990), Lovell (1993), Greene (1993), Ali and Seiford (1993) and Coelli (1995).
2. This metric was proposed by Allen and Diewert (1981) to measure the distance between price vectors in an index number context.
3. Fox et al. (2004) present some illustrative examples of the properties of outlier measures using mock data sets. They also present comparisons with the outlier detection method of Wilson (1993).
4. Zero observations in the dataset have been replaced with a very small number, namely 0.00000001, in order to avoid these fishers standing out as outliers simply because of a zero entry, but may not be extreme in any other way.
5. Fox et al. (2004) note that while price measures can be included as an 'input' or 'output' vector, since price and quantity variables can have very different scales, a separate measure of dissimilarity containing only the price variables may be desirable.
6. The variable 'Family weeks worked (weeks)' was left out as there are no quantity measures for contracted labour to capture the substitution between family and contracted labour.

REFERENCES

Aigner, D.J., C.A.K. Lovell and P. Schmidt (1977), 'Formulation and estimation of stochastic frontier production function models', *Journal of Econometrics*, **6**, 21–37.

Ali, A.I. and M. Seiford (1993), 'The mathematical programming approach to efficiency analysis', in H.O. Fried, C.A.K. Lovell and S.S. Schmidt (eds), *The Measurement of Productive Efficiency*, Oxford University Press, New York, 120–159.

Allen, R.C. and W.E. Diewert (1981), 'Direct versus implicit superlative index number formulae', *Review of Economics and Statistics*,**63**, 430–435.

Andrews, D.F. and D. Pregibon (1978), 'Finding the outliers that matter', *Journal of the Royal Statistical Society, Series B*, **40**, 85–93.

Bauer P.W. (1990), 'Recent developments in the econometric estimation of frontiers', *Journal of Econometrics*, **46**, 39–56.

Cason, T.N. and Gangadharan, L. (2006), 'An experimental study of compliance and leverage in auditing and regulatory enforcement', *Economic Inquiry*, **44**(2), 352–366.

Charnes, A., W.W. Cooper and E. Rhodes (1978), 'Measuring the efficiency of decision making units', *European Journal of Operations Research*, **2**, 429–444.

Coelli, T.J. (1995), 'Recent developments in frontier modelling and efficiency measurement', *Australian Journal of Agricultural Economics*, **39**, 219–245.

Fabricant, S. (1959) 'Basic facts on productivity change', National Bureau of Economic Research, Occasional paper no. 63, 1959.

Farrell, M.J. (1957), 'The measurement of productive efficiency', *Journal of the Royal Statistical Society, Series A*, 120(**3**), 253–290.

Førsund, F.R., C.A.K. Lovell and P. Schmidt (1980), 'A survey of frontier production functions and of their relationship to efficiency measurement', *Journal of Econometrics*, **13**, 5–25.

Fox, K.J., R.J. Hill and W.E. Diewert (2004), 'Identifying outliers in multi-output models', *Journal of Productivity Analysis*, **22**, 73–94.

Friesen, L. (2003), 'Targeting enforcement to improve compliance with environmental regulations', *Journal of Environmental Economics and Management*, **46**, 72–85.

Greene, W.H. (1993), 'The econometric approach to efficiency analysis', in H.O. Fried, C.A.K. Lovell and S.S. Schmidt (eds), *The Measurement of Productive Efficiency*, Oxford University Press, New York, 68–119.

Harrington, W. (1988),'Enforcement leverage when penalties are restricted', *Journal of Public Economics*, **37**, 29–53.

Lovell, C.A.K. (1993), 'Production frontiers and productive efficiency', in H.O. Fried, C.A.K. Lovell and S.S. Schmidt (eds), *The Measurement of Productive Efficiency*, Oxford University Press, New York, 3–67.

Schmidt, P. (1986), 'Frontier production functions', *Econometric Reviews*, **4**, 289–328.

Seiford, L.M. and R.M. Thrall (1990), 'Recent developments in DEA', *Journal of Econometrics*, **46**, 7–38.

Wilson, P.W. (1993), 'Detecting outliers in deterministic nonparametric frontier models with multiple outputs', *Journal of Business and Economic Statistics*, **11**(3), 319–323.

APPENDIX

Axioms for mix outlier indicators proposed by Fox et al. (2004) are as follows:

> **(M1)** $m(x_k, x_k) = 0$
> **(M2)** $m(x_j, x_k) \geq 0$
> **(M3)** $m(x_j, x_k) = m(x_k, x_j)$
> **(M4)** $m(\delta x_k, x_k) = m(x_k, \delta x_k) = 0$ where δ is a positive scalar
> **(M5)** $m(P[x_j, x_k]) = m(x_j, x_k)$, where $P[x_j, x_k]$ is a common permutation of the input-output vectors x_j, x_k
> **(M6)** $m(\lambda x_j, \mu x_k) = m(x_j, x_k)$ where λ and μ are positive scalars
> **(M7)** $m(x_j, x_k) = m(\tilde{x}_j, \tilde{x}_k)$, where $\tilde{x}_{ji} = \lambda_i x_{ji}$, $\tilde{x}_{ki} = \lambda_i x_{ki}$ and λ_i is a positive scalar, for all i (invariance to changes in the units of measurement).

Axioms for scale-outlier indicators proposed by Fox et al. (2004) are as follows:

> **(S1)** $s(x_k, x_k) = 0$
> **(S2)** $s(x_j, x_k) \geq 0$
> **(S3)** $s(x_j, x_k) = s(x_k, x_j)$
> **(S4)** $s(x_k, \delta x_k) = s(x_k, (1/\delta)x_k) = f[max(\delta, (1/\delta))]$, where f is a strictly increasing function and δ is a positive scalar. This ensures that large and small outliers are treated symmetrically.
> **(S5)** $s(P[x_j, x_k]) = s(x_j, x_k)$, where $P[x_j, x_k]$ is a common permutation of the input-output vectors x_j, x_k
> **(S6)** $s(x_j, x_k) = s(\tilde{x}_j, \tilde{x}_k)$, where $\tilde{x}_{ji} = \lambda_i x_{ji}$, and λ_i is a positive scalar, for all i (invariance to changes in the units of measurement).

5. Assessing stream health with respect to ecological connectivity

H. K. Edmonds, J. E. Lovell and
C. A. K. Lovell*

5.1 INTRODUCTION

Ecological connectivity, or landscape connectivity (Taylor et al., 1993), is the degree to which the landscape facilitates or impedes movement of biota between different locations that have sources of food, habitat, etc. necessary for carrying out their lifecycles. Ecological connectivity indicators are analysed in this study, and contrasted with other land-cover indicators in relation to their association with stream health. Created in a geographical information system (GIS), the newly developed ecological connectivity indicators considered here include metrics designed to capture the loss of stream and riparian zone to underground stormwater piping, and the fragmentation and loss of habitat which that may cause. In addition, in-stream connected stream extent metrics were introduced as measures of the longitudinal distance up to the first potential barrier to aquatic fauna dispersal (e.g., a culvert) associated with infrastructure on any stream segment upstream and/or downstream from each site.

Ecological connectivity has been found to influence the aquatic fauna of the urban, ephemeral, sub-tropical streams in southeast Queensland, Australia (SEQ) more than catchment-scale impervious area and associated hydrology (Millington, 2016). In particular, the extent of connected stream length upstream and the amount of piping and impervious surface in the upstream network that has replaced natural stream length were found to be relatively strongly associated with variation in macroinvertebrate diversity and abundance.

We extend our previous work on urban stream health (Millington et al., 2015) by including new ecological connectivity indicators; accounting for fish and macroinvertebrate diversity and abundance; applying additional performance measurement techniques; and expanding the areal extent of the study to ephemeral sub-tropical streams within 16 sub-catchments in

SEQ. Sites range from highly urbanised to relatively intact forest cover and therefore include a wide range of values for lumped catchment-scale impervious land cover and associated stormwater piping extents, as well as for tree, grass and impervious riparian land cover at the reach and catchment scales. Overall, however, the sites are highly urbanised, with mean lumped impervious cover of 23.5 per cent (min 0 per cent, max 48 per cent).

We measure stream health with macroinvertebrate and fish diversity and abundance indicators. We specify three influences on stream health based on metrics generated using GIS: an ecological connectivity index is created by aggregating two indicators of in-stream longitudinal connectivity; a land cover index is created by aggregating two indicators of land cover – a reach-scale tree cover metric and a catchment-scale impervious surface metric. Upstream sub-catchment drainage area also is included because it influences our health indicators and varies widely across sites. Data on macroinvertebrate abundance and diversity (SIGNAL2) and fish abundance and diversity (O/E_{50}) for 2010 were available from Brisbane City Council (BCC). We use three analytical techniques:

- data envelopment analysis (DEA) to aggregate three pairs of indicators into indices of stream health, ecological connectivity and land cover;
- stochastic frontier analysis (SFA) to evaluate the relative ecological performance of the sample sites in terms of explaining variation in the two stream health indicators in response to variation in the ecological connectivity and land-cover indices and upstream drainage area (UDA), with the one-sided error component capturing deviations from best practice; and
- ecological dominance analysis (EDA) to enrich the evaluation of the relative ecological performance of sample sites.[1]

A site dominates another site in an ecological sense if it is at least as healthy despite having no greater ecological connectivity, no more favourable land cover and no greater upstream drainage area. EDA is independent of the concepts of production technology and its structure, and of efficiency relative to a best practice frontier, and provides our ultimate evaluation of the ability of sites to convert ecological connectivity, land cover and UDA to stream health.

The chapter is organised as follows. In Section 5.2 we describe the setting and the data generation process. In Section 5.3 we provide the analytical details of our methods and approaches, which include DEA to aggregate indicators into indices, and SFA and EDA to provide evaluations of the performance of each site in the sample. Section 5.4 contains our empirical findings and discussion of stream health and its influences in our sample. Section 5.5 concludes.

5.2   THE SETTING AND THE DATA GENERATION PROCESS

This study area of medium areal extent – approximately 1150 km^2, encompassing 16 sub-catchments in the Lower Brisbane River catchment and surrounding coastal catchments (LBRCSCC) – overlapped the two sub-catchments in the previous study (152 km^2). Stream health data for 2010 came from a long-term data set generated by BCC as part of its Local Waterways Health Assessment (LWHA) city-wide stream health monitoring project encompassing 48 sites across the BCC Local Government Area, including sites within the LBRCSCC. Sites that did not have complete land cover and digital elevation model data and/or stream health data were removed from analysis, leaving a total of 30 sites for this study (Figure 5.1).

The two stream health indicators assessed are defined as follows: (i) 'family' level SIGNAL2 macroinvertebrate diversity and abundance (Chessman, 2003); and (ii) fish diversity and abundance, which were captured by a measure of community structure, O/E$_{50}$ (Kennard et al., 2006). The SIGNAL2 indicator assigns a score to aquatic invertebrate families based on their tolerance for pollution (scores range from 1 for most tolerant to 10 for least tolerant) and the O/E$_{50}$ indicator is a comparison of the species composition of the observed fish community, with the community composition predicted by a referential model fish assemblage.

Stream health influence indicators consisted of land-cover and connectivity metrics at the catchment, local and reach scales. A total of 43 candidate metrics were generated in a GIS, and included non-spatial (lumped) metrics and spatial metrics consisting of areal buffers and spatially explicit inverse-distance weighted metrics.

Generalised least squares (GLS) model testing and model averaging techniques were used for determining which of these influence indicators had the most explanatory power. Preliminary ordinary least squares (OLS) regression analysis to determine the direction and strength of association between each health indicator and a single influence indicator helped in the specification of the initial GLS model for each stream health indicator. These initial models included a maximum of three variables representing the categories of reach-scale land-cover metrics; catchment-scale land-cover and connectivity metrics; and catchment size metrics.

The possibility of spatial autocorrelation between neighbouring sites was accommodated by specifying a correlation structure within a GLS

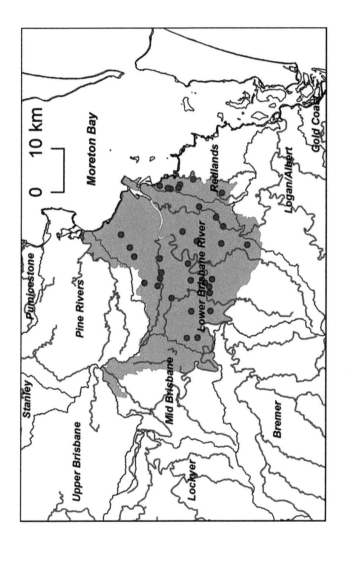

Notes:
Dots indicate site locations.
Grey lines indicate major waterways.
Black lines indicate major catchment boundaries.
The shaded area represents the Brisbane mainland local government area.

Figure 5.1   The study area

model.[2] Stepwise regression with backward selection of variables was performed to determine if a reduced model was better. Nested models were compared, and an analysis of variance (ANOVA) on the best model determined if the correlation structure was necessary. Finally, covariates in the best model from the previous step were systematically replaced by all other covariates in their co-linear set or metric category to create a set of a priori models or hypotheses. The best model or set of models were selected according to the Akaike Information Criterion statistic, and where no single model was clearly the best (which was generally the case) model averaging was applied to assess the relative importance of a particular variable of interest (Johnson and Omland, 2004).

In general, the newly developed connectivity metrics outperformed the impervious surface metrics. Two performed better than others and were chosen for aggregation into an ecological connectivity index (ECI):

- Extent of connected stream length upstream of each study site (CSL). This is the upstream mapped tributary extent until anthropogenic barriers (culverts and pipes) are reached (m).
- Percentage of upstream riparian buffer 30 m either side of the upstream stream network which is designated as either impervious surface or piped channel in the upstream mapped stream network (PIP). This is a catchment-scale effective riparian metric.

Two land-cover influence indicators that were relatively important for explaining variation in SIGNAL2 and O/E_{50} were selected for aggregation into a land-cover index (LCI): (i) catchment-scale impervious surface weighted by inverse flow-path distance to the stream (CIMP); and (ii) reach-scale tree cover in the riparian buffer 30 m either side of the stream network for a distance 200 m upstream (RTC). CIMP is a pure number or weight that ranges from 0 to 1, and RTC is a percentage.

Upstream sub-catchment area (km^2) (UDA) was selected for inclusion in the performance analysis because it had more explanatory power than all other candidate variables. These land-cover and ecological connectivity indicators and UDA are illustrated in Figure 5.2. This figure shows the different land-cover metrics (RTC, CIMP) and ecological connectivity metrics (CSL, PIP) used in the current study, as well as the landscape measure of upstream drainage area (UDA). These metrics are a subset of metrics considered in Millington (2016). Summary statistics for the variables used in this study appear in Table 5.1.

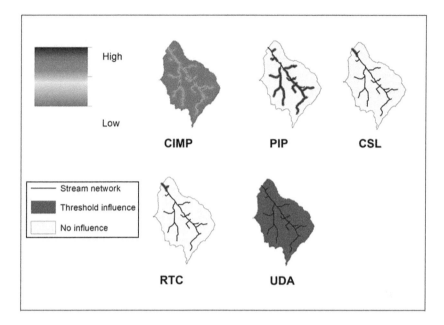

Figure 5.2   Land-cover and landscape metrics

5.3   METHODS AND APPROACHES

Our empirical analysis proceeds in three stages. We begin by using DEA to aggregate the two stream health indicators into a stream health index; to aggregate the two ecological connectivity indicators into an ecological connectivity index; and to aggregate the two land-cover indicators into a land-cover index, each motivated by a desire to conserve degrees of freedom in a small sample. We then use SFA and EDA to evaluate the relative ecological performance of each site. We describe the three techniques in this section, and report our findings in Section 5.4.

5.3.1   DEA Aggregation

DEA is a popular linear programming technique for estimating the relative efficiency of producers in a sample, but we do not use it for that purpose. We use it to aggregate variables in a manner consistent with the economic theory of index numbers, an application for which it is ideally suited, especially in non-market contexts where prices are non-existent.[3]

A linear program has primal and dual formulations, which are equal at optimum. In DEA the primal and dual formulations are called envelopment

Table 5.1   Descriptive statistics of sample data

Variable	Mean	Std. Dev.	Max.	Min.
Stream health index (GHI)	0.722	0.159	1	0.449
Macroinvertebrate abundance and diversity indicator (SIGNAL2)	3.428	0.752	4.755	2.135
Fish abundance and diversity indicator (O/E_{50})	0.312	0.233	0.93	0
Ecological connectivity index (ECI)	20.676	50.408	200	1
Catchment-scale length of connected stream upstream of site indicator (m) (CSL)	2.862	3.110	10.588	0.040
Catchment-scale piping and impervious surface in the upstream network that has replaced natural stream length indicator (PIP)*	68.996	241.242	1204.819	1.071
Land cover index (LCI)	3.906	3.494	11.299	1
Reach-scale tree cover in the riparian buffer indicator (%) (RTC)	0.590	0.301	0.998	0.079
Catchment-scale impervious surface distance-weighted to the stream indicator (CIMP)**	1061.386	5525.490	30303.030	2.161
Upstream sub-catchment drainage area (km²) (UDA)	2.247	3.596	13.566	0.197

Notes:
*   This variable is the reciprocal of the original variable (%).
**   This variable is the reciprocal of the original variable (a pure number), for which one zero value was replaced with the mean of zero and the smallest positive value in the sample prior to taking the reciprocal.

and multiplier problems. Let the two stream health indicator vectors be y_1 and y_2. An aggregate stream health index $y = f_y(y_1, y_2) = \varphi^{-1} \in (0,1]$ is constructed from the primal envelopment programme of the DEA output maximisation problem, as follows:

Envelopment Program	Multiplier Program
Max ϕ_o	Min δ_o
Subject to	Subject to
$\sum_{i=1}^{30} \alpha_i y_{mi} \geq \phi_o y_{mo} \quad m=1,2$	$\sum_{m=1}^{2} \gamma_m y_{mo} = 1$
$\sum_{i=1}^{30} \alpha_i = 1, \alpha_i \geq 0$	$-\sum_{m=1}^{2} \gamma_m y_{mi} + \delta_o \geq 0 \; i=1,...,30$
	$\gamma_m \geq 0, \delta_o$ free

This problem is solved 30 times, once for each site in the sample. The multipliers γ_m in the dual multiplier program are Lagrange multipliers associated with relaxing the inequality constraints in the envelopment maximisation program; they give the impact on the optimal value of the stream health index of marginal changes in each health indicator. They provide implicit valuations, or shadow prices, each site attaches to the two stream health indicators in constructing the aggregate stream health index. These multipliers are non-market analogues to the prices a market assigns to alternative goods serving a similar purpose. Azad and Ancev (2010) and Bellenger and Herlihy (2010) use similar techniques to estimate implicit valuations used to construct environmental indices.[4]

Let the two stream ecological connectivity vectors be x_1 and x_2. An aggregate ecological connectivity index $x^{EC} = f_{x^{EC}}(x_1, x_2) = \theta^{-1} \in [1, +\infty)$ is constructed from the primal envelopment program of the DEA input minimisation problem, as follows:

Envelopment Program	Multiplier Program
Min θ_o	Max μ_o
Subject to	Subject to
$\theta_o x_{no} - \sum_{i=1}^{30} \beta_i x_{ni} \geq 0 \quad n = 1, 2$	$\sum_{n=1}^{2} \rho_n x_{no} = 1$
$\sum_{i=1}^{30} \beta_i = 1, \beta_i \geq 0$	$\mu_o - \sum_{n=1}^{2} \rho_n x_{ni} \leq 0 \; i = 1, ..., 30$
	$\rho_n \geq 0, \mu_o \, \text{free}$

The multipliers ρ_n in the dual multiplier program are Lagrange multipliers associated with relaxing the inequality constraints in the envelopment minimisation program, and they identify the implicit valuations, or shadow prices, each site attaches to the two ecological connectivity indicators in constructing the aggregate ecological connectivity index.

An aggregate land cover index x^{LC} and its shadow prices are constructed and interpreted in the same way.

5.3.2 SFA Evaluation

SFA is a popular econometric technique for estimating the relative efficiency of producers in a sample, and we use it for that purpose. A generic SFA regression is

$ln \, y_i = \alpha_o + \sum_n \alpha_n ln \, x_{ni} + z_i + \upsilon_i - u_i,$

in which y_i is a scalar-valued measure of stream health at site i; x_{ni} are measures of ecological connectivity and land cover at site i; z_i is the sub-catchment drainage area upstream of site i; $v_i \sim N(0,\sigma_v^2)$ is normally distributed statistical noise; and $u_i \sim N^+(0,\sigma_u^2)$ is the inefficiency of site i, the failure of site i to generate maximum feasible stream health given (x_{ni}, z_i, v_i). Our small sample size prompts us to specify a single parameter half-normal distribution for u_i (Kumbhakar and Lovell, 2000). The stochastic frontier relative to which efficiency is estimated is $\ln y_i = \alpha_o + \sum_n \alpha_n \ln x_{ni} + z_i + v_i$.

5.3.3   EDA Evaluation

A site weakly dominates another site if it is at least as healthy even though it enjoys no more ecological connectivity, no more favourable land cover and no more upstream sub-catchment drainage area. Mathematically, site i dominates all sites j for which $y_{mi} \geq y_{mj}$, $x_{ni} \leq x_{nj}$ and $z_i \leq z_j$ for all variables m, n and z under consideration. The concept of dominance is independent of the concepts of production, its technology and structure, and of efficiency relative to a stochastic frontier: a site can dominate others without being efficient in DEA or SFA; and a site can be efficient in DEA or SFA without dominating any other site.

5.4   FINDINGS AND DISCUSSION: THE IMPACT OF ECOLOGICAL CONNECTIVITY ON STREAM HEALTH

We have applied DEA aggregation, SFA evaluation and EDA evaluation sequentially to the 30 sites in our sample, and we report our findings in this order.

5.4.1   DEA Aggregation

We have used DEA to create three aggregate indices. We are interested primarily in the shadow values each site attaches to the two indicators forming each index given in Table 5.2. These DEA-generated shadow values have guided our decisions whether or not to aggregate each pair of indicators.

In constructing an aggregate stream health index GHI, six sites attach positive value to both abundance and diversity indicators, and 24 sites attach positive value to macroinvertebrate abundance and diversity and zero value to fish abundance and diversity. On average, macroinvertebrate abundance and diversity is far more important than fish abundance and diversity in the construction of an index of aggregate stream health in our

Table 5.2   DEA multiplier weights for constructing aggregate indices

Site	GHI		ECI		LCI	
	SIGNAL2	O/E_{50}	CSL	PIP	CIMP	RTC
1	0.226	0.000	0.000	0.009	0.000	1.194
2	0.305	0.000	0.126	0.000	0.000	10.526
3	0.364	0.000	0.003	0.028	0.000	1.390
4	0.357	0.000	0.018	0.549	0.200	0.000
5	0.259	0.000	0.137	0.000	0.000	1.485
6	0.271	0.000	0.000	0.445	0.071	0.484
7	0.414	0.000	0.000	0.903	0.335	0.000
8	0.274	0.000	0.021	0.637	0.157	0.000
9	0.207	0.024	0.000	0.128	0.000	1.350
10	0.207	0.024	0.014	0.125	0.027	0.185
11	0.234	0.027	0.000	0.172	0.036	0.241
12	0.353	0.000	0.000	0.704	0.267	0.000
13	0.291	0.000	0.000	0.695	0.210	1.425
14	0.426	0.000	0.000	0.756	0.234	1.584
15	0.407	0.047	0.000	0.934	0.436	0.000
16	0.380	0.000	0.090	0.822	0.463	0.000
17	0.354	0.000	0.000	0.787	0.323	0.000
18	0.233	0.000	0.000	0.664	0.248	0.000
19	0.301	0.000	0.081	0.735	0.268	1.816
20	0.242	0.000	0.000	0.862	0.353	0.000
21	0.243	0.028	0.000	0.700	0.287	0.000
22	0.235	0.027	0.000	0.655	0.293	0.000
23	0.272	0.000	0.010	0.093	0.038	0.256
24	0.230	0.000	0.002	0.022	0.024	0.161
25	0.322	0.000	0.004	0.128	0.047	0.321
26	0.291	0.000	11.628	0.000	0.051	0.344
27	0.388	0.000	0.099	0.900	0.216	1.461
28	0.316	0.000	3.288	0.727	0.183	1.238
29	0.468	0.000	3.288	0.727	0.000	11.261
30	0.292	0.000	0.024	0.734	0.195	0.000
Mean	**0.305**	**0.006**	**0.649**	**0.488**	**0.165**	**1.224**
(Outlier(s)			**(0.270)**			**(0.533)**
deleted)						

sample; for most sites a marginal increase in fish abundance and diversity has no impact on an index of stream health. As a consequence, GHI and SIGNAL2 are highly collinear, with a simple correlation coefficient of 0.99[+], and so GHI adds no value over SIGNAL2 as a measure of stream health in our sample. On the basis of this pattern of shadow values we have decided not to aggregate the two stream health indicators SIGNAL2 and O/E$_{50}$. However, even though O/E$_{50}$ does not contribute significantly to GHI, we retain it together with SIGNAL2 for DEA and EDA evaluations to determine how the two stream health indicators SIGNAL2 and O/E$_{50}$ respond to variation in indices of ecological connectivity and land cover.[5]

The reasons for the lack of importance of the fish indicator in the stream health index are not clear, but are likely due to the distributions of the two indicators. While fish and macroinvertebrate diversity and abundance indicators are correlated (0.50), there is a lot of scatter; and around this scatter there are several 'outlier' sites for fish, which are the only six sites with non-zero weights in the DEA assessment. While the macroinvertebrate indicator was generally more strongly associated with land-cover indicators than the fish indicator was, the fish indicator was strongly associated with UDA. Indicators would be more useful in this preliminary DEA assessment if their ratios at each site (i.e. O/E$_{50}$ / SIGNAL2) varied more than they do.[6]

In contrast, in the ecological connectivity and land-cover indices both indicators contribute substantially to the construction of their respective index.

In the construction of an aggregate ecological connectivity index ECI, 13 sites attach positive value to both indicators; 14 sites attach positive value to PIP and zero value to CSL; and just three sites attach positive value to CSL and zero value to PIP. On average, the two indicators are of roughly comparable importance in the construction of ECI in our sample, regardless of whether one CSL outlier is excluded. On the basis of this pattern of shadow values we have no reason to ignore either indicator of ecological connectivity, which we measure with the ecological connectivity index ECI.

In the construction of the aggregate land-cover index LCI, 12 sites attach positive value to both indicators; 12 sites attach positive value to CIMP and zero value to RTC; and six sites attach positive value to RTC and zero value to CIMP. On average, RTC is more highly valued in our sample, even when two RTC outliers are excluded. On the basis of this pattern of shadow values again we have no reason to ignore either indicator of land cover, which we measure with the land-cover index LCI.

Consequently we conduct subsequent SFA and EDA evaluations of stream health separately for macroinvertebrate abundance and diversity and fish abundance and diversity, using ecological connectivity and land-cover indices and the upstream sub-catchment drainage area as potential influences on stream health.

These decisions whether or not to aggregate are motivated by an economic argument based solely on the DEA-generated shadow values attached to the three pairs of indicators in Table 5.2. In the case of stream health, a sufficient number of sites judge fish diversity and abundance to be unimportant, in the sense that these sites attach zero shadow value to a marginal increase in this indicator, prompting us not to aggregate. In the case of ecological connectivity and land cover, no indicator was judged to be unimportant by a sufficient number of sites, and so we chose to aggregate. However a stream ecology argument suggests an alternative strategy.

The stream ecology argument involves the different scales represented by the indicators. In the case of the ecological connectivity index, both indicators represent the catchment scale, and potentially represent similar ecological processes. However in the case of the land-cover index, one indicator represents the catchment scale and the other reach scale; and these two scales differ greatly in the area they include (see Figure 5.2), and may represent very different ecological processes. For example, reach-scale condition is associated with greater shading, and therefore reduced stream temperature and less variation in stream temperature (Pluhowski, 1970; Marsh et al., 2005), both of which are important for the diversity and abundance of biotic communities. Catchment-scale stream health stressors that would likely be represented by the catchment-scale indicators are associated with altered hydrology, elevated sediments, water quality contaminants, etc. (Paul and Meyer, 2001; Meyer et al., 2005; Wenger et al., 2009). The contrasting scales, the low explanatory power and the potential loss of information from aggregating such different metrics motivate the deletion of the land-cover indicator CIMP and replacing the land-cover index LCI with the land-cover indicator RTC.

An additional issue is that one of the ecological connectivity indicators, PIP, and the land-cover indicator CIMP both represent catchment scales and may also represent similar processes to some degree, which may render one of them superfluous. That is, the effective riparian buffer indicator PIP may also be representing some of these catchment-scale influences mentioned above, in addition to representing the loss of stream segments (and therefore the loss of ecosystem functions and physical and chemical processes) as well as fragmentation of dispersal paths for biota. In contrast, the other ecological connectivity indicator considered, the extent of connected stream length upstream of each site (CSL), is designed to target the fragmentation of dispersal paths more so than the loss of stream segments.

Motivated by the stream ecology argument, we have repeated the SFA and EDA ecological performance evaluations, replacing the land-cover index LCI with one of its components, the reach-scale tree cover indicator RTC. Results of the SFA and EDA evaluations are very similar, despite the fact that the simple correlation between LCI and RTC is just 0.64, and so we report findings based on the land-cover index LCI supported by the economic argument.

Table 5.3   SFA results for macroinvertebrate and fish abundance and diversity using land cover and ecological connectivity indices

Macroinvertebrate abundance and diversity
Dependent variable: ln SIGNAL2

	Estimate (SE)	Estimate (SE)	Estimate (SE)	Estimate (SE)
Intercept	1.111 (0.938)	1.266 (0.237)***	1.113 (0.688)	1.149 (0.346)***
ln ECI	0.005 (0.024)	0.034 (0.020)		−0.001 (0.027)
ln LCI	0.097 (0.046)*		0.103 (0.037)**	0.153 (0.052)**
ln UDA	0.081 (0.027)**	0.100 (0.028)***	0.080 (0.027)**	
σ^2	0.025 (0.011)*	0.038 (0.046)	0.025 (0.011)*	0.040 (0.061)
γ	0.00+ (0.356)	0.400 (1.366)	0.001 (0.373)	0.312 (1.840
ln L	12.795	10.961	12.776	8.890
χ_1^2				7.81***

Number of observations: 30
Significance: *** (0.001), ** (0.01), * (0.05)

Fish abundance and diversity
Dependent variable: ln O/E$_{50}$

	Estimate (SE)	Estimate (SE)	Estimate (SE)	Estimate (SE)
Intercept	−1.341 (1.145)	−1.331 (1.352)	−1.339 (1.276)	−1.569 (−3.275)
ln ECI	−0.037 (0.071)	−0.032 (0.053)		−0.064 (0.093)
ln LCI	0.017 (0.139)		−0.032 (0.109)	0.278 (0.175)
ln UDA	0.372 (0.076)***	0.375 (0.073)***	0.375 (0.078)***	
σ^2	0.219 (0.059)***	0.220 (0.058)***	0.221 (0.057)***	0.377 (0.106)***
γ	0.00+ (0.029)	0.00+ (0.032)	0.00+ (0.022)	0.00+ (0.157)
ln L	−19.815	−19.82222	−19.949	−27.946
χ_1^2				16.26***

Number of observations: 30
Significance: *** (0.001), ** (0.01), * (0.05)

5.4.2   SFA Evaluation

On the basis of the DEA aggregation exercise we have two indicators of stream health, SIGNAL2 and O/E$_{50}$; one index of ecological connectivity, ECI; one index of land cover, LCI; and a measure of the upstream sub-catchment drainage area, UDA. Since we chose not to aggregate SIGNAL2 and O/E$_{50}$, we ran two sets of SFA regressions: one with SIGNAL2 as the stream health indicator and one with O/E$_{50}$ as the stream health indicator. Results appear in Table 5.3.

The first column of SFA results includes all three influences; subsequent columns delete one influence each, which allows the use of likelihood ratio tests of nested models. The results of the macroinvertebrate abundance and diversity regressions and the fish abundance and diversity regressions coincide in several important respects:

- Upstream sub-catchment drainage area, UDA, is highly significant in all regressions that include it, suggesting that UDA is a critically important influence on both dimensions of stream health.
- Likelihood ratio tests strongly reject the hypothesis that UDA can be deleted from either stream health regression without significant loss of explanatory power (Table 5.3).
- ECI, an ecological focus of our study, is not significant in any regression that includes it.
- The inefficiency parameter γ, an economic focus of our study, is not statistically significant in any regression, implying that all residual (unexplained by ECI, LCI and UDA) performance variation relative to a single stream health standard is random.

The results of the macroinvertebrate abundance and diversity regressions and the fish abundance and diversity regressions differ in one respect: the land-cover index LCI is significant in the former but not the latter. This is roughly consistent with the GLS modelling study by Millington (2016), in which land-cover metrics were of marginal significance in the macroinvertebrate abundance and diversity regressions but no impervious surface metric at any scale was significant in the fish abundance and diversity regressions.

Summarising, the SFA evaluations are not as informative as we had expected, and some potential explanations come to mind. SFA imposes a lot of structure on an estimating model applied to just 30 observations. Also, the use of indices may conceal information contained in component indicators, although this is not the case for LCI and RTC. In addition, we measure stream health with SIGNAL2 and O/E_{50}, but other water-quality indicators such as temperature range and conductivity may be more responsive to variation in ECI and LCI than the indicators we have used. Finally, factors other than the explanatory landscape factors considered may be influencing the stream health of these sites. Perhaps good or bad terrestrial or floodplain connectivity (Rolls et al., 2012), historical land-use, other sources of local pollutants, or invasive species (Paul and Meyer, 2001) could be investigated. Furthermore, ecological assessments of urban streams may have unexplained aspects due to the complexity of the factors affecting them; the complexity of the responses of biota and water quality to complex interacting stressors; and the potential interactions of stressors and indicators (Walsh et al., 2005): for example, if altered conditions favour specific native or invasive taxa (Walters et al., 2003; Sheldon et al., 2012), they could thrive and affect the abundance of other taxa. In any event, omitted variables bias may be influencing the results.

5.4.3   EDA Evaluation

The SFA evaluations are conducted relative to stochastic frontiers, the deterministic kernels of which are common to all sites. This is a very restrictive assumption, unlikely to hold for 30 geographically dispersed sites the health of which is unlikely to be fully explained by the two indices LCI and ECI and upstream drainage area UDA. This assumption, in conjunction with the small sample size, may explain the paucity of information emerging from the SFA evaluations. EDA, by contrast, rests on no such assumption, and simply compares the performance of sites on the basis of their health indicators and their influences. Table 5.4 provides a suite of EDA results for macroinvertebrate abundance and diversity, and Table 5.5 does likewise for fish abundance and diversity. The acronyms at the top of each column indicate the influences included in each evaluation, and the combinations of influences are the same as in Table 5.3.

In Table 5.4 five sites stand out for their consistently strong or weak performance across all combinations of influences. Sites 18, 20 and 28 dominate several other sites (and are dominated by hardly any other sites); each has a higher SIGNAL2 score despite having less favourable influences. Conversely, sites 4 and 25 are dominated by several other sites (and dominate nearly no other sites); each has a lower SIGNAL2 score despite having more favourable influences. These five sites warrant further investigation, perhaps using a map or imagery to locate them in the catchment.

Five other sites stand out in Table 5.4 for a different reason. Sites 19, 21 and 22 exhibit little or no dominance unless UDA is deleted from the list of influences. These sites have relatively large upstream drainage areas, ranking #10, #7 and #4 in the sample. At the other extreme, sites 3 and 26 are dominated by just one site unless UDA is deleted from the list of influences. These sites have relatively small upstream drainage areas, ranking #28 and #22 in the sample. When stream health is measured with macroinvertebrate abundance and diversity, dominance is closely associated with upstream drainage area on this influence deletion criterion, a finding consistent with the SFA evaluations.

We have conducted the same experiment, retaining macroinvertebrate abundance and diversity as the stream health indicator, and deleting ecological connectivity and land-cover indices one at a time to explore the impacts on site rankings. Findings are similar to those for upstream drainage area, but in each case fewer sites are affected by the deletions.

Table 5.4   *Dominance results for macroinvertebrate abundance and diversity using land cover and ecological connectivity indices*

Influences	Number of sites each site dominates				Number of sites dominating each site			
	LCI, ECI, UDA	ECI, UDA	LCI, UDA	LCI, ECI	LCI, ECI, UDA	ECI, UDA	LCI, UDA	LCI, ECI
Site								
1	0	1	0	0	0	0	0	2
2	0	0	4	0	1	4	0	1
3	0	0	0	0	1	1	1	17
4	0	0	0	1	5	7	6	9
5	0	0	0	0	3	5	3	5
6	1	1	1	4	2	2	2	4
7	0	1	0	0	1	2	4	1
8	1	2	1	3	1	1	1	4
9	0	0	0	2	0	0	0	0
10	0	0	0	2	0	0	0	0
11	0	0	0	2	1	1	1	1
12	1	1	1	2	2	3	3	3
13	1	1	1	3	0	1	0	0
14	0	0	0	0	2	7	2	3
15	2	2	2	2	0	0	0	0
16	1	1	3	1	0	0	0	0
17	2	3	2	2	0	0	0	1
18	5	6	5	9	0	0	0	0
19	2	1	1	6	0	1	0	0
20	10	14	12	12	0	0	0	0
21	1	1	1	8	1	1	1	1
22	0	0	0	8	0	1	0	0
23	0	0	0	1	1	1	1	5
24	0	2	0	0	0	0	0	2
25	0	0	0	1	9	9	10	11
26	1	2	1	2	1	1	1	6
27	1	3	1	1	0	0	0	0
28	3	6	3	4	0	0	1	0
29	0	0	0	0	1	3	2	1
30	1	4	1	2	1	1	1	1
Mean	**1.1**	**1.73**	**1.33**	**2.6**	**1.1**	**1.73**	**1.33**	**2.6**

Table 5.5   Dominance results for fish abundance and diversity using land cover and ecological connectivity indices

Influences	Number of sites each site dominates				Number of sites dominating each site			
	LCI, ECI, UDA	ECI, UDA	LCI, UDA	LCI, ECI	LCI, ECI, UDA	ECI, UDA	LCI, UDA	LCI, ECI
Site								
1	0	0	0	0	6	6	6	10
2	0	0	3	0	4	7	1	4
3	0	0	0	0	2	2	2	23
4	0	0	0	2	8	10	9	13
5	0	0	0	0	1	1	1	3
6	1	1	1	5	8	8	8	13
7	1	1	1	4	3	3	5	3
8	4	5	4	7	0	0	0	2
9	0	0	1	2	0	0	0	0
10	0	0	0	2	1	1	2	2
11	0	0	0	5	0	0	0	0
12	5	6	5	9	3	3	3	3
13	1	1	1	8	4	7	4	4
14	3	2	2	11	1	4	1	2
15	18	20	18	18	0	0	0	0
16	0	0	1	1	0	2	0	0
17	11	15	12	11	0	0	0	1
18	3	3	3	7	6	6	6	10
19	3	2	2	12	0	4	0	0
20	9	13	11	12	0	0	0	0
21	3	4	3	12	0	0	0	0
22	0	0	0	10	0	1	0	0
23	0	0	0	1	8	8	9	19
24	0	1	0	0	3	3	3	19
25	0	0	0	3	13	13	13	15
26	2	3	2	4	4	4	4	14
27	11	16	11	12	1	1	1	1
28	0	0	0	1	2	2	5	3
29	7	6	6	12	1	2	1	1
30	1	3	1	2	4	4	4	8
Mean	**2.77**	**3.4**	**2.93**	**5.77**	**2.77**	**3.4**	**2.93**	**5.77**

When ecological connectivity is deleted from the list of influences, the dominance of two sites improves and that of one site declines. When land cover is deleted from the list of influences, the dominance of four sites improves and that of two sites declines. In each case sites whose dominance improves have relatively large values of that influence, and sites whose dominance declines have relatively small values of that influence. By this criterion, when stream health is measured with macroinvertebrate abundance and diversity, dominance is associated with ecological connectivity and land cover, but not as strongly as it is with upstream drainage area. This finding is partly consistent with the SFA evaluations, which finds LCI to be significant for macroinvertebrate abundance and diversity but not fish abundance and diversity, and ECI to be insignificant for both.

Table 5.5 presents analogous EDA results for fish abundance and diversity. A dozen sites stand out for their consistently strong or weak performance across all combinations of influences. Sites 12, 15, 17, 20, 27 and 29 dominate several other sites (and are dominated by few or no other sites). Conversely, sites 1, 4, 6, 18, 23 and 25 are dominated by several other sites (and dominate few or no others). These 12 sites also warrant further investigation, similar to that suggested in the SFA post-analysis: maps and imagery or local council knowledge could be used to identify potential additional influencing factors such as floodplain and terrestrial connectivity, invasive species, etc. (Paul and Meyer et al., 2001; Rolls et al., 2012).

In addition to the high- and low-performing sites for fish diversity and abundance noted above, sites 14, 19, 21 and 22 are mediocre performers unless UDA is deleted from the list of influences. Sites 3, 24 and 26 are very strong performers unless UDA is deleted from the list of influences. Once again, an explanation for these changes in performance is to be found in their ranking according to upstream drainage area: the former group have relatively large upstream drainage areas, ranking #11, #10, #7 and #4, while the latter group have relatively small upstream drainage areas, ranking #28, #25 and #22. When stream health is measured with fish abundance and diversity, dominance is closely associated with upstream drainage area, a finding consistent with the SFA evaluations and consistent with the dominance findings for macroinvertebrate abundance and diversity.

We have conducted the same experiment with fish abundance and diversity, deleting ecological connectivity and land-cover indices one at a time to explore the impacts on site rankings. Findings are similar to those for macroinvertebrate abundance and diversity. When ecological connectivity is deleted from the list of influences, the dominance of one site improves and that of one site declines. When land cover is deleted from the list of influences, the dominance of one site improves and that of four sites declines. In each case sites whose dominance improves have relatively large values of that influence, and sites whose dominance declines have relatively small values of that influence. By this criterion, when stream health is measured with fish abundance and diversity, dominance is associated with ecological connectivity and land cover, but not as strongly as it is with upstream drainage area. This finding also is partly consistent with the SFA evaluations.

Combining the results of Tables 5.4 and 5.5 generates two insights. First, site 20 is a dominant site for both stream health indicators, and sites 4 and 25 are frequently dominated for both stream health indicators. Site 20 ranks highly for both stream health indicators (8,8) and for all three influences (6,9,7); and sites 4 and 25 rank poorly for SIGNAL2 (23,22) and O/E_{50} (27,19), and for ECI (18,22), LCI (17,22) and UDA (18,23). Thus the superior or inferior ecological performance of these three sites is not associated with any single metric.

The second insight concerns specification of influences in the dominance analysis. For both stream health indicators, deletion of ECI or LCI makes little difference in dominance analysis; when either one is deleted, the performance of very few sites changes. However, when UDA is deleted, the performance of sites 19, 21 and 22 improves and the performance of site 26 declines, for both stream health indicators. This reinforces the impression that the extent of upstream drainage area is an important driver of stream health, whether measured by SIGNAL2 or by O/E_{50}.

Larger upstream catchment area is likely to be associated with the persistence of deeper pools of water during dry periods, providing refugia, as well as greater extent of upstream habitat during wet and dry periods, and higher flow rates (Rolls et al., 2012). Smaller upstream catchment sizes are consequently associated with the opposite aspects: less persistence of refugial pools; lesser extents of upstream stream habitat; and lower flow volumes – and potentially lower dissolved oxygen levels at sites with very low flows (e.g. Millington, 2016). However small upstream catchment size also may be associated with less upstream urban development (if upstream areas are hilly and difficult to build on), and may therefore include more pristine sites. In the ephemeral streams of SEQ, UDA is very important and likely interacts with the land-cover factors (e.g. lower UDA may be associated with a greater likelihood of extirpation or semi-extirpation events, compounded by urbanisation factors also associated with extirpation events, or with a lack of opportunity to recolonise after extirpation events); and so in Millington (2016) it was included as an explanatory metric in a separate category to the land-cover metrics in an attempt to control for it.

5.5 CONCLUSIONS

An efficiency-based analysis that assesses the relative ability of sites to cope with stream health stressors, not simply the health of streams at those sites independently of the stressors they face, can help guide managers in the allocation of scarce resources in their efforts to improve stream health. Such an approach can also offer insights to researchers on additional stream health stressors to investigate, by prompting them to consider what factors may be causing specific sites to dominate the performance of other sites based on existing data.

Ecological dominance analysis was our primary source of insights into the influence of ecological connectivity, land cover and upstream sub-catchment drainage area on two indicators of stream health. It revealed a very strong relationship between UDA and the two stream health indicators, particularly O/E_{50}, and a somewhat less strong relationship between ECI and LCI and the two stream health indicators. EDA also identified certain sites whose health depended critically on the inclusion or exclusion of each of the three influences separately. This information may help inform the policy debate concerning how to protect and improve the health of SEQ urban streams.

However nothing can be done about UDA (it is truly exogenous and immune to policy prescriptions), but management has played a role in the location and spatial configuration of the other four influences and can therefore make decisions that mitigate their impacts on stream health.

Based on our findings, future investigations might consider the role of EDA in identifying those sites that might be most responsive to policies aimed at improving land cover and ecological connectivity indicators. EDA, with its lack of formal structure, seems more useful than SFA (or DEA, for that matter), which is burdened by structure imposed by economic theory and statistical practice that hampers its usefulness in small samples.

There are two practical lessons to be learned from our findings. SFA requires a single dependent variable and, as we have demonstrated, it may be difficult to create a single dependent variable from a set of indicators by various means, including aggregation in non-market contexts. In addition, the benchmarking literature encourages managers to benchmark against the best, which in a frontier context means benchmarking against efficient peers. In our small sample, however, frontier analysis generated no efficient peers against which to benchmark. In situations such as this, benchmarking against dominating peers provides an alternative methodology for benchmarking against the best that is appealing in its simplicity and transparency.

NOTES

* We thank Brisbane City Council for their support in providing stream health data and GIS data sets for land cover and stormwater piping.
1. Tulkens (2006) introduced the acronym EDA, which he called efficiency dominance analysis. We have adapted the acronym to our setting and renamed it ecological dominance analysis.
2. Personal communication, Erin Peterson, CSIRO (2010).
3. Lovell (1995) and Lovell and Pastor (1999) were early proponents of the use of DEA to aggregate variables, and Färe et al. (2004) used DEA to create an environmental performance index as the ratio of an output quantity index to an emissions quantity index.
4. The Russian mathematician L. V. Kantorovich (1912–86) – one of the developers of linear programming and the 1975 recipient of the Nobel Prize in Economic Sciences (jointly with T. C. Koopmans) – called the multipliers 'resolving multipliers' and later, for political reasons, 'objectively determined valuations'; see Kantorovich (1965). According to Gardner (1990), Kantorovich obtained resolving multipliers for natural resources, including water, which Soviet planners had previously taken to be free goods.
5. Subsequent DEA and EDA evaluations based on GHI are virtually identical to those based on SIGNAL2, as one would expect in light of the strong correlation between the two series.
6. The distribution of O/E50 has mean 0.087 and standard deviation 0.049.

REFERENCES

Azad, M. A. S. and T. Ancev (2010), 'Using ecological indices to measure economic and environmental performance of irrigated agriculture', *Ecological Economics* **69**, 1731–1739.
Bellenger, M. J. and A. T. Herlihy (2010), 'Performance-based environmental index weights: are all metrics created equal?', *Ecological Economics* **69**, 1043–1050.
Chessman, B. (2003), 'SIGNAL 2: a scoring system for macro-invertebrates ('water bugs') in Australian rivers', Monitoring River Heath Initiative technical report no. 31, Department of Environment and Heritage, Commonwealth of Australia, Canberra. www.environment.gov.au/system/files/resources/a9ad51d4-a8a2-4e21-994d-c6381f7445ee/files/signal.pdf.
Färe, R., S. Grosskopf and F. Hernández-Sancho (2004), 'Environmental performance: an index number approach', *Resource and Energy Economics* **26**, 343–352.
Gardner, R. (1990), 'L. V. Kantorovich: the price implications of optimal planning', *Journal of Economic Literature* **28**, 638–648.
Johnson, J. B. and K. S. Omland (2004), 'Model selection in ecology and evolution', *Trends in Ecology and Evolution* **19**, 101–108.
Kantorovich, L. V. (1965), *Economic Calculation of the Best Use of Resources.* New York: Macmillan (originally 1959, *Ekonomicheskii Raschot Nailushego Ispolzovaniya Resursov.* Moscow: AN SSSR).
Kumbhakar, S. C., and C. A. K. Lovell (2000), *Stochastic Frontier Analysis.* Cambridge: Cambridge University Press.
Kennard, M. J., B. J. Pusey, A. H. Arthington, B. D. Harch and S. J. Mackay (2006), 'Development and application of a predictive model of freshwater fish assemblage composition to evaluate river health in eastern Australia', *Hydrobiologia* **572**, 33–57.

Lovell, C. A. K. (1995), 'Measuring the macroeconomic performance of the Taiwanese economy', *International Journal of Production Economics* **39**, 165–178.

Lovell, C. A. K., and J. T. Pastor (1999), 'Radial DEA models without inputs or without outputs', *European Journal of Operational Research* **118**, 46–51.

Marsh, N., C. Rutherford and S. Bunn (2005), 'The role of riparian vegetation in controlling stream temperature in a southeast Queensland stream' Technical report 05/3, Cooperative Research Centre for Catchment Hydrology. http://ewater.org.au/archive/crcch/archive/pubs/pdfs/technical200503.pdf.

Meyer, J. L., M. J. Paul, and W. K. Taulbee (2005), 'Stream ecosystem function in urbanising landscapes', *Journal of the North American Benthological Society* **24**, 602–612.

Millington, H. K., (2016), *Spatial Analysis of the Impacts of Urbanisation on the Health of Ephemeral and Perennial Streams in South East Queensland.* Nathan, Queensland: Griffith University.

Millington, H. K., J. E. Lovell and C. A. K. Lovell (2015), 'A framework for guiding the management of urban stream health', *Ecological Economics* **109**, 222–233.

Paul, M. J., and J. L. Meyer (2001), 'Streams in the urban landscape', *Annual Review of Ecology and Systematics* **32**, 333–365.

Pluhowski, E. J., (1970), 'Urbanization and its effect on the temperature of the streams on Long Island, New York', Geological Survey professional paper 627-D, US Department of the Interior. http://pubs.usgs.gov/pp/0627d/report.pdf.

Rolls, R. J., C. Leigh, and F. Sheldon (2012), 'Mechanistic effects of low-flow hydrology on riverine ecosystems: ecological principles and consequences of alteration', *Freshwater Science* **31**, 1163–1186.

Sheldon, F., D. Pagendam, M. Newham, B. McIntosh, M. Hartcher, G. Hodgson, C. Leigh, and W. Neilan (2012), 'Critical thresholds of ecological function and recovery associated with flow events in urban streams', Urban Water Security Research Alliance, Brisbane, Queensland. https://experts.griffith.edu.au/publication/n8d23507b0df8d4e817ad6835d693fa2f.

Taylor, P., L. Fahrig, K. Henein, and G. Merriam (1993), 'Connectivity is a vital element of landscape structure', *Oikos* **68**, 571–572.

Tulkens, H. (2006), 'Efficiency dominance analysis (EDA): basic methodology', in P. Chander, J. Drèze, C. K. Lovell and J. Mintz (eds), *Public Goods, Environmental Externalities and Fiscal Competition: Selected Papers on Competition, Efficiency and Cooperation in Public Economics by Henry Tulkens.* New York: Springer, Chapter 18.

Walsh, C. J., A. H. Roy, J. W. Feminella, P. D. Cottingham, P. M. Groffman and R. P. I. Morgan (2005), 'The urban stream syndrome: current knowledge and the search for a cure', *Journal of North American Benthological Society* **24**, 706–723.

Walters, D. M., D. S. Leigh and A. B. Bearden (2003), 'Urbanization, sedimentation, and the homogenization of fish assemblages in the Etowah river basin, USA', *Hydrobiologia* **494**, 5–10.

Wenger, S. J., A. H. Roy, C. R. Jackson, E. S. Bernhardt, T. L. Carter, S. Filoso, C. A. Gibson, W. C. Hession, S. S. Kaushal, E. Martí, J. L. Meyer, M. A. Palmer, M. J. Paul, A. H. Purcell, A. Ramírez, A. D. Rosemond, K. A. Schofield, E. B. Sudduth and C. J. Walsh (2009), 'Twenty-six key research questions in urban stream ecology: an assessment of the state of the science', *Journal of the North American Benthological Society* **28**, 1080–1098.

6. Accounting for nutrient pollution in measuring agricultural total factor productivity: a study of OECD economies

Viet-Ngu Hoang and Clevo Wilson*

6.1 INTRODUCTION

This chapter is based on the materials balance principle, which is used to derive environmental efficiency measures for agricultural production where nitrogen (N) and phosphorus (P) effluents and greenhouse gas (GHG) emissions are notable environmental stresses. These environmental efficiency measures are used to construct environmental Malmquist total factor productivity (TFP) indices in the same manner as the traditional Malmquist TFP indices are constructed (Hoang and Coelli, 2011). To demonstrate how an input use management strategy for environmentally sustainable agricultural production can be undertaken, we use panel data from 32 Organisation for Economic Co-operation and Development (OECD) economies covering 17 years from 1992 to 2008. This exercise can potentially be extended to include agricultural production systems around the world. It is important to account for these agricultural effluents and emissions, not only because they have a damaging impact on the environment but also because they impact on agricultural production itself. Moreover, some of them are known to be major anthropogenic pollutants contributing to climate change. Reducing input use, while maintaining current production levels, will also provide cost savings to farmers.

Since the theoretical and empirical literature on agricultural productivity is large, we limit the review to focus only on the most commonly used approaches. In particular, this chapter will focus attention on traditional and environmental Malmquist TFP indices. In doing so, it describes how the measure of input-orientated technical efficiency is used to construct the traditional Malmquist TFP indices. Environmental efficiency is then explained by incorporating the principle of material balance in this efficiency and productivity analysis framework. The environmental Malmquist TFP indices are shown to be built in the same manner as the traditional Malmquist TFP indices. While the literature indicates that this approach to measuring environmental TFP is yet to be used widely (Hoang and Coelli, 2011), it is shown to be useful in the context of agricultural production where the balances of N and P and the emissions of N and C composites are notable environmental stresses in the agricultural sector.

The selection of OECD member countries and the time periods studied are mainly due to data availability, although such an application could potentially be undertaken on a global scale. Furthermore, several other agricultural pollutants could be included (where adequate and reliable data are available) to make the analysis more robust. Data for this study are sourced from various datasets, including those of the United Nations Food and Agriculture Organization (FAO), the OECD and the International Fertilizer Association (IFA).

Data envelopment analysis (DEA) is used to calculate efficiency and TFP measures making two important assumptions: (1) production technology exhibits constant returns to scale; and (2) polluting effects of differing materials N, P and C are equal across economies and over the years. It is recognized that these two assumptions could be problematic due to the variability of agricultural production across countries and years. However, the first assumption is made because the Malmquist TFP index approach is biased if the production technology exhibits non-constant returns to scale (Grifell-Tatjé and Lovell, 1995). The second assumption is made because of the lack of better information about the relative polluting effects of each 'material' (namely, N, P and C) across countries and over time.

The findings reported in this chapter are useful for policy decision-making in the agricultural sector, and in devising policies to minimize agricultural-based effluents and emissions. The main findings of this study are:

● Existing agricultural production can use fewer inputs without a negative impact on current output levels. The results show that, on average, OECD agriculture should be able to produce current output with 23 per cent fewer inputs (i.e. labour, agricultural land, machinery, inorganic fertilizer, feed and seed, livestock and energy). In terms of N, P and C balances, OECD economies could reduce the total material balance further – by 52.6 per cent – if they were to adjust the combination of materials-containing inputs (livestock, fertilizers, feed and seed and energy). The low overall environmental efficiency scores imply that OECD economies should be able to produce the same output levels with inputs containing 63.5 per cent less materials of N, P and C.

- Positive growth in agricultural production is a product of using either or both traditional and environmental total factor productivity measures. In the period surveyed, OECD economies achieved an annual traditional TFP growth rate of 1.3 per cent. The environmental TFP growth, measured by the material efficiency in the Malmquist TFP index framework, was estimated to be only 0.95 per cent, which is smaller than the traditional TFP growth. This was found to be due to the decrease in the material-orientated allocative efficiency level. This observation implies that changes in input combinations could further contribute to environmental productivity growth in OECD agriculture.

The chapter also identifies the main drivers of environmental TFP growth, which can be attributed to three components: technical change (i.e. shifts in the production frontier); technical efficiency change (changes in the level of technical efficiency from one year to another relative to the frontier); and changes in the levels of material-based allocative efficiency (environmentally favourable changes in combination of materials-containing inputs). The main driving force, however, is the change in technical efficiency. The empirical results also reveal that technical efficiency and technical changes are subject to a degree of divergence. For example, in some years, while there was technical progress, it was accompanied by decreases in relative efficiency levels. One possible explanation for this pattern is a lagged effect of technological transfer. Therefore, technological transfer among OECD economies could have played a more important role in enhancing the environmental performance of OECD agriculture.

The results also suggest variations in the levels of material efficiency and productivity change across the 32 OECD economies in the period surveyed. This triggers an important empirical research question as to what are the main causes of these variations. While such a question goes beyond the scope of this chapter, further empirical investigations could provide useful inputs to policy development aimed at improving productive efficiency. It is evident that, in the years studied, many OECD economies implemented a number of important policies to tackle environmental effects of agricultural production (see, for example, Hoang and Coelli, 2011, for some discussions of these policies). Hence, there is an opportunity to carry out an empirical examination of the varying effects of these policies on environmental efficiency and productivity.

The chapter has six sections. Section 6.2 provides a methodological review of various approaches to measure environmental efficiency and productivity using the framework of input distance functions and production frontier. Section 6.3 provides descriptions of data and estimation techniques. Sections 6.4 and 6.5 provide the empirical results and discussions. Section 6.6 concludes.

6.2   METHODOLOGICAL REVIEW

This section provides a brief overview of the methodological approaches used in the empirical literature, with particular focus on the use of input distance functions in the construction of efficiency and productivity measures. We begin the discussion by defining the production technology used in measuring agricultural productivity, which involves several inputs and outputs.

6.2.1   Production Technology

A convenient way to describe a multiple input and output production technology is to use the technology set (T) in situations where decision-making units (DMUs) produce M outputs, $q \in \Re_+^M$ using K inputs, $x \in \Re_+^K$ where:

$$T = \{(q, x): x \text{ can produce } q\} \tag{6.1}$$

Technology set T consists of all input and output vectors (x, q) such that the input vector x can produce the output vector q. The production technology is assumed to satisfy standard axioms including convexity, strong disposability, closeness and boundedness (Färe and Grosskopf, 2000). The production technology can equivalently be described using output and input sets. The output set, $P(x)$, represents the set of all output vectors, q, that can be produced using the input vector, x. The feasible production set, P, is defined as:

$$P(x) = \{q: (x, q) \in T\} = \{q: x \text{ can produce } q\} \tag{6.2}$$

The input set, $L(q)$, consists of all input vectors x that can produce a given output vector q. The input set $L(q)$ is normally defined as:

$$L(q) = \{x: (x, q) \in T\} = \{x: x \text{ can produce } q\} \tag{6.3}$$

The properties of production technology, output and input sets are detailed in Färe and Primont (1995) and Coelli et al. (2005).

Since the output and input sets provide alternative descriptions of the same underlying production technology, these two sets are interrelated. If q belongs to the output set $P(x)$, then x belongs to the input set $L(q)$. The technology set, output set and input set are all equivalent representations as they contain the same information.

6.2.2   Input Distance Functions and Technical Efficiency

The input distance function can be defined using the input set, $L(\mathbf{q})$, or the production technology set, T. Thus:

$$D_1(\mathbf{x}, \mathbf{q}) = \max\{\rho: \rho > 0, (\mathbf{x}/\rho) \in L(\mathbf{q})\} = \max\{\rho: \rho > 0, (\mathbf{x}/\rho, \mathbf{q}) \in T\} \quad (6.4)$$

The input distance functions satisfy several important properties:

> non-increasing in $\mathbf{q}$ and non-decreasing in $\mathbf{x}$;
> linear homogeneous in $\mathbf{x}$;
> quasi-concave in $\mathbf{q}$ and concave in $\mathbf{x}$;
> if $\mathbf{x}$ belongs to $L(\mathbf{q})$ then $D_1(\mathbf{x}, \mathbf{q}) \geq 1$; and
> $D_1(\mathbf{x}, \mathbf{q}) = 1$ if $\mathbf{x}$ belongs to the frontier (more details are in Färe and Primont, 1995).

Input distance functions can be used to calculate input-orientated technical efficiency (ITE). ITE measures the proportional reduction of input quantities while producing a given level of outputs:

$$ITE = \frac{1}{D_1(\mathbf{x}, \mathbf{q})} = \frac{\mathbf{x}_{ITE}}{\mathbf{x}} = \frac{OB}{OA} \quad (6.5)$$

where $D_1(\mathbf{x}, \mathbf{q})$ is defined in Equation 6.4 and $\mathbf{x}_{ITE}$ is the technically efficient input vector.

Figure 6.1 presents the ITE concept in the case of two inputs (x_1 and x_2) and one output (q). The input set $L(\mathbf{q})$ is bounded below by the isoquant curve. Point A stays inside the input set, and its input distance is equal to the ratio OA/OB. The distance equals the factor by which the consumption of all inputs could be reduced proportionally while still holding the output level constant. Any points staying on the isoquant, such as points B and C, suggest that their distance values are unity and that they are technically efficient. Any points above the isoquant exhibit inefficiency, and their distance values are greater than unity. Graphically, Farrell's (1957) ITE of point A is the ratio of OB/OA, taking a value between 0 and 1. Higher value of ITE represents higher level of technical efficiency.

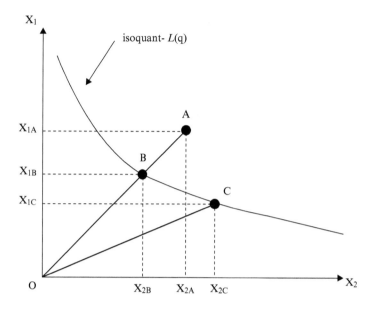

Figure 6.1   Input distance function and input requirement set

6.2.3   Environmental Efficiency Measures

Lauwers (2009) provides a review of three general groups of models used to measure environmental efficiency: environmentally adjusted production efficiency (EAPE), frontier eco-efficiency (FEE); and materials balance (MB)-based models. The environmentally adjusted production efficiency models use the production frontier to analyse the relationship between inputs and outputs. In these models, pollution is viewed as either environmentally detrimental inputs or undesirable outputs. By adding pollution as an extra input or output in conventional production models, technical efficiency measures can be estimated. Farms that have fewer pollution inputs are recorded with higher efficiency levels, *ceteris paribus*. In other words, these methods credit farms for the reduction of pollution. Also, technical efficiency can be interpreted as environmental efficiency.

The frontier eco-efficiency models use the frontier framework to derive eco-efficiency measures (Callens and Tyteca, 1999; Tyteca, 1999) which relate the economic value of outputs to the environmental pressures involved in production processes (Picazo-Tadeo et al., 2012). Empirical applications of these models can be seen as the frontier operationalization of the eco-efficiency concept in the analysis of sustainability (Lauwers, 2009).

There is a methodological distinction between the environmentally adjusted production efficiency and the frontier eco-efficiency models. The former models are based on the conventional production relationship between inputs and outputs, while the latter models are grounded on a hypothesized relationship between economic values of outputs and environmental pressures. They are often used in different research contexts. The primary use of the environmentally adjusted production efficiency models is to adjust efficiency measures to account for environmental pollution in the paradigm of costly environmental regulation. In this paradigm, efficiency analysis methods implicitly assume that efficiency improvements imply cost reduction (Lauwers, 2009). The frontier eco-efficiency models are used mainly to provide relative assessments among DMUs in terms of environmental performance where there are many types of environmental pressures caused by production and consumption activities.

The third approach to measuring environmental efficiency involves the use of the materials balance principle (MBP). The MBP stipulates that materials in inputs are transformed into desirable outputs and emissions that have potential to cause pollution (Ayres, 1995). The MBP holds true in many agricultural production systems. In a typical production system, farmers use various inputs to produce agricultural outputs. Some inputs – such as feed, seed, planting material, fertilizers, purchased animals, manure, soil, energy and water – contain various materials such as nitrogen (N), phosphorous (P) or carbon (C) to produce outputs. The principle of materials balance implies that the total amount of materials in the inputs must equate the total amount of materials in the outputs. In other words, after deducting the amount of materials in desirable outputs (i.e. agricultural produce), there remains the balance of materials, which equals the total amount of materials in inputs minus the amount of materials in the desirable outputs. In an open production system, the balance of materials goes into the land, air or water systems. Given that the balance has potential to cause pollution, the polluting potential of agricultural production can be represented by the balance of materials.

The MB-based models are distinct from the EAPE and FEE methods because the materials balance does not appear as either an input or an output as is the case for EAPE models. Nor does it appear as an indicator of environmental pressures as is the case for FEE models. The .MB-based models are grounded on the same production relationship between inputs and outputs; hence they are useful in analysing economic–environmental trade-offs faced by DMUs (Lauwers, 2009). In addition, the MB-based models are more suitable in situations where the MBP regulates the transformation of materials in production processes (Hoang and Coelli, 2011; Hoang and Alauddin, 2012; Hoang and Nguyen, 2013).

In the context of DMUs producing a vector of M outputs from a vector of K inputs, the amount of emission is represented by the balance of materials:

$$u = \mathbf{ax} - \mathbf{bq} \qquad (6.6)$$

where $\mathbf{a}$ and $\mathbf{b}$ are the vectors representing the materials contents of inputs and outputs. It is possible that some inputs could have zero materials (e.g. labour). When outputs are fixed, the materials balance is minimised when the total amount of materials in inputs (NC $= \mathbf{a}'\mathbf{x}$) is minimised. Instead of minimising inputs ($\mathbf{x}$), the total amount of materials contained in $\mathbf{x}$ will be minimised. This approach solves the following optimisation problem:

$$MC(\mathbf{q}, \mathbf{a}) = \min_{\mathbf{x}}\{\mathbf{a}'\mathbf{x}|\langle\mathbf{x},\mathbf{q}\rangle \in T\} \qquad (6.7)$$

MC_{NE} is a solution to (6.7) and the input vector is $\mathbf{x}_{ME}$ when $MC_{ME} = \mathbf{a}'\mathbf{x}_{ME}$. Materials balanced-based EE – hereafter called materials-based efficiency (ME) – for each DMU is the ratio of the minimum materials amount in optimised inputs to the material amount in the observed inputs:

$$ME = \frac{MC_{ME}}{MC} = \frac{\mathbf{a}'\mathbf{x}_{ME}}{\mathbf{a}'\mathbf{x}} \qquad (6.8)$$

From (6.5), input-orientated technical efficiency (ITE) is defined as:

$$ITE = \frac{\mathbf{x}_{ITE}}{\mathbf{x}} = \frac{\mathbf{a}'\mathbf{x}_{ITE}}{\mathbf{a}'\mathbf{x}} = \frac{MC_{ITE}}{MC} \qquad (6.9)$$

Hence:

$$ME = \frac{MC_{ME}}{MC} = \frac{\mathbf{a}'\mathbf{x}_{ME}}{\mathbf{a}'\mathbf{x}} = \frac{\mathbf{a}'\mathbf{x}_{ITE}}{\mathbf{a}'\mathbf{x}} \times \frac{\mathbf{a}'\mathbf{x}_{ME}}{\mathbf{a}'\mathbf{x}_{ITE}} = \frac{MC_{ITE}}{MC} \times \frac{MC_{ME}}{MC_{ITE}} = ITE \times MAE \qquad (6.10)$$

where

$$MAE = \frac{\mathbf{a}'\mathbf{x}_{ME}}{\mathbf{a}'\mathbf{x}_{ITE}} \qquad (6.11)$$

ITE can be estimated by a standard input-orientated framework, whereas ME can be estimated following a procedure similar to estimating cost efficiency in which the vector of material contents of inputs is used instead of prices. MAE can be estimated as a ratio of ME to ITE. The decomposition in (6.10) reveals two potential sources of improvements in environmental performance. ITE refers to the proportional decrease in inputs, while MAE relates to input combinations that have lower nutrient amounts. The values of these three efficiency measures are bounded between zero and one. The value of unity indicates full efficiency, whereas less than unity implies inefficiency.

6.2.4   Linkage between Environmental and Cost Efficiency

Cost efficiency is determined by the relationships between the unit price of each input and the unit price of each output. Environmental efficiency, on the other hand, is determined by the relationships between the unit amounts of materials contained in each input and the unit amounts of materials in each output. That is, cost efficiency is based on the relationship between prices, while environmental efficiency is based on the relationship between material amounts. Figure 6.2 is useful to illustrate these relationships for a simple case of two inputs (x_1 and x_2) and one output (q). There is an iso-cost line, an iso-material line and an isoquant curve in Figure 6.2. Point C is at the tangency of the iso-cost line with the isoquant, while the iso-material line is tangential to the isoquant at point N. Point C generates the lowest cost of production, while point N refers to the lowest consumption of materials.

Regarding the decomposition in Equation (6.10), Figure 6.2 depicts the ratio of distances from the origin (O) to points B and A as ITE (i.e. ITE = OB/OA). The movement from point B to point N relates to improve-

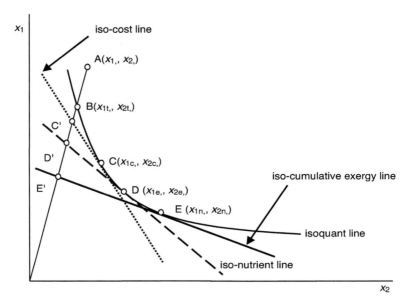

Figure 6.2   Minimization of cost and nutrient inputs

ment in MAE, which is the ratio of distances from the origin to points N and N′ (i.e. MAE = ON′/OB). The movement from point B to point C relates to improvement in cost allocative efficiency (CAE), which is the ratio of distances from the origin to points C and C′ (i.e. CAE = OC′/OB).

Given that the iso-material line is not identical to the iso-cost line, any observed data point such as point A exhibits three sources of inefficiency: (i) TE = OB/OA; (ii) cost allocative efficiency, CAE = OC/OB, which is derived from the ratio of cost efficiency to TE; and (iii) MAE = ON/OB, which is derived from the ratio of nutrient efficiency to TE. An improvement in cost efficiency could be associated with either an increase in TE or an increase in CAE, or both. Similarly, an improvement in NE could be caused by increases in TE and/or MAE. Improvements in TE, therefore, increase both cost and environmental efficiency. However, increases in CAE could result in a rise or fall in MB-based environmental efficiency, depending upon whether this movement is towards or away from the environmentally efficient operation (point N). Similarly, increases in MAE could result in higher or lower cost, depending upon the direction of movements towards or away from the cost efficient position (point C).

6.2.5 Traditional Productivity Measures

Caves et al. (1982) proposed the input distance functions approach to construct an input Malmquist total factor productivity (TFP) index by measuring the radial distances of an input vector in periods 's' and 't' relative to two reference technologies. First, using the reference technology in period 's', the input Malmquist TFP index is defined as:

$$M_{TFP}^{s} = \frac{ITE^{s,t}}{ITE^{s,s}} \tag{6.12}$$

where the first and second superscripts refer to the reference technology and time period respectively. For example, $ITE^{s,t}$ refers to the input-orientated technical efficiency score in (6.5) calculated using the observed data for a firm operating in period 't' relative to the output vectors of all firms operating in period 's'. Malmquist TFP in (6.12) measures a change in ITE scores between periods 's' and 't' using the same reference technology in period 's'.

Using the reference technology in period 't', the Malmquist TFP index, which refers to a change in ITE between periods 's' and 't' using the period 't' reference, is defined as:

$$M_{TFP}^{t} = \frac{ITE^{t,t}}{ITE^{t,s}} \tag{6.13}$$

The input Malmquist TFP change (TFPC) is the geometric mean of (6.12) and (6.13):

$$\text{TFPC} = [M^s_{TFP} \times M^t_{TFP}]^{1/2} = \left[\frac{ITE^{s,t}}{ITE^{s,s}} \times \frac{ITE^{t,t}}{ITE^{t,s}} \right]^{1/2} \tag{6.14}$$

All TE components in (6.14) are computable since reference technologies are observable, and input and output vectors are well defined in periods 's' and 't'. TFPC also can be decomposed into technical efficiency change (TEC) and technical change (TC):

$$\text{TFPC} = \frac{ITE^{t,t}}{ITE^{s,s}} \left[\frac{ITE^{s,s}}{ITE^{t,s}} \times \frac{ITE^{s,t}}{ITE^{t,t}} \right]^{1/2} = \text{TEC} \times \text{TC} \tag{6.15}$$

All TFPC, TEC and TC components in (6.15) can take any real positive values. The industry or economy experiences technical progress (or regress), as the value of TC is greater (or smaller) than unity. TEC measures change in ITE levels between two periods. TEC can take a greater (or smaller) value than unity, corresponding to the status of being more (or less) efficient relative to reference technologies in two respective periods. The value of unity means that there is no change in the efficiency scores. TFPC being greater (or smaller) than unity means that there is an increase (or decrease) in productivity.

6.2.6 Environmental Total Factor Productivity

While EE focuses on efficiency levels across many DMUs, temporal changes in EE and shifts in production technology over time are also important. Several studies proposed the use of EE scores to construct environmental total factor productivity (TFP) indexes (Yaisawarng and Klein, 1994; Chung et al., 1997; Ball et al., 2000; Hailu and Veeman, 2001a, b). Yaisawarng and Klein included pollution and the amount of materials causing pollution to compute EE scores, which are then used to construct a Malmquist TFP index. Hailu and Veeman constructed the Malmquist TFP index using input distance functions. Chung et al. used directional distance functions to construct the Malmquist-Luenberger productivity index.

Hoang and Coelli (2011) used ME to construct a new environmental total factor productivity (ETFP) measure by simply replacing ITE in (6.15) with ME defined in (6.8). Using the data observed in period 's' as the reference technology, the ETFP index for periods 's' and 't' is defined as a change in the materials balance-orientated efficiency in period 't' over period 's':

$$M^s_{ETFP} = \frac{ME^{s,t}}{ME^{s,s}} \tag{6.16}$$

Similarly, using the period 't' reference technology, the input Malmquist-type environmental TFP index (hereafter called materials-based TFP – MTFP) is:

$$M_{ETFP}^t = \frac{ME^{t,t}}{ME^{t,s}} \tag{6.17}$$

The changes in ETFP are the geometric mean of the two indexes in (6.16) and (6.17):

$$MTFPC^{s,t} = [M_{ETFP}^s \times M_{ETFP}^t]^{1/2} \left[\frac{ME^{s,t}}{ME^{s,s}} \times \frac{ME^{t,t}}{ME^{t,s}} \right]^{1/2} \tag{6.18}$$

Since $\mathbf{q}$, $\mathbf{x}$ and $\mathbf{a}$ are well defined, all ME components in (6.18) are computable. Further decompositions of these ME into ITE and MAE are available according to Equation (6.10):

$$ME^{s,s} = \frac{a'x_{ME}^{s,s}}{a'x^{s,s}} = \frac{a'x_{ITE}^{s,s}}{a'x^{s,s}} \times \frac{a'x_{ME}^{s,s}}{a'x_{ITE}^{s,s}} = ITE^{s,s} \times MAE^{s,s} \tag{6.19}$$

$ME^{s,s}$ and $ITE^{s,s}$ can be estimated in an input-oriented framework given an input vector $\mathbf{x}^{s,s}$ in period 's' corresponding to output vectors of all firms in period 's'. Similarly, we can have:

$$ME^{t,t} = \frac{a'x_{ME}^{t,t}}{a'x^{t,t}} = \frac{a'x_{ITE}^{t,t}}{a'x^{t,t}} \times \frac{a'x_{ME}^{t,t}}{a'x_{ITE}^{t,t}} = ITE^{t,t} \times MAE^{t,t} \tag{6.20}$$

$$ME^{s,t} = \frac{a'x_{ME}^{s,t}}{a'x^{s,t}} = \frac{a'x_{ITE}^{s,t}}{a'x^{s,t}} \times \frac{a'x_{ME}^{s,t}}{a'x_{ITE}^{s,t}} = ITE^{s,t} \times MAE^{s,t} \tag{6.21}$$

$$ME^{t,s} = \frac{a'x_{ME}^{t,s}}{a'x^{t,s}} = \frac{a'x_{ITE}^{t,s}}{a'x^{t,s}} \times \frac{a'x_{ME}^{t,s}}{a'x_{ITE}^{t,s}} = ITE^{t,s} \times MAE^{t,s} \tag{6.22}$$

Combining (6.18) to (6.22) results in:

$$MTFPC = TFPC \times \left[\frac{MAE^{s,t}}{MAE^{s,s}} \times \frac{MAE^{t,t}}{MAE^{t,s}} \right] \tag{6.23}$$

Combining (6.15) and (6.23) gives:

$$MTFPC = TC \times TEC \times \left[\frac{MAE^{s,t}}{MAE^{s,s}} \times \frac{MAE^{t,t}}{MAE^{t,s}} \right]^{1/2} = TC \times TEC \times MAEC \tag{6.24}$$

Technical change (TC) refers to the shift of the production frontier, while technical efficiency change (TEC) refers to changes in ITE levels.

Materials-based allocative efficiency change (MAEC) measures changes in the levels of MAE; TC and TEC capture the effects of technical and efficiency changes, while MAEC accounts for changes in combination of inputs in terms of materials.

6.3   DATA DESCRIPTION AND ESTIMATION TECHNIQUES

6.3.1   Environmental Pressures, Effluents and Emissions

The agricultural production volumes in OECD economies have risen over the last few decades, but at a cost to the environment (OECD, 2008). The commonly used indicators for the environmental pressures caused by agriculture in OECD economies include N and P effluent balances; emission of greenhouse gases (GHG) such as C (mainly through the consumption of energy and emissions from livestock manure); the use of toxic pesticides; and various aspects of land use diversity (OECD, 2008).

Among these pressures, eutrophication resulting from N and P effluents and GHG emissions are notable environmental issues in OECD economies (OECD, 2008). Eutrophication refers to excessive nutrient-induced increases in the production of organic matter in lakes, rivers and coastal waters. It promotes excessive growth of aquatic vegetation causing oxygen depletion, which in turn disrupts the normal functioning of the ecosystem and degrades the quality of water used for other economic and social activities (Gold and Sims, 2005). N and P are the two main polluting effluent nutrients, and management of both nutrients is necessary to control eutrophication (Paerl, 2009). The consumption of various types of energy such as fuel oil and coal as well as fertilizers in the agricultural production process releases greenhouse gases into the atmosphere, mainly in composites of C and N. Hence, it is desirable to assess environmental performance in terms of three materials: N, P and C.

When there is more than one nutrient involved in the analysis, aggregation of the varying effects of N, P and C into a single term can be effected as long as the information about the relative polluting powers of each material can be identified appropriately. This is a challenging task, especially in those studies using aggregate data.

In terms of eutrophication, the impacts of N and P depend on the nature of the aquatic system. Systems such as lakes and rivers tend to be limited more by P than by N; and the over-enrichment of P results in a more damaging effect than the enrichment of N (Gold and Sims, 2005). In contrast,

N is more commonly the key limiting nutrient in marine waters. Thus, N has greater eutrophication potential in saltwater systems than P (Howarth and Marino, 2006). Determination of the N:P weights should be based on the amount of phytoplankton which the available N and P will give rise to through photosynthesis in the photic zone of aquatic ecosystems (Seppälä et al., 2004). This N:P ratio differs between species, changes with time, and depends on the dominating species in the photic zone and on the nutrient status of the ecosystem (Seppälä et al., 2004). Soil and water experimental surveys can provide reliable scientific background information for reliable N:P weights; unfortunately, such experimental data are not available at regional and national levels. Many studies propose several weights (Redfield et al., 1963; Seppälä et al., 2004; Ptacnik et al., 2010); however, these weights are applicable to specific aquatic systems, such as fresh or marine water. At a national level, a country normally has more than one water system, making the aggregation of N and P eutrophying effects more difficult.

Identifying weights of materials in terms of the polluting effects of greenhouse gas emission may pose even greater problems, and, therefore, needs further investigation. Literature on varying impacts of differing GHGs such as N_2O vs CO_2 and CH_4 is available, but there is little discussion on comparing eutrophication and climate change impacts (see Hoang and Coelli, 2011 for more references).

The nature of aggregate data also means caution is needed in interpretation of the results. Material efficiency and productivity scores should not be interpreted as a specific amount of damage because the effects of equal amounts of N, P and C release on surrounding environments are heterogeneous. In our empirical study, this means that the actual effect of the same amount of N, P, and C balances varies across countries. One can also use differing sets of weights to capture the relative damaging powers of various materials and allow these sets of weights to vary across countries and over time. However, the current study simply used one set of weights (i.e. weights of N, P, and C are equal). This assumption means that there is no difference in the polluting potential of the three different elements (N, P and C), and their polluting powers remain the same over time and are the same in different countries.

6.3.2 Data Description and Estimation Method

National agricultural sectors can be divided into two sub-sectors: cropping and livestock. The whole industry is viewed as a 'large mixed farm' in which interactions between the two sub-sectors occur as shown in Figure 6.3.

Annual national data from 32 OECD countries between 1992 and 2008

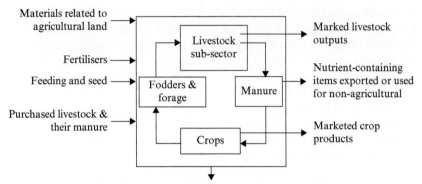

*Figure 6.3   Input and output flows for national crop and livestock
production system*

Table 6.1   Descriptive statistics of output and inputs

Variable	Arithmetic mean	Standard deviation	Min. value	Max. value
Output (price-weighted Fisher index)	1.271	1.939	0.006	11.641
Feed and seed	1.939	1.950	0.014	7.721
Price-weighted fertilizer ('000 tonnes)	1,621,997	3,537,051	18,911	22,000,000
Live cattle (livestock weighted for relative sizes,'000 heads)	15,300	26,900	210	153,000
Energy consumption ('000 tonnes oil-equivalent)	1,907	2,772	41	17,734
Labour ('000 active)	1,254	2,208	9	10,222
Land ('000 hectares)	39,600	104,000	490	469,000
Machinery (number)	923,837	1,512,819	9,993	7,613,311

were analysed. Belgium and Luxembourg were merged as a single country since data for each country were not available prior to 2000. Descriptive statistics of one single output index and seven inputs are given in Table 6.1. Data sources include the FAO, the OECD and the IFA.

Due to degrees of freedom constraints, all output commodities were aggregated into one term using a multilateral price-weighted Fisher quantity index. A multilateral price-weighted Fisher quantity index was also calculated for all *feed and seed* consumption as reported in FAO statistics.

Price and quantity data are from the FAO's statistics website. Missing quantities were filled as zeros, while missing prices were filled using the country product dummy method (Summers, 1973):

- *Labour* is the total economically active adult population (males and females) in agriculture.
- *Land* is the total area in permanent crops, annual crops and permanent pasture. No adjustment was made for differences in quality across agricultural land types.
- *Cattle* input is the aggregate number of animals held in farm inventories, weighted by their relative sizes: cattle (1 per head); camels (1.381 per head); water buffalo (1.25 per head); horses, asses and mules (1 per head); sheep and goats (0.13 per head); pigs (0.25 per head); and chickens, ducks and turkeys (12.50 per 1000 head) (Hayami and Ruttan, 1985).
- *Fertilizer* is the total amount of inorganic nutrients (N, P2O5 and K2O) weighted for relative prices: 1.00 for N, 1.36 for P2O5 and 0.85 for K2O (Fuglie and Rada, 2013).
- *Machinery* is the total number of various types of machinery in use, including tractors, balers, ploughs, harvesting machines, seeders, threshing machines and milking machines.
- *Energy* is direct on-farm energy consumption (1000 tonnes oil equivalent).

These seven inputs account for the major part of total agricultural input use, and they have been used in previous studies (Coelli and Rao, 2005; Hoang and Coelli, 2011; Fuglie and Rada, 2013). However, there are other inputs (e.g., buildings, water, chemical pesticides, veterinary pharmaceuticals, etc.) which are not included due to lack of complete data.

Labour, machinery and land are assumed to have zero material contents. The aggregate materials content for feed and seed input was the ratio of the weighted sum of nitrogen, phosphorous and carbon hydrate contents in feed and seed commodities to the Fisher quantity index input. The material content of fertilizers was calculated as the ratio of the sum of N, P and C (equal weights) content to the total price-weighted amount of fertilizer. The aggregate material content of size-weighted cattle equivalent was calculated as the total N, P and C emission of livestock manure.[1]

This chapter uses DEA to calculate efficiency scores. As a non-parametric method, DEA does not require assumptions about the decision-making units' behaviour, the functional form of production functions or efficiency distribution. In this study, the production technology is assumed to exhibit constant return to scale (CRS) given the Malmquist TFP is biased under variable return to scale technology (Grifell-Tatjé and Lovell, 1995; Coelli and Rao, 2005). The use of DEA in the present chapter has several limitations. First, data noise and random errors are not accounted for; hence, they might be embedded in efficiency scores. Second, DEA assumes that all countries have the same production technology at a given time period. This assumption is only reasonable if climate conditions (e.g., sunlight, average daily temperature, rainfall) and the quality of other inputs such as land (e.g., soil quality), labour and machinery are all taken into consideration. These limitations imply that measurement errors may exist, which would have caused errors in the reported results. Stochastic frontier analysis (SFA) may be used to address the issue of data noise, and it allows the incorporation of variables such as average sun exposure, rainfall or diurnal temperature range into the production function. By such incorporation the accuracy of estimation may be improved, but SFA may suffer from the problem of misspecification. Consequently there are possibilities for future research to improve this empirical application.[2]

6.4   EMPIRICAL RESULTS

6.4.1   Environmental Efficiency

Table 6.2 provides summary results for ITE, MAE and ME in the case where the polluting effects of N, P and C are equal. The mean ITE score of 0.7694 suggests that, on average, OECD agriculture should be able to produce its current output with 23 per cent fewer inputs (i.e. the seven inputs in Table 6.1). In terms of N, P and C balances, the mean MAE score of 0.4743 indicates that these economies could reduce the total material balance by 52.6 per cent if they were to adjust the combination of materials-containing inputs (cattle, fertilizers, feed and seed, energy).

Table 6.2   Mean values of efficiency measures for 32 OECD countries

Efficiency measures	Geometric mean	Arithmetic mean	Minimum	Maximum
Technical efficiency (ITE)	0.7694	0.8082	0.1370	1.00
Allocative efficiency (MAE)	0.4743	0.5343	0.1150	1.00
Material efficiency (ME) = ITE × MAE for geometric mean)	0.3649	0.4163	0.0940	1.00

Table 6.3   Annual geometric mean values of efficiency levels, 1992–2008

Year	Technical efficiency	Allocative efficiency	Material efficiency
1992	0.7772	0.4985	0.3874
1993	0.7796	0.4587	0.3575
1994	0.7875	0.5108	0.4024
1995	0.7570	0.4558	0.3449
1996	0.7419	0.4882	0.3623
1997	0.7135	0.4523	0.3229
1998	0.7229	0.4246	0.3069
1999	0.7480	0.4107	0.3072
2000	0.6509	0.5403	0.3517
2001	0.7763	0.4935	0.3831
2002	0.8123	0.4731	0.3844
2003	0.8106	0.5481	0.4443
2004	0.7863	0.4470	0.3514
2005	0.7869	0.4696	0.3697
2006	0.8185	0.4709	0.3855
2007	0.8082	0.4835	0.3907
2008	0.8237	0.4587	0.3778

The overall ME score of 0.3649 indicates that OECD agriculture should be able to produce the same output levels with inputs containing 63.5 per cent less materials of N, P and C. Smaller total amounts of materials in the inputs means the smaller the balance of materials sent to the environment, which implies less potential to pollute the environment. In other words, by improving ME, these countries could have reduced potential damage to their air, water and land systems.

Table 6.3 and Figure 6.4 show the temporal trends of ITE, MAE and ME scores from 1992 to 2008. In general, these three measures move in the same direction over the surveyed period, except in 1999–2001. Technical efficiency exhibited a slight decrease in the late 1990s but a slight increase in the late 2000s. Material efficiency showed more fluctuations over the period, mainly due to allocative efficiency; but its level did not change significantly over the period 1992–2008.

Table 6.4 shows that the rankings of OECD countries changed significantly between ITE and ME. ITE-based rankings placed Belgium/Luxembourg, Denmark, Israel, the Netherlands, Poland, Switzerland and the United States of America in the most favourable positions. In terms of ME, only Poland and Israel retained their top rankings. Several countries such as Germany, Finland and Japan achieved high rankings in terms of ME even though their TE levels were relatively

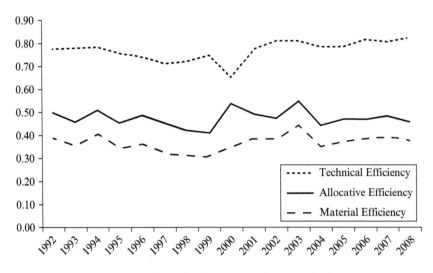

Figure 6.4   Trends in technical, allocative and material efficiency

low. The statistical tests rejected a null hypothesis that there is no agreement between the three rankings at the 5 per cent level of significance (Friedman=47.66; Kendall=0.51; p-value=0.03). Correlation analysis also shows a strong positive relationship (r=0.7529) between allocative efficiency and material efficiency, suggesting that improvements in allocative efficiency would have a strong direct impact on the overall material efficiency level.

6.4.2   Traditional Malmquist Total Factor Productivity Change

The mean values of traditional total factor productivity change for the 32 OECD economies from 1992 to 2008 are reported in Table 6.5. Changes in traditional TFP were decomposed into technical change (TC) and technical efficiency change (TEC) according to Equation (6.15). The estimation of traditional Malmquist TFP showed that, on average, OECD countries achieved an annual growth rate of 1.3 per cent, which was decomposed into technical change of 0.36 per cent (i.e. the upward shift of the production frontier) and 0.97 per cent improvement in year-to-year technical efficiency levels.

Figure 6.5 shows temporal trends in the three measures of efficiency changes. Technical progress occurred in most years of the late 1990s but fluctuated since then until 2008. Technical efficiency change, on the other hand, exhibited greater fluctuations. More importantly, Figure 6.5 displays

Table 6.4   Efficiency levels and ranking of OECD countries: geometric
means in 1992–2003

Country	Technical efficiency	Allocative efficiency	Material efficiency	Ranking (TE)	Ranking (AME)	Ranking (ME)
Australia	0.7267	0.1509	0.1096	22	31	32
Austria	0.7739	0.5581	0.4320	20	17	13
Belgium-Luxembourg	1.0000	0.3355	0.3355	1	25	21
Canada	0.8190	0.3800	0.3113	16	23	23
Czech Republic	0.8081	0.6739	0.5445	17	9	7
Denmark	1.0000	0.4173	0.4173	1	22	14
Estonia	0.7357	0.6937	0.5103	21	7	8
Finland	0.8947	0.7182	0.6427	13	5	4
France	0.8631	0.3422	0.2954	15	24	24
Germany	0.9977	0.6563	0.6548	9	11	3
Greece	0.5829	0.8575	0.4999	29	2	9
Hungary	0.6868	0.7048	0.4841	24	6	12
Iceland	0.1902	0.6836	0.1300	32	8	30
Ireland	0.9165	0.2031	0.1861	11	29	28
Israel	1.0000	0.7674	0.7674	1	3	2
Italy	0.6300	0.6466	0.4074	26	13	15
Japan	0.9742	0.6254	0.6093	10	15	5
Mexico	0.8029	0.1458	0.1171	18	32	31
Netherlands	1.0000	0.4900	0.4900	1	20	11
New Zealand	0.9996	0.1861	0.1860	8	30	29
Norway	0.5060	0.7557	0.3826	31	4	19
Poland	1.0000	1.0000	1.0000	1	1	1
Portugal	0.6037	0.5391	0.3255	28	18	22
Republic of Korea	0.8016	0.4894	0.3923	19	21	17
Slovakia	0.6909	0.5757	0.3978	23	16	16
Slovenia	0.6672	0.2898	0.1933	25	27	27
Spain	0.6116	0.6392	0.3911	27	14	18
Sweden	0.9018	0.6611	0.5961	12	10	6
Switzerland	1.0000	0.4993	0.4993	1	19	10
Turkey	0.5655	0.6506	0.3677	30	12	20
United Kingdom	0.8911	0.2960	0.2638	14	26	26
United States of America	1.0000	0.2714	0.2714	1	28	25

the opposite movements of TEC and TC. In many years when there was positive technical change (upward shift in the frontier), change in the efficiency levels (i.e. distances to the frontier) was negative. Technical change was negative in eight years (1993, 1998, 2001, 2002, 2003, 2005, 2006 and

Table 6.5   Summary values of Malmquist total factor productivity change

TFP change measures	Geometric mean	Arithmetic mean	Minimum	Maximum
Technical efficiency change (TEC)	1.0097	1.0160	0.4386	2.1702
Technical change (TC)	1.0036	1.0138	0.4766	1.8063
TFP change (TFPC = TEC × TC for geometric mean)	1.0133	1.0226	0.4902	1.5131

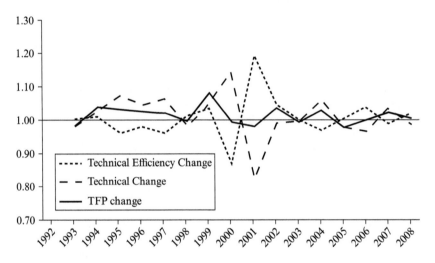

Figure 6.5   Trends in traditional Malmquist total factor productivity change, 1993–2008

2008), but its effects on the traditional TFP growth was compensated by improvements in ITE levels. In years when ITE levels declined, these reductions were outweighed by technological progress. There are at least two possible explanations for this observation: first, the failure to capture data noise and random errors of DEA (which can be overcome by using SFA); and second, time lags in the responses of OECD countries to technological progress, which implies that faster technological transfer (e.g., the transfer of farming practices/experiences/governmental policies and management) may help OECD countries reduce lags and enhance further efficiency improvements.

Table 6.6 shows annual change in the traditional Malmquist TFP across 32 countries. Most of the economies experienced annual Malmquist TFP growth, except France, Hungary, Israel, Japan and Turkey. Exceptionally,

Table 6.6   Measures of traditional productivity changes in 32 OECD economies

Country	Technical efficiency change (TEC)	Technical change (TC)	TFP change (= TEC × TC)
Australia	0.9924	1.0121	1.0045
Austria	1.0091	1.0238	1.0330
Belgium-Luxembourg	1.0000	1.0077	1.0077
Canada	1.0072	1.0210	1.0283
Czech Republic	0.9915	1.0092	1.0006
Denmark	1.0000	1.0166	1.0166
Estonia	1.0292	1.0068	1.0363
Finland	1.0021	0.9986	1.0007
France	0.9732	1.0010	0.9742
Germany	1.0025	1.0544	1.0570
Greece	0.9974	1.0034	1.0008
Hungary	0.9794	0.9971	0.9766
Iceland	0.9906	1.0177	1.0081
Ireland	1.0039	1.0295	1.0336
Israel	1.0000	0.9828	0.9828
Italy	1.0345	0.9926	1.0268
Japan	0.9989	0.9915	0.9904
Mexico	1.0221	1.0080	1.0303
Netherlands	1.0000	1.0011	1.0011
New Zealand	1.0000	1.0082	1.0082
Norway	0.9910	1.0101	1.0010
Poland	1.0000	1.0118	1.0118
Portugal	1.0298	0.9931	1.0226
Republic of Korea	0.9911	1.0232	1.0141
Slovakia	0.9943	1.0134	1.0076
Slovenia	1.0393	1.0355	1.0761
Spain	1.0448	0.9932	1.0376
Sweden	1.0083	1.0064	1.0147
Switzerland	1.0000	1.0170	1.0170
Turkey	0.9803	0.9957	0.9760
United Kingdom	1.0077	1.0153	1.0231
United States of America	1.0000	1.0147	1.0147

Germany achieved an annual growth of 5.7 per cent due to substantial technical change. Hoang and Coelli (2012) and Hoang (2011) reported similar findings for Germany due to the significant output expansion with little increase in input consumption in the mid-1990s.

Table 6.7   Decomposition of environmental total factor productivity change

Environmental TFP change measures	Geometric mean	Arithmetic mean	Minimum	Maximum
Technical efficiency change (TEC)	1.0097	1.0160	0.4386	2.1702
Technical change (TC)	1.0036	1.0138	0.4766	1.8063
TFP change (TFPC = TEC × TC for geometric mean)	1.0133	1.0226	0.4902	1.5131
Material allocative efficiency change (MAEC)	0.9962	1.0010	0.6561	1.6519
Material TFP change (MTFPC = TFPC × MAEC for geometric mean)	1.0095	1.0157	0.5168	2.4318

6.4.3   Environmental Total Factor Productivity Change

The geometric mean values of material-orientated TFP change across 32 OECD economies for the years from 1992 to 2008 are reported in Table 6.7. MTFPC was decomposed into changes in the traditional Malmquist TFP and changes in nutrient allocative efficiency (MAEC) according to Equation (6.24). The environmental TFP was estimated to be an annual growth rate of 0.95 per cent across 32 economies. This MTFP growth was lower than the traditional TFP growth because of reductions in material allocative efficiency levels (MAEC).

Figure 6.6 presents the pattern of movements of the environmental TFP change and its three components – technical change (TC), technical efficiency change (TEC) and material allocative efficiency change (MAEC) – for 32 OECD economies from 1991 to 2008. Negative growth occurred in five years (2001/2000, 2003/2002, 2005/2004, 2006/2005 and 2008/2007), which was caused by negative change in the technical change measure.

As shown in Table 6.8, the main driving force of changes in environmental TFP is the change in technical efficiency change (TEC) component of the traditional Malmquist TFP. This finding is important because significant technological improvement may not have originated in all economies, and hence technological transfer among economies could play a more important role in enhancing the environmental performance of OECD agriculture.

The environmental TFP growth varied across countries, as shown in Table 6.9. Only seven countries – Denmark, France, Greece, Ireland, Norway, Korea and Sweden – experienced decreases in the mean values of environmental TFP in the period from 1992 to 2008. In all these countries

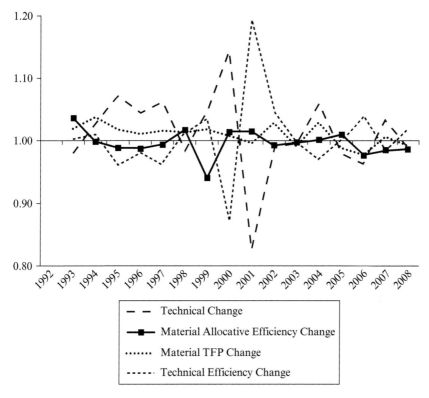

*Figure 6.6   Trends in traditional and environmental total factor
productivity change*

*Table 6.8   Correlation matrix for various measures of efficiency and
productivity change*

	TEC	TC	TFPC	MAEC	MTFPC
Technical efficiency change (TEC)	1.000				
Technical change (TC)	−0.466	1.000			
TFP change (TFPC)	0.625	0.375	1.000		
Material allocative efficiency change (MAEC)	−0.325	−0.202	−0.516	1.000	
Material TFP change (MTFPC)	0.487	0.246	0.725	0.118	1.000

Table 6.9   Measures of traditional and material productivity changes in 32 OECD economies

Country	TFP change (TFPC)	Material allocative efficiency change (MAEC)	Material TFP change (= TFPC × MAEC)
Australia	1.0045	1.0219	1.0264
Austria	1.0330	0.9758	1.0080
Belgium-Luxembourg	1.0077	0.9941	1.0018
Canada	1.0283	0.9860	1.0139
Czech Republic	1.0006	1.0181	1.0188
Denmark	1.0166	0.9833	0.9996
Estonia	1.0363	1.0075	1.0440
Finland	1.0007	1.0051	1.0058
France	0.9742	1.0161	0.9898
Germany	1.0570	0.9594	1.0141
Greece	1.0008	0.9920	0.9928
Hungary	0.9766	1.0438	1.0194
Iceland	1.0081	0.9967	1.0049
Ireland	1.0336	0.9573	0.9895
Israel	0.9828	1.0203	1.0028
Italy	1.0268	0.9810	1.0073
Japan	0.9904	1.0140	1.0042
Mexico	1.0303	0.9959	1.0260
Netherlands	1.0011	1.0032	1.0044
New Zealand	1.0082	1.0116	1.0199
Norway	1.0010	0.9956	0.9966
Poland	1.0118	0.9988	1.0105
Portugal	1.0226	0.9899	1.0123
Republic of Korea	1.0141	0.9804	0.9943
Slovakia	1.0076	1.0245	1.0323
Slovenia	1.0761	0.9278	0.9984
Spain	1.0376	0.9857	1.0229
Sweden	1.0147	0.9815	0.9960
Switzerland	1.0170	0.9843	1.0010
Turkey	0.9760	1.0694	1.0438
United Kingdom	1.0231	0.9798	1.0024
United States of America	1.0147	0.9891	1.0036

(except France) it appears that the negative change in the level of material allocative efficiency was the main cause of decreased environmental TFP change – regardless of the fact that there was technological progress. This suggests that technological progress (in terms of shifts in the production frontier) could well have occurred but did not always lead to increase in the material allocative efficiency. Hence, in developing relevant policies attention should be paid to innovations which would reduce inputs and the combinations of material-containing inputs which could yield better environmental performance.

6.5   DISCUSSION OF MAIN FINDINGS

6.5.1   Technological Transfer

As highlighted in Hoang and Coelli (2011), the hypothesis of slow agricultural technological spillover during the surveyed period may be surprising given only modest differences in the levels of agricultural modernization among OECD countries. While empirically testing this hypothesis goes beyond the scope of this work, it is useful to provide some elaboration.

First, the hypothesis is in line with theories of economic growth introduced by Atkinson and Stiglitz (1969) and Basu and Weil (1998), who emphasize that spillover depends on past and current local conditions. International spillovers may therefore not have occurred at a fast pace because domestic conditions were not ready to adopt new technologies from overseas. For example, because of skill mismatches, farmers are unlikely to adopt crop-specific technologies until they receive enough training. In order to provide proper training, local scientists need to conduct pilot testing for new technologies and 'localize' them. This suggests that research and development (R&D) might be localized rather than 'globalized'. Using GDP and R&D expenditure data, empirical studies report that the majority of innovations are indeed localized (Keller 2002). Unfortunately, there appears to be few empirical studies that investigate this issue in the agricultural sector. For example, Dowrick and Gemmell (1991) found that technological advances by leading producers (the United States, Canada and Australia) did not transfer to other countries in the 1975–85 period.

Second, while measuring the contribution of technological transfer in TFP is difficult due to data and methodological inadequacies (Alston et al., 2010), many studies investigate the lag in the impacts of R&D on production. Marra et al. (2000), in a review of 289 articles and reports (of which 50 per cent involved field crop studies), revealed that only 19 per cent of them considered the spillover effect on the rates of return, and that nearly 50 per cent of the estimates had a research lag length of 11–30 years. Considered together, the localization of technical development, the small spillover evident during previous periods and the long lags in R&D impacts, the hypothesis of slow technological transfer makes sense.

6.5.2   Determinants of Variations in Environmental Efficiency and Productivity Change

The empirical results presented in Section 6.4 show variations in the environmental performance across economies and over time. Two questions arise: are these variations significant? and what are the factors that explain these variations? While this study does not provide the answers, it is important to note that empirical investigations into these questions could provide useful inputs into the development of relevant policies. For example, it is worth considering the impacts of environmental policies on environmental efficiency and productivity growth. This is particularly important given that, during the years surveyed, many OECD economies had been particularly active in developing policies to tackle environmental problems.

6.6   CONCLUSIONS

Environmental performance of agriculture in the OECD has received increasing attention in the last few decades. The OECD community has published several reports on this issue which provide useful information relating to the use of a range of environmental indicators to measure environmental performance of agricultural production. However, research in measuring environmental total factor productivity is still in its infancy. This chapter, therefore, provides a simple application of the use of material balance-based environmental efficiency to construct an environmental productivity index. In particular, the chapter estimates environmental efficiency and TFP change using the Malmquist index approach, with a focus on three materials: nitrogen, phosphorus and carbon.

   Empirical results were based on data of 32 OECD countries from 1992 to 2008 using the input-orientated DEA framework under the assumption of constant returns to scale and equal weights of the polluting effects of N, P and C. These results provide several important findings. First, there is considerable potential for OECD countries to improve their material-based environmental efficiency by either improving their technical efficiency (i.e. reducing the consumption of physical inputs) or, more importantly, by changing the combination of material-containing inputs. In turn, improved material efficiency would considerably reduce the extent of pollution caused by N and P balances entering water, air and land systems.

   Second, the OECD countries considered in this study achieved an annual traditional TFP growth rate of 1.3 per cent. Third, the environmental TFP growth is estimated to be smaller than the traditional TFP growth caused by reductions in the material-orientated allocative efficiency level. This finding implies that changes in the input combinations could improve the environmental productivity performance of OECD countries.

These empirical results pose several important hypotheses. First, international technological transfer may not be effective among OECD countries during the period surveyed. This slow international spillover might be a consequence of the nature of "localized" innovations, long lags in local R&D, and the low level of transfer in the previous periods. Policies that target faster transfer and deployment of new technologies would help these countries achieve higher efficiency and productivity growth. Second, better environmental performance in several countries might be the result of environmental policies that these countries have implemented. In this study the potential effects of such policies on the material efficiency and productivity performance across the 32 economies was not empirically assessed. However, such studies would be worthwhile. Third, government interventions to change the relative prices of inputs are worth considering given our empirical results indicate that changes in the combinations of inputs could have a strong impact on the environmental performance of the agricultural sector. Furthermore, the empirical study has enabled us to show that such analysis could potentially be undertaken to cover the rest of the world. Such a study could highlight how agricultural input use could be significantly reduced while maintaining current output levels and at the same time reducing GHG emissions and reducing agricultural pollution.

There are, however, important shortcomings in this study. They include:

- the issue of data noise due to aggregation of data;
- the use of a non-parametric framework;
- the assumption of constant return to scale;
- the assumption of equal polluting powers of the three concerned materials (N, P and C);
- non-inclusion of other pollutants and GHG emissions such as methane.

Improvements in these five areas could enhance the accuracy of environmental efficiency and productivity estimates for better interpretation of results in the context of policy development and environmental conservation.

NOTES

*   Substantial portion of this chapter is drawn from a report made to the Trade and
    Agriculture Directorate OECD in the context of the OECD Green Growth Indicators
    for Agriculture project. The report has received generous inputs from Dr Dimitris
    Diakosavvas. The first author also presented the report in the OECD Expert Workshop:
    Measuring Environmentally Adjusted Total Factor Productivity for Agriculture, 14–15
    December 2015, Paris, France.
1. OECD statistics report N, P effluents from livestock manure in its 2013 edition of the
    OECD Environmental Database at http://stats.oecd.org/.
2. The model can be best applied to datasets of farms located in similar geographic
    locations.

REFERENCES

Alston, J.M., M.A. Anderson, S.J. James and P.G. Pardey (2010). *Persistence Pays: U.S. Agricultural Productivity Growth and the Benefits from Public R&D Spending*. Springer, New York.

Alston, J.M., M.C., Marra, P.G. Pardey and T.J. Wyatt (2000), 'Research returns redux: a meta-analysis of the returns to agricultural R&D', *Australian Journal of Agricultural and Resource Economics*, **44** (2), 185–215.

Atkinson, A.B. and J.E. Stiglitz (1969), 'A new view of technological change', *Economic Journal*, **79** (315), 573–578.

Ayres, R.U. (1995), 'Thermodynamics and process analysis for future economic scenarios' *Environmental and Resource Economics*, **6** (3), 207–230.

Ball, V. Eldon, R. Färe, S. Grosskopf and R.F. Nehring (2000), 'Productivity of the U.S. agricultural sector: the case of undesirable outputs', in Charles R. Hulten, Edwin R. Dean and Michael J. Harper (eds), *New Developments in Productivity Analysis*. University of Chicago Press, Chicago and London, pp. 541–586.

Basu, S. and D.N. Weil (1998), 'Appropriate technology and growth', *Quarterly Journal of Economics*, **113**, 1025–1054.

Callens, I. and D. Tyteca (1999), 'Towards indicators of sustainable development for firms: a productive efficiency perspective', *Ecological Economics*, **28**, 41–53.

Caves, D.W., L.R. Christensen and W.E. Diewert (1982), 'Multilateral comparisons of output, input, and productivity using superlative index numbers', *Economic Journal*, **92**, 73–86.

Chung, Y.H., R. Fare and S. Grosskopf (1997), 'Productivity and undesirable outputs: a directional distance function approach', *Journal of Environmental Management*, **51**(3), 229–240.

Coelli, T.J. and D.S.P. Rao (2005), 'Total factor productivity growth in agriculture: a Malmquist index analysis of 93 countries, 1980–2000', *Agricultural Economics*, **32**, 115–134.

Coelli, T. J., D.S.P. Rao, C.J. O'Donnell and G. Battese (2005), *An Introduction to Efficiency and Productivity Analysis*, Springer, New York.

Dowrick, S. and N. Gemmell (1991), 'Industrialisation, catching up and economic growth: a comparative study across the world's capitalist economies', *Economic Journal*, **101** (405), 263–275.

Färe, R. and S. Grosskopf (2000), 'Theory and application of directional distance functions', *Journal of Productivity Analysis*, **13** (2), 93–103.

Färe, R. and D. Primont (1995), *Multi-Output Production and Duality: Theory and Applications*, Kluwer Academic Publishers, Boston.

Farrell, M.J. (1957), 'The measurement of productive efficiency', *Journal of the Royal Statistical Society, Series A*, **120** (3), 253–281.

Fuglie, K. and N. Rada (2013), 'ERS data product: international agricultural productivity', USDA, available at www.ers.usda.gov/data-products/international-agri cultural-productivity.

Gold, A.J. and J.T. Sims (2005), 'Eutrophication', in D. Hillel (ed.), Encyclopedia of Soils in the Environment. Elsevier, Oxford, pp. 486–494.

Grifell-Tatjé, E. and C.A.K. Lovell (1995), 'A note on the Malmquist productivity index', *Economics Letters*, **47**(2), 169–175.

Hailu, A. and T.S. Veeman (2001a), 'Alternative methods for environmentally adjusted productivity analysis', *Agricultural Economics*, **25** (2–3), 211–218.

Hailu, A. and T.S. Veeman (2001b), 'Non-parametric productivity analysis with undesirable outputs: an application to the Canadian pulp and paper industry', *American Journal of Agricultural Economics*, **83** (3), 605–616.

Hayami, Y. and V.W. Ruttan (1985), Agricultural development: an international perspective. Johns Hopkins University Press, Baltimore.

Hoang, V.-N. (2011), 'Measuring and decomposing changes in agricultural productivity, nitrogen use efficiency and cumulative exergy efficiency: application to OECD agriculture', *Ecological Modelling*, **222** (1), 164–175.

Hoang, V.-N. and M. Alauddin (2012), 'Input-orientated data envelopment analysis framework of measuring and decomposing economic, environmental and ecological efficiency: an application to OECD agriculture', *Environmental and Resource Economics*, **51** (3), 431–452.

Hoang, V.N. and T. Coelli (2011), 'Measurement of agricultural total factor productivity growth incorporating environmental factors: a nutrients balance approach', *Journal of Environmental Economics and Management*, **62** (3), 462–474.

Hoang, V.N. and T.T. Nguyen (2013), 'Analysis of environmental efficiency variation: a materials balance approach', *Ecological Economics*, **86**, 37–46.

Howarth, R.W. and R. Marino (2006), 'Nitrogen as the limiting nutrient for eutrophication in coastal marine ecosystems: evolving views over three decades', *Limnology and Oceanography*, **51** (1), 364–376.

Keller, W. (2002), 'Geographic localization of international technology diffusion', *American Economic Review*, **92** (1), 120–142.

Lauwers, L. (2009), 'Justifying the incorporation of the materials balance principle into frontier-based eco-efficiency models', *Ecological Economics*, **68** (6), 1605–1614.

Marra, M.C., P.G. Pardey, T.J. Wyatt and J.M. Alston (2000), Research returns redux: a meta analysis of the returns to agricultural R&D, *Australian Journal of Agricultural and Resource Economics*, 44, 185–215.

OECD (2008), *Environmental Performance of Agriculture in OECD Countries since 1990*. Organisation for Economic Co-operation and Development, Paris.

Paerl, H.W. (2009), 'Controlling eutrophication along the freshwater–marine continuum: dual nutrient (N and P) reductions are essential', *Estuaries and Coasts*, **32**(4), 593–601.

Picazo-Tadeo, A.J., M. Beltrán-Esteve and J.A. Gómez-Limón (2012), 'Assessing eco-efficiency with directional distance functions', *European Journal of Operational Research*, **220** (3), 798–809.

Ptacnik, R., T. Andersen and T. Tamminen (2010), 'Performance of the redfield ratio and a family of nutrient limitation indicators as thresholds for phytoplankton N vs. P limitation', *Ecosystems*, **13** (8), 1201–1214.

Redfield, A.C., B.H. Ketchum and F.A. Richards (1963), 'The influence of organisms on the composition of sea water', in M.N. Hill (ed.), *The Composition of Sea-Water: Comparative and Descriptive Oceanography*. Wiley, New York, pp. 26–77.

Seppälä, J., S. Knuuttila and K. Silvo (2004), 'Eutrophication of aquatic ecosystems a new method for calculating the potential contributions of nitrogen and phosphorus', *International Journal of Life Cycle Assessment*, **9** (2), 90–100.

Summers, R. (1973), 'International price comparisons based upon incomplete data', Review of *Income and Wealth*, **19** (1), 1–16.

Tyteca, D. (1999), 'Sustainability indicators at the firm level', *Journal of Industrial Ecology*, **2** (4), 61–77.

Yaisawarng, S. and D.J. Klein (1994), 'The effects of sulfur dioxide controls on productivity change in the U.S. electric power industry', *Review of Economics and Statistics* **76** (3), 447–460.

7. Incorporating the environment in agricultural productivity: applying advances in international environmental accounting

Carl Obst and Mark Eigenraam*

7.1 INTRODUCTION

In light of the ongoing realities of climate change and the increasing demand for food around the world, understanding the capacity of the environment to support agricultural production is of upmost concern. From an ecological perspective, the relevant factors in assessing capacity include soil quality, nutrient and water availability and the biodiversity of pollinators among many other factors. From an economic perspective, the factors most commonly considered are output and input prices, labour input, produced capital requirements and land availability.

A priori, it is hard to deny that both ecological and economic factors are relevant in understanding the capacity for agricultural production. However, although ecological factors are taken into account in some approaches to agricultural productivity – for example, linear programming approaches – most current measures of agricultural productivity, particularly at economy-wide level, either exclude ecological factors or consider only specific flows such as nitrogen balances or greenhouse gas (GHG) emissions. The resulting measures must therefore be seen as providing a restricted view on productivity and the potential for increases or sustainability in agricultural output.

The explicit incorporation of environmental considerations into productivity measures, especially for the agricultural industry, would support a more complete understanding of the factors that drive output and input growth, and hence support the development of more integrated policy responses. This chapter proposes a way forward to fill this gap in current productivity measures by providing a systematic framework for integrating ecological information.

Since the mid-1990s there have been important advances in the measurement of natural capital and environmental assets, encapsulated in the recent international standard, the System of Environmental-Economic Accounting (SEEA) (United Nations et al., 2014a). The SEEA applies the principles of accounting for the economy to facilitate the organization and integration of environmental data. Of particular interest is the most recent extension that applies national accounting principles to the integration of information on ecosystem condition and ecosystem services. This advance is referred to as ecosystem accounting (United Nations et al., 2014b).

In concept, ecosystem accounting provides information that can directly extend the measurement of productivity. In effect, measures of the ecosystem assets (i.e. the underlying natural capital) that underpin agricultural activity can be included as a new factor of production in deriving the volume of inputs – in addition to the traditional factors of labour and produced capital. For agriculture, the enhancement allows recognition of the changing quality of agricultural land and the use of ecosystem services. This chapter articulates a conceptual approach to the integration of ecosystem services and ecosystem assets into standard growth accounting measures to generate measures of environmentally adjusted agricultural productivity.

The chapter is structured to provide an overview of the SEEA (section 7.2) and an explanation of ecosystem accounting. In section 7.3, the standard approaches to economy-wide measurement of productivity are introduced, and a brief summary of approaches to agricultural productivity and common environmental extensions to these measures is provided. Section 7.4 presents an ecosystem accounting based approach to deriving environmentally adjusted productivity measures. Section 7.5 discusses a series of conceptual and measurement issues that remain to be further explored, and section 7.6 concludes.

7.2   OVERVIEW OF THE SEEA FRAMEWORK AND ITS DEVELOPMENT

7.2.1   Development of the SEEA[1]

The potential and need to better integrate measures relating to natural capital within the national accounts framework emerged through the 1970s and 1980s (see Bartelmus, 1987; Ahmad et al., 1989). Consistent with a request from the first United Nations Conference on Environment and Development, held in Rio de Janeiro in 1992 (United Nations, 1992), the United Nations Statistical Division led the drafting of the first international document on environmental-economic accounting (United Nations, 1993). This document, Integrated Environmental and Economic Accounting, became known as the System of Environmental-Economic Accounting, or SEEA. It was an interim document prepared by the world's official statistics community to propose ways in which the System of National Accounts (SNA) might be extended to better take natural capital into consideration.

Since the 1990s there has been an important broadening of focus in SEEA-related work (United Nations et al., 2014a). Through the 1980s and early 1990s the primary focus was on extensions and adjustments to gross domestic product (GDP) (Obst, 2015), for example measures of depletion and degradation adjusted GDP, and recording environmental expenditures. Discussion considered the range of ways in which depletion and degradation might be estimated, valued and subsequently incorporated within the structure of the standard national accounts and its various measures of production, income, saving and wealth.

Through the 1990s this focus started to broaden to consider ways in which accounting approaches and structures may be useful in the organization of physical information on environmental stocks and flows such as water, energy and waste. This broader application of accounting, which has been expanded further in recent years through the development of ecosystem accounting, confronts the common conception that adoption of accounting approaches necessarily relies on the valuation of nature in monetary terms. Certainly there are questions that must be answered using monetary valuation, for example adjusting measures of GDP; but there are some important advantages of applying accounting principles in the organization of data in physical terms.

7.2.2   The SEEA Family

The SEEA 2012 comprises three volumes: SEEA Central Framework; SEEA Experimental Ecosystem Accounting (SEEA EEA); and SEEA Applications and Extensions (United Nations et al., 2014a, b, c).[2] In addition, various thematic SEEA publications have been developed, including SEEA for Forestry (EC and Eurostat, 2002); SEEA Fisheries (FAO and UN, 2004); and SEEA Water (UN, 2012). Work has also been completed on the development of SEEA Energy and SEEA for Agriculture, Forestry and Fisheries (SEEA AFF) (FAO, 2015).

All of these various publications within the SEEA "family" are connected through their common basis in the national accounting principles and structures of the international standard for economic accounting – the SNA (European Commission et al., 2009). It is the SNA that defines the measurement boundaries for GDP and many other common economic aggregates that form the basis for much macro-economic assessment and policy. Indeed, the logic driving the development of the SEEA is: (i) that the SNA's accounting for the environment is insufficient and (ii) that highlighting the significance of the environment may be best achieved by mainstreaming environmental information via the standard framework for economic measurement. Thus the SEEA is envisioned as a complementary system to the SNA rather than a competing accounting approach.

The recent work to develop the SEEA AFF emerged from ongoing interest in organizing information for the purpose of analysing the relationship between the economy and the environment for agriculture, forestry and fisheries activities. The work has been led by the United Nations Food and Agriculture Organization (FAO), which is the leading international agency concerning data on these activities. The data framework of the SEEA AFF encompasses a range of information of direct relevance to the estimation of environmentally adjusted measures of agricultural productivity. The SEEA AFF was endorsed by the United Nations Committee of Experts on Environmental-Economic Accounting in June 2016.

7.2.3   The SEEA EEA Model

SEEA EEA was developed through 2011 and 2012 to provide an approach to the measurement and integration of environmental degradation within the standard economic accounts (United Nations et al., 2014b). The definition and measurement of degradation has been an area of discussion and contention within national accounting circles since the mid-1990s. The work on SEEA EEA was able to take advantage of the more recent developments in the measurement of ecosystem services, such as presented in the Millennium Ecosystem Assessment (MA) (2005), The Economics of Ecosystems and Biodiversity study (TEEB, 2010) and the National Ecosystem Assessment of the United Kingdom (UK NEA, 2011). SEEA EEA represents a synthesis of approaches to the measurement of ecosystems designed to enable integration with standard national accounting concepts and measurement boundaries.

The full ecosystem accounting model is described at length in SEEA EEA Chapter 2 (United Nations et al., 2014b), and readers are referred to that document for a detailed description.[3] For the purposes of discussion here, Figure 7.1 provides a depiction of the general model.

Five key features of the ecosystem accounting model are noted:

1.   The delineation of spatial areas. Ecosystem accounting is focused on accounting for ecosystem assets, each delineated by a spatial area.

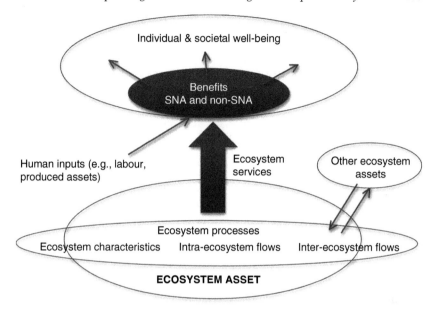

Source: United Nations et al. (2014b, Figure 2.2).

Figure 7.1   General ecosystem accounting model, SEEA EEA

In the case of agriculture this could equate to a single farm or to a broader area, such as a rice-farming area, with the understanding that each spatial area would consist of a similar vegetation type and cover. From a measurement perspective, defining the spatial boundaries is fundamental, since without such boundaries it is not possible to consistently measure the condition and changes in condition of the asset or to appropriately attribute flows of ecosystem services. Further, by establishing a mapping of mutually exclusive ecosystem units across a region or country, the ecosystem accounting model supports aggregation of ecosystem data from micro to macro levels, and hence integration with macro-economic measures.

The use of a spatial basis for accounting is the embodiment of a systems approach to accounting wherein both economic and environmental stocks and flows are considered in a holistic fashion. However, the delineation of an ecosystem asset should not be equated with definition of a farming or agricultural system which would commonly be considered to also encompass additional socio-economic factors (e.g. markets, institutions, government policies, etc.). Indeed, it is likely that description of a complete agricultural system would comprise more than one type of ecosystem asset. For example, in a rice production system there would be rice fields as well as neighbouring water sources and perhaps forest ecosystems.

For the purposes of integrating ecosystem information about defined spatial areas with standard economic accounts and productivity measures, it is most useful to consider each ecosystem asset as a type of quasi-producing unit – i.e. additional producing units to the standard economic units that comprise industries and households.

2. Measuring the condition of ecosystem assets. Each ecosystem asset (e.g. a contiguous set of rice fields) has numerous characteristics (climate, soil, vegetation, species diversity, etc.) and performs various ecosystem functions (see, e.g. Odum and Barrett, 2005). The integrity and functioning of the asset is measured by its condition. It is the decline in overall condition, in biophysical terms, that underpins the measurement of ecosystem degradation. Asset accounts for ecosystem condition and ecosystem extent (i.e. the area of the ecosystem asset) are described in SEEA EEA. These accounts are compiled in biophysical terms. Asset accounts for ecosystems in monetary terms are compiled indirectly based on the valuation of ecosystem services.

3. Measuring the flow of ecosystem services. Based on both the ecosystem asset's condition and the use made of the ecosystem asset (e.g. for rice production), a basket of ecosystem services will be supplied. The ecosystem services supplied are consumed by users/beneficiaries – i.e. economic units including businesses, households and governments. An ecosystem services supply and use account is developed in ecosystem accounting. The coverage of ecosystem services includes provisioning services (e.g. food, fibre, water), regulating services (e.g. air filtration, pollination, water flow regulation, carbon sequestration) and cultural services (e.g. tourism, spiritual connections).

The focus in SEEA EEA is on final ecosystem services following the approach taken in TEEB (2010) and Banzhaf and Boyd (2012), among others. Consequently, ecosystem services are considered contributions to benefits rather than equivalent to benefits as in the definition used in the Millennium Ecosystem Assessment (2005). A consequence is that in valuation a distinction must be made between the price of a marketed good, such as rice, and the value of the contribution of the ecosystem. For rice, the contribution would be estimated by deducting growing and harvesting costs (labour, pesticides, fertilizer, machinery, etc.) from total sales of harvested rice.

In concept, by estimating the monetary value of all ecosystem services supplied by an ecosystem asset, and then estimating the associated net present value of this basket of services, the value of the ecosystem asset itself is derived. The value of ecosystem degradation will be related to the change in the value of the ecosystem asset over an accounting period, noting that the value of the asset may change for reasons other than a decline in condition (e.g. through changes in land use) and that a loss in condition may not be due to human activity (e.g. storm damage), and hence would be excluded from ecosystem degradation for accounting purposes.[4]

4. Relating ecosystem services to standard measures of economic activity. The supply of all final ecosystem services is outside the production boundary of the SNA as they are considered natural processes (see European Commission et al., 2009, 6.24). At the same time, many ecosystem services contribute to the production of goods and services that are included in the SNA production boundary, for example the contribution of water to rice production. To understand the impact on measures of GDP, it is necessary to recall that GDP is a measure of value added – i.e. output less intermediate inputs. Thus, where final ecosystem services contribute to existing measures of output (as in the rice production case), the net effect of recording the supply of ecosystem services on GDP is zero, since the ecosystem services are considered both as additional outputs (of the ecosystem asset) and additional inputs to currently recorded production.[5]

    SEEA EEA also goes an additional step by including the output of ecosystem services that are not inputs to currently recorded goods and services – e.g., the carbon sequestration service of plants. It is this additional output, and associated value added, attributable to ecosystem assets that directly increases measures of GDP.

5. The use of exchange values. The ecosystem accounting model reflects relationships between stocks and flows that exist without regard for the unit of measurement. Thus, in concept, the accounting relationships can be reported in both physical and monetary units. Measurement in monetary terms requires the use of various valuation techniques, since prices for ecosystem services and assets are not directly observed in markets as for standard economic products.

Economists have developed many valuation techniques to support analysis of environmental issues, including for the valuation of ecosystem services. These techniques include pricing based on production and cost functions, hedonic pricing, resource rent, replacement and damage costs and stated preference methods.[6] For accounting purposes, some of these techniques (e.g. production and cost functions, hedonic pricing and resource rent) are appropriate as they estimate the *exchange value* or transaction price of an ecosystem service – i.e. the price at which a willing buyer and willing seller would complete a transaction of a single ecosystem service. Exchange values are required for accounting since they allow a balance between estimates of supply and demand to be maintained in monetary terms. However, other techniques that are commonly used for environmental valuation, such as stated preference methods, are usually applied to estimate the change in welfare of economic units due to a change in policy or situation that arises in relation to an ecosystem service or asset. The use of these welfare valuations is not directly appropriate for accounting purposes since they will include estimates of consumer surplus. However, there are likely connections that can be made to utilize or adapt these valuation approaches for accounting purposes. Research is ongoing, for example in the context of the World Bank's Wealth Accounting and Valuation of Ecosystem Services (WAVES) programme, into the best ways to utilize different valuation techniques for accounting purposes (Atkinson and Obst, 2016).

These five key elements of ecosystem accounting provide the conceptual basis for extending the current approaches to measuring multifactor productivity (MFP) to incorporate ecosystem services, and hence provide coherent measures of environmentally adjusted agricultural MFP. Before describing this integration, the following section provides an introduction to the growth accounting approach to measuring MFP.

7.3   MEASURING MFP AND ENVIRONMENTALLY ADJUSTED MFP FOR AGRICULTURE

7.3.1   Economy-Wide Approaches

Multifactor productivity (MFP) is a well-accepted and widely compiled estimate of productivity that takes into account the extent to which the volume all of the inputs to production (labour, capital and intermediate inputs) are changing in relation to the volume of output. In short, MFP growth occurs when the growth in the volume of output is greater than the combined volume of inputs. Under various assumptions, including that markets are competitive, the so called MFP "residual" reflects changes in technical progress – i.e. that part of the growth in output that cannot be explained by the growth in inputs (OECD, 2001).

The measurement of MFP can be undertaken in a number of ways, and has been compiled for individual firms and industries and for countries as a whole. At national or economy wide level, the standard approach used across Organisation for Economic Co-operation and Development (OECD) countries is known as growth accounting (see OECD, 2001). The growth accounting approach was originally developed in the 1950s and 1960s by Solow (1957), Jorgenson (1963) and others, and has been continually refined since that time.

Key aspects of growth accounting, particularly the measurement of capital services, have been integrated into the standard national accounts framework (see European Commission et al., 2009, Chapter 20). Because of this conceptual integration and the associated availability of time series of economic data, since the 1980s many countries, particularly in the OECD, have steadily adopted and published economy wide MFP estimates as extensions of the core national accounts dataset (e.g. ABS, 2015; Statistics Canada, 2015).

Two approaches to measuring economy wide MFP can be applied. The first involves measuring the change in the volume of value added for each industry (i.e. output less intermediate inputs) and to compare this to the change in the combined volume of the two factors of production – labour and capital. Since the volume of value added by industry is the same measure used in the derivation of GDP, this information is readily available. The volumes of labour and capital are weighted together using national accounts information on the cost shares of each, namely compensation of employees for labour inputs and gross operating surplus (GOS) for capital.

The second approach, known as KLEMS (capital, labour, energy, materials and services), uses output by industry as the left-hand side variable of interest, and compares growth in output with the combined growth in inputs of labour, capital and three categories of intermediate inputs (energy, materials and services). Due to the use of underlying national accounting information to determine input cost shares, the resulting MFP estimates from either approach are mathematically related (OECD, 2001).

7.3.2   Approaches to Measuring Agricultural MFP

These economy wide MFP estimates described above include estimates for the agricultural industry, and this enables an understanding of the contribution of agricultural MFP to overall MFP growth. However, notwithstanding the direct use of environmental assets by the agriculture industry, the measurement of capital's contribution to MFP growth in agriculture has commonly been undertaken using the same methods as for other industries – i.e. including only produced (or manufactured) capital. In some countries, such as Australia, a variation has been adopted with the inclusion of the area of agricultural land as a capital input to the agricultural industries within economy wide measures (ABS, 2016). However, even with this important extension, no account has been taken for the changing quality of land, for example through declines in soil fertility and soil erosion.

Experts in the measurement of the agriculture industry have also developed measures of productivity. The approaches range from farm level analysis to national and international level studies, and encompass both parametric and non-parametric approaches. This chapter does not attempt a review of these methods, except to note that there is a close conceptual link between the approaches used by agricultural experts in, for example, the USA (Ball et al., 2014), Canada (Cahill and Rich, 2012) and Australia (Zhao et al., 2012) and the economy wide growth accounting described above. Given this link, the methods proposed in this chapter should be broadly amenable to consideration by those experts.

One important note is that these agriculture specific approaches have taken into consideration the area of land as an input to production, and in the USA some adjustment has been made for the relative quality of land in different regions (Ball et al., 2014). However, no direct input of biophysical information concerning the use of environmental resources has been incorporated.

7.3.3   Approaches to Accounting for Environmentally Adjusted MFP

More recently, interest has grown in establishing measures of MFP that take into account environmental factors. Of particular importance has been the work of the OECD as part of its Green Growth initiative in which a leading indicator of green growth is defined as environmentally adjusted MFP (OECD, 2014). With this indicator concept in mind, the OECD has advanced work in this direction and developed MFP measures adjusted for the use of mineral and energy resources and GHG emissions (see Brandt et al., 2013, 2014).

In the same context of green growth, the OECD held a workshop on environmentally adjusted measures of agricultural MFP in December 2015 with the aim of assessing the current state of methods, and hence determining ways to develop an indicator relevant for measuring progress towards green growth in agriculture (OECD, 2015).

The workshop revealed a range of approaches, with papers by Hoang (2015) and Kuosmanen (2015) summarizing the current state of play. Generally, the focus of environmentally adjusted agriculture MFP measures has been to consider adjustment of standard MFP measures for specific environmental factors – including land, the impacts of nitrogen (N) and phosphorous (P), residuals and byproducts from agricultural activities, including GHG emissions, and the impacts of changes in weather patterns, for example due to climate change. For some of these factors the measurement approaches take into consideration accounting issues, for example the integration of material balance considerations in measuring the impact of N and P flows. However, there is no apparent broader conceptual model for the integration of environmental factors into the standard MFP measures. In effect, the approaches reflect a case-by-case approach, with the use of different methods depending on the environmental factor under consideration. The purpose of this chapter is to present a broader conceptual model that would facilitate measuring environmentally adjusted agricultural MFP for the types of factors listed above and for others that might be deemed relevant in understanding MFP growth, for example the role of pollination.

7.4 INTEGRATING ECOSYSTEM ACCOUNTING AND GROWTH ACCOUNTING FOR AGRICULTURE

7.4.1 The Analogy between Ecosystem and Produced Capital

In concept, ecosystem accounting provides information that can directly extend current measures of agricultural MFP to incorporate environmental factors. The addition of environmental factors is appropriate in either a value added based approach to measuring MFP or a KLEMS based approach. In cases where land is already included as a capital input, the enhancement provided through ecosystem accounting is to recognize changes in the quality of agricultural land.

The basis for the extension lies in recognizing that the flows of ecosystem services from agricultural land (in line with the flow of ecosystem services from ecosystem assets in Figure 7.1) are directly analogous, in accounting terms, to the capital services that flow from produced capital and which are already included in the standard growth accounting MFP measures.

This analogy to capital services of produced assets generally underlies the development of wealth accounting and the associated theory for the valuation of ecosystems and natural capital (see, for example, Hamilton and Clemens, 1998; Dasgupta and Mäler, 2000; Arrow et al., 2012). However, since these studies have generally focused on balance sheet entries (i.e. wealth) of natural capital and taken measurement of produced capital as given; the more specific question of the consistency of approaches to measuring natural and produced capital has not been considered in the wealth accounting literature.

However, two recent developments have identified this connection. The first arose through the development of the SEEA Central Framework, wherein defining the accounting for depletion of natural resources using an analogous approach to measuring depreciation of fixed capital was applied (see Schreyer and Obst, 2015). This advance in the SEEA Central Framework and the connection to the theory underpinning wealth accounting was recently established in Hamilton (2015). Separately, the research by Fenichel and Abbot (2014) has applied the underlying Jorgenson capital accounting framework to the valuation of natural capital, in essence finding that an analogy between accounting for natural and produced capital exists. In both cases, however, the extension to the environmental adjustment of MFP using ecosystem accounting principles has not been considered.[7] It is this extension that is made here.

7.4.2   Incorporating "Direct" Ecosystem Services into MFP Calculations

The incorporation of ecosystem services into MFP calculations should be considered in a number of stages where different types of ecosystem services are progressively included. The most straightforward inclusion concerns ecosystem services where there is the direct use of an ecosystem by an agricultural unit. Examples include the abstraction of water for irrigation; the pollination of crops by wild pollinators; native grasses eaten by livestock; and the absorption of soil nutrients in plant growth. For each of these types of ecosystem service there is an associated flow entry that reflects the flow of services that can be included in the standard growth accounting formulation.

There are two key challenges in incorporating these ecosystem services. First, there is challenge of understanding and measuring the relationship between the physical flows of ecosystem services and the associated agricultural outputs. Commonly, there are no simple linear relationships involved with the supply of ecosystem services. The flows will be dependent on a range of factors, including the relative condition of the ecosystem asset (and neighbouring assets); the weather patterns that may arise in any given season; and the extent to which produced inputs are used, for example the application of fertilizer and pesticides. However, while the precise articulation of the link between ecosystem services and agricultural output may be difficult to measure, this challenge also arises for produced capital (although perhaps to a lesser extent) whereby assumptions about the link between assets and capital service flows are made following generalized models (OECD, 2001).

The second challenge lies in estimating the cost share relevant for these inputs. Since these ecosystem services flow directly into the production of agricultural outputs that are included in standard measures of industry value added, in concept the value of these inputs should be incorporated implicitly in estimates of the gross operating surplus. It is therefore a matter of partitioning the gross operating surplus between the return to produced capital and the return to ecosystem assets. This is akin to the measurement of resource rent as applied in standard natural resource accounting and also to the valuation of ecosystem services via production function methods (Freeman, 2013).

7.4.3 Example of Incorporating Direct Ecosystem Services

To give a sense of the extended production function to incorporate ecosystem services that underpins the proposal, the following tables provide a stylized example demonstrating the changes that would be reflected in the standard supply and use entries for an apple farmer who utilizes pollination services.

In the standard supply and use table (Table 7.1) no pollination services are recorded and there are simply crop outputs – in this case apples (800) – and purchased intermediate inputs of fertilizer (200) and fuel (150). The estimated industry value added is thus 450 (800–350). The apples are pur-

Table 7.1   Standard supply and use table for an apple farmer

	Apple farmer	Other industries	Household final consumption	Total
Supply table				
Apples	800			800
Apple products		2000		2000
Fertilizer		200		200
Fuel		150		150
Total output (1)	800	2350		3350
Use table				
Apples		800		800
Apple products			2000	2000
Fertilizer	200			200
Fuel	150			150
Total input (2)	350	800	2000	3350
Gross value added (3 = 1–2)	450	1550	na	2000
Labour input: wages and salaries (4)	150	600		750
Gross operating surplus (5 = 3–4)	300	950		1250

Table 7.2   Extended supply and use table for an apple farmer

	Apple farmer	Other industries	Ecosystem asset: forest	Household final consumption	Total
Supply table					
Apples	800				800
Apple products		2000			2000
Fertilizer		200			200
Fuel		150			150
Ecosystem services: pollination			200		200
Total output *(1)*	800	2350	200		3350
Use table					
Apples		800			800
Apple products				2000	2000
Fertilizer	200				200
Fuel	150				150
Ecosystem services: pollination	200				200
Total input *(2)*	550	800	0	2000	3350
Gross value added (3 = 1–2)	250	1550	200	na	2000
Labour input: wages and salaries (4)	150	600	0		750
Gross operating surplus (5 = 3–4)	100	950	200		1250

chased by other industries to produce apple products that are subsequently sold to households (2000). The resulting total gross value added (GVA) is 2000.

In Table 7.2, the supply and use table is extended to record the outputs of pollination services supplied by the neighbouring forest ecosystem and the use of those ecosystem services by the apple farmer. To make the extension, a column is added reflecting the "industry" of the forest ecosystem, and rows are added to record the supply and use of pollination services. The additional output of pollination services is estimated at 200. There are no inputs required to produce the pollination services, and hence the value added of the forest equals its output – i.e. 200.

This additional output recorded in the extended supply and use table must also be recorded as an input to maintain a balance in the table. Thus, in the use table the pollination services are recorded as an input for the apple farmer. Since the output of apples remains at 800 but the inputs have increased, the value added of the apple farmer is reduced from 450 in Table 7.1 to 250 in Table 7.2.

The net effect of these various inclusions is that the value added that was previously attributed solely to the apple farmer is now partitioned across two producing units – the apple farmer and the forest ecosystem. From an MFP perspective, in looking at the column pertaining to the apple farmer, we now see that additional inputs have been recorded – the pollination services – that can now be taken into account in measuring the productivity of the apple farmer.

In this example, the use of pollination services is recorded in a manner analogous to the leasing of machinery from a rental company. An alternative, but entirely consistent, recording might be considered if the ecosystem asset supplying the services was considered to be under the control of the apple farmer. In this case, the flow of ecosystem services would not be recorded as a part of intermediate inputs but rather as a flow of capital services, which would, in effect, be shown in a partitioning of the apple farmer's gross operating surplus, together with the capital services of any machinery and equipment for example.

The benefit of partitioning the ecosystem asset as shown in Table 7.2 is that it facilitates not only understanding inputs to the apple farmer but also the recording of other ecosystem service outputs that would be supplied by the partitioned ecosystem asset, for instance carbon sequestration services by the forest ecosystem. Allowing for recording multiple services and multiple beneficiaries in the measurement of environmentally adjusted MFP is a fundamental aspect of using an ecosystem accounting approach.

7.4.4   Incorporating "Sink" Services

A second stage in the incorporation of ecosystem services is recognizing the role of ecosystem assets in dealing with the residual flows generated as a result of agricultural production. These services are often considered in economics in the context of negative production externalities, and represent the use of the environment as a "sink" for pollutants and waste. Examples of relevant flows include GHG emissions and excess flows of nitrogen and phosphorous into local water catchments. In these cases, the relevant "receiving" ecosystems provide a service to agricultural producers by capturing the residual flows. If ecosystems were not playing this role, costs (reductions in profit) would be incurred by the producer.

Unlike the previous case of direct use, it will be uncommon for the cost of these sink ecosystem services to be incorporated in the market prices for the outputs from agricultural production, and hence the value of the services will not be incorporated into the operating surplus that might serve as a base for estimating the cost share of these inputs. Thus from an accounting perspective it becomes necessary to recognize additional outputs and inputs related to these services. Further, where the release of residuals leads to a decline in the condition of ecosystem assets, it is likely to be appropriate to allocate an amount of degradation, i.e. a cost of natural capital. As noted in the following section, further research is required to understand fully the accounting implications of these proposals.

There is a connection between the description of these sink ecosystem services and the OECD work on environmentally adjusted MFP noted in the previous section (Brandt et al., 2014). In their approach, emissions are treated as a negative output rather than additional input of ecosystem services. Further comparison of the approaches is required, especially with respect to valuation of flows.

7.4.5   Incorporating Broader Benefits Arising from Agricultural Land

A third stage of potential extension of the ecosystem accounting approach is recognizing that there will be a range of positive externalities of agricultural production that could be considered in understanding the full production function and relevant trade-offs. Thus, the incorporation of ecosystem services could be extended to include, for example:

- the carbon sequestration services of farms which provide benefits globally;
- the role that agricultural areas play in the regulation of water flows within a water catchment; and
- the cultural benefits obtained from the good management of agricultural landscapes.

As in the previous stage, the key challenge is estimating the appropriate adjusted measure of agricultural output that reflects the production of these additional services by ecosystem assets managed by agricultural units.

7.4.6   Summary

Overall, the incorporation of ecosystem services into the derivation of MFP should support a more extensive analysis of agricultural production processes. For example, trade-offs between the use of fertilizer and the maintenance of soil fertility (and hence obtaining nutrients from the soil) should become explicit since both become inputs within scope of the system. More broadly, there is thus the potential to reflect, in the measures of MFP, the effect of investments in best practice land management as part of the productivity equation both in the context of measuring agricultural outputs and also in the broader benefits that agricultural areas can be managed to provide. This simply was not possible in a fully integrated manner in the past.

7.5   KEY QUESTIONS FOR FUTURE RESEARCH

It is considered that the broad approach of integrating ecosystem accounting and growth accounting has considerable potential, but there remain important measurement issues to overcome. This section outlines some key research questions.

First, a much more detailed mathematical representation of the conceptual model is needed with regard to the application to MFP measurement. In particular, it will be necessary to take the ecosystem accounting concepts and blend them with the standard capital and growth accounting theory and related index number approaches. An important aspect in this work will be to understand the alignment between ecosystem accounting and the production and consumption theory that underpins growth accounting. It is likely that research in this area will have related benefits in the ongoing research to develop valuation techniques for ecosystem services that are required for national accounting uses.

Second, there are many data – including biophysical data on land cover, water flows, natural resource stocks and measures of ecosystem condition – that need to be brought together to compile environmentally adjusted MFP measures. Ecosystem accounting approaches have only been trialled on a large scale in the UK (UK NEA, 2011), although some important pilot work is being undertaken in a number of locations – including the Netherlands, Indonesia, the Philippines, South Africa, Peru and Australia – and the number of studies is steadily growing (London Group, 2016).[8] Experience to date suggests that progress on ecosystem accounting will generally involve bringing together a wide range of existing data. Consequently, there is the potential to utilize data that are currently applied in the estimation of agricultural models, such as linear programming models (for example, see the modelling in Strappazzon et al., 2002). These models combine information on physical and ecological flows with economic data. Integrating these types of data within an accounting framework would be a positive first step.

Of particular relevance in this regard is the ongoing development and testing of the SEEA for Agriculture, Forestry and Fisheries (SEEA AFF). The SEEA AFF has been under development by the FAO since 2013 as an application of the SEEA Central Framework to the integration of data for assessing the connection between agriculture, forestry and fisheries activity and the associated environmental assets and flows (FAO, 2015) The integration of environmental and economic data envisaged in the SEEA AFF provides the basic information source for compiling extended measures of agricultural MFP using generally available data, and provides a bridge to the implementation of ecosystem accounting for these sectors.

Third, the most challenging area of measurement is likely to be the valuation of ecosystem services such that relevant cost shares within an accounting framework can be determined. Given that ecosystem services are not exchanged on markets, it will be important to advance the testing and implementation of appropriate valuation techniques. A particularly interesting aspect here will be to understand the connections between values for agricultural land and values for associated ecosystem services.

Fourth, an important aspect of the work will be considering spatial detail. Aggregate measures within the ecosystem accounting framework reflect an aggregation of information about different types of ecosystem assets. Thus, while the concepts are applicable at a farm level, it is possible in theory to measure productivity for different regions and for different types of farming operation – e.g. irrigated and rainfed agriculture, cropping and grazing. Building the information set that would support integrated macro and micro measurements of agricultural MFP is an important aspect of the research programme for ecosystem accounting.

Overall, while these are challenging research tasks, the broadening of the MFP framework to incorporate environmental adjustments using ecosystem accounting provides an excellent platform for undertaking an integrated research programme that can utilize findings from many different areas of work.

7.6   CONCLUSION

This chapter provides an introduction to two important fields of national accounting: the measurement of MFP through growth accounting approaches, and the work on environmental-economic accounting. To this point, these two fields have not been connected in any direct sense. Given this lack of connection, the intent of this chapter is to describe how recent developments in environmental-economic accounting described in the SEEA EEA – i.e. the integration of the measurement of ecosystem condition and ecosystem services into national accounts frameworks – might be considered in an MFP context. Improved measurement of agricultural MFP provides a very relevant test case given the direct use of ecosystems and natural capital by the agricultural industry.

Conceptually, the accounting equivalence between ecosystem services in ecosystem accounting and capital services of produced capital used in standard economy wide MFP measurement represents a fundamental insight and is the basis for the potential to extend standard MFP measures. At the same time, there remain important future research questions that must be advanced to consider this extension in more depth and to test the approach in practice. An important avenue for taking forward this research is that ecosystem accounting can be applied at a relatively detailed spatial level, for example at farm or landscape level, and finding suitable test cases at a more detailed level may be a good starting place before taking on the challenges of aggregation to national level.

It is intended that this chapter provides a basis for further exchanges between relevant experts. A key finding from work on the SEEA since 2011 has been the need to bring together experts from a range of disciplines – including economics, statistics, accounting, ecology and geography. The further inclusion of agricultural specialists, such as agronomists and soil scientists, would be particularly relevant in the context of advancing measures of environmentally adjusted agricultural MFP.

NOTES

*   The work in this chapter builds on the conceptual framework for ecosystem accounting established in the United Nations System of Environmental-Economic Accounting Experimental Ecosystem Accounting (SEEA EEA) published in 2014. The authors recognize the important contributions from the experts from numerous disciplines and countries involved in the ecosystem accounting discussions. Further, the chapter builds on discussions at recent workshops on environmentally adjusted multifactor productivity (MFP) measurement held at the OECD (December 2015) and the University of Sydney (February 2016). The authors acknowledge the inputs from experts at these workshops in developing the ideas in this chapter.

1.   This brief history is taken from Obst (2015), which summarizes the longer description in United Nations et al. (2014a).

2.   The third volume focuses on ways in which data organized following the SEEA Central Framework can be applied to the analysis of various policy questions and linked to other datasets. It is not discussed further here.

3.   The references section of the SEEA EEA provides an extensive listing of the literature on which the various aspects of the ecosystem accounting model have been based. This includes research in relation to ecosystem condition, ecosystem services, ecological economics, geospatial statistics and national accounting.

4.   In national accounting degradation, like the depreciation of manufactured assets, is considered a cost against income from production, and hence only the change in asset value that is attributable to the production activity should be deducted. Other changes in value are recorded in the accounts but not as a deduction from income.

5. Note that it is by recognizing ecosystem services as both outputs (of ecosystem assets) and inputs (to farming units) that double counting is avoided. The treatment is exactly analogous to the treatment of outputs and inputs through the standard supply chains recorded in standard input-output tables.
6. For an extensive discussion on environmental valuation techniques see Freeman (2013).
7. It is noted that the work of Brandt et al. (2013) on extended measures of MFP builds, in part, on the developments presented in the SEEA Central Framework and Schreyer and Obst (2015).
8. Although a complete inventory is not available, the authors are aware of ecosystem accounting work underway covering more than 30 countries, both developed and developing, including both national initiatives and projects co-ordinated by the World Bank, the UN, the EU and Conservation International. See www.wavespartnership.org.

REFERENCES

Ahmad, Y.J., S. El Serafy and E. Lutz (eds) (1989), *Environmental Accounting For Sustainable Development*, Washington, DC: World Bank.

Arrow, K., P. Dasgupta, L.H. Goulder, K.J. Mumford and K. Oleson (2012), 'Sustainability and the measurement of wealth', *Environmental and Development Economics*, **17**, 317–353.

Atkinson, G. and C. Obst (2016), 'Defining exchange values for non-market transactions in ecosystem accounting using environmental economics', Paper prepared for the Policy and Technical Expert Committee of the World Bank WAVES program, April, Washington DC.

Australian Bureau of Statistics (ABS) (2016), *Australian System of National Accounts: Concepts, Sources and Methods 2015*, ABS cat no. 5216.0, Canberra: ABS.

Australian Bureau of Statistics (2015), *Estimates of Industry Multi-Factor Productivity*, ABS cat no. 5260, Canberra: ABS.

Ball, E., S.L. Wang and R. Nehring (2014), 'Productivity and economic growth in U.S. agriculture', Economic Research Service, U.S. Department of Agriculture.

Banzhaf, S. and J. Boyd (2012), 'The architecture and measurement of an ecosystem services index', *Sustainability*, **4**, 430–461.

Bartelmus, P. (1987), 'Beyond GDP: new approaches to applied statistics', *Review of Income and Wealth*, **33**(4), 347–358.

Brandt, N., P. Schreyer and V. Zipperer (2013), 'Productivity measurement with natural capital', OECD Economic Department working papers, no. 1092, Paris: OECD.

Brandt, N., P. Schreyer and V. Zipperer (2014), 'Productivity measurement with natural capital and bad outputs', OECD Economic Department working papers, no. 1154, Paris: OECD.

Cahill, S. and T. Rich (2012), 'Measurement of Canadian agricultural productivity growth', in *Productivity Growth in Agriculture: An International Perspective*, K.O. Fuglie, S.L. Wang and V.E. Ball (eds), Wallingford: CAB International.

Dasgupta, P. and K.-G. Mäler (2000), 'Net national product, wealth and social wellbeing', *Environmental and Development Economics*, **5**(1), 69–93.

European Commission (EC) and Eurostat (2002), *The European Framework for Integrated Environmental and Economic Accounting for Forests: IEEAF, 2002*, Luxembourg: Office for Official Publications of the European Communities.

European Commission, International Monetary Fund, Organisation for Economic Co-operation and Development, United Nations and World Bank (2003), *Handbook of National Accounting: Integrated Environmental and Economic Accounting 2003*, New York: United Nations.

European Commission, International Monetary Fund, Organisation for Economic Co-operation and Development, United Nations and World Bank (2009), *System of National Accounts 2008*, New York: United Nations.

Fenichel, E.P. and J.K. Abbott (2014), 'Natural capital: from metaphor to measurement', *Journal of the Association of Environmental and Resource Economists*, **1**(1), 1–27.

Food and Agriculture Organization of the United Nations and United Nations (FAO) (2004), *Handbook of National Accounting: Integrated Environmental and Economic Accounting for Fisheries (SEEA Fisheries)*, New York: United Nations.

Food and Agriculture Organization of the United Nations and United Nations (2015), *System of Environmental-Economic Accounting for Agriculture, Forestry and Fisheries*, Consultation draft. Available at http://unstats.un.org/unsd/envaccounting/aff/chapterList.asp.

Freeman, A.M. (2013), *The Measurement of Environmental and Resource Values: Theory and Methods* (3rd edition), Washington, DC: RFF Press.

Hamilton, K. (2015), 'Measuring sustainability in the UN system of environmental-economic accounting', *Environment and Resource Economics*, May, doi: 10.1007/210640-015-9924-y.

Hamilton, K. and M. Clemens (1998), 'Genuine saving in developing countries', *World Bank Economic Review*, **13**(2), 333–356.

Hoang V. (2015), 'Traditional and environmental agricultural total factor productivity in OECD countries', Paper presented to the OECD Expert Workshop: Measuring Environmentally Adjusted TFP for Agriculture TFP, December.

Jorgenson, D. (1963), 'Capital theory and investment behavior', *American Economic Review*, **53**, 247–259.

Kuosmanen, T. (2015), 'Green productivity in agriculture: a critical synthesis', Paper presented to the OECD Expert Workshop: Measuring Environmentally Adjusted TFP for Agriculture TFP, December.

London Group (2016), Papers prepared for the 22nd meeting of the London Group on Environmental Accounting, Oslo, Norway, September. http://unstats.un.org/unsd/envaccounting/londongroup/meeting22.asp.

Millennium Ecosystem Assessment (2003), *Ecosystems and Human Well-Being: A Framework for Assessment*. Washington, DC: Island Press.

Obst, C. (2015), 'Reflections on advances in accounting for natural capital', *Sustainability Accounting, Management and Policy Journal*, **6**(3), 315–339.

Odum, E.P. and G.W. Barrett (2005), *Fundamentals of Ecology* (5th edition), Belmont, CA: Thompson Brooks/Cole.

OECD (2001), *Measuring Productivity: Measurement of Aggregate and Industry-Level Productivity Growth*, Paris: OECD.

OECD (2014), *Green Growth Indicators 2014*, OECD Green Growth Studies, Paris: OECD, doi: http://dx.doi.org/10.1787/9789264202030-en.

OECD (2015), OECD Expert Workshop: Measuring Environmentally Adjusted Total Factor Productivity for Agriculture, December 2015, Paris. www.oecd.org/tad/events/environmentally-adjusted-total-factor-productivity-in-agriculture.htm.

Schreyer, P. and C. Obst (2015), 'Towards complete balance sheets in the national accounts: the case of mineral and energy resources', *OECD Green Growth Papers*, 2015–02.

Solow, R. (1957), 'Technical change and the aggregate production function', *Review of Economics and Statistics*, **39**, 312–320.

Statistics Canada (2015), *Multifactor Productivity Growth Estimates and Industry Productivity Database, 1961 to 2013*, Ottawa: Statistics Canada.

Strappazzon, L., M. Eigenraam, R. Wimalasuriya and G. Stoneham (2002), 'Estimating research benefits when there is input and output substitution: an applied analysis', Economics Branch, Victorian Department of Natural Resources and Environment, Melbourne: Victorian Government.

TEEB (2010), *The Economics of Ecosystems and Biodiversity: Mainstreaming the Economics of Nature – a Synthesis of the Approach, Conclusions and Recommendations of TEEB*, Geneva: UNEP.

TEEB (2015), *TEEB for Agriculture and Food: Towards a Global Study on the Economics of Eco-Agri-Food Systems*, Geneva: UNEP.

UK NEA (2011), *The UK National Ecosystem Assessment: Synthesis of Key Findings*, Cambridge: UNEP-WCMC.

UN (1992), *Agenda 21: Programme of Action for Sustainable Development*, UN Conference on Environment and Development, Rio de Janeiro, 3–14 June 1992, New York: United Nations.

United Nations (1993), *Handbook of National Accounting: Integrated Environmental and Economic Accounting, Interim Version*, New York: United Nations.

United Nations (2012), *SEEA-Water: System of Environmental-Economic Accounting for Water*, New York: United Nations.

United Nations, European Commission, Food and Agricultural Organization of the United Nations, International Monetary Fund, Organisation for Economic Co-operation and Development and World Bank (2014a), *System of Environmental-Economic Accounting 2012: Central Framework*, New York: United Nations.

United Nations, European Commission, Food and Agricultural Organization of the United Nations, International Monetary Fund, Organisation for Economic Co-operation and Development and World Bank (2014b), *System of Environmental-Economic Accounting 2012: Experimental Ecosystem Accounting*, New York: United Nations.

United Nations, European Commission, Food and Agricultural Organization of the United Nations, Organisation for Economic Co-operation and Development and World Bank (2014c), *System of Environmental-Economic Accounting 2012: Applications and Extensions*, New York: United Nations.

Zhao, S, Y. Sheng and E.M. Gray (2012), 'Measuring productivity of the Australian broadacre and dairy industries: concepts, methodology and data', in K.O. Fuglie, S.L. Wang and V.E. Ball (eds), *Productivity Growth in Agriculture: An International Perspective*, Wallingford: CAB International.

8. Climate adjusted productivity on Australian cropping farms

Neal Hughes and Kenton Lawson*

8.1 INTRODUCTION

Climatic conditions are the single most important factor affecting the productivity of Australian cropping farms (Kokic et al., 2006, Hughes et al., 2011). This is probably true for agriculture in many parts of the world, but Australia's climate is particularly variable, with lower mean rainfall and higher rainfall variability than other comparable regions (Peel et al., 2004). As a result, Australian agriculture is subject to more revenue volatility than almost any other country in the world (Keogh, 2012).

The Australian Bureau of Agricultural and Resource Economics and Sciences (ABARES) estimates total factor productivity (TFP) for Australian farms with data from its long-running survey programmes. These TFP figures measure the technical performance of the industry over time, including gains achieved through adoption of new technologies and improved management practices. As such, TFP is often used to evaluate agricultural research and development activities.

Previous studies have shown that these farm productivity estimates are strongly correlated with climate variables (Kokic et al., 2006; Hughes et al., 2011). In particular, farm TFP indexes are subject to large decreases in drought years. These climate effects tend to obscure underlying trends in farm technical performance. Noise in the data due to climate variation makes it difficult to identify short-term trends in productivity. Instead, attention is usually placed on long-term trends (i.e. 10–20 years), with an implicit assumption that climate effects average out over this time scale. However, this approach becomes problematic in the presence of climate change.

According to the Commonwealth Scientific and Industrial Research Organisation (CSIRO) and the Australian Bureau of Meteorology (BOM), climate change models predict large changes in the global distribution of rainfall. In Australia, lower mean rainfall is predicted for much of southern Australia. Greater climatic volatility is also predicted, particularly more frequent and more severe droughts. Large changes have already been observed over the last 10 to 15 years, including higher average temperatures and lower winter rainfall in parts of south-western and south-eastern Australia (CSIRO and BOM, 2014). In order to provide an unbiased measure of farm productivity, it is now necessary to control for the effects of climate variability and change.

This study presents a method of controlling for exogenous climate effects on firm level TFP indexes. The approach is applied to the case of Australian cropping farms, but may also be of relevance to other industries where productivity is affected by exogenous changes in weather conditions. The approach is best suited to large spatio-temporal data sets, where firm TFP is observed for extended time periods across a range of locations.

The approach involves the estimation of predictive models using non-parametric (machine learning) regression methods. Spatio-temporal data on productivity is matched to climate observation data (rainfall, temperature, etc.) in order to develop models that can predict productivity conditional on climate conditions. These models can then be used to generate estimates of productivity under long-run average climate conditions.

This method is applied to the Australian broadacre cropping industry, using ABARES farm survey data for the period 1977–78 to 2014–15 and climate data from the Australian Water Availability Project (AWAP) (Raupach et al., 2009). Estimates of climate adjusted productivity are presented, along with estimates of the effects of climate on productivity and changes in the sensitivity of farms to climate over the period. These results provide a clearer picture of how the cropping industry is performing and adapting in response to the unfolding climate change trends within the region.

8.2   PREVIOUS RESEARCH

8.2.1   Productivity and Climate

Previous work has demonstrated a strong correlation between Australian cropping farm productivity and climate indicators (Alexander and Kokic, 2005; Kokic et al., 2005, 2006; Hughes et al., 2011; Sheng et al., 2011). Kokic et al. (2006) regressed cropping farm TFP indexes against a range of predictors, including a regional wheat water stress index as a proxy for moisture availability. Moisture availability was found to be the dominant factor influencing TFP. Estimates of average TFP adjusted for moisture showed evidence of a decline in productivity growth beginning in the late 1990s.

Hughes et al. (2011) combined output and input indexes for cropping farms, with spatial climate data including rainfall and temperature. The study presented estimates of productivity growth adjusted for climate effects, which were then decomposed further into technical change (expansion of the production frontier) and technical efficiency change (movement of farms relative to the frontier). This study found that a deterioration in climate conditions contributed to a decline in productivity growth over the post-2000 period. However, after adjusting for climate effects, a slowdown in productivity growth was still observed. This slowdown was attributed to a gradual decline in the rate of technical change.

Sheng et al. (2011) looked at the effect of climate on aggregate productivity, using a wheat water stress index. After controlling for climate effects, a structural break (i.e., a slowdown) in productivity growth was still observed. This slowdown was attributed to a decline in research and development investment.

A number of other studies have examined the effect of climate on broadacre farm productivity in Western Australia (Salim and Islam, 2010; Che et al., 2012; Islam et al., 2014; Kingwell, 2014). Islam et al. and Kingwell et al. employed index number methods, Che et al. a stochastic frontier model, and Salim and Islam a TFP regression model. A common finding is that Western Australian broadacre farms have managed to offset the effects of adverse climate conditions with productivity improvements. Kingwell et al. found that increases in farm scale have been a key driver of these gains.

8.2.2   Recent Climate Trends

In recent times, increased attention has been placed on observed climate trends and their effects on agriculture. Several studies have documented changes in Australian climate over the last 15 to 20 years, including a reduction in average winter rainfall in southern Australia and general increases in temperature.

Increasingly, these trends are being linked with long-term climate change. For example, Cai et al. (2012) and the South Eastern Australian Climate Initiative (2012) concluded that the decline in winter rainfall in southern Australia is at least partly explained by a climate change induced expansion of the tropical zone/contraction of the sub-tropical (higher winter rainfall) zone. Nidumolu et al. (2012) and the Australian Export Grains Innovation Council (AEGIC, 2016) discuss these recent climate trends in the context of Australian broadacre cropping zones. AEGIC documents a contraction of the traditional Australian winter cropping zone over the period post-2000 consistent with the contraction of the sub-tropical zone.

8.2.3   Crop Yields and Climate

There exists a large body of scientific research on the effect of climate on crop yields in Australia. Much of this literature involves biophysical modelling of crop growth, such as the Agricultural Production Systems sIMulator (APSIM).[1] These models have frequently been applied to evaluate the effect of long-term climate change predictions on crop yield (Potgieter et al., 2013; Ghahramani et al., 2015). A number of previous studies have linked these biophysical models with economic models (Nelson et al., 2007, 2010).

Research has also focused on the effects of observed climate on crop yields (Stephens et al., 2011; Hochman et al., 2017). Stephens et al. found that declining climate conditions had a significant negative effect on wheat yields during the 2000s. However, even after controlling for these climate effects, a significant decline in the rate of growth in wheat yield was still observed.

More recently, Hochman et al. (2017) found that climate effects have reduced potential wheat yield in Australia by around 27 per cent since 1990. Most of this decline was attributed to reductions in rainfall and rising temperatures, while elevated CO_2 concentrations prevented a further 4 per cent loss. This climate effect was found to be offset by productivity improvements such that actual yields remained relatively constant.

8.3   DATA

8.3.1   Farm Data

Farm-level data are drawn from the Australian Agricultural and Grazing Industries Surveys (AAGIS) for the period 1977–78 to 2014–15. The data provide coverage of broadacre farms across all regions of Australia for five industry categories: cropping specialists, mixed-cropping livestock, beef, sheep and sheep-beef. For this study, attention is limited to cropping and mixed farms.

A total of 49,159 farm observations were obtained from the AAGIS data, with 20,689 classified as either cropping or mixed farms. The sample was further reduced to eliminate outliers and farms with inadequate location data. The final sample contains 20,508 observations, an average of around 555 per year. The data set variables are defined in Table 8.1.

Annual sample means for selected variables are shown in Figure 8.1. Key trends of note include:

Table 8.1   Variables included in the farm data set

Variable name	Description
TFP	Farm level total factor productivity (TFP) index, defined as *OUTPUT/INPUT*
INPUT	Farm level aggregate input index
OUTPUT	Farm level aggregate output index
YEAR	Financial year
INDUSTRY	Industry code (1 = cropping, 2 = mixed)
LAT	Latitude
LONG	Longitude
GRDC	Grains Research and Development Corporation (GRDC) region (1 = North, 2 = South, 3 = West)
AREA	Average of opening and closing land area operated (ha)
LIVESTOCK	Farm livestock contribution to total input: the ratio of a livestock quantity index (an aggregation of sheep, beef and other livestock numbers) to *INPUT*
AGE	Age of the farm operator / manager (years)
INVEST	Farm capital investment per unit land: the ratio of net capital expenditure (excluding land transactions) to *AREA* ($ per ha)
LAND_PRICE	Price of farm land ($ per ha)
IRRIG	1 if the farm reported any irrigation activity in that year

- the 'slowdown' in cropping farm TFP growth during the 1990s;
- a similar slowdown in the rate of wheat yield improvement;
- increasing farm scale – growth in average land areas and wheat areas;
- greater cropping specialization/reduced livestock activity, increasing average farmer age; and
- large increases in land prices and in on-farm investment from the mid-2000s.

8.3.2   Climate Data

When selecting the appropriate climate variables to include, the researcher faces a trade-off between model-based and data-driven approaches. At one end of the spectrum there are biophysical simulation models – such as APSIM – which predict crop or pasture growth as a function of climate factors and farm management practices. At the other extreme we could rely on raw weather station observations. Data-driven approaches exploit all available information, but may suffer from a high degree of *noise*,

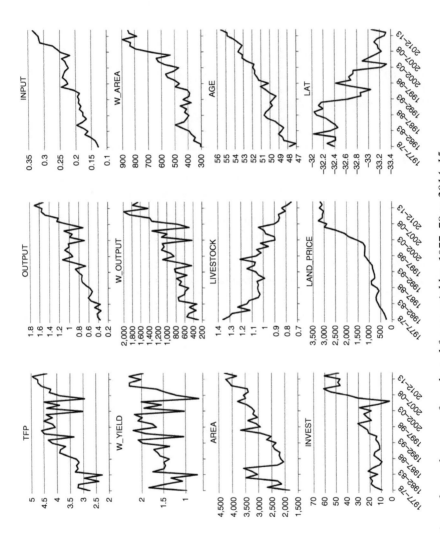

Figure 8.1   Annual sample means for selected farm variables, 1977–78 to 2014–15

178

whereas model-based approaches involve less noise but involve additional assumptions that may introduce *bias*.

This study follows a data-driven approach, drawing climate data from the Australian Water Availability Project (AWAP) (Raupach et al., 2009). The AWAP data set is based on weather station data but involves basic modelling assumptions, including interpolation to estimate rainfall at locations between weather stations and water balance modelling to estimate soil moisture.

AWAP provides data across Australia on a 0.05 degree (around 5km) grid. Farm-level climate variables were obtained by matching the spatial coordinates for each farm to the AWAP grids. The following climate variables were obtained for each farm in the sample:

> *RAIN* – precipitation (mm)
> *TMAX* – average maximum temperature (degrees C)
> *TMIN* – average minimum temperature (degrees C)
> *UMOIST* – upper layer relative soil moisture (fraction 0–1)
> *LMOIST* – lower layer relative soil moisture (fraction 0–1).

Monthly data for each variable were matched to each farm for the period 1900 to 2014–15. These monthly observations were then aggregated into various periods of relevance to broadacre farms:

> *WINTER* – winter cropping season (April to October)
> *SUMMER* – summer cropping season (November to March)
> *SUMMER_LAG* – previous summer cropping season
> *YEAR* – financial year (July to June)
> *ONE_YEAR_LAG* – previous financial year
> *TWO_YEAR_LAG* – previous two financial years
> *WIN* – winter quarter (June to August)
> *SPR* – spring quarter (September to November)
> *SUM* – summer quarter (December to February)
> *AUT* – autumn quarter (April to May).

Variables were constructed for each combination of climate measures (*RAIN, TMAX*, etc.) and each time window (*WINTER, SUMMER . . .*), resulting in a total of 60 climate variables (*WINTER_RAIN, SUMMER_TMAX . . .*). These 60 variables are constructed for each farm location and for each financial year over the period 1914–15 to 2014–15.

8.4   METHOD

8.4.1   The Effect of Climate on Productivity

Climate variability can affect farm productivity in two ways:

- Output effects – for a given level of inputs, climate will affect the amount of farm outputs produced (e.g. a decline in rainfall will reduce crop yield).
- Input effects – input decisions will depend to some extent on prevailing climate conditions and vice versa (e.g. a farmer may reduce input use in anticipation of adverse conditions).

The effect of climate on farm production can be complex. In Australia, moisture is the primary limiting factor on crop growth. However, the effect of climate on crop growth will depend on many variables (rainfall, soil type, evaporation, temperature and farm management practices and so on), each of which may be subject to complex non-linear interactions.

On the input side, farmers make decisions subject to expected climate conditions. In practice, farmers make input decisions at different stages across the year, subject to different information about current and future climate. Some input decisions may occur late in the year with knowledge of final climate conditions, while others may be made early (i.e. at crop planting) subject to uncertainty over seasonal conditions. While farmer expectations of climate are unobservable, they are likely to be correlated with actual conditions. As such, all variable farm inputs are likely to be correlated with observed climate data.

8.4.2   A Data-Driven Approach

To control for the effect of climate on productivity we estimate a regression of the form:

$$Y_{it} = g(Z_{it}, X_{it}, t) \tag{8.1}$$

where Y_{it} is the *TFP* index for farm i in period t, Z_{it} is a vector of farm specific climate variables, X_{it} a vector of farm characteristics and g is an unknown functional form to be estimated. Here Z_{it} is a subset of the 60 climate variables defined above and X_{it} includes the variables *LAT, LONG, AREA, LIVESTOCK, AGE* and *IRRIG*.

Given the complexities outlined above, it is difficult to know the appropriate parametric form for the function g. We adopt a 'data-driven' approach, borrowing from the field of machine learning (see Varian, 2014). Here non-parametric regression methods are used to estimate g without making prior assumptions about the functional form.

In this study, we employ two popular 'regression tree' based methods: 'random forests' (Breiman, 2001) and 'gradient boosted regression trees' (Friedman, 2002) as implemented in the Python machine learning software package scikit-learn (Pedregosa et al., 2011). Large-scale empirical testing has found that well-calibrated Gradient Boosted Regression Trees (GBRT) models consistently outperform other standard machine learning algorithms including random forests (Caruana and Niculescu-Mizil, 2006).

In order to evaluate the accuracy of our models, we employ standard out-of-sample testing (cross-validation) techniques, specifically ten-fold cross validation. Here, the data is divided into ten sub-samples. At each step, nine of the sub-samples are used to fit the model, and one is withheld as the testing set. This process is repeated ten times, so that each sub-sample is used for testing once. The final score (cross-validated R^2) is taken as the mean of the scores from each sub-sample.

This study employs a recursive feature elimination method to select an appropriate subset of climate variables. The process begins by estimating the model with the full set of climate variables. The performance of the model is assessed by cross-validation, and subsequently the climate variables with the lowest importance (the bottom 5th percentile) are eliminated. This process is repeated for 12 iterations. The final set of climate variables is that which achieves the highest cross-validated performance score.

GBRT and random forest models involve a number of meta-parameters that need to be 'tuned' to maximize performance, including the *number of samples per split*, the *number of trees* and, in the case of GBRT, the *learning rate*. A search of the meta-parameter space was completed as summarized in Figure 8.2, with the final values being those that maximized the cross-validated performance measure.

8.4.3 Model Testing

The two non-parametric methods were compared against a benchmark quadratic regression model fit by Ordinary Least Squares (OLS), using a set of climate variables including *WINTER_RAIN, SUMMER_RAIN, SUMMER_LAG_RAIN, WINTER_TMAX, SUMMER_TMAX, WINTER_TMIN, SUMMER_TMIN*. GBRT achieved a cross-validated R^2 of 0.324, compared with random forests at 0.294 and the quadratic model at 0.199. On this basis GBRT was selected as the preferred regression method.

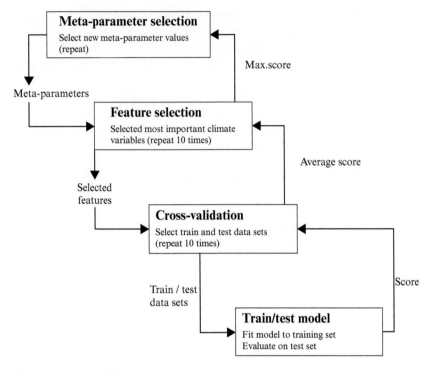

Figure 8.2   Model estimation process

While these cross-validated R^2 scores may seem low, they need to be considered in the particular context. Firstly, the in-sample R^2 of the final model is much higher, at around 0.6. Secondly, this farm level data set is subject to a high degree of heterogeneity and noise. When the cross-validated predictions are averaged over the sample (for each year), the model accounts for over 98 per cent of annual variation in TFP.

8.4.4   Climate Adjusted Productivity

Once an estimate for the function g is obtained, we can generate predictions of farm performance measures under differing climate conditions:

$$\hat{Y}_{it}^{s} = g(Z_{is}, X_{it}, t) \tag{8.2}$$

Here $\hat{Y}_{it}^{s}$ is an estimate of what farm performance (i.e. TFP) would have been for farm i under the climate conditions of a given year s. This type of counterfactual prediction can be used to isolate the effects of climate variation for particular years. In particular, we can define climate adjusted productivity Y_{it} as:

$$\overline{Y}_{it} = 1/101 \sum_{s=1915}^{s=2015} \hat{Y}_{it}^s \tag{8.3}$$

That is, we predict farm performance for each observation under the climate conditions prevailing for each of the last 101 years, and then take the average across those 101 years. $\overline{Y}_{it}$ is then a measure of the performance of farm i in period t under long-run average climate conditions. Note that Y_{it} controls for temporal variation in climate (annual variability and climate change), but does not control for persistent spatial differences in climate (i.e. lower rainfall in particular areas).[2]

In addition, we also define Y_{it}^{dry} and Y_{it}^{wet} as the 5th and 95th percentiles of $\hat{Y}_{it}^s$ for each observation: Y_{it}^{dry} and Y_{it}^{wet} measure the performance of farms under unfavourable and favourable conditions, respectively, as opposed to Y_{it}, which measures performance under average conditions.

Next we define the climate effect index C_{it} as:

$$C_{it} = \hat{Y}_{it}^t / \overline{Y}_{it} \tag{8.4}$$

Here C_{it} measures the total effect of climate on the productivity of farm i for year t. For each observation we also define C_{it}^s as the effect of year s climate conditions on farm i in year t. As before, we also define C_{it}^{dry} and C_{it}^{dry} as the 5th and 95th percentiles of C_{it}^s for each observation: C_{it}^{dry}, for example, is a measure of the sensitivity of a farm to adverse climate conditions (e.g. the effect of a 1 in 20 year drought). Note that given the nature of the model, this sensitivity to climate can change over time.

In the results section, farm level estimates are presented mostly as simple annual averages, for example:

$$Y_t = 1/n \sum_{i=1}^{n} Y_{it} \tag{8.5}$$

8.4.5 Decomposing Climate Adjusted Productivity

The estimated models can be also used to decompose climate adjusted productivity further, in order to isolate the effect of technology change (time t), the effects of changes in the spatial distribution of sampled farms (spatial coordinates *LAT* and *LONG*) and the effect of changes in farm control variables (farm land area *AREA*, the extent of grazing activity *LIVESTOCK* and farmer age *AGE*). To do this, two alternative sets of model predictions are generated. One set is where the year is held constant (at 2015):

$$\hat{Y}_{it}^{2015} = g(\mathbf{Z}_{is}, \mathbf{X}_{it}, 2015) \tag{8.6}$$

Here $\hat{Y}_{it}^{2015}$ predicts the productivity of each farm in each year s climate conditions, but with 2015 technology. The other set of predictions holds both the year (technology) and other farm control variables (*AREA, LIVESTOCK, AGE*) constant:

$$\hat{\bar{Y}}_{it}^{2015} = g(\mathbf{Z}_{is}, \overline{\mathbf{X}}_{it}, 2015) \tag{8.7}$$

Here $\mathbf{X}_{it}$ is as defined previously, but with variables *AREA, LIVESTOCK* and *AGE* for each farm replaced with a long-run average value. For *AGE* the long-run average value is simply the long-run average sample mean. For the other variables, the long-run average value is location specific, based on a model fit by GBRT.

Indexes are generated for these new sets of predictions following the same method described above. The effects of changes in farm location (*SPACE*) are given by the sample average of $\hat{\bar{Y}}_{it}^{2015}$ (where the only variables allowed to change over time are *LAT* and *LONG*). Given this, the effects of other farm controls (denoted by *OTHER* and including *AREA, LIVESTOCK, AGE*, etc.) and technological change (denoted by *TIME*) are then defined as:

$$SPACE_t = \hat{\bar{Y}}_t^{2015} \tag{8.8}$$

$$OTHER_t = \hat{Y}_t^{2015} - SPACE_t \tag{8.9}$$

$$TIME_t = \hat{Y}_t^{2015} - SPACE_t - OTHER_t \tag{8.10}$$

8.5   RESULTS

8.5.1   Climate Adjusted Productivity

Average climate adjusted productivity for cropping farms is shown in Figure 8.3 and Table 8.2.

After controlling for climate effects, the well-documented slowdown in productivity is apparent, with productivity growth decreasing considerably post-1993–94. However, a positive story also emerges, with evidence of a resurgence in productivity growth in recent years. After controlling for climate, productivity growth has averaged over 1 per cent per year since 2006–07. This productivity growth has helped the cropping sector to offset the effects of a deterioration in average climate conditions since 2000.

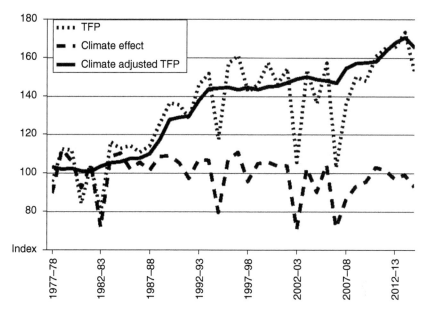

Figure 8.3   Average climate adjusted productivity, 1977–78 to 2014–15

Table 8.2   Average annual growth in climate-adjusted productivity for selected periods, regions and industries

	1977–78 to 1993–94	1993–94 to 2006–07	2006–07 to 2014–15	1977–78 to 2014–15
All cropping	2.09	0.05	1.10	1.16
Crop specialists	2.47	0.01	1.30	1.34
Mixed farms	1.80	0.14	0.72	0.98
NSW	1.92	−0.40	1.49	1.01
VIC	2.01	0.47	1.01	1.25
QLD	2.43	0.04	1.59	1.40
SA	2.45	0.16	0.74	1.27
WA	1.83	0.14	0.54	0.95
Southern GRDC	2.12	0.20	0.98	1.20
Northern GRDC	2.39	−0.21	1.54	1.29
Western GRDC	1.79	0.23	0.45	0.95

The results demonstrate the importance of controlling for climate when measuring agricultural productivity. These trends are difficult to observe in the underlying TFP data, given annual variability and the longer-term deterioration in average climate conditions.

The results suggest that the vast majority of productivity growth in the cropping sector has occurred within two key periods: 1987–88 to 1993–94 (with average growth of around 4 per cent per year) and 2010–11 to 2013–14 (around 2 per cent per year). Together these periods account for 93 per cent of the total productivity gain between 1977–78 and 2014. A very similar pattern is observed in Australian wheat yields using the same data sources and methodology (Hughes et al., 2017).

At a regional level, the productivity rebound since 2006–07 has been strongest in the northern Grains Research and Development Corporation (GRDC) region and lowest in the western GRDC region (Table 8.2). In line with previous studies (e.g. Hughes et al., 2011) we also find that cropping specialists typically outperform mixed cropping farms.

8.5.2   Potential Causes of Productivity Trends

The causes of the productivity slowdown post-1993–94 have been considered in a number of previous studies. Sheng et al. (2011) point to a decline in agricultural research and development investment, while Jackson (2010) identified a range of other factors, including the loss of a profitable break crop and a shift in research priorities away from productivity enhancement.

Another potential cause is farmers' terms of trade (the ratio of output to input prices). As discussed in Hughes et al. (2011), productivity tends to be inversely related to the terms of trade: farmers have an incentive to improve productivity in response to terms of trade decline. The average terms of trade for grain farms declined consistently between 1980 and 1991, but have remained relatively stable since (Hughes et al., 2017).

The causes of the recent rebound in productivity growth remain an open question. A partial explanation can be found in recent increases in farm investment. Average farm capital investment (e.g. in machinery and equipment) has increased significantly on a per hectare basis since 2006–07 (see Figure 8.1). This followed a dramatic rise in farm land prices, beginning around 2002, which allowed many farms to increase debt levels in order to finance new investment (ABARES, 2016). Further, increases in investment have been highest in the northern GRDC region (where productivity gains since 2006–07 have been highest) and lowest in the western region (where productivity gains since 2006–07 have been lowest).

As Stephens et al. (2011) note, the slowdown in productivity in the mid-1990s coincided with a shift in climate conditions (including the 1994–95 drought year and subsequent 'Millennium' drought), while the resurgence has more or less coincided with the end of drought conditions. This observation suggests a possible, indirect effect of climate on productivity. For example, a run of poor climate years might limit the capacity or willingness of farmers to innovate, by worsening their financial position or making them more pessimistic about the future.

However, the above results control for lagged climate conditions (up to two years prior) so that persistent effects of drought should already be taken into account. In addition, trends in the financial position of cropping farms are inconsistent with this story, with high equity ratios during the late 1990s and early 2000s in the midst of the productivity slowdown (Martin et al., 2014). Further, while the 1994–95 drought was followed by a period of low growth, the 1982–83 and 2006–07 droughts were both followed by periods of strong growth.

8.5.3   Climate Effects on Productivity

Figure 8.4 shows the average effect of climate on TFP since 2000 (relative to the period 1914–15 to 2014–15). Results for other time periods are summarized in Table 8.3. The results show a significant deterioration in climate conditions for Australian cropping farms since the mid-1990s.

The decline in conditions has been most pronounced in southern Australia, particularly in southern New South Wales (NSW) and in the northern parts of the western GRDC region. Relative to the long-run average, the biggest decline has been in the western GRDC region (8.2 per cent since 2000). However, relative to the period 1977–78 to 1993–94 the decline has been as dramatic, or worse in NSW and Victoria (VIC), given the period 1977–78 to 1993–94 was significantly above average in these regions.

Figure 8.5 shows how the sensitivity of farms to climate variation has changed over time.

Climate sensitivity (as measured by the gap between productivity in representative 'wet' and 'dry' years) decreased between 1977–78 and 1989–90, then increased until around 2005–06. Since 2007–08 the sensitivity of farms to climate variability has decreased significantly.

These results are consistent with previous observations on productivity in the cropping sector during the 1990s (Stephens et al., 2011). During this period productivity gains were associated with increases in intensification (i.e. higher input use, particularly fertilizers), increased specialization in cropping and earlier planting times. These changes helped farms to

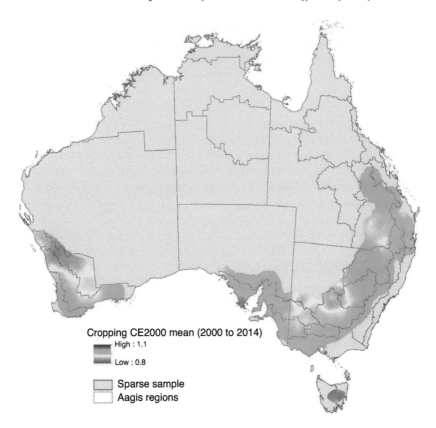

Cropping CE2000 mean (2000 to 2014)
High : 1.1
Low : 0.8

Sparse sample
Aagis regions

Figure 8.4   Map of climate effect on productivity since 2000–01

increase productivity in good years, but also increased exposure to negative climate shocks.

As Stephens et al. (2011: iv) noted:

> In the four southern mainland States the technology of the 1980s and 1990s was appropriate for the climate resources, but an abrupt change to a drier and more variable climate imposed severe constraints on technology which has limited yield increases. In fact, it appears that the very factors that underpinned record yield increases in the 1990s produced a cropping system that was vulnerable to the changed climate experienced in the 2000s. High rates of nitrogenous fertilisers, early sowing and higher adoption of grain legumes and oilseeds were all restricted with unfavourable conditions and record levels of yield variability. Modern cropping systems were also vulnerable to frosts, especially in southern Western Australia where frost frequency and severity appeared to increase. Consequently, the interaction between technology and climate reached record levels in the 2000s after a minimum in the 1990s.

Table 8.3 *Percentage change in average annual climate effect (TFP) for selected periods, regions and industries*

	1977–78 to 1993–94	1993–94 to 2014–15	2000–01 to 2014–15	1977–78 to 2014–15
All cropping	2.37	−2.76	−4.71	−0.70
Crop specialists	2.98	−2.56	−5.04	−0.39
Mixed farms	1.95	−3.04	−4.45	−0.97
NSW	4.69	−1.96	−4.78	0.57
VIC	4.06	−3.19	−4.67	−0.31
QLD	1.15	−4.27	−4.92	−1.74
SA	1.10	−1.76	−1.20	−0.45
WA	−0.15	−3.60	−7.63	−2.29
Southern GRDC	2.88	−2.60	−4.21	−0.40
Northern GRDC	3.45	−2.64	−4.07	−0.12
Western GRDC	−0.10	−3.89	−8.20	−2.45

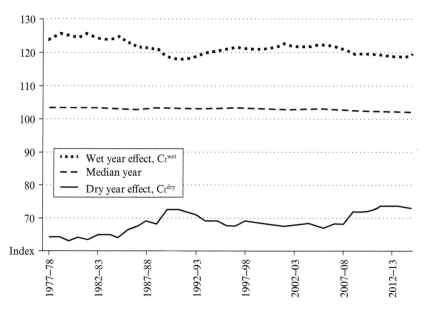

Figure 8.5 *Effect of dry and wet years on TFP, 1977–78 to 2014–15*

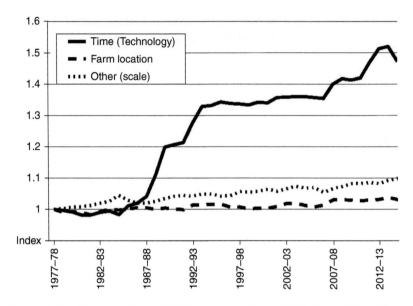

Figure 8.6   Climate adjusted TFP decomposition, 1977–78 to 2014–15

8.5.4 Decomposing Climate Adjusted Productivity

Figure 8.6 shows the results of a decomposition of climate adjusted productivity. Here the effects assigned to time (notionally related to technological change) are isolated from the effects of other control variables (including *AREA*, *LIVESTOCK* and *AGE*) and changes in the location of sampled farms. The time (i.e. technology) index shows a clear pattern, with essentially all productivity gains occurring within two periods: 1984–95 to 1993–94 and 2006–07 to 2013–14.

Changes in control variables (driven predominantly by scale effects) have provided consistent gains in productivity, accounting for around 15 per cent of total productivity growth over the period. Hughes et al. (2017) provide more detail on the relationship between control variables and TFP within the model: *AREA* typically has a positive effect on *TFP* for smaller farms, giving way to a negative effect for very large farms.

Changes in the distribution of sample farms have accounted for around 5 per cent of the improvement in average productivity levels over the period. At a regional level these effects have been strongest in the southern GRDC region (Hughes et al., 2017). A closer examination of the data shows a consistent increase in the number of cropping farms in south-western Victoria, beginning around 1990. The results provide evidence for a shift of cropping activity in Victoria and WA toward higher rainfall areas and away from inland areas more affected by the decline in climate conditions. While further research is required to confirm these trends, they are at least partially supported by ABS crop area data (Hughes et al. 2017).

8.6 CONCLUSIONS

This study presented a simple method of controlling for the effect of climate variability on productivity. The approach involved applying non-parametric machine learning regression models to large firm level spatio-temporal data sets. The method was applied to the Australian broadacre cropping industry, a sector well known for its exposure to climate variability (i.e. drought) and, in more recent times, climate change.

While the data sets used here – drawn from ABARES farm surveys – are relatively small for this type of analysis, the approach showed promise. Machine learning methods are appropriate in this context for a number of reasons. Firstly, the focus is on prediction (i.e. predicting farm productivity under alternative climate conditions), with little need to understand the marginal responses of specific climate variables. Secondly, there is a high degree of spatial and temporal variation in the explanatory variables. Thirdly, there are few if any concerns around causality/endogeneity, as the weather is clearly exogenous.

The results showed deterioration in climate conditions, particularly in southern Australia since 2000. This change in climate has had a significant negative effect on cropping farm productivity (around 5 per cent on average since 2000). After controlling for climate, farm productivity has remained relatively strong, particularly since 2007, with average annual growth in climate adjusted productivity of over 1 per cent. The non-parametric models provide a detailed picture of productivity trends across time, with two key periods of growth identified as 1984–85 to 1993–94 and 2007–08 to 2013–14, each preceded by periods of relative stagnation.

The approach enabled us to identify changes in the sensitivity of farms to climate over time. These results proved consistent with past studies and with anecdotal observations. During the 1990s there was an industry focus on intensification and maximizing productivity under good climate conditions. However, this focus increased the exposure of the sector to climate variability. Following the dramatic shift in climate conditions during the 2000s this trend appears to have reversed, with farmers reducing their climate sensitivity and improving performance under adverse climate conditions (particularly post-2007).

Climate adjusted productivity change was also decomposed into time effects, location effects and farm type effects (land area, farmer age, etc.). The decomposition attributed most productivity growth over the period to technological change, with a consistent contribution from farm type effects (largely increases in farm scale). The study also found that changes in the spatial distribution of farms in the sample had a small positive effect on average productivity over the period. ABARES survey data suggests that a shift of cropping activity in NSW and Victoria from lower to higher rainfall areas has occurred since 1990. However, further research is required to confirm this trend.

Overall, the study demonstrates the importance of controlling for climate when measuring productivity in agriculture, particularly on cropping farms. The results provide a clear picture of how the industry is adapting to the climate change trends unfolding in the region. There is little doubt that climate change is already having a large effect on the cropping industry in Australia. At the same time, there is good evidence to suggest that farmers are adapting. In the longer term, the ability of farmers to continue adapting to the changing climate will remain crucial to the success of this important sector of the economy.

NOTES

*   This project has benefited from discussions with Australian Bureau of Agricultural and Resource Economics and Sciences (ABARES) staff, including Alistair Davidson, Mathew Miller, Tom Jackson and Peter Gooday. Haydn Valle at ABARES helped with the extraction of farm survey data. Helpful comments on a draft of this chapter were received from Tiho Ancev (University of Sydney) and Samad Azad (University of Tasmania). This project has also benefited from discussions with staff at the Commonwealth Scientific and Industrial Research Organisation (CSIRO), including Zvi Hochman and Phil Kokic.
1.   See Pearson et al. (2011) for a detailed review.
2.   Using the same model, an alternative measure could be constructed to control for spatial differences in climate (this was not required in this study as temporal rather than cross-sectional comparisons were the main focus). One problem with this approach is that farms in persistently lower rainfall areas are likely to adopt different technologies such that direct comparisons (even when controlling for rainfall) may be problematic.

REFERENCES

Alexander, F. and P. Kokic (2005), *Productivity in the Australian Grains Industry*, Australian Bureau of Agricultural and Resource Economics and Sciences, Canberra.
ABARES (2016), 'Australian farm survey results 2013–14 to 2015–16', Australian Bureau of Agricultural and Resource Economics and Sciences, Canberra.
AEGIC (2016), 'New Australian climate developing', Australian Export Grains Innovation Council, http://aegic.org.au/new-australian-climate-developing/.

Breiman, L. (2001), 'Random forests', *Machine Learning*, **45**, 5–32.

Cai, W., T. Cowan and M. Thatcher (2012), 'Rainfall reductions over southern hemisphere semi-arid regions: the role of subtropical dry zone expansion', *Scientific Reports*, **2**, article 702.

Caruana, R. and A. Niculescu-Mizil (2006), 'An empirical comparison of supervised learning algorithms', Paper presented at the 23rd International Conference on Machine Learning, Pittsburgh, June 25–29.

Che, N., T. Kompas, V. Xayavong, and D. Cook (2012), 'Profitability, productivity and the efficiency of grain production with climate impacts: a case study of Western Australia', Crawford School Research Paper.

CSIRO and BOM (2014) 'State of the climate 2014', Commonwealth Scientific and Industrial Research Organisation and Australian Bureau of Meteorology, www. bom.gov.au/state-of-the-climate/.

Friedman, J. (2002), 'Stochastic gradient boosting', *Computational Statistics and Data Analysis*, **38**, 367–378.

Ghahramani, A., P. Kokic, A. Moore, B. Zheng, S. Chapman, M. Howden and S. Crimp (2015), 'The value of adapting to climate change in Australian wheat farm systems: farm to cross-regional scale', *Agriculture, Ecosystems and Environment*, **211**, 112–125.

Hochman, Z., D.L Gobbett and H. Horan (2017), 'Climate trends account for stalled wheat yields in Australia since 1990', *Global Change Biology*, doi:10.1111/gcb.13604.

Hughes, N., K. Lawson, A. Davidson, T. Jackson and Y. Sheng (2011), 'Productivity pathways: climate-adjusted production frontiers for the Australian broadacre cropping industry', Paper presented at the Australian Agricultural and Resource Economics Society Conference, Melbourne, February 8–11.

Hughes, N., K. Lawson and H. Valle (2017), 'Farm performance and climate: climate adjusted productivity on broadacre cropping farms', Australian Bureau of Agricultural and Resource Economics and Sciences, Canberra.

Islam, N., V. Xayavong, L. Anderton and D. Feldman (2014), 'Farm productivity in an Australian region affected by a changing climate', Paper presented at Australian Agricultural and Resource Economics Society Conference, Port Macquarie, NSW, February 4–7.

Jackson, T. (2010), *Harvesting Productivity: ABARE-GRDC Workshops on Grains Productivity Growth*, Australian Bureau of Agricultural and Resource Economics, Canberra.

Keogh, M. (2012), 'Including risk in enterprise decisions in Australia's riskiest businesses', Paper presented at the 56th Annual Conference of the Australian Agricultural and Resource Economics Society, Fremantle, Western Australia, February 7–10.

Kingwell, R., L. Anderton, N. Islam, V. Xayavong and A. Wardell-Johnson, D. Feldman and J. Speijers (2014), 'Broadacre farmers adapting to a changing climate', in J.P. Palutikof, S.L. Boulter, J. Barnett and D. Rissik (eds), *Applied Studies in Climate Adaptation*, Wiley, Chichester, pp. 130–138.

Kokic, P., A. Davidson and V. B. Rodriguez (2006), 'Australia's grains industry: factors influencing productivity growth', *Australian Commodities: Forecasts and Issues*, **13**, 705–712.

Kokic, P., A. Heaney, L. Pechey, S. Crimp and B. Fisher (2005), 'Climate change: predicting the impacts on agriculture: a case study', *Australian Commodities: Forecasts and Issues*, **12**, 161–170.

Martin, P., E. Gray and T. Thompson (2014), *Australian Grains: Financial Performance of Grain Producing Farms 2011–12 to 2013–14*, Australian Bureau of Agricultural and Resource Economics and Sciences, Canberra.

Nelson, R., P. Kokic and H. Meinke (2007), 'From rainfall to farm incomes: transforming advice for Australian drought policy, II. Forecasting farm incomes', *Crop and Pasture Science* **58**, 1004–1012.

Nelson, R., P. Kokic, S. Crimp, P. Martin, H. Meinke, M. Howden, P. De Voil and U. Nidumolu (2010), 'The vulnerability of Australian rural communities to climate variability and change: Part II – Integrating impacts with adaptive capacity', *Environmental Science and Policy*, **13**, 18–27.

Nidumolu, U., P. Hayman, M. Howden and B. Alexander (2012), 'Re-evaluating the margin of the South Australian grain belt in a changing climate', *Climate Research*, **51**, 249–260.

Pearson, L., R. Nelson, S. Crimp, J. Langridge (2011) 'Interpretive review of conceptual frameworks and research models that inform Australia's agricultural vulnerability to climate change', *Environmental Modelling and Software* **26**, 113–123.

Pedregosa, F., G. Varoquaux, A. Gramfort, V. Michel, B. Thirion, O. Grisel, M. Blondel, P. Prettenhofer, R. Weiss and V. Dubourg (2011), 'Scikit-learn: machine learning in Python', *Journal of Machine Learning Research*, **12**, 2825–2830.

Peel, M., T. McMahon and B. Finlayson (2004), 'Continental differences in the variability of annual runoff-update and reassessment', *Journal of Hydrology*, **295**, 185–197.

Potgieter, A., H. Meinke, A. Doherty, V. Sadras, G. Hammer, S. Crimp and D. Rodriguez (2013), 'Spatial impact of projected changes in rainfall and temperature on wheat yields in Australia', *Climatic change*, **117**, 163–179.

Raupach, M., P. Briggs, V. Haverd, E. King, M. Paget and C. Trudinger (2009), 'Australian Water Availability Project (AWAP): CSIRO Marine and Atmospheric Research Component: Final Report for Phase 3', CAWCR Technical Report No. 013.

Salim, R. and N. Islam (2010), 'Exploring the impact of R&D and climate change on agricultural productivity growth: the case of Western Australia', *Australian Journal of Agricultural and Resource Economics*, **54**, 561–582.

Sheng, Y., J. Mullen and S. Zhao (2011), *A Turning Point in Agricultural Productivity: Consideration of the Causes*, Australian Bureau of Agricultural and Resource Economics and Sciences, Canberra.

South Eastern Australian Climate Initiative (2012), 'Climate and water availability in south-eastern Australia: a synthesis of findings from Phase 2 of the South Eastern Australian Climate Initiative (SEACI)', CSIRO.

Stephens, D., A. Potgieter and J. Walcott (2011), *GRDC Strategic Planning for Investment Based on Agro-Ecological Zones: Second Phase*, Department of Agriculture and Food, South Perth, WA.

Varian, H. (2014), 'Big data: new tricks for econometrics', *Journal of Economic Perspectives*, 28, 3–27.

9. Environmentally adjusted efficiency of municipal water suppliers

Francesc Hernández-Sancho and Águeda Bellver-Domingo

9.1 INTRODUCTION

Urban water demand is growing together with population density in large urban areas. This phenomenon has numerous economic, environmental and social implications. Supply of drinking water should be provided to the entire population, and for this reason the efficient operation of water utilities becomes very relevant. Efficient operation of water utilities is important due to it is direct relation to social and environmental costs. Implementing methodologies to analyse the efficiency of the supply network allows utility companies or regulators to assess the vulnerabilities of the system that cause social and environmental impacts (Molinos-Senante et al., 2016b).

From a functional point of view, the task of water utilities is complex. Their aim is to deliver drinking water to households and at the same time comply with quality controls (Marques et al., 2015). Achieving that goal means taking into account the particularities of the urban water cycle: water storage, treatment, distribution, wastewater collection and treatment, and disposal and management of residues. At the end of this cycle the water returns to the ecosystem, closing the cycle. In addition, the particularities of the geographic scope of a specific water supply area are relevant for the efficiency of water utilities (González-Gómez and García-Rubio, 2008). In this light, utilities have to deliver drinking water to households not only in a technically efficient way but also in a way that is environmentally and economically efficient (Faust and Baranzini, 2014; Guerrini et al., 2015).

Achieving efficiency is not an easy task: rapid expansion that the drinking water distribution network has had to sustain in most countries in order to meet the growing demand for water carries many problems (Medellín-Azuara et al., 2007; Worthington, 2014). Specifically, three main problems that water utilities must solve are: (i) inefficiencies at the level of output; (ii) inefficiencies at the level of cost; and (iii) inefficiencies at the level of product quality (Seppälä et al., 2001). Estimation of the efficiency of water utilities requires knowing the extent to which their costs will result in a suitable water supply process, because efficiency is strongly related to the cost structure of water utilities (Garcia and Thomas, 2001). In general, excessive costs borne by the water utility will mean a low efficiency, and the investment needed to correct this situation will likely result in increase in the water bill to the public (Guerrini et al., 2013). Calculating efficiency permits us to identify the water utilities that have overruns (i.e. low efficiency) and which part of the processes needs to be corrected in order to remove the irregularities in the production process (Kumar et al., 2015).

The studies of Saal and Parker (2000, 2001) highlight the importance of analysing the quality of the service provided by water utilities. From a practical point of view, efficiency analysis is a very effective tool for managers to monitor the work and to control the activity of water utilities. The results obtained from an efficiency analysis allow us to design and modify public policies that govern the water supply sector. However, the estimation of efficiency involves a large number of variables that influence it (Picazo-Tadeo et al., 2008).

According to a study by Hernández-Sancho et al. (2009), variables that are most commonly used in conducting efficiency studies in developed countries are: the price of water, energy, household composition, weather and the particularities of the water utility. Of these, price is often considered the most important variable. Carvalho and Marques (2011) also looked at the source of water used for supply;[1] the topography of the region where the water utility operates; and the destination of the drinking water (residential vs. non-residential use). Hernández-Sancho et al. (2009) emphasize that although the price of water is a key indicator used in measuring efficiency, it does not adequately reflect the real cost of water because it does not take into account other factors associated with water supply (e.g. environmental factors).

Put differently, one may say that the water sector is heavily influenced by externalities. Its operation results in a series of social and environmental impacts that should be taken into account when estimating the efficiency of water utilities. These have typically not been considered in the classical analysis of efficiency because they do not have a direct economic impact on the balance of company assets (Molinos-Senante and Sala-Garrido, 2015). Water utilities change their operation and management according to changes in the social, environmental and political context. In fact, the calls for universal access to drinking water and sanitation come at the same time as the demand for water grows. This combination of factors means a challenge for managers of enterprises and for the public administration, where improved efficiency of water supply is paramount. This chapter aims at presenting the current state of estimating the efficiency of water utilities and presenting the main existing methodologies for its calculation, emphasizing the importance of environmental factors in the operation of water utilities.

In this context, analysing efficiency with respect to the ownership of the water utility, the existence of economies of scale and scope (González-Gómez and García-Rubio, 2008), and identifying the environmental impact associated with the extraction, treatment and distribution of drinking water are some of the most important issues for the efficient management of water utilities.

9.2   AN OVERVIEW OF RESEARCH QUESTIONS

The work of González-Gómez and García-Rubio (2008) raises three questions that are relevant when understanding how the management of water utilities affects their efficiency. These questions are addressed based on scientific evidence presented in the literature.

Question 1: Are economies of scale well utilized in this industry? Is there any limit to the possibility of current economies of scale?

The existence of economies of scale is one of the aspects most analysed in the literature. Its relevance is significant in that it is indicative of efficiency. The general theory tells us that larger companies are more efficient in using their assets. In the case of water, economies of scale are related to the structure of costs when production varies depending on the size of the distribution network and the number of users connected, while population density and the volume of water demanded remains constant (Garcia and Thomas, 2001). Quantitative assessment of economies of scale is complicated. It is a variable that is highly sensitive to the particularities of each water utility and, consequently, each empirical work typically comes with conclusions that lack generality.

There are a number of authors who provide evidence for the existence of economies of scale in the water sector (Ashton, 2000; Benito et al., 2010; Carvalho and Marques, 2014; Mercadier et al., 2016; Torres and Morrison Paul, 2006). By contrast, there are other authors who provide evidence of diseconomies of scale, which is the situation where the larger the size of the water utility, the more inefficient it is (Ashton, 2003; Mizutani and Urakami, 2001; Saal and Parker, 2000; Sauer and Frohberg, 2007). Despite this differentiation Saal et al. (2013) argue that there are economies of scale in the water utilities to a certain level of produced output. From a given level of output, the economies of scale are no longer relevant and the diseconomies of scale take centre stage because the size of the water utility increases.

Sauer (2005) shows that the right size for water utilities in rural areas in Germany is around 3,600 million cubic meters of water per year, which is delivered to some 18,500 connected users. By calculating the efficiency, one can show that the dimensioning of drinking water distribution network has not been appropriate. Results show that the size of water utilities analysed should be three times larger than their current size so that the utilities could achieve efficiency in their drinking water distribution network. This dimensioning is dependent on the country; the characteristics of the distribution network of drinking water; the characteristics of the water utilities themselves; and the regulatory framework, the estimated efficiency changes, and with it the evidence of the presence of the economies of scale (Zschille 2015).

The presence of economies of scale should be properly studied, since there is no universal formula to solve the problems of efficiency in the water sector. As Zschille (2015) argues, the quest to achieving economies of scale is often a justification for mergers between water utilities, or for joint public/private management of utilities. However, there is a risk if this approach does not properly assess the economies of scale and the efficiency. For each particular case it requires a detailed investigation of the characteristics of water utilities and the environment in which they operate.

Question 2: Is there any relation between ownership and efficiency? Is privatization a way to achieve improvements in business practice? Is it more efficient to have a single company that manages all of the phases in the urban water cycle or to have several companies specialized in each of the phases in the cycle?

The main challenge in the water sector is that it needs large investment to sustain good performance. A common situation is when the same company (or a consortium combining public and private partnership, PPP) is responsible for water supply and also for sewage collection and wastewater treatment. Water managers and water utilities prefer to group costs with the aim of enhancing the efficiency of water utility management (González-Gómez and García-Rubio, 2008). However, there is an ongoing debate about which type of ownership is conducive to achieving a greater level of efficiency (Molinos-Senante and Sala-Garrido, 2016).

Saal et al. (2007) quantify efficiency changes by calculating the total factor productivity (TFP) and its relation to the presence of scale economies during the period 1985–2000. They apply the methodology to a sample of water sewage companies (WaSCs) and water only companies (WoCS) in England and Wales, subsequently focusing their attention on the performance of WaSCs. These companies have undergone a progressive privatization process in order to implement a tightening of drinking water quality. Efficiency analysis has the aim of verifying whether there were inefficiencies in WaSCs performance in the period prior to privatization (where ownership was public) and in the post-privatization period, given that the WaSCs are under conditions of natural monopoly. Results show that WaSCs are characterized by decreasing returns to scale that have negatively affected TFP (both prior to and post-privatization). Hence, a water sector consisting of a small number of companies but with large size would have difficulties saving costs through scale economies. The authors note that although technical improvement has been achieved, privatization of WaSCs was not able to improve efficiency at the initial stages. However, thanks to the tightening of the regulatory framework for the water sector, WaSCs achieved cost recovery over time by improving their efficiency. This work demonstrates that the existence of a monopoly goes with a regulatory framework whose aim is to control water utilities performance (Molinos-Senante and Sala-Garrido, 2015).

The dilemma facing society about whether public or private ownership of water utilities is more desirable is a long-standing and ongoing discussion in the water sector, and its implications for efficiency are significant. Historically, but not exclusively, ownership has tended to be public, since water supply has always been considered a common good. However, the rate of growth of the urban water supply has contributed to raising the question of whether privately owned utilities should have a role in improving technological innovation in the sector. The argument for privatization is strongly related to efficiency, since it is considered that privatization reduces operational costs due to the ability to invest capital and the ability to improve work practices.

However, there is no clear scientific evidence that private ownership of water utilities is more efficient, so there is no universal solution to the existing dilemma (Seppälä et al. 2001). Some authors, like Anwandter and Ozuna (2002), point out that there may be situations where a private company seeks to remain at a low efficiency level in order to increase its income through demands for higher water tariffs. Romano and Guerrini (2011) break with the classical belief that private management is more efficient; their study shows that water utilities under public ownership reach higher levels of efficiency than public–private partnerships. On the other hand, authors like Benito et al. (2010) conclude that regulatory framework for the water sector has more influence on efficiency than ownership of the water utility. The regulatory framework becomes the cornerstone of the water sector because, regardless of ownership, the fact that the water sector is a regulated monopoly implies no competition and no market forces to rely on.

Question 3: What are the environmental factors that must be taken into account in the water industry, and what is their importance in terms of explaining differences in efficiency?

The effects that the water sector is having on the environment are becoming ever more clear. This is reflected in the numerous efforts to seek an integrated management of the water cycle (GWP, 2012). The existence of highly urbanized areas has created a new water cycle, the urban water cycle. This cycle is no longer natural, including all the infrastructure that allows us to have drinking water at home as well as the treatment of wastewater. The urban water cycle has a major impact on the environment, as growing demand for water means that extraction rates for water supply are increasing and, therefore, the water volume stored in the water bodies is reducing. All components of ecosystems are intertwined, and the decrease in the volume of stored water brings negative effects on society (e.g. the need to search for alternative water sources, including desalination or water reuse) and on the environment (imbalance in the ecosystems). These are the reasons that drive the need to include environmental effects in efficiency studies.

These environmental effects pertaining to the urban water sector vary significantly across space: a utility located in an area with high rainfall has a different set of environmental effects compared to a utility operating in an area characterized by water stress (Lannier and Porcher, 2014). A common tendency of water utilities has been not to consider the environment in their efficiency studies. The result has been an unrealistic efficiency estimation because, if environmental parameters are included in the assessment, estimated efficiency is bound to be negatively affected (Carvalho and Marques, 2011; Saal et al., 2007). Consideration of environmental aspects is a relatively new and emerging field, mainly because the environment is 'something' exogenous and heterogeneous that influences the performance of utilities, but it cannot be directly managed by water utility managers (Faust and Baranzini, 2014).

Water loss is one type of environmental indicator that is detectable from the difference between water inflow in the distribution system and the water volume that reaches users – the so-called 'billed volume' (Alexander,

2010; Molinos-Senante et al., 2014). Leaks greatly affect distribution efficiency for different reasons. The first reason is that water lost through leaks is non-revenue water, which causes losses in direct income for water utilities. Quantifying water volumes lost due to leaks in the network has always been a difficult task; however, it is clear that they are directly related to efficiency losses of water utilities (Frauendorfer and Liemberger 2010; Garcia and Thomas 2001; Kumar 2010). The second reason is the drop in piping pressure. The drop in pressure has two aspects: first, low water quality because lower pressure in the pipe creates a risk of water contamination (Hernández-Sancho et al., 2012). The second consequence is that the utility has to increase the amount of water flowing through the system so that users will get the same amount of water without repairing the leaks. The latter is typically more attractive for the water utility because environmental costs are not considered (Garcia and Thomas, 2001). The environmental impact in this case involves two aspects: increase in the water volume withdrawn from the environment and the increase in energy use associated with additional pumping of water (Brunone et al., 2014).

A common method that companies use to recover the lost revenue due to water leaks is asking the regulator to increase the water tariff. This implies distortion of the price of water (Hernández-Sancho et al., 2009). The ideal situation would be when water utilities detect and repair leaks to improve their efficiency and so water prices would not be affected. From an environmental point of view, a drinking water network without leaks produces an environmental benefit because it is not necessary to increase the volume of water withdrawn to meet demand (Frauendorfer and Liemberger, 2010; Molinos-Senante et al., 2016c). The study by Delgado-Galván et al. (2010) analyses the impact of leaks on water utility efficiency, but not only from the economic point of view; it also seeks to assess the costs of monitoring leaks to achieve environmental and social benefits. Results reveal that the absence of leakage management has high social and environmental costs. In that case, the solution to achieving efficiency in the drinking water distribution network is to repair leakages.

This study reinforces the idea that non-revenue water should be included in efficiency analysis as a non-desirable output from a drinking water network (Abrate et al., 2011; Garcia and Thomas, 2001). It is clear that non-revenue water directly affects efficiency. In fact, the only incentive to manage leaks is the loss of revenue to the water utilities. From an institutional point of view, water loss through leaks is free of charge, and water utilities have no duty to repair them. However, by including leaks as non-desirable outputs in an efficiency analysis of a drinking water network, the efficiency of water utilities can be evaluated in a more adequate fashion. Thus, correcting and preventing leakages would become important for water utilities to increase efficiency and internalize environmental externalities of water abstraction, purification and distribution processes (Frauendorfer and Liemberger, 2010). The above discussion shows that the study of technical efficiency is important not only from an economic point of view, but also from an environmental point of view.

European countries operate under a common regulatory framework where the required levels of environmental quality of surface and groundwater for drinking water supply are stipulated. This is a great starting point for the inclusion of environmental externalities and, at the same time, it allows that environmental criteria are taken into account when establishing the legal framework in each country. Inclusion of the environment in efficiency analysis is a complicated issue due to the difficulty of quantifying the impacts.

However it is necessary to consider the inclusion of environmental externalities to evaluate the actual efficiency of water utilities, as Ananda (2014) has done for the Australian water utilities. Few authors have considered the environment in their efficiency analyses as an influential part in the process of water abstraction, purification and distribution. We review some of this work in the section below.

9.3   EMPIRICAL CONTRIBUTIONS

Methodologies used for calculating efficiency are based on the process of benchmarking (Molinos-Senante et al., 2016a). The efficiency of a company is estimated by comparison to another company with the aim of analysing each company's behaviour, taking into account the market dynamics (Filippini et al., 2008; Maziotis et al., 2016b). The relevance of benchmarking methodologies is also apparent in the monitoring processes of regulatory bodies in the water sector. They help carry out the monitoring of the service quality provided by water utilities, and allow the preparation of legislative instruments that will frame the functioning of the water sector (Walter et al., 2009).[2] They also help in adjusting the water tariff in order to achieve a fair and equitable structure of the water supply sector (Molinos-Senante et al., 2016a).

Nonparametric approaches are the most commonly used of the benchmarking methodologies because it is not necessary to define the behaviour of the units of analysis, or the relationship between the variables (Carvalho and Marques, 2011). The implementation of benchmarking methodologies makes it possible to obtain information about structural and operating differences and variations in inputs and outputs that allow us to identify the causes of inefficiencies of the units under analysis (Zschille and Walter, 2012).

The problem with benchmarking methodologies is that the results obtained vary between different studies. This is because comparing different water utilities is difficult since there is heterogeneity in the sample with respect to the characteristics of the water distribution network and due to environmental characteristics (Filippini et al. 2008). Moreover, within the benchmarking methodologies it is possible to use a parametric approach and a nonparametric approach. As with other aspects of efficiency assessment, there is no consensus on whether implementation of one or the other approach is better. This is because the nonparametric methods are based on mathematical programming, while parametric methods are based on econometric techniques (Mellah and Ben Amor, 2016). Below, we discuss the methodologies most commonly used to measure efficiency and those empirical studies in which they have been implemented.

9.3.1   Data Envelopment Analysis (DEA)

DEA is a linear programming methodology that estimates efficiency by measuring the proportion of inputs used that generate outputs of the production process. DEA allows us to estimate the relative efficiency of a tested sample and identify those producers who provide a quality service or quality product (Abbott and Cohen, 2009; Worthington, 2014). Furthermore, DEA evaluates the performance of water utilities given that there is limited knowledge about the production function of the water sector, because DEA does not require assumptions about the functional relationship between costs and outputs. The most commonly analysed aspects of water utilities are ownership, company size, geographic location and searching for economies of scale and scope, depending on the country or region (Romano and Guerrini, 2011).

The usefulness of DEA to conduct efficiency studies is clear through the large number of authors who have used it in their water utilities research (Anwandter and Ozuna, 2002; Byrnes et al., 2010; Deng et al., 2016; Guerrini et al., 2015; Marques et al., 2014; Molinos-Senante et al., 2015a; Mugisha, 2013; Picazo-Tadeo et al., 2009; See, 2015; Thanassoulis, 2000a, 2000b; Tupper and Resende, 2004; Woodbury and Dollery, 2004; Zschille, 2015).

9.3.2   Stochastic Frontier Analysis (SFA)

From the point of view of urban water management, this methodology is useful to distinguish between inefficiency and unobserved heterogeneity that influences costs (since conventional models tend to confuse the unobserved heterogeneity with inefficiency, which generates biased results).

Environmental factors are often responsible for unobserved heterogeneity. The performance of water utilities depends on both environmental conditions where they are operating (topography and climate) and on typology of their drinking water distribution network (population density and water network shape); all of these influence the costs (Farsi et al., 2005a; Filippini et al., 2008). Hence, the results of efficiency analyses vary significantly (Daraio and Simar, 2005), and it is difficult to distinguish when inefficiency exists and when unobserved heterogeneity exists. Due to this, unobserved heterogeneity is often confounded with inefficiency, and results are biased (Filippini et al., 2008). This situation has to be corrected to avoid problems related to the use of the results in decision-making processes (Farsi et al., 2005b).[3]

There is a wide variety of authors who have implemented SFA for calculating efficiency of water utilities. The literature can be divided into authors who have included environmental variables in their analysis (Bottasso and Conti, 2003; Faust and Baranzini, 2014; Lin, 2005; Mellah and Ben Amor, 2016) and authors who have not included environmental variables (Antonioli and Filippini, 2001; Corton, 2003; Horn, 2011; Mande Buafua, 2015; Mugisha, 2014).

9.3.3   Life Cycle Assessment (LCA)

LCA is a quantitative methodology that allows evaluation of environmental effects associated with an output, production process or activity throughout the entire life of the output. In case of the water sector, the cycle would comprise the processes starting from the raw water being withdrawn from the environment and finishing with the wastewater being processed in a treatment plant. This methodology provides an overview of interrelationships and various conditions of the production process (Landu and Brent 2006). LCA is not a methodology for calculating efficiency, but it is included in this chapter because there are empirical studies that have used it to see the relevance of environmental factors in terms of efficiency of water utilities. The use of LCA enables an analysis of existing technological alternatives to improve water supply with a lower environmental cost, facilitating the work of decision makers (Schulz et al., 2012). Some studies that have implemented this methodology for the water sector are Ashbolt et al. (2006), Landu and Brent (2006), Lundie et al. (2004), Schulz et al. (2012) and Sharma et al. (2009); all of them consider environmental variables in their analysis.

9.3.4 Shadow Prices

One way of measuring efficiency in the water sector is to consider the non-desirable outputs in the assessment of the performance of water utilities. Some undesirable outputs are service outages, customer complaints and quality of water supplied (Molinos-Senante et al., 2016b). Using the method of shadow prices for measuring efficiency allows researchers to consider the negative effects of the water sector that reduce the efficiency of water utilities (Hernández-Sancho et al., 2012). This allows us to estimate the efficiency considering not only economic characteristics but also environmental factors (Molinos-Senante et al., 2016b).

Shadow prices methodology follows the approach of Färe et al. (1993), which is based on distance functions that represent the production technology at the same time, allowing modelling the simultaneous generation of multiple outputs. This methodology seeks to maximize production of desired output and, at the same time, avoid the generation of non-desirable output (Wei et al., 2013), all depending on available technology (Hernández-Sancho et al., 2010). Given a set of inputs $X = (x_1, \ldots, x_N)$, a set of outputs $U = (u_1, \ldots, u_M)$ and a production set $P(x) = \{u \in \mathfrak{R}_+^M : x \text{ can produce } u\}$, it is assumed that the reference technology satisfies the conditions proposed by Färe et al. (1988). An output distance function is defined by Shephard (1970) as:

$$D_0(x, u) = \inf\{\theta: (u/\theta) \in P(x)\} \qquad (9.1)$$

satisfying that $u \in P(x) <=> D_0(x, u) \leq 1$.

Define a price vector $r = (r_1, \ldots, r_M)$ of outputs with $r \neq 0$. Given r, revenue function is defined as:

$$R(x, r) = sup_u \{ru: D_0(x, u) \leq 1\} \qquad (9.2)$$

Under the assumption that the functions $D_0(x, u)$ y $R(x, r)$ are distinguishable, and according to Shephard (1970), it is possible to show that:

$$\nabla_u D_0(x, u) = r^*(x, u) \qquad (9.3)$$

Denote $r^*(x, u)$ to be the maximum income achievable through the price outputs vector $\nabla_u D_0(x, u)$. To obtain the shadow prices of non-desirable outputs it is necessary to assume that the shadow price of a desirable output is the same value as its market price (the observed market price of the mth output $r_m^0 = r_m$, where r_m is the shadow price of the mth desirable output). Hence, for all $m \neq m'$ we will have the shadow prices formula (Färe et al., 1993):

$$r'_m = r^0_m \frac{\partial D_0(x,u)/\partial u'_m}{\partial D_0(x,u)/\partial u_m} \tag{9.4}$$

where m is the desirable output with a market price of r_m.

Färe et al. (1993) use a translog function optimization (estimate a distance function taking into account that the aim of distance function is to maximize production of desirable output). The translog function is defined by:

$$
\begin{aligned}
lnD_0(x^k,u^k) = \alpha_0 &+ \sum_{n=1}^{N} \beta_n ln x_n^k + \sum_{m=1}^{M} \alpha_m ln u_m^k \\
&+ \frac{1}{2} \sum_{n=1}^{N} \sum_{n'=1}^{N} \beta_{nn'} (ln x_n^k)(ln x_{n'}^k) \\
&+ \frac{1}{2} \sum_{m=1}^{M} \sum_{m'=1}^{M} \alpha_{mm'} (ln u_m^k)(ln u_{m'}^k) \\
&+ \sum_{n=1}^{N} \sum_{m=1}^{M} \gamma_{nm} (ln x_n^k)(ln u_m^k)
\end{aligned}
\tag{9.5}
$$

Linear programming is used to estimate parameters (α, β, γ) of the distance function, looking to minimize the sum of the deviations between the function estimated for each unit and the frontier (Färe et al. 1993; Hernández-Sancho et al., 2010) as follows:

$$Min \sum_{k=1}^{K} [lnD_0(x^k,u^k) - ln1] \tag{9.6}$$

s.t.:

i $lnD_0(x^k, u^k) \geq 0$

ii $\dfrac{\partial lnD_0(x^k,u^k)}{\partial ln x_n^k} \geq 0$

iii $\dfrac{\partial lnD_0(x^k,u^k)}{\partial ln u_m^k} \leq 0, (m = 1)$

iv $\dfrac{\partial lnD_0(x^k,u^k)}{\partial ln u_{m'}^k} \geq 0, (m' = 2,3,4...)$

v $\sum_{m=1}^{M} \alpha_m = 1; \sum_{n'=1}^{N} \beta_{nn'} = \sum_{n=1}^{N} \gamma_{nm} = 0$

vi $\alpha_{mm'} = \alpha_{m'm}; m=1,...,M; m'=1,...,M$ $\beta_{nn'} = \beta_{n'n}; n=1,...,N; n'=1,...,N$

As with all linear programming, there are several restrictions, as defined by Hernández-Sancho et al. (2010). Various authors have implemented shadow price methodology in the context of the water cycle (Djukic et al.,

2016; Garrido-Baserba et al., 2016; Hernández-Sancho et al., 2009; Hernández-Sancho et al., 2010; Molinos-Senante et al., 2013, 2016b and c).

One specific implementation of shadow price methodology within the water cycle consists of taking into account the water quality, which is altered by the presence of pollutants in the water. Many water polluting substances are anthropogenic and reach aquatic ecosystems through effluents from wastewater treatment plants (WWTPs). Here, the approach considers the marginal value of reducing the pollutants in WWTP effluent. These pollutants are negative externalities of the wastewater treatment process that are not quantified by the traditional economic approaches. The efficiency with which pollutants are removed is not 100 per cent (there are pollutants that are capable of going through WWTPs without sustaining degradation). Thus WWTP effluent contains pollutants that cause environmental damage. The European Urban Wastewater Directive (Directives 91/271/EEC and 98/15/EEC) mandates all municipalities to have collections and wastewater treatment systems, particularly municipalities that are close to sensitive areas (wetlands and lakes). The EU Water Framework Directive (Directive 2000/60/EC) goes further, making the economic analysis of wastewater management relevant. Governments have to implement the principle of full cost recovery through cost-benefit analysis. Given that shadow prices estimate the marginal cost of pollutants, the shadow price is a proxy for the environmental benefit associated with removing these pollutants from the WWTP effluent (and improving water quality). Shadow price methodology for WWTP pollutants allows environmental externalities to be internalized within the decision-making process.

Methodologies discussed in this chapter allow us to estimate the environmental efficiency of municipal water suppliers. Using this approach, efficiency assessment can be integrated into decision-making processes. It represents a significant advantage when developing concrete measures for water resources management. Efficiency may be included within a feasibility analysis – like the cost-benefit analysis (Bark et al. 2016) – to assess the feasibility of management measures analysed under different scenarios (Busch et al. 2012). The final result will be the design of economic incentives (such as tariffs, for the specific case of water) that allow changing water suppliers' behaviour toward more sustainable practices, improving the provision and exploitation of water sources, and ensuring the continuity of ecosystems over time through improved environmental quality.

9.4   EMPIRICAL APPLICATIONS

This section presents an overview of several empirical studies that are specifically pertinent to measuring efficiency of the urban water sector.

The study by Guerrini et al. (2013) evaluated the efficiency of water utilities through calculation of economies of scale and scope. The estimated efficiency takes into account inputs such as investment costs, labour cost, population served and water network length. The aim of this study was to determine the most efficient way to manage water utilities in Italy. A nonparametric DEA analysis was implemented with variable returns to scale and input-orientation to determine the efficient production frontier. The authors conclude that economies of scope have a strong influence on the efficiency of water utilities in the sample, such that if companies provide services in addition to drinking water (e.g. wastewater treatment, gas or electricity supply) they can reach a higher efficiency level compared with water utilities that only focus their efforts in the drinking water sector.

Despite the fact that the existence of scope economies was also evident in a study by Molinos-Senante et al. (2015b) on the UK water industry, the number of other empirical studies that support this finding is limited (Abbott and Cohen, 2009). Another finding of the study by Guerrini et al. (2013) is that economies of scale also influence the estimated efficiency. The size of population served by water utilities influences their efficiency scores. This is because cost reductions can be achieved in terms of lower marginal energy requirements as well as lower marginal infrastructure costs when a more densely populated area is served (Lannier and Porcher 2014). This is in line with the study by Carvalho and Marques (2011), who found that water utilities are more efficient in areas where the population density is higher. That is, the water sector is influenced by the existence of economies of density. The significance of the economies of density is also corroborated by the work of Walter et al. (2009). If only population density is taken into account, drinking water supply in large urban areas would be more efficient, as pointed out in Mellah and Ben Amor (2016). However, the existence of other external variables, as discussed previously, may affect the estimated efficiency results substantially.

Molinos-Senante et al. (2015c) consider efficiency of water utilities through the evaluation of the service quality using undesirable outputs and DEA methodology. One of the objectives of this study is the identification of variables that affect the efficiency of 18 water utilities in Chile. Results show that peak water demand and the density of the population supplied (among other factors) influence positively the efficiency of water utilities. However, the non-revenue water (quantified at 33.7 per cent, of which

74 per cent is due to leaks in the drinking water supply network) adversely affects the efficiency of evaluated water utilities.

Through DEA methodology and SFA, the work of Lannier and Porcher (2014) analysed technical efficiency of 177 French water utilities (both public and private ownership). As the main input they use the water tariff. The authors argue that water tariffs are designed to recover cost; so, if water utilities have excessive revenues, there are management inefficiencies. As a main output, the study considered billed water volume. They take into account leakages in the water supply network, considering that this output entails considering water service quality provided in the form of non-revenue water. Overall results show that public water utilities are slightly more efficient than private ones (the score for public ownership is 0.883 and for private ownership 0.823). Efficiency differences reflect differences in the management of water utilities, which translate into differences in water tariff depending on the region and on the ownership of the water utilities.

Taking into account environmental considerations related to performance of water utilities can be based on several approaches. The most common approach has been to consider the non-desirable outputs derived from water services of the urban water cycle. In the work by Ananda and Hampf (2015) emissions of greenhouse gases resulting from energy consumption of Australian water facilities during the period 2006 to 2011 are analysed. For this purpose, the authors use a Malmquist-Luenberger productivity growth index. This index is a variant of the Malmquist index, which is one of the approaches based on the DEA methodology that allows determining the evolution of productivity though time (Wang and Lan, 2011).

The Malmquist index is combined with directional distance functions to obtain the Malmquist-Luenberger index that can measure the variation in productivity associated with environmental effects over time (Oh, 2010). The results show that productivity decreased by 4 per cent a year if GHG emissions are included in the efficiency analysis. The interpretation of this result should take into account the efficiency loss of water utilities due to the influence that weather has on the Australian water cycle. Drought increases water cycle costs because it is necessary to meet the water demand with a scarce water source, and it is necessary to apply high-quality wastewater treatment to guarantee environmental standards and environmental safety, implying a negative impact on the efficiency of water utilities. The contribution of this study is that it clearly shows that ignoring non-desirable outputs in productivity analysis implies an overestimation of the levels of efficiency of water utilities. This strengthens the case for inclusion of environmental externalities in methodologies for efficiency analysis to be able to assess the real situation of water utilities and achieve the technological and environmental improvements in the urban water cycle.

9.5   CONCLUSIONS

This chapter has presented the state of efficiency measurement in the urban water sector, with an emphasis on including environmental variables. In addition, it has presented a number of empirical cases in which these environmental efficiency methodologies have been implemented.

One of the problems of most concern to water utilities is the non-revenue water associated with leaks. Their presence in the distribution water network is a situation where water utility is far from efficiency. Its existence harms both the water utility (increasing water and energy consumption to meet demand) and the consumer (the water tariff increases to recover the costs incurred by the water utility). Efficiency methodologies allow water utilities to monitor their efficiency level according to their water process characteristics.

The use of methodologies to quantify the efficiency of water utilities enables monitoring of the production process and the management of the urban water cycle. Inclusion of environmental considerations in the development of these efficiency methodologies is a very important facet to internalize environmental externalities associated with the operation of the urban water cycle.

The internalization of environmental externalities is a challenge facing water utilities. This chapter presented the available efficiency valuation methodologies and various empirical studies where environmentally adjusted efficiency has been used. This shows that it is possible to consider the environmental aspects within efficiency analysis, reinforcing the current trend of not only considering and accounting purely economic costs and benefits. This approach means a more realistic efficiency analysis that takes into account the influence of environmental factors on water utilities performance.

NOTES

1. Compared with groundwater, surface water requires more effort for treatment. While it is true that the conditions of the ecosystem in which the body of water lies can reduce this effort, the raw water quality has a direct impact on the operating costs (Carvalho and Marques, 2011).
2. Evaluating the quality of service has been one of the first factors that have been studied to understand the efficiency of companies in the water sector. In this context, quality of

service refers to factors such as continuity of service, leakage, the number of users connected and the ability to meet the demand for water supply (Maziotis et al., 2016a).
3. Both unobserved heterogeneity and inefficiency have been analysed by a wide range of authors in other contexts not related to the water sector (Hailu and Tanaka, 2015; Kellermann, 2015; Kopsakangas-Savolainen and Svento, 2011).

REFERENCES

Abbott, M. and B. Cohen (2009), 'Productivity and efficiency in the water industry', *Utilities Policy*, **17**, 233–244.
Abrate, G., F. Erbetta and G. Fraquelli (2011), 'Public utility planning and cost efficiency in a decentralized regulation context: the case of the Italian integrated water service', *Journal of Productivity Analysis*, **35**, 227–242.
Alexander, J. (2010), 'Reducing unaccounted-for or non-revenue water', *EngineerIT*, October, 49–54.
Ananda, J. (2014), 'Evaluating the performance of urban water utilities: robust nonparametric approach', *Journal of Water Resources Planning and Management*, **140** (9), doi: 10.1061/(ASCE)WR.1943-5452.0000387.
Ananda, J. and B. Hampf (2015), 'Measuring environmentally sensitive productivity growth: an application to the urban water sector', *Ecological Economics*, **116**, 211–219.
Antonioli, B. and M. Filippini (2001), 'The use of a variable cost function in the regulation of the Italian water industry', *Utilities Policy*, **10**, 181–187.
Anwandter, L. and T.J. Ozuna (2002), 'Can public sector reforms improve the efficiency of public water utilities?' *Environment and Development Economics*, 7, 687–700.
Ashbolt, N., D. Livingston, G. Peters, E. Lai and S. Lundie (2006), 'A sustainability framework for the Australian water industry', *Water: Journal of the Australian Water Association* **33**, 83–88.
Ashton, J.K. (2003), 'Capital utilisation and scale in the English and Welsh water industry', *Service Industries Journal* **23**, 137–149.
Ashton, J.K. (2000), 'Total factor productivity growth and technical change in the water and sewerage industry', *Service Industries Journal* **20**, 121–130.
Bark, R.H., M.J. Colloff, D.M. Hatton, C.A. Pollino, S. Jackson and N.D. Crossman (2016), 'Integrated valuation of ecosystem services obtained from restoring water to the environment in a major regulated river basin', *Ecosystem Services*, 22, Part B, 381–391.
Benito, B., F. Bastida and J.A. García (2010), 'Explaining differences in efficiency: an application to Spanish municipalities', *Applied Economics*, **42**, 515–528.
Bottasso, A. and M. Conti (2003), 'Cost Inefficiency in the English and Welsh water industry: an heteroskedastic stochastic cost frontier approach, Economics Discussion Papers', University of Essex, Department of Economics.
Brunone, B., O. Giustolisi, M. Ferrante, D. Laucelli, S. Meniconi, L. Berardi, A. Campisano, L. Berardi, S. Liu, D. Laucelli, S. Xu, P. Xu, W. Zeng and O. Giustolisi (2014), 'Energy saving and leakage control in water distribution networks: a joint research project between Italy and China', 12th International Conference on Computing and Control for the Water Industry, CCWI2013, *Procedia Engineering*, **70**, 152–161.

Busch, M., A. La Notte, V. Laporte and M. Erhard (2012), 'Potentials of quantitative and qualitative approaches to assessing ecosystem services', *Ecological Indicators*, **21**, 89–103.

Byrnes, J., L. Crase, B. Dollery and R. Villano (2010), 'The relative economic efficiency of urban water utilities in regional New South Wales and Victoria', *Resource and Energy Economics*, **32**, 439–455.

Carvalho, P. and R.C. Marques (2014), 'Computing economies of vertical integration, economies of scope and economies of scale using partial frontier nonparametric methods', *European Journal of Operational Research*, **234**, 292–307.

Carvalho, P. and R.C. Marques (2011), 'The influence of the operational environment on the efficiency of water utilities', *Journal of Environmental Management*, **92**, 2698–2707.

Corton, M.L. (2003), 'Benchmarking in the Latin American water sector: the case of Peru', *Utilities Policy*, **11**, 133–142.

Daraio, C. and L. Simar (2005), 'Introducing environmental variables in nonparametric frontier models: a probabilistic approach', *Journal of Productivity Analysis*, **24**, 93–121.

Delgado-Galván, X., R. Pérez-García, J. Izquierdo and J. Mora-Rodríguez (2010), 'An analytic hierarchy process for assessing externalities in water leakage management', *Mathematical and Computer Modelling*, **52**, 1194–1202.

Deng, G., L. Li and Y. Song (2016), 'Provincial water use efficiency measurement and factor analysis in China: based on SBM-DEA model', *Ecological Indicators*, **69**, 12–18.

Djukic, M., I. Jovanoski, O.M. Ivanovic, M. Lazic and D. Bodroza (2016), 'Cost-benefit analysis of an infrastructure project and a cost-reflective tariff: a case study for investment in wastewater treatment plant in Serbia', *Renewable and Sustainable Energy Reviews*, **59**, 1419–1425.

Färe, R., S. Grosskopf and C.A.K. Lovell (1988), 'An indirect approach to the evaluation of producer performance', *Journal of Public Economics*, **37**, 71–89.

Färe, R., S. Grosskopf, C.A.K. Lovell and S. Yaisawarng (1993), 'Derivation of shadow prices for undesirable outputs: a distance function approach', *Review of Economics and Statistics*, **75**, 374–380.

Farsi, M., M. Filippini and W. Greene (2005a), 'Efficiency measurement in network industries: application to the Swiss railway companies', *Journal of Regulatory Economics*, **28**, 69–90.

Farsi, M., M. Filippini and M. Kuenzle (2005b), 'Unobserved heterogeneity in stochastic cost frontier models: an application to Swiss nursing homes', *Applied Economics*, **37**, 2127–2141.

Faust, A. and A. Baranzini (2014), 'The economic performance of Swiss drinking water utilities', *Journal of Productivity Analysis*, **41**, 383–397.

Filippini, M., N Hrovatin and J. Zoric (2008), 'Cost efficiency of Slovenian water distribution utilities: an application of stochastic frontier methods', *Journal of Productivity Analysis*, **29**, 169–182.

Frauendorfer, R. and R. Liemberger (2010), *The Issues and Challenges of Reducing Non-Revenue Water*, Mandaluyong City, Philippines: Asian Development Bank.

Garcia, S. and A. Thomas (2001), 'The structure of municipal water supply costs: application to a panel of French local communities', *Journal of Productivity Analysis*, **16**, 5–29.

Garrido-Baserba, M., R. Reif, M. Molinos-Senante, L. Larrea, A. Castillo, M. Verdaguer and M. Poch (2016), 'Application of a multi-criteria decision model to select of design choices for WWTPs', *Clean Technologies and Environmental Policy*, **18** (4), 1097–1109.

González-Gómez, F. and M.A. García-Rubio (2008), 'Efficiency in the management of urban water services: what have we learned after four decades of research?', *Revista de Economía Pública (Hacienda Pública Española)*, **185**, 39–67.

Guerrini, A., G. Romano and B. Campedelli (2013), 'Economies of scale, scope, and density in the Italian water sector: a two-stage data envelopment analysis approach', *Water Resources Management*, **27**, 4559–4578.

Guerrini, A., G. Romano, C. Leardini and M. Martini (2015), 'The effects of operational and environmental variables on efficiency of Danish water and wastewater utilities', *Water*, **7**, 3263.

GWP (2012), 'What is IWRM?', Global Water Partnership. Accessed 5 October 2016 at www.gwp.org/the-challenge/what-is-iwrm/.

Hailu, K.B. and M. Tanaka (2015), 'A "true" random effects stochastic frontier analysis for technical efficiency and heterogeneity: evidence from manufacturing firms in Ethiopia', *Economic Modelling*, **50**, 179–192.

Hernández-Sancho, F., M. Molinos-Senante, R. Sala-Garrido and S. Del Saz-Salazar (2012), 'Tariffs and efficient performance by water suppliers: an empirical approach', *Water Policy*, **14**, 854–864.

Hernández-Sancho, F., S. Del Saz-Salazar and R. Sala-Garrido (2009), 'Economic and technical efficiency of drinking water systems: an empirical approach for Spain', in Hlavinek, P., Popovska, C., Marsalek, J., Mahrikova, I. and Kukharchyk, T. (eds), *Risk Management of Water Supply and Sanitation Systems*. Springer, Dordrecht, pp. 115–124.

Hernández-Sancho, F., M. Molinos-Senante and R. Sala-Garrido (2010), 'Economic valuation of environmental benefits from wastewater treatment processes: an empirical approach for Spain', *Science of the Total Environment*, **408**, 953–957.

Horn, T. (2011), 'Incorporating water purification in efficiency evaluation: evidence from Japanese water utilities', *Applied Economics Letters*, **18**, 1789–1794.

Kellermann, M.A. (2015), 'Total factor productivity decomposition and unobserved heterogeneity in stochastic frontier models', *Agricultural and Resource Economics Review*, **44**, 124–148.

Kopsakangas-Savolainen, M. and R. Svento (2011), 'Observed and unobserved heterogeneity in stochastic frontier models: an application to the electricity distribution industry', *Energy Economics*, **33**, 304–310.

Kumar, S. (2010), 'Unaccounted for water and the performance of water utilities: an empirical analysis from India', *Water Policy*, **12**, 707–721.

Kumar, S., A. Groth and L. Vlacic (2015), 'Cost evaluation of water and wastewater treatment plants using water price index', *Water Resources Management*, **29**, 3343–3356.

Landu, L. and A.C. Brent (2006), 'Environmental life cycle assessment of water supply in South Africa: the Rosslyn industrial area as a case study', *WATER SA* **32**, 249–256.

Lannier, A.L. and S. Porcher (2014), 'Efficiency in the public and private French water utilities: prospects for benchmarking', *Applied Economics*, **46**, 556–572.

Lin, C. (2005), 'Service quality and prospects for benchmarking: evidence from the Peru water sector', *Utilities Policy*, **13**, 230–239.

Lundie, S., G.M. Peters and P.C Beavis (2004), 'Life cycle assessment for sustainable metropolitan water systems planning', *Environmental Science and Technology*, **38**, 3465–3473.

Mande Buafua, P. (2015), 'Efficiency of urban water supply in sub-Saharan Africa: do organization and regulation matter?' *Utilities Policy* **37**, 13–22.

Marques, R.C., S. Berg and S. Yane (2014), 'Nonparametric benchmarking of Japanese water utilities: institutional and environmental factors affecting efficiency', *Journal of Water Resources Planning and Management*, **140**, 562–571.

Marques, R.C., N.F. da Cruz and J. Pires (2015), 'Measuring the sustainability of urban water services', *Environmental Science and Policy*, **54**, 142–151.

Maziotis, A., M. Molinos-Senante and R. Sala-Garrido (2016a), 'Assessing the impact of quality of service on the productivity of water industry: a Malmquist-Luenberger approach for England and Wales', *Water Resources Management*, 1–21, doi: 10.1007/s11269-016-1395-6.

Maziotis, A., D.S. Saal, E. Thanassoulis and M. Molinos-Senante (2016b), 'Price-cap regulation in the English and Welsh water industry: a proposal for measuring productivity performance', *Utilities Policy*, **41**, 22–30.

Medellín-Azuara, J., L.G. Mendoza-Espinosa, J.R. Lund and R.J. Ramírez-Acosta (2007), 'The application of economic-engineering optimisation for water management in Ensenada, Baja California, Mexico', *Water Science and Technology*, **55**, 339–347.

Mellah, T. and T. Ben Amor (2016), 'Performance of the Tunisian water utility: an input-distance function approach', *Utilities Policy*, **38**, 18–32.

Mercadier, A.C., W.A. Cont and G. Ferro (2016), 'Economies of scale in Peru's water and sanitation sector', *Journal of Productivity Analysis*, **45**, 215–228.

Mizutani, F. and T. Urakami (2001), 'Identifying network density and scale economies for Japanese water supply organizations', *Papers in Regional Science*, **80**, 211–230.

Molinos-Senante, M., R. Reif, M. Garrido-Baserba, F. Hernández-Sancho, F. Omil, M. Poch and R. Sala-Garrido (2013), 'Economic valuation of environmental benefits of removing pharmaceutical and personal care products from WWTP effluents by ozonation', *Science of the Total Environment*, **461–462**, 409–415.

Molinos-Senante, M., F. Hernández-Sancho, M. Mocholí-Arce and R. Sala-Garrido (2014) 'A management and optimisation model for water supply planning in water deficit areas', *Journal of Hydrology*, **515**, 139–146.

Molinos-Senante, M. and R. Sala-Garrido (2015), 'The impact of privatization approaches on the productivity growth of the water industry: a case study of Chile', *Environmental Science and Policy*, **50**, 166–179.

Molinos-Senante, M., A. Maziotis, M. Mocholí-Arce and R. Sala-Garrido (2015a), 'Accounting for service quality to customers in the efficiency of water companies: evidence from England and Wales', *Water Policy*, **18** (2), doi: 10.2166/wp.2015.062.

Molinos-Senante, M., A. Maziotis and R. Sala-Garrido (2015b), 'Assessing the relative efficiency of water companies in the English and Welsh water industry: a metafrontier approach', *Environmental Science and Pollution Research*, **22**, 16987–16996.

Molinos-Senante, M., R. Sala-Garrido and M. Lafuente (2015c), 'The role of environmental variables on the efficiency of water and sewerage companies: a case study of Chile', *Environmental Science and Pollution Research*, **22**, 10242–10253.

Molinos-Senante, M. and R. Sala-Garrido (2016), 'Performance of fully private and concessionary water and sewerage companies: a metafrontier approach', *Environmental Science and Pollution Research*, **23**, 11620–11629.

Molinos-Senante, M., R.C. Marques, F. Pérez, T. Gómez, R. Sala-Garrido and R. Caballero (2016a), 'Assessing the sustainability of water companies: a synthetic indicator approach', *Ecological Indicators*, **61** (2), 577–587.

Molinos-Senante, M., A. Maziotis and R. Sala-Garrido (2016b), 'Estimating the cost of improving service quality in water supply: a shadow price approach for England and Wales', *Science of the Total Environment*, **539**, 470–477.

Molinos-Senante, M., M. Mocholí-Arce and R. Sala-Garrido (2016c), 'Estimating the environmental and resource costs of leakage in water distribution systems: a shadow price approach', *Science of the Total Environment*, **568**, 180–188.

Mugisha, S. (2014), 'Frontier distance function analysis for water supply systems', *Proceedings of the Institution of Civil Engineers: Municipal Engineer*, **167**, 11–21.

Mugisha, S. (2013), 'Data envelopment analysis in target setting of water utilities', *Proceedings of the Institution of Civil Engineers: Municipal Engineer*, **166**, 157–166.

Oh, D. (2010), 'A global Malmquist-Luenberger productivity index', *Journal of Productivity Analysis*, **34**, 183–197.

Picazo-Tadeo, A.J., F.J. Sáez-Fernández and F. González-Gómez (2008), 'Does service quality matter in measuring the performance of water utilities?' *Utilities Policy*, **16**, 30–38.

Picazo-Tadeo, A., F.J. Sáez-Fernández and F. González-Gómez (2009), 'The role of environmental factors in water utilities' technical efficiency: empirical evidence from Spanish companies', *Applied Economics*. **41**, 615–628.

Romano, G. and A. Guerrini (2011), 'Measuring and comparing the efficiency of water utility companies: A data envelopment analysis approach', *Utilities Policy*, **19**, 202–209.

Saal, D.S., P. Arocena, A. Maziotis and T. Triebs (2013), 'Scale and scope economies and the efficient vertical and horizontal configuration of the water industry: a survey of the literature', *Review of Network Economics*, **12**, 93–129.

Saal, D.S. and D. Parker (2001), 'Productivity and price performance in the privatized water and sewerage companies of England and Wales', *Journal of Regulatory Economics*, **20**, 61–90.

Saal, D.S. and D. Parker (2000), 'The impact of privatization and regulation on the water and sewerage industry in England and Wales: a translog cost function model', *Managerial and Decision Economics*, **21**, 253–268.

Saal, D.S., D. Parker and T. Weyman-Jones (2007), 'Determining the contribution of technical change, efficiency change and scale change to productivity growth in the privatized English and Welsh water and sewerage industry: 1985–2000', *Journal of Productivity Analysis*, **28**, 127–139.

Sauer, J. (2005), 'Economies of scale and firm size optimum in rural water supply', *Water Resources Research*, **41** (11), doi: 10.1029/2005WR004127.

Sauer, J. and K. Frohberg (2007), 'Allocative efficiency of rural water supply: a globally flexible SGM cost frontier', *Journal of Productivity Analysis*, **27**, 31–40.

Schulz, M., M.D. Short and G.M. Peters (2012), 'A streamlined sustainability assessment tool for improved decision making in the urban water industry', *Integrated Environmental Assessment and Management*, **8**, 183–193.

See, K.F. (2015), 'Exploring and analysing sources of technical efficiency in water supply services: some evidence from Southeast Asian public water utilities', *Water Resources and Economics*, **9**, 23–44.

Seppälä, O.T., J.J. Hukka and T.S. Katko (2001), 'Public–private partnerships in water and sewerage services: privatization for profit or improvement of service and performance?' *Public Works Management and Policy*, **6**, 42–58.

Sharma, A.K., A.L. Grant, T. Grant, F. Pamminger and L. Opray (2009), 'Environmental and economic assessment of urban water services for a greenfield development', *Environmental Engineering Science*, **26**, 921–934.

Shephard, R.W. (1970), *Theory of Cost and Production Functions*, Princeton University Press, Princeton.

Thanassoulis, E. (2000a), 'DEA and its use in the regulation of water companies', *European Journal of Operational Research*, **127**, 1–13.

Thanassoulis, E. (2000b), 'The use of data envelopment analysis in the regulation of UK water utilities: water distribution', *European Journal of Operational Research*, **126**, 436–453.

Torres, M. and C.J. Morrison Paul (2006), 'Driving forces for consolidation or fragmentation of the US water utility industry: a cost function approach with endogenous output', *Journal of Urban Economics*, **59**, 104–120.

Tupper, H.C. and M. Resende (2004), 'Efficiency and regulatory issues in the Brazilian water and sewage sector: an empirical study', *Utilities Policy*, **12**, 29–40.

Walter, M., A. Cullmann, C. von Hirschhausen, R. Wand and M. Zschille (2009), 'Quo vadis efficiency analysis of water distribution? A comparative literature review', *Utilities Policy*, **17**, 225–232.

Wang, Y. and Y. Lan (2011), 'Measuring Malmquist productivity index: a new approach based on double frontiers data envelopment analysis', *Mathematical and Computer Modelling*, **54**, 2760–2771.

Wei, C., A. Löschel and B. Liu (2013), 'An empirical analysis of the CO2 shadow price in Chinese thermal power enterprises', *Energy Economics*, **40**, 22–31.

Woodbury, K. and B. Dollery (2004), 'Efficiency measurement in Australian local government: the case of New South Wales municipal water services', *Review of Policy Research*, **21**, 615–636.

Worthington, A.C. (2014), 'A review of frontier approaches to efficiency and productivity measurement in urban water utilities', *Urban Water Journal*, **11**, 55–73.

Zschille, M. (2015), 'Consolidating the water industry: an analysis of the potential gains from horizontal integration in a conditional efficiency framework', *Journal of Productivity Analysis*, **44**, 97–114.

Zschille, M. and M. Walter (2012), 'The performance of German water utilities: a (semi)-parametric analysis', *Applied Economics*, **44**, 3749–3764.

10. Valuing environmental and health impacts from no action in wastewater management

Francesc Hernández-Sancho, Birguy Lamizana-Diallo and William Ingram

10.1 INTRODUCTION

'Wastewater' is a somewhat misleading term. With proper management, the energy, the nutrients, the other valuable materials, together with the water itself, need not go to waste at all. Wastewater could instead generate significant dividends for economies, societies and the environment. Therefore, proper management of wastewater is not only a challenge but also an opportunity. An integrated approach to water resources management favours wastewater reuse, as outlined in various policy frameworks such as the European Water Framework Directive (Bixio, 2006). The Global Wastewater Initiative (GW^2I), a multi-stakeholder platform under the United Nations Environment Programme (UNEP) Global Programme of Action for the Protection of the Marine Environment from Land-Based Activities (GPA), is working to promote the potential of wastewater reuse for greater economic, societal and food security.

The composition of wastewater effluent is typically at least 99 per cent water, with suspended, colloidal and dissolved solids making up the remaining 1 per cent. Municipal wastewater can contain organics, minerals, nutrients and inorganics, along with toxic chemicals and pathogenic microorganisms. Quality of industrial wastewater varies depending on the process that the water is used for, and the industry itself. Such contaminated waters can contain pollutants that can at the same time be valuable resources, like precious metals and heavy metals. For example, a wastewater treatment plant in Suwa, Japan, situated near a significant number of precision equipment manufacturers, reported nearly 2 kilograms of gold per tonne of ash from burning sludge, which is a higher percentage of gold than that found in the ore in many gold mines.

The success of wastewater reclamation and reuse relies on careful planning, detailed economic calculation and thorough social and political considerations and assessment (Huertas et al., 2008). This review will concisely outline some of the approaches promoted by the Global Wastewater Initiative, their benefits and also the risks in the context of 'cost of no action'.

Agriculture is the top user of reclaimed wastewater, with reuse ranging from individual household applications (such as at-source separation of urine and its dilution and application to crops) to large-scale irrigation systems. Nutrients from wastewater – especially nitrogen, phosphorus and potassium – can benefit crop yields and reduce synthetic fertiliser use and the associated costs of environmental damage. For example, increasingly expensive and non-renewable mined phosphate fertilisers can be supplemented by human organic sewage, of which about 0.5 per cent by weight is phosphorus.

Another potential output of wastewater is energy. Organics in wastewater can be stabilised by anaerobic digestion, a bacterial process with by-products of methane and carbon dioxide. This is commonly practised in wastewater treatment plants. The methane can be burnt as an energy source, and the stabilised sludge can be used in agriculture (Stillwell et al., 2010). The common practice at wastewater treatment plants of anaerobic digestion being combined with aerobic digestion means that only a portion of the potential energy can be captured, and methods to improve this efficiency are being developed (McCarty et al., 2011). It has been shown that the potential energy available in raw municipal wastewater can far exceed the electricity requirements of the treatment process – in one study by a factor of 9.3 (Shizas and Bagley, 2004).

Suspended solids can be collected from wastewater, compressed into briquettes and burnt as fuel. This was one approach promoted by one of the GW²I's projects in Georgia. Wastewater reuse is also related to energy embedded in the production of fertilisers. Around 2 per cent of the world's energy expenditure goes towards the Haber-Bosch process to satisfy demand for nitrogen (N) fertiliser. Closing the loop and applying nutrients directly to crops, alongside reductions in associated fertiliser transport, would reduce fossil fuel use, making this a climate-smart practice. This is especially relevant in energy insecure countries.

The use of heat pumps to capture thermal energy of wastewater has high potential for low-energy requirements, such as heating buildings. Here, electrical energy is used to extract heat from the wastewater source and transfer it to where it is required. The ratio of the heat energy transferred to the electrical energy used typically has values of between 2 and 5 (McCarty et al., 2011). Removing thermal energy will still allow for the wastewater to be used for other beneficial purposes. This has the potential to satisfy energy, agricultural and water demands, sitting in the centre of the food–energy–water nexus.

Turning wastewater into drinking water is also showing promising application with direct potable reuse (DPR) and indirect potable reuse (IPR). IPR can be achieved by mixing treated wastewater into a reservoir or through aquifer recharge. This can replenish groundwater and reduce local water scarcity. DPR requires treating wastewater to drinking standards by filtration, reverse osmosis and treatment with ultraviolet (UV) and hydrogen peroxide. One DPR system currently provides 250,000 people in Windhoek, Namibia, with safe drinking water. However, the uptake of these systems around the world is still slow. A significant reason for this is the public perception of water quality associated with reuse systems.

Resolving the complexities in wastewater reuse management could benefit from rigorous multi-criteria decision analyses. A change of mindset across different levels of decision-making is needed before wastewater moves from being an expensive waste to a valuable resource. While in developing countries the main challenge is the implementation of wastewater treatment systems, in developed countries the objective is to treat wastewater without harming the environment – i.e. by generating the lowest possible environmental impact. In this sense, since the mid-2000s, the existing systems in the developed world have been increasingly criticised from the viewpoint of sustainability (Kärrman, 2001).

The conventional sanitary systems in developed countries in effect transform a concentrated domestic health and environmental problem into a diffuse problem for the entire settlement and/or region (Bdour et al., 2009). According to Van Lier et al. (1998), the criteria for sustainable wastewater treatment technology must include:

- no dilution of high-strength wastes with clean water;
- maximum recovery and reuse of treated water and by-products obtained from the pollution substances (i.e. irrigation, fertilization);
- application of efficient, robust and reliable treatment/conversion technologies, which are low cost (in construction, operation and maintenance), have a long lifetime and are plain in operation and maintenance;
- being applicable at any scale, very small as well as very big;
- leading to a high self-sufficiency in all respects; and
- being acceptable to the local population.

Regions affected by water scarcity have another challenge, which is the regeneration of the wastewater with a certain quality allowing their reuse for different purposes. In this context, several research studies have shown that treated wastewater, if appropriately managed, is viewed as a major component of the water resources supply to meet the needs of a growing economy (El Fadel et al., 2002).

Investments in wastewater management are required both in developed and developing countries. Sound decision-making involves adopting criteria based on policies, specific projects and/or interventions which are judged appropriate for the region, and subsequently performing an appraisal of how alternative options compare (Pearce et al., 2012). Under the current global economic crisis, an economic investment criterion has become essential to support improvements in sustainable wastewater management. While it is national policies that typically determine which programmes are implemented, a need for consistent economic standards to review and establish competitive water interventions should be considered in the current economic climate (Ward, 2012).

In order to develop effective policies and instruments in the management of wastewater, it is necessary to understand the total benefits from avoided pollutant discharge into the environment, and to incorporate them into the policy design. Economic valuation is often used as a tool to understand the costs and benefits of different choices, and it can contribute to sustainable development. The fact that both costs and benefits use a common metric – money – can help overcome fragmentation in cross-sectoral decision-making and build a broad alliance of stakeholders by quantifying the common interests and mutual dependence of different stakeholders (Lange and Jiddawi, 2009).

The monetary valuation of environmental benefits provides an enhanced understanding for improving the economics of wastewater management and treatment. Therefore, stakeholders and planners are now equipped with knowledge for planning and decision-making processes. These results will also be valuable in selecting the most feasible intervention strategy when several alternatives are available.

10.2   COST OF NO ACTION APPROACH

Agricultural use of wastewater has been common practice for centuries, and now around 50 countries report benefitting from it. Global water scarcity, along with poverty in the developing world, is helping to drive this. Untreated wastewater reuse is not limited to the developing world, and is also common practice elsewhere (Raschid-Sally and Jayakody, 2008).

It is estimated that around 7 per cent of the world's total irrigated land (20 million ha) is under irrigation with untreated or partially treated wastewater, particularly in arid regions (UN-Water, 2013). Unreported use is likely to be much higher. In many cities, peri-urban agriculture benefits from wastewater irrigation and, despite only having small areas available for crops, can show high productivity. A study in Accra, Ghana, demonstrated that 200,000 urban dwellers benefit from vegetables grown on only 100 ha of land (Raschid-Sally and Jayakody, 2008).

Wastewater management and treatment involves potentially significant benefits (avoided costs); therefore, the cost of no action in terms of treatment may be interpreted as benefits not achieved due to the discharge of wastewater without treatment. These potential benefits associated with improving wastewater management can be grouped into market and non-market benefits. While market benefits are easily identifiable and quantifiable, non-market benefits are difficult to measure, and require economic valuation methods.

The cost of no action in the context of wastewater management can be also classified into costs due to adverse human health effects associated with poor quality of drinking water, and into negative environmental effects.

10.2.1 Human Health Effects

Health problems related to untreated wastewater are a major challenge. They are typically caused by the presence of pathogenic microorganisms transmitted to humans through food, water or other vectors. Additionally, non-communicable diseases can arise due to significant concentrations of toxic chemicals from industrial wastewater, such as heavy metals and salts, or from household and pharmaceutical products (Salgot et al., 2006).

It is well known that unmanaged wastewater can be a source of pollution, a hazard for the health of human populations and the environment alike. It is therefore understandable that the newly adopted 2030 agenda for Sustainable Development Goals (SDGs) put emphasis on addressing the unsustainable patterns of pollution, such as in wastewater, as highlighted in Goal 6, target 6.3: 'By 2030, improve water quality by reducing pollution, eliminating dumping and minimizing release of hazardous chemicals and materials, halving the proportion of untreated wastewater and substantially increasing recycling and safe reuse globally.' This entails improved and adequate sanitation facilities and wastewater treatment technologies.

It should be highlighted that inadequate sanitation is one of the biggest contributing factors to child mortality under the age of five (Cumming, 2009). In fact, at least 1.8 million children under five die every year due to water-related disease (WHO, 2008). Ten years after the adoption of the Millennium Development Goals (MDGs), 2.5 billion people were still without improved sanitation. Nevertheless, great disparities between regions should be noted: virtually the entire population of the developed regions use improved facilities (95 per cent), but in developing regions only half of the population (56 per cent) has access to improved sanitation facilities. Among the people in the world who do not use improved sanitation facilities, by far the greatest number are in Sub-Saharan Africa and South Asia, where only 30 per cent and 41 per cent of people, respectively, are covered (WHO-UNICEF, 2012).

Sanitation has the potential to accelerate progress towards the most MDGs in which society lags behind, and to multiply existing investment in these sectors. For example, Education for All (EFA) reported the disproportionate effect that poor sanitation has on female student enrolment and attendance, and called on national governments to address gender disparities by building schools with proper sanitation (UNESCO, 2008).

Subsistence farmers who stand to gain the most from wastewater irrigation with increased food security and nutrition are also likely to have the highest risk from health impacts from the use of untreated wastewater. High costs of healthcare and missed days of work may counterbalance the economic gains of reusing wastewater, and increase poverty. UNEP's 'Sick Water?' report (2010) outlines the policy recommendation that 'Financing should take account of the fact that there are important livelihood opportunities in improving wastewater treatment processes.'

Irrigation with untreated wastewater risks the addition of toxins such as heavy metals into the soil and groundwater, alongside nutrient loading. This could directly influence aquatic fauna and bio-magnify in species higher up the food chain. Uptake by crops or pasture could result in direct human ingestion or indirect ingestion via the consumption of cows' milk, for example, which puts many infants in the developing world at risk (Pilarczyk et al., 2013). Contamination of produce is highlighted as an example of a cost of no action in terms of wastewater treatment in the 2015 UNEP report 'Economic Valuation of Wastewater'.

Agricultural application of wastewater is largely done on an unplanned basis, as outlined in the Wastewater Analytical Brief by UN-Water, often resulting in poorly treated wastewater being reused. WHO promotes an integrated risk assessment and management approach, which covers the chain from the wastewater source to the point of crop consumption. When wastewater treatment is not available, a multi-barrier approach should be applied, considering crop choice, type of irrigation, harvesting time and protection for farmers. The largest risks to health are from crops eaten raw that have been in close proximity to the irrigated soil, with intestinal helminths (parasitic worms) being the most likely cause of infection. WHO, the UN Food and Agriculture Organization (FAO) and UNEP published a series of reports, the *2006 WHO Guidelines*, for the safe use of wastewater, excreta and greywater which have served as references for good practices.

Wastewater may pollute drinking water if it is discharged in water bodies that are also sources of drinking water. The adverse health effects include the following economic components:

- direct medical expenditures for illness treatment;
- indirect costs resulting from illness, which includes the value of time lost from work, decreased productivity, increased possibility of facing demotion, money spent as caregivers, and premature death (Calhoun and Bennet, 2003); and
- pain and suffering associated with illness.

The first two effects refer to market value. These effects can be directly quantified, e.g. the health costs generated by increasing drinking water contamination. However, the last effect is a non-market value that can only be quantified by economic valuation methods.

The medical costs of caring for illnesses associated with drinking unsafe water have been widely studied (Hutton et al., 2007; Kim et al., 2012; Gordon et al., 2011). The methodology to analyse medical costs are diverse, and dependent on the type of illness. Therefore, to quantify a particular cost type the first step is to identify the most significant diseases associated with water contamination; here, cooperation between regional economic and health professionals is vital.

In general, many factors affect patient medical costs, including gender, age and geographic region, among others. All available variables should be considered to characterise patient medical costs. The value of productivity lost through illness or premature mortality results in substantial losses to society. Consequently, an economic assessment of interventions to improve water quality should integrate avoided costs. Despite several approaches to estimating indirect costs associated with illness, the human capital approach is most widely applied. It relies on earnings as a measure of productivity. The methodology calculates expected lifetime earnings that would have been earned had disease or death been avoided (Bradley et al., 2008). Consequently, lost earnings are used as a proxy for loss in productivity. Wage and production structure data for this purpose can be obtained from national or regional bureaus of statistics.

In relation to non-market values, the methods used to estimate the economic value of risk reductions are based on willingness to pay (WTP). Many studies have examined WTP for reducing different types of risk, including air pollution (Roman et al., 2012), road safety (Hakes and Viscusi,

2007) and accidents in the workplace (Tsai et al., 2011). Contributions to drinking water quality have been more limited, and served to estimate the economic value of health costs avoided derived from risk reductions associated with improving drinking water quality (Adamowick et al., 2011; Maddison et al., 2005).

The health effects, i.e., the cost of no action from a health perspective, can be expressed as:

$$HAC = \sum_{t=1}^{T} \frac{\left(\sum_{k=1}^{K} ME_{kt} * n_{kt}\right) + \left(\sum_{j=1}^{J} AW_{jt} * n_{jt}\right) + (WTPR_t * N_t)}{(1+r)^t} \tag{10.1}$$

where HAC are the health costs (€); ME_k is the direct medical expenditure for one person to treat the illness k (€ person^{-1} year^{-1}); n_k is the number of cases of the illness k; AW_j is the average wage of the productive sector j (€ person^{-1} year^{-1}); n_j is the number of cases of the illness in the productive sector j; $WTPR$ is the average WTP for risk reduction (€ person^{-1} year^{-1}); N is the total population of an area affected by the polluted water; r is the discount rate; t is the year; and T is the time horizon.

10.2.2 Environmental Effects

The discharge of reused wastewater into water bodies causes major impacts on the environment. Eutrophication is one of the most prevalent risks to freshwater around the globe, and wastewater contributes to the 80 million tonnes of nitrogen and 10 million tonnes of phosphorus already entering aquatic ecosystems each year (UN-Water, 2013). This far outweighs natural inputs, leading to economic losses from denigrated ecosystem services.

Additionally, nutrients in reused wastewater that supplement fertiliser use may not be present in ideally balanced concentrations. An excess of some nutrients over others has been shown to reduce productivity (UN-Water, 2014). Better information about crop requirements and wastewater nutrient concentrations would allow for better integrated management. Massive soil quality reductions from salts have been documented in China, attesting to a lack of suitable systemic risk management platforms that cover all aspects of wastewater treatment, transport, distribution and use (Yi et al., 2011).

If wastewater is not treated and managed adequately, significant environmental damage is generated. The assessment of this environmental impact requires application of economic valuation methods. Consequently, economic theory has developed a wide range of techniques to value non-market goods, including placing a value on environmental damage.

Economic valuation of wastewater reuse and management is complex and incomplete, but is nonetheless an important tool for policy makers and operators at all levels. Because some benefits to reuse have not been assigned market values, for example broader environmental implications, they have not traditionally been included in economic assessments. The GW²I promotes methodologies that allow a comparison of estimated cost of no action (benefits lost) with costs of action on wastewater treatment, to provide useful information to decision-makers.

Traditional valuation techniques are based on the notion of demand. In the field that concerns us, stated preference methods are the most common (Bateman et al., 2006). These approaches are based on simulating a hypothetical market by conducting surveys. Surveying techniques are used to elicit individuals' WTP for the hypothetical provision of an environmental good (e.g. an improvement in water quality as a consequence of wastewater treatment). The values obtained are taken to represent the economic benefits or costs avoided of the proposed change in environmental quality, and can be aggregated in a cost-benefit framework to obtain the social benefits of public policies aimed at improving social welfare.

Therefore, the empirical results from valuation studies provide a wealth of information about the value that the population of interest is placing on a programme of providing an environmental good (Carson and Hanemann, 2005). These studies usually generate information about the broad shape of the WTP distribution and how that distribution varies with respondent characteristics such as income, education and age. The primary categories of stated preference methods are the contingent valuation (CV) method and choice modelling techniques. CV is a survey-based method widely used for placing monetary values on environmental goods. This survey approach relies on asking respondents in a hypothetical market how much they are willing to pay for a specific public good. Different elicitation formats can be used; however the most commonly used question format is the discrete choice model, first introduced in CV analysis by Bishop and Heberlein (1979) and ratified by the National Oceanic and Atmospheric Administration (NOAA) Blue Ribbon Panel (Arrow et al., 1993).

Respondents are directly questioned regarding their WTP for increases in public goods in the contingent valuation method. Alternatively, the choice modelling techniques are based on ranking or rating a series of 'product profits' that characterise products.

Based on CV methodology, the environmental benefits associated with an improvement of wastewater treatment can be expressed as follows:

$$EB = \sum_{t=1}^{T} \frac{(WTPE_t * NH_t)}{(1+r)^t} \qquad (10.2)$$

where *EB* are the environmental benefits (€); *WTPE* is the average willingness to pay for improving the quality of water bodies (€/household-year); *NH* is the number of households in the area affected by the intervention; *r* is the discount rate; *t* is the year; and *T* is the intervention time horizon.

10.2.3   Other Methodologies: Shadow Price Approach

Despite the popularity of the stated preference methods for economic valuation of water quality, there are other methodologies that can be used for the purpose. In this context, using the concept of a distance function (Färe et al., 1993) it is possible to calculate the shadow prices for undesirable outputs – the pollutants to be removed from the wastewater – that have a clear negative impact on the environment. In this sense, wastewater treatment is considered as a productive process in which a desirable output (treated water) is obtained together with a series of undesirable outputs (suspended solids, nitrogen, phosphorus and so on).

A shadow price for these undesirable outputs can be considered as the equivalent of the environmental damage avoided, since if they are dumped without control they would cause a negative impact on the environment (Hernández-Sancho et al., 2010). So, the avoided costs estimated with the methodology of shadow prices represent an estimation of the economic value of the environmental benefits obtained from the treatment process aimed at improving water quality. These benefits, as in the case of CV, can also be incorporated in a cost-benefit framework.

The shadow price approach was used previously to estimate the economic value of atmospheric pollutants (Coggin and Swinton, 1996; Swinton, 1998); but, more recently, several empirical applications have been developed to calculate shadow prices of pollutants removed from wastewater during treatment (Hernández-Sancho et al., 2010; Molinos-Senante et al., 2011a). In this approach, pollutants extracted from wastewater are undesirable outputs that can generate a negative impact on the environment. Therefore, shadow prices for these contaminants could be representative of the environmental benefits of wastewater treatment.

The literature on environmental benefits of wastewater treatment using the shadow price methodology is quite recent. Adaptation of the methodology developed by Färe et al. (1993) to the wastewater framework was carried out by Hernández-Sancho et al. (2010). The authors calculated the shadow price of five pollutants: nitrogen (N); phosphorus (P), suspended solids (SS), biological demand of oxygen (BOD) and chemical demand of oxygen (COD). The various economic values of the contaminants are affected by the type of water body into which the effluent is discharged. Furthermore, Molinos-Senante et al. (2011b) compare the environmental benefits of improving wastewater treatment obtained using shadow price methodology on one hand, and contingent valuation on the other. This comparison has been applied in the Serpis River Basin (Spain) in order to fulfil the European Water Framework Directive. It is important to note that shadow prices are the avoided costs resulting from the removal of pollutants during the wastewater treatment. For example, the shadow price of nitrogen if it is discharged to wetlands is -65.209 €/kg, meaning that every kilogram of this nutrient that is not dumped into a wetland results in environmental damage prevented, or the environmental benefit generated by removing it from wastewater equals €65.209 (UNEP, 2015).

The suitability of each methodology will depend on several factors. CV is a very flexible technique that can be applied to a great variety of non-market goods. Even though the distance function methodology has a more limited scope, it may be useful to quantify the environmental impacts from the production processes. We also have to consider budget constraints since CV studies, which rely upon survey responses, are very expensive to carry out. In this case, the distance function methodology has an advantage since obtaining the necessary information is more direct and less costly (Färe et al., 2001). The results obtained from CV studies are very much dependent on the assumptions made with regard to the elicitation format chosen and the empirical model used for estimating the mean WTP (Bengochea-Morancho et al., 2005). However, using the distance function methodology, shadow prices are obtained based on objective parameters associated with the production process. Finally, the CV method could be more appropriate than the distance function method when we try to estimate the total economic value of clean water, given it is the only technique that in theory is capable of estimating both use and non-use values.

10.3 CONCLUSIONS

The Global Wastewater Initiative is making progress in coordinating efforts to transition towards a world where wastewater is not waste, but a resource. Its position to assist national policy making and international agenda setting is powerful. In a world increasingly subject to water scarcity, the effective treatment and reuse of wastewater can satisfy multiple demands. The current damage to the environment can be avoided with good management, which will bring far-reaching benefits.

The environmental and health benefits from sustainable wastewater management typically have no market prices. For this reason, they have not been considered in financial analyses of wastewater treatment projects in the past. However, monetary valuation of these non-market impacts is required in order to analyse the feasibility of any wastewater treatment project. In other words, the economic valuation of the environmental and health costs of no action is necessary to justify suitable investment policies in wastewater treatment.

As is well known, wastewater treatment is a desirable process since it provides many health and environmentally beneficial effects. However, one of the main barriers to investing in wastewater treatment projects is the absence of economic incentives due to the benefits derived from avoiding discharge of untreated effluent not having a market value. This chapter illustrates that there are several methodologies that allow estimating the cost of no action (benefits lost) in the context of wastewater treatment. The comparison with the cost of action provides essential information for decision-making processes. In this sense, some empirical applications developed have demonstrated that implementing wastewater treatment processes in developing countries is feasible from an economic point of view if environmental and health effects are integrated into the assessment.

In spite of this, further efforts are needed to quantify the cost of no action in developing countries, since most of the studies so far have focused on developed countries. To promote the implementation of wastewater treatment processes in developing countries, it is fundamental to assess their economic feasibility – estimating the cost of no action taking into account the particularities of each case.

REFERENCES

Adamowick, W., Dupont, D., Krupnick, A. and Zhanj, J. (2011), 'Valuation of cancer and microbial disease risk reductions in municipal drinking water: an analysis of risk context using multiple valuation methods', *Journal of Environmental Economics and Management* **61**, 213–226.

Arrow, K., Solow, R., Portney, P., Leamer, E., Radner, R. and Schuman, H. (1993), 'Report of the National Oceanic and Atmospheric Administration Panel on Contingent Valuation', *Federal Register*, **58**, 4602–4614.

Bateman, I.J., Cole, M.A., Georgiou, S. and Hadley, D.J. (2006), 'Comparing contingent valuation and contingent ranking: a case study considering the benefits of urban river water quality improvements', *Journal of Environmental Management*, **79**, 221–231.

Bdour, A.N., Hamdi, M.R. and Tarawneh, Z. (2009), 'Perspectives on sustainable wastewater treatment technologies and reuse options in the urban areas of the Mediterranean region', *Desalination*, **237**, 162–174.

Bengochea-Morancho, A., Fuertes-Eugenio, A.M. and Del Saz-Salazar, S. (2005), 'A comparison of empirical models to infer the willingness to pay in contingent valuation', *Empirical Economics*, **30** (1), 235–244.

Bishop, R.C. and Heberlein, T.A. (1979), 'Measuring values of extra-market goods: are indirect measures biased?', *American Journal of Agricultural Economics*, **61**, 926–930.

Bixio D., Thoeye, C., De Koning J., Joksimovic, D., Savic, D., Wintgens, T. and Melin, T. (2006), 'Wastewater reuse in Europe', *Desalination*, **187**, 89–101.

Bradley, C.J., Yabroff, K.R., Dahman, B., Fener, E.J., Mariotto, A. and Brown, M.L. (2008), 'Productivity costs of cancer mortality in the United States: 2000–2020', *Journal of the National Cancer Institute*, **100** (24), 1763–1770.

Calhoun, E.A. and Bennett, C.L. (2003), 'Evaluating the total costs of cancer: the Northwestern University costs of cancer program', *Oncology* **17** (1), 109–114.

Carson, R.T. and Hanemann, W.M. (2005), 'Contingent valuation', in K.-G. Mäler and J.R. Vincent (eds), *Handbook of Environmental Economics, Vol. 2*, Amsterdam: Elsevier, pp. 821–936.

Coggin, J.S. and Swinton, J.R. (1996), 'The price of pollution: a dual approach to valuing SO2 allowances', *Journal of Environmental Economics and Management*, **30** (5), 58–72.

Cumming, O. (2009), 'The sanitation imperative: A strategic response to a development crisis', *Desalination*, **248**, 8–13.

El-Fadel, M., Zeinati, M. and Jamali, D. (2002), 'Water resources in Lebanon: characterization, water balance, and constraints, *Journal of Water Resources and Development*, **16** (4), 619 – 642.

Färe, R., Grosskopf, S., Lovell, C.A.K. and Yaisawarng, S. (1993), 'Derivation of shadow prices for undesirable outputs: a distance function approach', *Review of Economics and Statistics*, **75** (2): 374–380.

Färe, R., Grosskopf, S. and Webwe, W.L. (2001), 'Shadow prices of Missouri public conservation land', *Public Finance Review*, **29** (6), 444–460.

Gordon, L.G., Eckermann, S., Hirst, N.G., Watson, D.I., Mayne, G.C., Fahey, P. and Whiteman, D.C. (2011), 'Healthcare resource use and medical costs for the management of oesophageal cancer', *British Journal of Surgery*, **98** (11): 1589–1598.

Hakes, J.K. and Viscusi, W.K. (2007), 'Automobile seatbelt usage and the value of statistical life', *Southern Economic Journal*, **73**(3), 659–676.

Hernández-Sancho, F., Molinos-Senante, M. and Sala-Garrido, R. (2010), 'Economic valuation of environmental benefits from wastewater treatment processes: an empirical approach for Spain', *Science of Total Environment*, **408**, 953–957.

Huertas, E., Salgot, M., Hollender, J., Weber, S., Dott, W., Khan, S., Schäferd, A., Messalem, R., Bis, B., Aharoni, A. and Chikurel, H. (2008), 'Key objectives for water reuse concepts', *Desalination*, **218**, 120–131.

Hutton, G., Haller, L. and Bartram, J. (2007), 'Global cost-benefit analysis of water supply and sanitation interventions', *Journal of Water and Health*, **5** (4), 481–501.

Kärrman, E. (2001), 'Strategies towards sustainable wastewater management', *Urban Water*, **3** (1–2), 63–72.

Kim, J.H., Kim, S.H., Joo, J.S. and Lee, K.S. (2012), 'Factors associated with medical cost among patients with terminal cancer in hospice units', *Journal of Palliative Care*, **28** (1), 5–12.

Lange, G.M. and Jiddawi, N. (2009), 'Economic value of marine ecosystem services in Zanzibar: implications for marine conservation and sustainable development', *Ocean and Coastal Management*, **52** (10), 521–532.

230 New directions in productivity measurement and efficiency analysis

Maddison, D., Catala-Luque, R. and Pearce, D. (2005), 'Valuing the arsenic contamination of groundwater in Bangladesh', *Environmental and Resource Economics* **31**, 459–476.

McCarty, P. L., Bae J. and Kim J. (2011), 'Domestic wastewater treatment as a net energy producer: can this be achieved?', *Environmental Science and Policy*, **45**, 7100–7106.

Molinos-Senante, M., Hernández-Sancho, F. and Sala-Garrido, R. (2011a), 'Cost-benefit analysis if water-reuse projects for environmental purposes: a case study for Spanish wastewater treatment plants', *Journal of Environmental Management*, **92**, 3091–3097.

Molinos-Senante, M., Hernández-Sancho and F., Sala-Garrido, R. (2011b), 'Assessing disproportionate costs to achieve good ecological status of water bodies in a Mediterranean river basin', *Journal of Environmental Monitoring*, **13** (8), 2091–2101.

Pearce, J., Albritton, S., Grant, G., Steed, G. and Zelenika, I. (2012), 'A new model for enabling innovation in appropriate technology for sustainable development', *Sustainability: Science, Practice, and Policy*, **8** (2), 42–53.

Pilarczyk, R., Wójcik, J., Czerniak, P., Sablik, P., Pilarczyk, B. and Tomza-Marciniak, A. (2013), 'Concentrations of toxic heavy metals and trace elements in raw milk of Simmental and Holstein-Friesian cows from organic farm', *Environmental Monitoring and Assessment*, **185**, 8383–8392.

Raschid-Sally, L. and Jayakody, P. (2008), 'Drivers and characteristics of waste-water agriculture in developing countries: results from a global assessment', International Water Management Institute (IWMI) research report 127, Colombo, Sri Lanka.

Roman, H.A., Hammitt, J.K., Walsh, T.L. and Stieb, D.M. (2012), 'Expert elicitation of the value per statistical life in an air pollution context', *Risk Analysis*, **32** (12), 2133–2151.

Salgot, M., Huertas, E., Weber, S., Dott, W. and Hollender, J. (2006), 'Wastewater reuse and risk: definition of key objectives', *Desalination*, **187**, 29–40.

Shephard, R.W. (1970), *Theory of Cost and Production Functions*. Princeton: Princeton University Press.

Shizas I. and Bagley, D.M. (2004), 'Experimental determination of energy content of unknown organics in municipal wastewater streams', *Journal of Energy Engineering*, **130**, 45–53.

Stillwell, A.S., Hoppock, D.C. and Webber, M.E. (2010), 'Energy recovery from wastewater treatment plants in the United States: a case study of the energy–water nexus', *Sustainability*, **2**, 945–962.

Swinton, J.R. (1998), 'At what cost do we reduce pollution? Shadow price of SO2 emissions', *Energy Journal*, **19** (4), 63–83.

Tsai, W.J., Liu, J.T. and Hammitt, J.K. (2011), 'Aggregation biases in estimates of the value per statistical life: evidence from longitudinal matched worker-firm data in Taiwan', *Environmental and Resource Economics*, **49** (3), 425–443.

UNEP (2010), *Sick Water? The Central Role of Wastewater Management in Sustainable Development*, Arendal, Norway: United Nations Environment Programme/GRID-Arendal.

UNEP (2015), *Economic Valuation of Wastewater: The Cost of Action and the Cost of No Action*, Nairobi: United Nations Environment Programme.

UNESCO (2008), *Education for All Global Monitoring Report*, United Nations

Educational, Scientific and Cultural Organization. Available from: http://unesdoc.unesco.org/images.pdf.

UN-Water (2013), 'Safe use of wastewater in agriculture', Proceedings of the UN-Water Decade Programme on Capacity Development, United Nations Water, Germany.

UN-Water (2014), *Wastewater Management: A UN-Water Analytical Brief*, United Nations Water. Available from: www.unwater.org/publications/publications-detail/en/c/275896/.

Van Lier, J., Seeman, P. and Lettinga, G. (1998), *Decentralized Urban Sanitation Concepts: Perspectives for Reduced Water Consumption and Wastewater Reclamation for Reuse*, Wageningen, The Netherlands, Agricultural University: EP&RC Foundation.

Ward, F.A. (2012), 'Cost-benefit and water resources policy: a survey', *Water Policy*, **14** (2), 250–280.

WHO (2008), *The Global Burden of Disease: 2004 Update*, Geneva: World Health Organization. Available from: www.who.int/healthinfo/gll.pdf.

WHO-UNICEF (2012), *Progress Sanitation and Drinking-Water 2012 Update*. Geneva: World Health Organization/United Nations Children's Fund. Available from: www.unicef.org/media/files/JMPreport2012.pdf.

Yi, L., Jiao, W., Chen, X. and Chen W. (2011) 'An overview of reclaimed water reuse in China', *Journal of Environmental Sciences*, **23**, 1585–1593.

11. Estimating the cost of carbon abatement for China

Atakelty Hailu and Chunbo Ma

11.1 INTRODUCTION

China is now the leading source of carbon emissions and is facing mounting domestic and international pressure to reduce its carbon emissions. As a result, it has become the subject of a growing number of studies attempting to estimate marginal carbon abatement costs using distance function frameworks. These models use historical data, and do not need to make widely varying and strong assumptions about future economic development and technological progress. This is in contrast to the larger part of the existing literature typically based on the use of integrated systems forecasting models that derive marginal abatement cost (MAC) as shadow prices representing the economic growth that would be forgone as a result of mitigation targets (Repetto and Austin, 1997; Weyant and Hill, 1999; Lasky, 2003; Fischer and Morgenstern, 2005; Kuik et al., 2009).

Du et al. (2015) provide a critical review of the distance function based literature on China, most of which focuses on carbon mitigation costs—except for a few studies that also investigate the cost of abating sulfur dioxide. Most of these are recent (Ma and Hailu, 2016) and are summarized in Table 11.1. The types of data that have been used are disaggregated plant level or aggregated data at the provincial and industry level. In terms of methods, about half of the studies have employed nonparametric data envelopment analysis (DEA) methods (Wang et al., 2011; Choi et al., 2012; Yuan et al., 2012; Wei et al., 2012), while the remaining studies have used directional output distance functions (Wei et al., 2012, 2013; Du et al., 2015)—with the exception of Lee and Zhang (2012), who use an input distance function.

As shown in the last column of Table 11.1, the estimated carbon abatement costs differ greatly. Three studies estimate the cost to be under US$20 per tonne of CO_2 equivalent. The lowest estimate among these is the one from the input distance function based study by Lee and Zhang (2012), which generates an estimate of US$3 per tonne of CO_2 equivalent.

Table 11.1   Empirical estimates of marginal abatement cost (MAC) for China

Studies	Approach	Period	DMU	US$/tonne
Nonparametric Methods				
Wang et al., 2011	DEA	2007	Province	**77**
Choi et al., 2012	DEA	2001–2010	Province	**7**
Yuan et al., 2012	DEA	2004; 2008	Industry	**33~19561**
Wei et al., 2012	DEA	1995–2007	Province	**19**
Parametric Methods				
Lee and Zhang, 2012	Input distance	2009	Industry	**3**
Wei et al., 2013	Directional output (deterministic)	2004	Plant	**335**
Wei et al., 2013	Directional output (stochastic)	2004	Plant	**100**
Du et al., 2015	Directional output	2001–2010	Province	**163~341**

Note: All monetary values converted to constant 2010 US dollars per tonne of CO_2 equivalent.

Estimates from other studies range from the low thirties to the hundred (and even higher) US dollars per tonne. Results from these studies are not directly comparable, however, as the studies differ in the chosen distance function, the period covered and the level of decision making unit (DMU). Nevertheless, available empirical MAC estimates for carbon emissions in China obtained from the distance function approach vary widely, from merely a few US dollars into the hundreds and thousands of US dollars per metric tonne.

Using the DEA approach to measure shadow prices suffers from non-differentiability problems. There are no unique slope values for extreme observations (at vertices) and thus no unique shadow prices can be defined at those points. Recently, Chambers and Färe (2008) have shown how the bounds for the shadow prices can be derived. The bounds reflect the willingness to pay (lower value) and the willingness to accept (upper value) for changes in input or output quantities. While these new developments are significant and useful for some purposes, the values generated are bounds and not estimates of shadow prices defined in the usual way, where the focus is on smooth and infinitesimal changes in quantities (and related trade-offs).

Thus, parametric distance functions offer a more useful approach for estimating shadow prices (Hailu and Veeman, 2001). Among these, the directional distance function has been the preferred approach among studies on China (Table 11.1). The choice is often justified on the grounds that the directional output distance function is a more appropriate metric for measuring performance in the presence of bad output under regulation (Färe et al., 1993, 2005). However, one could argue that, since all distance functions provide alternative representations of the same underlying technology, the trade-offs between bad and good outputs (shadow prices) should be properly captured by all forms.

Further, environmental regulations in China are mostly specified in terms of desirable inputs or outputs. For example, before the pilot markets for carbon trading were introduced, China's regulations were mostly specified in terms of changes in energy intensities. However, energy intensity targets can be achieved by either reducing energy consumption or by increasing GDP growth. Energy intensity targets have no direct binding effect on carbon emissions. Thus, even if one is willing to relate distance function type choice to regulation, it is not clear if the output directional distance function is appropriate for the Chinese context (Ma and Hailu, 2016). Further, compared with (radial) output-based measures, input-based measures of efficiency are always unambiguous measures of performance, whether the technology includes undesirable outputs or not (Hailu and Veeman, 2000).[1] For example, whether a 20 percent increase in both desirable and undesirable outputs is socially beneficial depends on the values of desirable outputs relative to undesirable outputs. A 20 percent reduction in inputs, on the other hand, has unambiguous benefits as a 20 percent cost saving. Lee and Zhang (2012) is the only paper on China that uses an input distance function.

Ma and Hailu (2016) estimate and compare results from different types of distance functions: radial input, radial output and directional output. The MAC estimates they obtained from radial input and output distance functions were similar. However, the estimates from directional output distance functions were much higher. They argue that the substantial heterogeneity in cost estimates can be explained in terms of inherent differences in the nature (or economic interpretation) of the estimates from different studies. In particular, they argue that radial measures imply little change in the input or output mix, and thus reflect short-run MACs, while nonradial measures are evaluated at input/output mixes that are a transformation of observed values and therefore are more akin to long-run MACs.

In this chapter, we improve upon the study by Ma and Hailu in three ways. First, we use revised CO_2 emission estimates that are based on the 'apparent consumption approach' to energy statistics. The apparent consumption is calculated from an overall balance of domestic production, interprovincial trade, international refueling and changes in stocks. The method provides a comprehensive account of fossil fuels consumed in an economy of a province, i.e. final consumption, consumption in the transformation of secondary energy and losses in transformation. Our revised national carbon emission data are very close to estimates recently reported by Liu et al. (2015). Second, both stochastic and deterministic distance function frontiers are estimated subject to monotonicity, homogeneity and symmetry constraints. The stochastic frontier is estimated using Bayesian methods, while the deterministic distance function frontier is estimated using mathematical programming. Third, we impose concavity curvature conditions, which were not part of the estimation in the previous study, or any other studies in the literature to our knowledge. Carbon abatement cost estimates from both estimation methods are compared with each other and also with observed carbon prices in the Chinese pilot markets for CO_2 emission permits.

The chapter is organized into four sections. The next section describes the distance function representation of the technology, estimation methods and the data used in the study. Results are presented in the third section. The final section concludes the chapter.

11.2 METHODS

11.2.1 Representation of Production Technology

For the case of a production technology using a vector x of N inputs to produce a vector u of M marketable and pollutant outputs, Shephard's (1953, 1970) input distance function can be defined as follows:

$$D(u^{it}, x^{ti}, t) = \max_\theta \left\{ \theta : \left(u^{it}, \frac{x^{it}}{\theta} \right) \in Y(t), \theta \in R^+ \right\} \qquad (11.1)$$

where x and u are, respectively, the input output vectors; t is the time trend variable; $Y(t)$ is the technology (or production possibility) set at time t; and i represents the region or province in our case. In other words, the value of the input distance function measures the maximum amount by which the input vector can be deflated, given the output vector. Thus, by definition, the reciprocal of the value of the input distance function provides the standard input-based Farrell (1957) measure of technical efficiency (TE), as shown in (11.2). A value greater than unity for the input distance function indicates that the observed input-output vector is technically inefficient.

$$TE_x^{it}(u^{it}, x^{ti}, t) = \frac{1}{D(u^{it}, x^{ti}, t)} \qquad (11.2)$$

The input distance function has the following properties: it has a finite value for $u \geq 0$; it is an increasing and continuous function of x for $u \in R^M_+$; it is concave and homogeneous of degree one in x; it is an upper semi-continuous and quasi-concave function of u. See Shephard (1970) or Färe and Primont (1995) for more on the characteristics of the function. The first derivative, or the monotonicity property of the input distance function with respect to desirable and undesirable outputs, needs also to be distinguished. By definition, the value of the distance function measures the maximum proportion by which all inputs can be proportionally reduced without a change in the output vector. The distance function should, therefore, be non-decreasing in inputs and non-increasing in desirable (or freely disposable) outputs. On the other hand, a reduction in pollutant outputs requires the use of inputs for abatement, other outputs remaining the same. Therefore, the input distance function should be non-decreasing in pollutant outputs. Finally, the input distance function provides a complete representation of the production technology in the sense that $IDF(u^{it}, x^{it}, t) \geq 1 \Leftrightarrow (u^{it}, x^{it}) \in Y(t)$.

The above theoretical restrictions are difficult to incorporate in a classical econometric estimation. Most studies to date have therefore employed mathematical programming approaches to parameter estimation (also known as goal programming) first used by Aigner and Chu (1968). These methods rely on the minimization of the sum of deviations of the values of the function from the production frontier that is being estimated. Linear programming does not account for noise in the data (i.e. frontier is deterministic), and it does not provide statistical measures of goodness of fit or significance. However, it is a very flexible method that allows us to impose both equality and inequality restrictions very easily. The ability to impose inequality restrictions is of prime importance in the case of this study because the asymmetric treatment of desirable and undesirable outputs in the specification of the technology requires the imposition of restrictions on the first derivative signs of the input distance function. In this sense, the linear programming approach allows us to build in a degree of sophistication in the specification of the systematic component of the function much more easily than is possible with econometric techniques. The approach to parameter estimation has been used in several recent studies (e.g., Serot, 1993; Färe et al., 1993; Coggins and Swinton, 1996; Hailu and Veeman, 2000; Hailu, 2003; Hailu and Chambers, 2012; Tang et al., 2016).

A translog functional form is chosen because it is flexible and thus provides a second-order approximation to the technology of unknown production for the input-based distance function. Furthermore, the linear homogeneity property can be imposed globally with a translog functional form, which could be written as follows, suppressing region/year identifiers to reduce notation complexity:

$$
\begin{aligned}
\ln D(u,x,t) = \alpha_o &+ \sum_{n=1}^{N} \alpha_n \ln x_n + \sum_{m=1}^{M} \beta_m \ln u_m \\
&+ 0.5 \sum_{n=1}^{N} \sum_{n'=1}^{N} \alpha_{nn'} \ln x_n \ln x_{n'} + 0.5 \sum_{m=1}^{M} \sum_{m'=1}^{M} \beta_{mm'} \ln u_m \ln u_{m'} \\
&+ 0.5 \sum_{n=1}^{N} \sum_{m=1}^{M} \gamma_{nn'} \ln x_n \ln u_m + \alpha_t.t + 0.5\,\alpha_{tt}.t^2 + \sum_{n=1}^{N} \alpha_{nt}.t.\ln x_n \\
&+ \sum_{m=1}^{M} \beta_{mt}.t.\ln u_m
\end{aligned}
\tag{11.3}
$$

The objective of the mathematical programming approach is to minimize the sum of the logarithmic values of the distance function (Hailu and Veeman 2000):

$$
\text{Minimize} \sum_{i=1}^{R} \sum_{t=1}^{T} \ln D(u^{it}, x^{it}, t)
\tag{11.4}
$$

where R is the number of provinces and T is the number of years. Equation (11.4) is solved under the following constraints:

$(C_1)\ln D(u^{it}, x^{it}, t) \geq 0, \qquad$ *for all i, t*

$(C2)\dfrac{\partial \ln D(u^{it}, x^{it}, t)}{\partial x_n^{it}} \geq 0, \qquad$ *for all i,t, and input n*

$(C3)\dfrac{\partial \ln D(u^{it}, x^{it}, t)}{\partial u_m^{it}} \leq 0, \qquad$ *for all i,t, and good output m*

$(C4)\dfrac{\partial \ln D(u^{it}, x^{it}, t)}{\partial u_m^{it}} \geq 0, \qquad$ *for all i,t, and bad output m*

$(C5)\displaystyle\sum_{n=1}^{N} \alpha_n = 1, \sum_{n=1}^{N} \alpha_{nn'} = 0, \sum_{n=1}^{N} \gamma_{nm} = 0, \sum_{n=1}^{N} \alpha_{nt} = 0, n' = 1, ..., N; m = 1, ..., M$

$(C6)\; \alpha_{nn'} = \alpha_{n'n}; \beta_{mm'} = \beta_{m'm}, n, n' = 1, . . . , N; m, m' = 1, . . . M$

Constraint C1 ensures that all observations are feasible, implying that each observation is located either on or within the technology frontier. Constraint C2 imposes the monotonicity condition indicating that the input distance function is non-decreasing in inputs. Constraint C3 requires that the distance function is non-increasing in desirable outputs, while C4 ensures that the function is non-decreasing in undesirable outputs. That is, desirable outputs can be freely disposed but pollution abatement is costly. Constraints C5 and C6 ensure the homogeneity and symmetry conditions, respectively.

Recent advances in Bayesian simulation techniques offer attractive alternatives. First, theoretical restrictions can be incorporated in the parameter estimation problem more easily than in classical estimation methods. Second, unlike the LP- or MP-based estimations, the Bayesian approach provides an indication of the robustness of the parameter estimates. What is provided is a distribution of the parameters rather than just point estimates without any indication of their variability. Third, exact finite sample properties of efficiency and other measures of interest can be determined (O'Donnell and Coelli, 2005).

11.2.2   Stochastic Frontier Model

Below, we describe how the stochastic frontier model is specified for Bayesian estimation of the distance function parameters. For a particular province i, we can represent the actual production frontier as a stochastic frontier incorporating an element s^{it} that accounts for noise, measurement errors or any unknown peculiarities of observation i in period t:

$$D(u^{it}, x^{it}, t).s^{it} = 1 \qquad (11.5a)$$

The stochastic variable s^{it} has a symmetric distribution around one (its log value has a symmetric distribution around 0). If s^{it} is greater (less) than unity, the actual location of the input isoquant frontier for i is closer to (further from) the origin than the average technology frontier, $D(u^{it}, x^{it}, t)$, indicating that the actual frontier faced by this firm/observation is more (less) productive than the average frontier. Actual observed input-output vectors are not necessarily efficient (do not lie on the stochastic frontier), i.e. for observed input-output vectors (u^{it}, x^{it}) we have:

$$D(u^{it}, x^{it}, t).s^{it} \geq 1 \qquad (11.5b)$$

We can introduce technical efficiency terms into the stochastic frontier formulation using the fact that the input vector multiplied by the technical efficiency score should lie on the stochastic frontier. Thus, if we have an input-output vector (u^{it}, x^{it}) for province i in period t and its input-oriented efficiency score is TE^{it}, then we have:

$$D(u^{it}, TE_x^{it}.x^{it}, t).s^{it} = 1 \qquad (11.6a)$$

Using the linear homogeneity in inputs property of the input distance function, we can factor out the efficiency score and rewrite (11.6a) as:

$$D(u^{it}, x^{it}, t).TE_x^{it}.s^{it} = 1 \qquad (11.6b)$$

or, in logs:

$$lnD(u^{it}, x^{it}, t) + \ln TE_x^{it} + \ln s^{it} = 0 \qquad (11.6c)$$

Since we will be using a translog functional form for the distance function, it is convenient to relabel the terms in the equation. Using τ^{it} to denote $-\ln TE_x^{it}$ and v^{it} for $\ln s^{it}$, we can rewrite (11.6c) as:

$$lnD(u^{it}, x^{it}, t) - \tau^{it} + v^{it} = 0 \qquad (11.6d)$$

τ^{it} is an asymmetric term that is always non-negative since efficiency has a maximum value of 1. The stochastic term v^{it} will also be assumed to be symmetric around zero. Exploiting the linear homogeneity property of distance function further, we can reduce the number of parameters to be estimated by normalizing the input vector x^{it} by, say, the last input x_N^{it} to get:

$$lnD(u^{it}, \bar{\bar{x}}^{it}, t) + lx_N^{it} - \tau^{it} + v^{it} = 0 \qquad (11.6e)$$

where $\bar{\bar{x}}^{it}$ is the normalized input vector with size $N - 1$ and $lx_N^{it} = \ln x_N^{it}$. The Bayesian model can be developed based on (11.6e).

11.2.3 Bayesian Priors

As in Hailu and Chambers (2012) and Koop et al. (1997), a hierarchical prior Bayesian model is used where the efficiency variable τ^{it} is assumed to be exponentially distributed with mean λ_i, that is:

$$\tau^{it} \sim Expon(\lambda^{-1}) \qquad (11.7a)$$

Or, equivalently, τ^{it} is gamma distributed with a shape parameter of 1:

$$\tau^{it} \sim f_G(1, \lambda^{-1}) \qquad (11.7b)$$

where $f_G(a, b)$ is the gamma distribution with mean $\frac{a}{b}$ and variance $\frac{a}{b^2}$. The prior distribution of the efficiency distribution parameter λ^{-1} is assumed to be exponential:

$$\lambda^{-1} \sim f_G(1, -\ln r^*) \qquad (11.7c)$$

The prior on the distance function parameter vector β requires that monotonicity and curvature conditions be satisfied, or:

$$p(\beta) = I(\beta \in B) \tag{11.7d}$$

where B is the subset of the parameter space satisfying these regularity conditions. $I(z)$ is an indicator function assuming a value of 1 when z is true and zero otherwise. The prior distribution of the precision parameter $h = \sigma^{-2}$ is assumed to be gamma:

$$\sigma^{-2} \sim f_G\left(\frac{\eta_o}{2}, \frac{c_o}{2}\right) \tag{11.7e}$$

This prior distribution is made uninformative by setting η_o and c_o to zero or to very low levels.

11.2.4 Bayesian Simulation

Based on the distribution of υ^{it} in equation (11.6), the likelihood function for the panel data set of K regions and T time periods is:

$$L(Z, lx_N, \tau; \sigma^{-2}, \lambda, \beta) = \prod_{i=1}^{R} \prod_{t=1}^{T} f_G(\tau^{it}|\lambda^{-1}) . exp\left\{-\frac{\sigma^{-2}}{2}(- lx_N^{it} + \tau^{it} - Z^{it}\beta)^2\right\} \tag{11.8}$$

This likelihood is combined with the priors to derive the conditional distributions of interest that form the basis for the Bayesian simulation. The posterior distribution is:

$$p(Z, lx_N, \tau; \sigma^{-2}, \lambda, \beta) = p(\sigma^{-2}).p(\lambda^{-1}).p(\beta).L(Z, lx_N, \tau; \sigma^{-2}, \lambda, \beta) \tag{11.9}$$

A Marcov Chain Monte Carlo (MCMC) Bayesian simulation of the above posterior can be conducted in two ways. The first is to derive the conditional distributions for the parameters and variables of interest—namely, β, σ^{-2}, λ^{-1}, τ—based on the specifications above. The partitioning of the parameters and variables into these blocks allows for Gibbs sampling with data augmentation where samples of model parameters, as well as unobservable or latent variables such as the efficiency variables, are generated. This approach would require writing and implementing the Gibbs sampling code, and this can be a tedious and difficult task. The second, and more convenient, approach is to use packaged Gibbs sampling software such as WinBUGS to do the posterior simulation as in Hailu and Chambers (2012). We follow this second approach in this study.

11.2.5 Shadow Prices

Shadow prices for bad outputs can be derived from the different distance functions as implied marginal rates of transformation between a good output and a bad output transformed into dollar values using the market price for the good output (e.g. Färe et al., 1993; Hailu and Veeman, 2000). In our case, the shadow price r_j for a bad output u_j expressed in terms of a good output u_i derived from an input distance function would be given by:

$$r_j = p_i \cdot \left[\frac{\partial D(.)}{\partial u_j} \middle/ \frac{\partial D(.)}{\partial u_i} \right] \qquad (11.10)$$

where p_i is the market price for a good output, while the good output is GDP as discussed below and this price would be unity. Similar formulae are used in the case of the radial output and the directional distance functions.

11.3 DATA AND VARIABLES

Existing studies on the MAC of carbon dioxide all include energy as a separate production input variable. These studies typically calculate energy-related carbon emissions based on the Intergovernmental Panel on Climate Change reference approach (IPCC, 2006). Wei et al. (2013) also calculated emissions from the production of cement. Calculated CO_2 emissions as such will inevitably exhibit high correlation with energy consumption. Adding the carbon emissions from the production of cement will not reduce the correlation by much, as the proportion of emissions from cement production is usually small compared with energy-related emissions. In fact, the correlation is so high as to make the estimation of marginal effects via the radial measures extremely difficult and unreliable, if not totally impossible.

We include two inputs (labor and capital), one good output (provincial GDP), and three bad outputs—carbon dioxide (CO_2) emission, sulfur dioxide (SO_2) emission, and total provincial soot emission. We use Chinese provincial data for the ten-year period from 2001 to 2010. Table 11.2 presents the definition and summary statistics of these variables. Below we explain how the data were collected and constructed.

11.3.1 Inputs

Labor data were collected from the National Bureau of Statistics of China *China's Statistical Yearbooks* (NBSCa 2002–11). Provincial capital data

Table 11.2   Summary statistics for data used in the analysis, 2001–10 (30 provinces)

Variables	Definition	Unit	Mean	S.D.	Min	Max
Inputs						
Labor	Total employment	10^6 persons	23	15.2	2.4	60
Capital	Total capital stock	10^6 \$US	436	358	41	2138
Outputs						
GDP	Gross domestic product	10^9 \$US	135	120	7	694
CO_2	Energy related CO_2	10^6 tonnes	161	119	0	586
CO_2	CO_2 with cement	10^6 tonnes	172	127	0	628
SO_2	SO_2 emission	10^4 tonnes	75	46	2	200
Soot	Soot emission	10^4 tonnes	34	24	1	112

Notes:
All variables are defined as annual provincial statistics.
All monetary variables are converted to constant 2010 prices and Chinese renminbi (RMB) converted to US dollars at 1US\$=6.6227RMB.

were collected from Wu (2009), with updates for recent years obtained from the author through personal communication.

11.3.2   Outputs

Provincial GDP was also collected from *China's Statistical Yearbooks* (NBSCa, 2002–11). Emission data on SO_2 and soot are available from *China's Environmental Statistical Yearbooks* (NBSCb, 2002–11).

Energy consumption data were collected from *China's Energy Statistical Yearbooks* (NBSCc, 2002–11). We adopt the 'apparent consumption approach' to energy statistics. The apparent consumption is calculated from an overall balance of domestic production, interprovincial trade, international refueling, and changes in stocks. The method provides a comprehensive account of fossil fuels consumed in the provincial economy—i.e. final consumption, consumption in the transformation of secondary energy, and losses in transformation. This is a better indicator of energy consumption than primary energy consumption or final energy consumption typically used in this literature.

China's statistical authority does not report emission or inventory data on carbon dioxide. Previous studies typically calculated Chinese carbon emissions based on emission factor values recommended by the IPCC (2006). Yet, estimates of Chinese emissions remain subject to great uncertainty due to conflicting estimates of energy consumption and emission factors. Recent research finds that China's CO_2 emissions from coal consumption and cement production are notably lower than those reported by other prominent inventories (Liu et al., 2015). We thus use updated carbon emission factors that are consistent with the latest research (Liu et al., 2015). We also calculated carbon emissions from the process of cement production.

11.3.3   Carbon Prices

China has already launched seven regional pilot markets for carbon trading in a bid to gain experience ahead of a nationwide scheme. The pilot markets include Beijing, Shanghai, Tianjin, Guangzhou, Shenzhen, Hubei and Chongqing. Daily trading prices for these pilots are available from the China Carbon Trading Network (CCTN, 2016).

11.4   RESULTS AND DISCUSSIONS

We estimated the input distance function both as a deterministic frontier using mathematical programming and as a stochastic frontier using Bayesian methods. Marginal abatement costs for both cases are summarized in Table 11.3. The mean and median values for the MP method are found to be US\$35.30 and US\$31.59 per tonne, respectively. The corresponding figures for the Bayesian method are lower, at US\$23.62 and US\$21.42, respectively. There are other differences between the two estimates. While for the Bayesian method the lowest value obtained is US\$2.89, it is zero for the MP method. The range is wider for MP, with the maximum MAC estimate being US\$91.81. The maximum for the Bayesian method is US\$79.20.

Figure 11.1 plots the provincial MAC estimates from both methods. It shows that there are some cases for which the two values are similar (along the 45 degree line). However, these are limited to cases of relatively low MAC, with the bulk of them being under US\$40. For the majority of cases, and for almost all MAC estimates that are above US\$40 according to the MP estimates, the Bayesian estimates are found to be lower.

Table 11.3   Summary statistics for MACs, 2001–2010 (30 provinces)

Estimation method	Mean	Median	Min	Max
MP	35.30	31.59	0.00	91.81
Bayesian	23.62	21.42	2.89	79.20

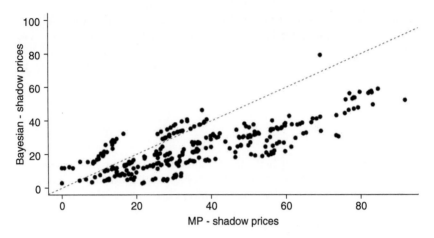

Figure 11.1   Provincial MACs: Bayesian vs. MP (US$/tonne)

There is no national carbon market in China; but the CO_2 permit prices observed in the seven regional pilot spot markets reflect short-run MACs. For reference purposes, one could compare observed carbon prices with the estimates obtained. While recognizing the limitation of liquidity and low participation in the pilot markets, a report released at the 2014 United Nations Climate Change Conference held in Lima indicated that carbon prices in China have converged to a range of 20–70 Yuan per tonne after a year of operation, and that this could be indicative of future price fluctuation ranges for a national carbon market (Wang, 2014). As can be seen from Figure 11.2, observed carbon prices mostly lie within the range of US$5–15 per tonne. Our average estimates are higher, but the Bayesian estimates are closer to the observed range of prices. However, this could be partly explained by two factors (Ma and Hailu, 2016). First, our CO_2 calculation only considers energy-related emissions and emissions from cement production, while the emissions covered in the pilot trading schemes are much broader. Most schemes cover traditionally energy-intensive and emission-intensive manufacturing industries, and some also include building and construction and tertiary industries. Broader coverage would drive down the marginal abatement cost.

11.5   CONCLUSIONS

As the number of countries seriously considering incentive-based policies for pollution control grows, there is increasing recognition of the major

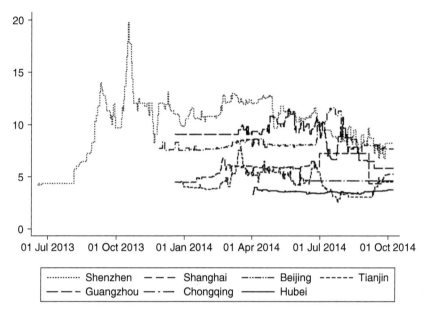

Figure 11.2   Carbon prices in China's pilot markets (US$/tonne)

challenges posed by the lack of adequate knowledge about the cost to industry of pollution abatement activities. Such cost estimates are either unavailable or uncertain. When results are available they vary widely, as in the case of China. Estimates obtained from using similar frameworks, namely distance function approaches, have led to very different estimates, potentially undermining the support for policies. Further, there has been limited amount of research aimed at explaining the variability. Ma and Hailu (2016) recently showed, using the same dataset as this study but with a different definition for the CO_2 variable, that the variability can be partly attributed to differences in the input/output coverage of estimated models and the inclusion/exclusion of pollutants other than CO_2. That study argued that the substantial heterogeneity in cost estimates can be explained in terms of inherent differences in the nature (or economic interpretation) of the estimates from different studies, especially whether the reductions envisaged are akin to short-run or long-run type reductions.

The current study has shown that the choice of estimation method and the theoretical restrictions imposed have important implications for the results. By using Bayesian methods that impose concavity (curvature) conditions on the estimation, we have obtained abatement cost estimates that are lower than those obtained using the most commonly applied methods.

Our mean MAC estimate is closer to the carbon prices observed in China's pilot markets. Further, the results appear to be more realistic, with cost estimates being all strictly positive (no zeros) and with the maximum cost estimates being substantially lower. The findings suggest that methods which combine the strengths of econometric estimation (i.e. allowing for noise) and the mathematical programming methods that have been widely used (ease with which theoretical constraints are imposed) generate better MAC estimates and should be used in empirical studies to provide better information for policy.

NOTE

1. And, as shown clearly in Hailu and Veeman (2000), the input distance based measures of efficiency do credit producers for reductions in bad outputs.

REFERENCES

Aigner, D.J. and S.F. Chu (1968) 'On estimating the industry production function', *American Economic Review*, 58 (4), 826–839.

Chambers, R.G. and R. Färe (2008), 'A "calculus" for data envelopment analysis', *Journal of Productivity Analysis*, **30** (3), 169–175.

CCTN (2016), *China Carbon Trading Network*, accessed 20 September 2016 at http://k.tanjiaoyi.com [in Chinese].

Choi, Y., N. Zhang, and P. Zhou (2012), 'Efficiency and abatement costs of energy-related CO2 emissions in China: a slacks-based efficiency measure', *Applied Energy*, **98** (1), 198–208.

Coggins, J.S. and J.R. Swinton (1996), 'The price of pollution: a dual approach to valuing SO2 allowances', *Journal of Environmental Economics and Management*, **30** (1), 58–72.

Du, L.M., A. Hanley and C. Wei (2015), 'Marginal abatement costs of carbon dioxide emissions in China: a parametric analysis', *Environmental and Resource Economics*, **61** (2), 191–216.

Färe, R. and D. Primont (1995), *Multi-Output Production and Duality: Theory and Applications*, Boston, MA: Kluwer Academic Publishers.

Färe, R., S. Grosskopf, C.A.K. Lovell and S. Yaisawarng (1993), 'Derivation of shadow prices for undesirable outputs: a distance function approach', *Review of Economics and Statistics*, **75** (2), 374–80.

Färe, R., S. Grosskopf, D.W. Noh and W. Weber (2005), 'Characteristics of a polluting technology: theory and practice', *Journal of Econometrics*, **126** (2), 469–492.

Farrell, M.J. (1957), 'The measurement of productive efficiency', *Journal of the Royal Statistical Society, Series A*, **120** (3), 253–290.

Fischer, C. and R.D. Morgenstern (2005), *Carbon Abatement Costs: Why the Wide Range of Estimates?*, Washington, DC: Resources for the Future.

Hailu, A. (2003), 'Pollution abatement and productivity performance of regional Canadian pulp and paper industries', *Journal of Forest Economics*, **9** (1), 5–25.

Hailu, A. and R.G. Chambers (2012), 'A Luenberger soil quality indicator', *Journal of Productivity Analysis*, **38** (2), 145–154.

Hailu, A. and T.S. Veeman (2000), 'Environmentally sensitive productivity analysis of the Canadian pulp and paper industry, 1959–1994: an input distance function approach', *Journal of Environmental Economics and Management*, **40** (3), 251–274.

Hailu, A. and T.S. Veeman (2001), 'Alternative methods for environmentally adjusted productivity analysis', *Agricultural Economics*, **25** (2), 211–218.

Intergovernmental Panel on Climate Change (IPCC) (2006), 'IPCC guidelines for national greenhouse gas inventories', accessed 15 October 2015 at www.ipcc-nggip.iges.or.jp/public/2006gl/.

Koop, G, J. Osiewalski and M.F.J. Steel (1997) 'Bayesian efficiency analysis through individual effects: hospital cost frontiers', *Journal of Econometrics* **76** (1), 77–105.

Kuik, O., L. Brander and R.S.J Tol (2009), 'Marginal abatement costs of greenhouse gas emissions: a meta-analysis', *Energy Policy*, **37** (4), 1395–1403.

Lasky, M. (2003), *The Economic Costs of Reducing Emissions of Greenhouse Gases: A Survey of Economic Models*, Washington, DC: Congressional Budget Office.

Lee, M. and N. Zhang (2012), 'Technical efficiency, shadow price of carbon dioxide emissions, and substitutability for energy in the Chinese manufacturing industries', *Energy Economics*, **34** (5), 1492–1497.

Liu, Z., D. Guan, W. Wei, S.J. Davis, P. Ciais, J. Bai, S. Peng, Q. Zhang, K. Hubacek, G. Marland, R.J. Andres, D. Crawford-Brown, J. Lin, H. Zhao, C. Hong, T.A. Boden, K. Feng, G.P. Peters, F. Xi, J. Liu, Y. Li, Y. Zhao, N. Zeng and K. He (2015), 'Reduced carbon emission estimates from fossil fuel combustion and cement production in China', *Nature*, **524** (7565), 335–338.

Ma, C. and A. Hailu (2016), 'The marginal abatement cost of carbon emissions in China', *Energy Journal*, **37** (S), 111–127.

National Bureau of Statistics of China (NBSCa) (2002–11), *China Statistical Yearbooks*. Beijing: China Statistical Press.

National Bureau of Statistics of China (NBSCb) (2002–11), *China Environmental Statistical Yearbooks*. Beijing: China Statistical Press.

National Bureau of Statistics of China (NBSCc) (2002–11), *China Energy Statistical Yearbooks*. Beijing: China Statistical Press.

O'Donnell, C.J. and T.J. Coelli (2005), 'A bayesian approach to imposing curvature on distance functions', *Journal of Econometrics*, **126** (2): 493–523.

Repetto, R. and D. Austin (1997), *The Costs of Climate Protection: A Guide for the Perplexed*, Washington, DC: World Resources Institute.

Serot, D. E., (1993), 'Estimating total factor productivity using parametric, nonstochastic cost frontiers', *Journal of Productivity Analysis*, **4** (4), 407–418.

Shephard, R.W. (1953), *Cost and Production Functions*, Princeton, NJ: Princeton University Press.

Shephard, R.W. (1970), *Theory of Cost and Production Functions*, Princeton, NJ: Princeton University Press.

Tang, K., A. Hailu, M.E. Kragt and C. Ma (2016), 'Marginal abatement costs of greenhouse gas emissions: broadacre farming in the Great Southern Region of Western Australia', *Australian Journal of Agricultural and Resource Economics*, **60** (3), 459–475.

Wang, Y. (2014), 'China carbon finance development report', *United Nations Climate Change Conference*, Lima.

Wang, Q.W., Q.J. Cui, D.Q. Zhou and S.S. Wang (2011), 'Marginal abatement costs of carbon dioxide in China: a nonparametric analysis', *Energy Procedia*, **5**, 2316–2320.

Wei, C., L. Andreas and B. Liu (2013), 'An empirical analysis of the CO2 shadow price in Chinese thermal power enterprises', *Energy Economics*, **40** (1), 22–31.

Wei, C., J. Ni and L. Du (2012), 'Regional allocation of carbon dioxide abatement in China', *China Economic Review*, **23** (3), 552–565.

Weyant, J.P. and J.N. Hill (1999), 'Introduction and overview', *Energy Journal*, 20, Special Issue, The costs of the Kyoto Protocol: a multi-model evaluation, vii–xliv.

Wu, Y.R. (2009), 'China's capital stock series by region and sector', Discussion paper 09.02, University of Western Australia Business School, Perth.

Yuan, P., W.B. Liang and S. Cheng (2012), 'The margin abatement costs of CO2 in Chinese industrial sectors', *Energy Procedia*, **14**, 1792–1797.

12. Environmentally adjusted efficiency of shrimp farming in Bangladesh

Hasneen Jahan and Tiho Ancev

12.1 INTRODUCTION

Shrimp aquaculture is the fastest growing agricultural sector in terms of value added and the second largest export earning sector in Bangladesh. It has experienced a spectacular growth in the coastal areas of Bangladesh since the mid-1990s. This expansion of shrimp aquaculture can be attributed to the suitable climatic conditions and the availability of resources such as feed, seed, water and an inexpensive labour force (Islam, 2003a; Wahab, 2003). The rapid increase of shrimp farming after the 1980s is due to high profitability as a result of high demand for shrimp on the international market (Deb, 1998). The economy of Bangladesh has benefited enormously from the rapid development of aquaculture production, in particular from shrimp cultivation. In 2013/14, Bangladesh earned about US$550 million from shrimp export, which is about 3 per cent of the value of total national export (EPB, 2014). There are about 1 million people employed directly in shrimp aquaculture, who support approximately 4.8 million dependants (USAID, 2006). According to the country's Department of Fisheries, the shrimp farming area in Bangladesh has increased from 51,812 hectares in 1983/84 to 246,198 hectares in 2009/10, and the production of farmed shrimp has increased from 4,386 tonnes to 82,044 tonnes over the same period (DOF, 2010).

In the same time, it is widely reported that the rapid growth of shrimp farming has led to adverse environmental, social and health effects, causing considerable national and international concerns about its environmental and social cost. Reported environmental consequences related to shrimp farming in Bangladesh are numerous and include:

- salinisation of soil and saltwater intrusion into freshwater aquifers;
- loss of wild fish stock; destruction of mangrove forests;
- effluent discharge of shrimp feed and waste, indiscriminate use of polluting chemicals, and

- the spread of human infectious diseases (NACA, 1995; Nijera Kori, 1996; Deb, 1998; Bhattacharya et al., 1999; Banks, 2002; Karim, 2003; Haque, 2004; Rahman et al., 2006).

Shrimp farming has serious adverse effects on soil quality: the soil salinity level in many areas seriously hampers crop cultivation (Islam et al., 1999). Shrimp farming-induced salinity has a significant negative impact on paddy rice productivity (Umamaheswar et al., 2009). In addition, the rapid expansion of shrimp farming has drastically reduced stocks of indigenous fish varieties and destroyed mangrove flora and fauna (Gain, 1998). The Bangladesh Fisheries Research Institute (BFRI, 2002) found that during the collection of shrimp fry, a substantial number of valuable aquatic organisms are being indiscriminately destroyed and as a consequence, fish catch has gradually decreased in many shrimp farming areas. The ecological problems created by unplanned shrimp cultivation, particularly in the Chakaria Sundarbans, resulted in significant degradation of mangroves in this area (Gregow, 1997).

Given the significant economic and environmental effects associated with shrimp farming, there is a need to examine the environmentally adjusted efficiency of shrimp farms if there are ambitions for sustainable development of this industry. Quantification of environmentally adjusted efficiency can help in proposing, designing and enacting policies aimed at achieving sustainable shrimp farming. This chapter presents an environmentally adjusted efficiency measurement of shrimp farming by applying a data envelopment analysis (DEA) model based on a directional distance function approach. This approach is particularly useful to assess the efficiency of production units that generate negative environmental effects in the course of their normal production process aimed at producing the usual, 'desirable' outputs (Chambers, 1998; Färe and Grosskopf, 2004). The approach relies on identifying and quantifying the negative environmental effects – referred to as 'undesirable' outputs – that are the unintended consequences of the production process. Overall, this efficiency measurement will address the joint economic and environmental performance of shrimp farming that will help to explore the direction of improvement in performance. Moreover, the efficiency measurement of shrimp farming by alternatively considering weak and strong disposability assumptions will help to point out the weaknesses of efficiency measurement when undesirable outputs are not considered.

The ensuing empirical work is based on the use of directional distance functions within a DEA framework. Traditional production theory does not account for the joint production of desirable and undesirable outputs. Since the 1980s a significant body of literature has emerged recognizing the need to take into account both desirable and undesirable outputs of a production technology, and to modify the conventional measures of efficiency and productivity of decision-making units accordingly (Färe et al., 1989, 1993; Ball et al., 1998; Tyteca, 1996). DEA-based distance and directional distance function approaches have useful qualities for measuring environmental performance (Tyteca, 1996). Distance functions do not depend on price information, removing the need to estimate shadow prices for typically non-marketed environmental attributes. DEA methods also allow the data to 'reveal' how multiple attributes contribute jointly to overall environmental performance, as opposed to imposing a priori weighting (Bellenger and Herlihy, 2009).

More recently, directional distance function has been increasingly implemented as a useful functional representation of the production technology that incorporates both desirable and undesirable outputs (Chung et al., 1997; Chambers, 1998; Chambers et al., 1996, 1998). Following Luenberger's benefit function (1992), Chung et al. (1997) provide the basis for representing the joint production of desirable and undesirable outputs by extending the concept of Shephard's output distance function (Shephard, 1970) to the concept of directional output distance function to measure productivity changes. The directional distance function provides an adequate technique that can be used to approach economic and environmental performance together, and can provide an indication of overall performance. The flexibility of this technique enhances its usefulness in policy-oriented applications (Picazo-Tadeo et al., 2005). Another advantage of the directional distance function is that it allows evaluation of levels of efficiency in any direction from the observation point, as opposed to the distance function, which is used to measure efficiency only in a fixed direction, typically a radial one (Watanabe and Tanaka, 2007).

Estimating shrimp farming efficiency is an important issue to be addressed in its own right, but the estimation of shrimp farming efficiency including environmental affects has not yet been reported in the literature, and the present study fills that gap. The study also investigates the effect of 'weak' and 'strong' disposability assumptions in applying directional distance functions. The efficiency analysis reflects how these assumptions make differences in efficiency scores when measuring the environmentally adjusted efficiency of any farm or enterprise.

12.2 CONCEPTUAL FRAMEWORK

Following Chung et al. (1997), suppose that $x = (x_1,...,x_N) \in \Re_+^N$ denotes a vector of inputs, $y = (y_1,...,y_M) \in \Re_+^M$ denotes a vector of desirable outputs, and $b = (b_1,...,b_I) \in \Re_+^I$ denotes a vector of undesirable outputs. Production takes place in $k = 1, . . .,K$ observations. The production technology can be described using the output set as:

$$P(x) = \{(y, b): x \text{ can produce } (y, b)\} \qquad (12.1)$$

Where $P(x)$ is a convex and compact set and satisfies the standard properties of 'no free lunch', i.e. $P(0) = (0, 0)$; possibility of inaction, i.e. $(0, 0) \in P$; and that desirable outputs are freely disposable, i.e. $(y, b) \in P(x)$ and $y' \leq y$ imply $(y', b) \in P(x)$.

To take into account the joint production of desirable and undesirable outputs, two additional assumptions are needed:

i.   Null jointness of the output set: if $(y, b) \in P(x)$ and $b = 0$, then $y = 0$, implying that no desirable output can be produced without producing some undesirable outputs. Here, the undesirable outputs $b = (b_1, . . .,b_I)$ are assumed to be by-products of the intended desirable outputs $y = (y_1, . . ., y_M)$ (Murty et al., 2012). In fact, the only feasible way to completely eliminate the undesirable outputs is by shutting down production of the desirable outputs all together.

ii.   The desirable and the undesirable outputs are considered as being jointly weakly disposable: $(y, b) \in P(x)$ and $0 \leq \theta \leq 1$ implies $(\theta y, \theta b) \in P(x)$. This means that, if x can produce outputs (y, b), then it is feasible to reduce these outputs proportionally by θ; a proportional contraction of desirable and undesirable outputs is feasible, and the reduction of undesirable outputs is not costless and negatively influences the production of desirable outputs. Further, assumption (ii) emphasizes the asymmetry between the desirable and undesirable outputs insofar as desirable outputs are costlessly disposable, but undesirable outputs are not (Färe et al., 2001).

A production technology that satisfies these assumptions can be represented by a directional output distance function (Chung et al., 1997; Chambers et al., 1998) as:

$$\vec{D}_T(x,y,b;g_y,-g_b) = \sup\{\beta:(y+\beta g_y, b-\beta g_b) \in P(x)\} \qquad (12.2)$$

Where $g = (g_y, -g_b)$ is the directional vector in which desirable and undesirable outputs can be scaled up or down. Given the production technology $P(x)$ and the directional vector g, the directional output distance function represents the maximum feasible expansion of desirable outputs in the g_y direction, and the largest feasible contraction of undesirable outputs in the $-g_b$ direction. The directional output distance function is also a measure of efficiency, since it simultaneously accounts for reduction of undesirable outputs and improvement of desirable outputs. In other words, it is a combined environmental and technical efficiency measure (Färe et al., 2005). In Equation (12.2), β is an expansion factor that indicates the maximal feasible proportional expansion of desirable outputs and contraction of undesirable outputs for a given decision-making unit relative to a point on the production frontier. If an observation is completely efficient in maximizing desirable outputs and minimizing undesirable outputs, then the observation is operating on the production possibility frontier, and consequently β is zero. Therefore, β may be considered as a measure of the decision-making unit's inefficiency, and $(1 - \beta)$ a measure of its efficiency (Macpherson et al., 2010).

The current study evaluates the efficiency of shrimp farms by considering four models with different directional vectors in the output set $P(x)$, and compares them to identify differences in the estimated efficiency scores. In Model 1, a directional distance function $\vec{D}_o(x,y,b;1,-1)$ is estimated, with a view to increasing desirable outputs and decreasing undesirable outputs at the same time by the same proportion with a directional vector $g = (1, -1)$. In Model 2, $\vec{D}_o(x,y,b;1,0)$ is estimated, with a view to increasing desirable outputs while undesirable outputs are kept at their current level with a directional vector $g = (1, 0)$. In Model 3, $\vec{D}_o(x,y,b;0,-1)$ is estimated, with a view to reducing undesirable outputs while keeping desirable outputs at their current level with a directional vector $g = (0, -1)$. These three models follow the assumption of weak disposability of outputs, which explicitly stipulates that disposal of undesirable outputs is not free, as per assumption (ii) discussed above.

In contrast, Model 4 follows the assumption of strong disposability of desirable and undesirable outputs implying that undesirable outputs can be costlessly disposed. Model 4 takes the form $\vec{D}_o(x,y;1)$, which effectively excludes undesirable outputs from the output set $P(x)$ and uses the directional vector $g = (1)$. This model completely ignores the harmful environmental effects and solely reflects the potential increase in desirable outputs, in this case production of shrimp.

12.2.1 Efficiency Error (EE)

When measuring efficiency from a perspective of increasing desirable outputs, the efficiency scores are significantly affected by the disposability assumptions made with respect to the undesirable output. Both in Model 2 and Model 4, desirable outputs are assumed to be increasing in the same direction. However, the undesirable outputs are assumed to be weakly disposable in Model 2 but strongly disposable in Model 4. Given these assumptions, the production set $P(x)$ itself will differ significantly between Model 2 and Model 4. It can be noted here that by excluding undesirable outputs from the production technology (as in Model 4), undesirable outputs are assumed to be freely disposable (Färe et al., 2001). If efficiency is measured by considering the assumption of strong disposability, i.e. ignoring the undesirable outputs, when in reality a weak disposability assumption would be more appropriate, there will be an error in estimated efficiency scores. This error can be represented by the difference of two directional distance functions: $EE = \vec{D}_o(x,y;1) - \vec{D}_o(x,y,b;1,0)$. The higher this difference is, the more biased the result is as a result of not considering the undesirable outputs.

12.3   EMPIRICAL METHODS

The purpose of using directional distance functions based on DEA is to measure environmentally adjusted efficiency of shrimp farming considering both desirable and undesirable outputs. The DEA approach can provide an indicator of the environmentally adjusted performance without any *priori* arbitrary assumption about how to weight economic versus environmental efficiency (Tyteca, 1996). To evaluate the performance of shrimp farming in Bangladesh, this study considers the four models described above.

In Model 1, credit is given to simultaneous expansion of desirable outputs and contraction of undesirable outputs. In this case the maximization problem for the directional output distance function $\vec{D}_o(x,y,b;1,-1)$ is solved by the following linear programming setup:

$$\vec{D}_o(x^{k'},y^{k'},b^{k'};g_y,-g_b) = \max \beta \qquad (12.3a)$$

s.t.

$$\sum_{k=1}^{K} z_k y_{km} \geq (1 + \beta) y_{k'm}, m = 1, ..., M \qquad (12.3b)$$

$$\sum_{k=1}^{K} z_k b_{ki} = (1 - \beta) b_{k'i}, i = 1,..., I \qquad (12.3c)$$

$$\sum_{k=1}^{K} z_k x_{kn} \leq x_{k'n}, n = 1, ..., N \qquad (12.3d)$$

$$z_k \geq 0, k = 1,...,k \qquad (12.3e)$$

Where $k = 1, \ldots, K$ indexes the observations in the dataset, β is an (in) efficiency score to be estimated for each unit, i.e. shrimp farming *upazila* (sub-district).[1] In this case, the unit of observation is an *upazila*, since the data were collected at *upazila* level, effectively representing average farm-level data for a specific sub-district. The variable z_k is an intensity or weighting variable assigned to each observation in constructing the production possibility frontier. The non-negativity of this variable imposes an assumption of constant returns to scale on technology (Chung et al., 1997). Weak disposability is imposed by applying an inequality sign in the case of desirable outputs in (12.3b), and an equality sign in the case of undesirable outputs in (12.3c). The value of the directional output distance function is positive for inefficient observations that are found below the frontier. In contrast, the value of the directional output distance function is zero for those observations that are technically efficient, as they are found right on the frontier. This is represented by the (in)efficiency score β. Since desirable outputs are being expanded and undesirable outputs contracted by the same proportion, the value of β is bounded between 0 (for efficient units) and 1 (for the least efficient units) (Färe et al., 2006). The model presented in Equations (12.3a–e) is run for each observation in the dataset to identify the inefficiency levels for all units, $k = 1, \ldots, K$.

A linear programming setup similar to the one given in Equations (12.3a–12.3e) is used for Models 2–4 with appropriate modifications. In Model 2, credit is given only to the expansion of desirable outputs when the undesirable outputs are present in the production set. The difference between Model 1 and Model 2 is that in Model 2 $((\overrightarrow{D}_o(x^{k'},y^{k'},b^{k'};g_y,0) = \max \beta))$, the undesirable outputs are not scaled by a directional vector, and therefore credit is only given to the desirable outputs. In Model 3 $((\overrightarrow{D}_o(x^{k'},y^{k'},b^{k'};0,-g_b) = \max \beta))$, credit is only given to the contraction of the undesirable outputs, while the desirable outputs are kept constant in the production set – i.e. desirable outputs are not scaled by β.

In Model 4 $((\overrightarrow{D}_o(x^{k'},y^{k'};g_y) = \max \beta))$, credit is only given to the expansion of desirable outputs by completely excluding the undesirable outputs from the production technology. Therefore, all together four different sets of linear programming problems have been solved. A description of the formulations of those problems that correspond to Models 2, 3 and 4 is presented in the Appendix. The General Algebraic Modeling System (GAMS)/Cplex solver was used to solve the optimization problems (GAMS, 2011).

12.4   DATA AND VARIABLES

The empirical study covers major shrimp farming regions in Bangladesh. This includes the coastal areas of Khulna, Bagerhat, Satkhira and Jessore districts in the southwest region; Chittagong and Cox's Bazar districts in the southeast region; and Patuakhali and Pirojpur districts in the southern region. To take into account the changes in economic and environmental efficiency of shrimp farming areas, the study focuses on two distinct time points – the years 2000 and 2010. Data were collected for 31 *upazilas* within the above-mentioned eight districts. On average, the area of *upazilas* varies from 200 to 1000 sq. km, and the population varies from 100,000 up to 300,000 (GOB, 2015). The southwest region of Bangladesh comprises over 75 per cent of the total shrimp farming area in the country; the remaining 25 per cent are found in the southeast and the southern regions (DOF, 2013).

The study covers all the *upazilas* that practise commercial shrimp farming. Each *upazila* is considered as an observation unit, resulting in 62 observation units for the two time periods analysed. Shrimp farming is commonly practised in the coastal districts, with over 90 per cent of all farms in Bangladesh using an extensive shrimp farming system, which is a low-input, low-output system. The environmental-economic assessment will be carried at *upazila* level because environmental data were available only at this level, which is the reason we treat *upazilas* as observation units in this study. Since data for undesirable outputs were only available at *upazila* level, per hectare cost and return data for shrimp farming needed to be transformed to *upazila* level so that those data corresponded directly with data on undesirable outputs.

For the purpose of measuring the efficiency of shrimp farming, three types of variables are considered: desirable outputs, inputs and undesirable outputs. Typically, desirable outputs are marketable goods, whereas undesirable outputs are those that have harmful effects on the environment.

12.4.1   Desirable Outputs

Gross return from shrimp farming was considered to be the desirable output. It is the average revenue from shrimp farming of an *upazila* and expressed in US$. The per hectare return for each *upazila* is multiplied by the respective shrimp farming area of that *upazila* to obtain its gross return. The average annual catch of subsistence fishery operations per *upazila* is considered to be another desirable output. This is a valuable activity that many households in the study area practise. However, one of the effects of shrimp farming is that it results in substantial loss of finfish and shellfish as a consequence of catching tiger shrimp (*Penaeus monodon*) fry along the length of the coastline. By-catch is a significant feature of catching tiger shrimp fry. This by-catch leads to large quantities of discarded fish that subsequently die. For every tiger shrimp fry collected, an estimated 160 fry of fish and other shrimps are lost (EJF, 2003; BFRI, 2002). Given that subsistence fish catch cannot be treated as an undesirable output – its reduction attributable to shrimp farming could, but data on that were not available – the quantity of average fish catch per household was treated as a desirable output. This ensures that in areas where subsistence fish catch has declined, the reduction in this desirable output is accounted for when calculating environmentally adjusted efficiency. Subsistence fish catch data were collected from Fisheries Statistical Yearbooks published by the Department of Fisheries of Bangladesh.

12.4.2 Inputs

Total cost (a price weighted quantity index of inputs) of shrimp farming is considered as input in this study. For each *upazila* the total cost was calculated by adding up the costs for individual inputs. Major items that were included in the total cost are labour, land rent, post larvae (shrimp seed), feed and fertilizer.[2] Average per hectare cost and return data were collected for each *upazila* from different secondary sources (Ahmed et al., 2008; Barman and Karim, 2007; BCAS, 2001; DOF, 2000, 2010; Feroz, 2009; Gordon et al., 2009; Islam, 2003b; Jahan, 2008; NACA, 2006, 2010; Nuruzzaman, 2006). The average per hectare data for an *upazila* were multiplied by the total shrimp farming area of that *upazila* (DOF, 2000, 2010; PDO-ICZMP, 2005). Consumer Price Index (CPI) was used to get the deflated real value for cost and return data.

12.4.3 Undesirable Outputs

It is widely perceived that shrimp farming is the main reason for increased soil salinity, impaired soil fertility and land degradation in Bangladesh (Deb, 1998; Islam, 2003a; Dutta and Iftekhar, 2004). Shrimp aquaculture has raised serious concerns about the impact of saltwater intrusion into the surrounding agricultural lands (Flaherty and Karnjakesom, 1995; Flaherty and Vandergeest, 1998). Soil salinity in shrimp growing areas is in the order of five times higher than in areas where shrimp are not grown (Islam et al., 1999). Therefore, soil salinity is considered as one of the undesirable outputs for the present study. The percentage of soil affected by salinity is calculated by considering the land area that has a salinity level of 4 dS/m or more as a proportion of the total land area for that *upazila*.[3] The data for soil salinity were collected from the Soil Research Development Institute (SRDI, 2000, 2010) and the Bangladesh Fisheries Research Institute (BFRI, 2002).

The need for saltwater for shrimp farming is satisfied by digging narrow canals to carry seawater to the farms during the shrimp-growing season. This practice significantly affects the surrounding freshwater bodies through intrusion of saline water (BCAS, 2001; Islam, 2003a; Chowdhury et al., 2006). Moreover, the brackish water from shrimp farms infiltrates the surrounding areas through seepage and inundation, increasing the salinity of ground and surface water (EJF, 2004; Shamsuddin et al., 2006). This is also affecting freshwater fish farming, irrigation and drinking water, and can contribute to transmitting waterborne diseases. Therefore, surface water salinity is considered as another undesirable output in this study. Surface water salinity is measured in electric conductivity (EC) of water in different water bodies in a particular *upazila*. The data for water salinity were collected from the Department of the Environment, the BFRI and from a study by Ahmed et al. (2010).

Shrimp culture is often regarded as the silent destroyer of mangrove forests (Primavera, 1994; NACA, 1995; Deb, 1998; Gain, 1998; Barbier and Cox, 2004). Many coastal areas of Khulna, Barisal, Patuakhali and Chittagong were once ornamented with dense mangrove vegetation, but mangroves over large areas have been cleared and converted to other land uses, particularly to shrimp farming (Deb, 1998). In the southeastern parts of Bangladesh an area of 18,200 ha of mangrove (Chakaria Sundarbans) has almost completely been destroyed to make way for shrimp aquaculture (Akhtaruzzaman, 2000). Consequently, loss of mangrove forest is considered to be one of the undesirable outputs for the present study. However, as most of the mangrove forest destruction took place before 2000, and there has been no evidence of further significant decrease of mangrove forest in Bangladesh post-2000, it is expected that this variable will have a limited influence on environmental efficiency scores of shrimp farms over the considered sample period (Shahid and Islam, 2003; Emch and Peterson, 2006; Giri et al., 2008). Consequently, mangrove destruction was only taken into account for a few *upazilas* where it was proven that shrimp farming was responsible for the destruction. In those cases, the percentage loss of mangrove forest is accounted as the variable for mangrove loss. The data for mangrove forest area were collected from the Department of Forestry in Bangladesh and the Bangladesh Space Research and Remote Sensing Organization (SPARRSO).

In summary, the following variables were used in the present study: gross return from shrimp farming and subsistence fish catch per household are considered as desirable outputs (y); proportion of soil salinity affected land area, water salinity in EC units and loss of mangrove forests area are considered as undesirable outputs (*b*); total cost of shrimp farming is considered as input variable (*x*). Aggregated descriptive statistics by district of the included variables are presented in Table 12.1.

12.5 RESULTS

A summary of the empirical findings on the efficiency of shrimp farming under the considered four models is presented in Table 12.2, displaying the aggregated efficiency scores by district. The detailed disaggregated results, displaying efficiency scores for all *upazilas* from all four models, are presented in Appendix Table 12A.1.

Table 12.2 shows that the efficiency level across eight shrimp farming districts ranges from 80 per cent to 100 per cent in the case of Model 1, *g* = (1, −1), which credits both expansion of desirable outputs and contraction of undesirable outputs. At a disaggregate level in 2000, shrimp farming in seven *upazilas* attained the best practice frontier, while most of the *upazilas* were exhibiting up to 20 per cent inefficiency. This implies that there is substantial scope for improvement in both economic and environmental efficiency. In the Khulna district, the average efficiency score was 0.796 in the year 2000 – that is, shrimp farming was only 80 per cent efficient. However, the average environmentally adjusted efficiency across *upazilas* in Khulna dropped to 73 per cent in 2010, implying an efficiency loss of 7 per cent in a decade. The other two districts of the southwest region, Bagerhat and Satkhira, had average efficiency levels of 93 per cent and 84 per cent respectively in 2000. The efficiency score for these two districts was 88 per cent in 2010; i.e. the average efficiency level of shrimp farms in Bagerhat slightly worsened, and in Satkhira it slightly improved (see Table 12.2). On the other hand, the *upazilas* within Cox's Bazar and the Chittagong districts in the southeast region had average efficiencies of 86 per cent and 81 per cent respectively in 2000, and attained an increased level of efficiency in 2010– 93 per cent and 100 per cent respectively. A positive rate of efficiency change indicates an outward shift towards the best practice frontier. In these districts, there is no competition for land with other alternative uses (such as rice farming), and farms are situated in a naturally saline belt, adjacent to the sea; the soil and water are naturally suitable for shrimp farming. Therefore, environmental degradation due to shrimp farming has been of much less concern in this region.

Model 2 produced similar relative patterns of average environmentally adjusted efficiency scores (see Table 12.2), although at different levels. In Model 2, the magnitudes of efficiencies are lower compared to Model 1.

Table 12.1 Descriptive statistics of shrimp farms and the associated environmental effects by districts in Bangladesh

District	Shrimp area (ha)		Gross return (US$/ha/year)		Total cost (US$/ha/year)		% of salinity affected area		Water salinity (EC units)		Mangrove forest area (ha)		Annual fish catch (kg/household/ upazila)	
	2000	2010	2000	2010	2000	2010	2000	2010	2000	2010	2000	2010	2000	2010
Khulna (6)	37,630	36,235	1986	3333	1362	2287	69	70	13–27	15–34	181,600	189,993	31.26	23.61
Bagerhat (7)	42,941	46,571	1680	2778	1032	1852	61	65	0.5–22	4–26	230,919	243,145	27.4	29.21
Satkhira (6)	51,537	64,761	1919	2963	1282	1978	64	67	12–33	17–36	164,525	167,348	34.2	25.87
Jessore (2)	34	825	1704	2315	1204	1589	11	16	5–7	15–22	0	0	24.45	66.78
Cox's Bazar (5)	29,048	51,334	2088	3703	1370	2104	29	34	23–39	32–49	133,731	132,063	29.46	53.38
Chittagong (2)	1548	2895	1861	2407	1278	1709	17	28	2–3	2–6	66802	82,773	22.82	69.88
Patuakhali (2)	2821	1630	1717	2170	1149	1461	44	50	1–32	2–30	16882	33,085	53.22	42.52
Pirojpur (1)	2623	240	1623	2183	901	1391	21	28	7–9	10–12	989	2429	28.56	24.87

Table 12.2 Average efficiency scores across shrimp farms within districts obtained from directional distance functions

District	Model 1 (g = 1, −1)			Model 2 (g = 1, 0)			Model 3 (g = 0, −1)			Model 4 (g = 1)		
	2000	2010	% change	2000	2010	% change	2000	2010	% change	2000	2010	% change
Khulna	0.796	0.732	−6.4	0.756	0.711	−4.5	0.453	0.277	−17.5	0.593	0.630	3.38
Bagerhat	0.931	0.880	−5.08	0.941	0.875	−6.5	0.716	0.504	−21.2	0.793	0.778	−1.5
Satkhira	0.839	0.879	4.05	0.819	0.867	4.8	0.519	0.406	−11.6	0.657	0.746	8.8
Jessore	1	1	0	1	1	0	1	1	0	0.939	0.727	−21
Cox's Bazar	0.855	0.932	7.7	0.852	0.931	7.8	0.518	0.713	19.6	0.680	0.727	4.7
Chittagong	0.805	1	19.4	0.560	1	43	0.676	1	32.4	0.319	0.571	25.18
Patuakhali	0.914	1	8.6	0.932	1	6.8	0.555	1	44.5	0.692	0.432	−26.03
Pirojpur	1	0.624	−37.6	1	0.532	−46.8	1	0.415	−58.4	.909	0.480	−42.85

Note: The efficiency scores are presented as a calculation of (1−β).

The reason is that credit was given only for expanding the desirable outputs, while undesirable outputs were held constant rather than contracting as in Model 1.

All calculated efficiency scores were much lower when desirable outputs were held constant and only a movement towards the frontier in the direction of reducing undesirable outputs was considered (Model 3). This indicates that, in general, all *upazilas* considered in the sample are far from the efficiency frontier when it comes to purely environmental performance, and that there is substantial room for improvement in that direction. Specifically, the *upazilas* in Khulna show a very poor average environmental performance (only 45 per cent efficient in 2000), which even worsened over time (only 27 per cent efficient in 2010). The *upazilas* in Jessore, Cox's Bazar, Chittagong and Patuakhali on the other hand show an improvement of environmental performance over time. Given that shrimp farming is relatively new in the Jessore district, the high score of this district indicates that the environmental impacts have not yet been significant enough to be reflected in the efficiency scores.

The calculated efficiency scores when undesirable outputs are completely ignored (Model 4, corresponding to the strong disposability assumption) are relatively lower. This indicates that shrimp farming *upazilas* are not technically efficient, as observations are well below the efficiency frontier when considering only desirable outputs. However, as discussed earlier, if we measure efficiency by considering desirable outputs only, when in fact undesirable outputs are present in the production process, the resulting efficiency scores are erroneous. In Model 4, shrimp farming in the southern districts of Patuakhali and Pirojpur are particularly inefficient in terms of technical efficiency. This may explain why there has been a recent dwindling trend in shrimp farming area in these districts. For example, the shrimp farming area in Pirojpur district was some 2600 ha in 2000, and it declined to 240 ha in 2010. Similarly, the shrimp farming area in Patuakhali district was some 2800 ha in 2000 and dropped to some 1600 ha in 2010. Shrimp farming in Chittagong district also shows poor economic performance, but there is an improvement over time. It is noticeable that shrimp farming in Khulna shows an average positive change in economic performance (Model 4), but when environmental factors are considered in the other three models, the change in performance over time is poor. This indicates that environmental factors are significantly affecting the efficiency of shrimp farming.

As expected, the efficiency scores vary across the four models considered. Models that take into account undesirable outputs and either measure the potential for their reduction (Model 1) or hold them constant (Model 2) while at the same time measuring the potential to increase desirable output produce similar efficiency scores in a given time period. The efficiency scores are higher than those in the other two models where either only environmental performance (Model 3) or only economic performance (Model 4) is considered.

Although the shrimp farms are following the same technology (extensive farming system) across regions, the bio-physical characteristics in the specific locations have an impact on the estimated technical efficiency. In the southwest and southern regions, shrimp farming is practised on land that was previously used for crop cultivation. Therefore, environmental degradation due to shrimp farming is a concern in these regions, adversely affecting the efficiency of shrimp farms. On the other hand, shrimp farms in the southeast region are situated on naturally saline land which has no alternative uses. Hence, shrimp farming results in relatively small environmental consequences in this region.

The errors in efficiency measurement that can be attributed to the existence of undesirable outputs are presented in Table 12.3, which shows aggregated inefficiency scores by district. The same directional vectors for desirable outputs are considered for this comparison. It is evident from the table that there is a wide variation in measuring efficiency when alternative assumptions are considered. When weak disposability assumption is considered in measuring efficiency the result shows higher efficiency scores compared to the efficiency scores that followed strong disposability assumption. This implies that in an economic-environmental assessment, environmental factors play an important role in evaluating efficiency of the farms. If these factors are not considered, their performance might be underestimated. The errors in measurement at a disaggregated *upazila* level are presented in Appendix Table 12A.2.

Table 12.3   *Error in estimated inefficiency score due to considering strong disposability assumption instead of weak disposability assumption*

District	$\vec{D}_0\,(y,b,x;1,0)$		$\vec{D}_0(y,x;1)$		Error in efficiency	
	2000	2010	2000	2010	2000	2010
Khulna	0.2435	0.2892	0.4043	0.37049	0.1608	0.0813
Bagerhat	0.0592	0.1246	0.2069	0.2218	0.1477	0.0971
Satkhira	0.1814	0.1332	0.3429	0.2544	0.1616	0.1211
Cox's Bazar	0.1479	0.0691	0.3201	0.2729	0.1721	0.2038
Chittagong	0.4399	0	0.6806	0.4287	0.2406	0.4287
Jessore	0	0	0.0612	0.27294	0.0612	0.2729
Patuakhali	0.0683	0	0.3078	0.5682	0.2394	0.5682
Pirojpur	0	0.4685	0.0909	0.5195	0.0909	0.0510

12.6 CONCLUSIONS

The overall economic and environmental performance of shrimp farming is of great importance for Bangladesh, given the significance of this industry to the economic life of the country and to its environmental health. The estimated efficiency values in this chapter reflect both the economic performance and the environmental performance of shrimp farms as the estimation considers models that sequentially include and exclude undesirable outputs in the production technology. Using directional distance functions, this study measured the efficiency of the shrimp farming industry. Four different directional vectors are used to evaluate the possible directions for improving economic and environmental performance of shrimp enterprises. The results show that there is a significant variation in efficiency when different directions of movement towards the efficiency frontier are considered. The results also show that there is a significant difference of efficiency when weak and strong disposability assumptions are considered, and there is a room for improvement of both economic and environmental performance. The efficiency errors (EEs) show that environmentally adjusted efficiency should be considered in order to accurately reflect the performance of shrimp farming.

Existing public policy on shrimp production in Bangladesh does not adequately address the need of the industry to improve its environmental and economic performance. Environmental performance is a great concern for the southwest region, which includes the Khulna, Bagerhat and Satkhira districts. Therefore, more focus should be given on improving the environmental performance of shrimp farming in this region. Environmentally adjusted efficiency measurement can help policy makers to take steps to increase overall efficiency of the farms. The current policy does not give farmers any incentives for reducing undesirable outputs, and without incentives the farmers are not going to change their practices, as undesirable outputs have no direct effect on their own production. Farmers should be motivated by incentive-based policies to reduce undesirable outputs and to adopt and develop new environmentally friendly production methods.

Conversely, farms in the southeast region (Cox's Bazar and Chittagong districts) are doing fairly well in terms of environmental issues, and more focus should be given to improve their economic performance, especially in Chittagong. The experience and information from the identified high-performing *upazilas* (e.g. Moheshkhali and Ukhiya) can be shared and exchanged with the low-performing *upazilas* (e.g. Bashkhali and Anowara) to improve their operation. For some districts (e.g. Pirojpur), focus should be given to both economic and environmental improvement. Emphasis should be put on those *upazilas* where the overall improvement can be made with lower cost in terms of shrimp revenue foregone. The findings from this study could provide the basis for implementing more region-specific policies for the shrimp industry, which will be useful to improve environmental performance of shrimp farms in conjunction with their economic performance.

NOTES

1. Sub-unit of district or sub-district. It is a geographical region used for administrative or other purposes.
2. The individual cost items for each sub-district are not presented here for brevity, but are available from the authors upon request.
3. Deci Siemens per meter (dS/m) is an electrical conductivity unit to measure soil salinity: 1 dS/m 5 1000 μS/cm.

REFERENCES

Ahmed, N., J.H. Brown and J.F. Muir (2008), 'Freshwater prawn farming in gher systems in southwest Bangladesh', *Aquaculture Economics and Management*, **12**(3), 207–223.
Ahmed, M.J., M.R. Haque, A. Ahsan, S. Siraj, M.H.R. Bhuiyan, S.C. Bhattacharjee and S. Islam (2010), 'Physiochemical assessment of surface and groundwater quality of the greater Chittagong region of Bangladesh', *Pakistan Journal of Analytical and Environmental Chemistry*, **11**(2), 1–11.
Akhtaruzzaman, A.F.M. (2000), 'Mangrove forestry research in Bangladesh', Paper presented at the Research for Conservation of Mangroves International Workshop, Asia-Pacific Corporation, 26–30 March, Okinawa, Japan.
Ball, E., R. Färe, S. Grosskopf and R. Nehring (1998), 'Productivity of the U.S. agricultural sector: the case of undesirable outputs', Paper presented at the Conference on Research in Income and Wealth: New Developments in Productivity Analysis, 20–21 March, Maryland.
Bangladesh Bureau of Statistics (2010), *Statistical Yearbook of Bangladesh*, Bangladesh Bureauof Statistics (BBS), Government of the People's Republic of Bangladesh.
Banks, R. (2002), 'Brackish and marine water aquaculture', Report from the Fisheries Sector Review, Department for International Development (DFID), Bangladesh.
Barbier, E.B. and M. Cox (2004), 'An economic analysis of shrimp farm expansion and mangrove conversion in Thailand', *Land Economics*, **80**(3), 389–407.
Barman, B.K. and M. Karim (2007), 'Analysis of feeds and fertilizers for sustainable aquaculture development in Bangladesh', in M.R. Hasan, T. Hecht, S.S. De Silva and A.G.J. Tacon (eds), *Study and Analysis of Feeds and Fertilizers for Sustainable Aquaculture Development*, Rome: UN Food and Agriculture Organization (FAO), pp. 113–140.

BCAS (2001), 'The cost and benefit of *bagda* shrimp farming in Bangladesh: an economic, financial and livelihood assessment', Prepared as part of the Fourth Fisheries Project by the Bangladesh Centre for Advanced Studies (BCAS), August, Dhaka, p. 143.

Bellenger, M.J. and A.T. Herlihy (2009), 'An economic approach to environmental indices', *Ecological Economics*, **68**(8), 2216–2223.

BFRI (2002), 'Studies on the impact of shrimp farming on mangrove and estuarine environment of greater Khulna', Final report, Bangladesh Fisheries Research Institute, Brackishwater Station, Paikgacha, Khulna.

Bhattacharya, D., M. Rahman and F.A. Khatun (1999), *Environmental Impacts of Trade Liberalization and Policies for the Sustainable Management of Natural Resources: A Case Study on Bangladesh's Shrimp Farming Industry*, New York: United Nations Environmental Programme (UNEP).

Chambers, R.G. (1998), 'Input and output indicators', in Färe, R., S. Grosskopf and R.R. Russell (eds), *Index Numbers: Essays in Honour of Sten Malmquist*, Boston: Kluwer Academic Publishers, pp. 241–271.

Chambers, R.G., Y. Chung and R. Färe (1996), 'Benefit and distance functions', *Journal of Economic Theory*, **70**(2), 407–419.

Chambers, R.G., Y. Chung and R. Färe (1998), 'Profit, directional distance functions and Nerlovian efficiency', *Journal of Optimization Theory and Applications*, **98**(2), 351–364.

Chowdhury, M.A., G.P. Shivakoti and M. Salequzzaman (2006), 'A conceptual framework for the sustainability assessment procedures of the shrimp aquaculture industry in coastal Bangladesh', *International Journal of Agricultural Resources, Governance and Ecology*, **5**(2/3), 162–184.

Chung, Y., R. Färe, and S. Grosskopf (1997), 'Productivity and undesirable outputs: a directional distance function approach', *Journal of Environmental Management*, **51**(3), 229–240.

Deb, A.K. (1998), 'Fake blue revolution: environmental and socioeconomic impact of shrimp culture in the coastal areas of Bangladesh', *Ocean and Coastal Management*, **41**(1), 63–88.

DOF (2000, 2010, 2013), *Fishery Statistical Yearbook of Bangladesh*, Department of Fisheries, Dhaka.

Dutta, A.K. and M.S. Iftekhar (2004), 'Tree species survival of the homestead forests of salt affected areas: a perception analysis for Bangladesh', *Journal of Biological Sciences*, **4**(3), 309–313.

EJF (2003), 'Smash and grab: conflict, corruption and human rights abuses in the shrimp farming industry', Report by the Environmental Justice Foundation (EJF) in partnership with WildAid, London.

EJF (2004), 'Desert in the delta: a report on the environmental, human rights and social impacts of shrimp production in Bangladesh', Report by the Environmental Justice Foundation (EJF), London.

EPB (2014), *Bangladesh Export Statistics*, Export Promotion Bureau (EPB), Ministry of Commerce, Government of the People's Republic of Bangladesh, Dhaka.

Färe, R. and S. Grosskopf (2004), *New Directions: Efficiency and Productivity*. Springer, New York.

Färe, R., S. Grosskopf, C.A.K. Lovell and C. Pasurka (1989), 'Multilateral productivity comparisons when some outputs are undesirable: a non-parametric approach', *Review of Economics and Statistics*, **71**(1), 90–98.

Färe, R., S. Grosskopf, C.A.K. Lovell and S. Yaisawarng (1993), 'Derivation of shadow prices for undesirable outputs: a distance function approach', *Review of Economics and Statistics*, **75**(2), 374–380.

Färe, R., S. Grosskopf, D.W. Noh and W. Weber (2005), 'Characteristics of a polluting technology: theory and practice', *Journal of Econometrics*, **126**(2), 469–492.

Färe, R., S. Grosskopf and C. Pasurka, (2001), 'Accounting for air pollution emissions in measures of state manufacturing productivity growth', *Journal of Regional Sciences*, **41**(3), 381–409.

Färe, R., J.E. Kirkley and J.B. Walden (2006), 'Adjusting technical efficiency to reflect discarding: the case of the U.S. Georges Bank multi-species otter trawl fishery', *Fisheries Research*, **78**(2–3), 257–265.

Feroz, A.N.M.W. (2009), 'An economic study on shrimp farming and its environmental effects in selected areas of Satkhira district', MS thesis, Department of Agricultural Economics, Bangladesh Agricultural University, Mymensingh.

Flaherty, M. and C. Karnjanakesorn (1995), 'Marine shrimp aquaculture and natural resource degradation in Thailand', *Environmental Management*, **19**(1), 27–37.

Flaherty, M. and P. Vandergeest (1998), '"Low-salt" shrimp aquaculture in Thailand: goodbye coastline, hello Khon Kaen!', *Environmental Management*, **22**(6), 817–835.

Emch, M. and M. Peterson (2006), 'Mangrove forest cover change in the Bangladesh Sundarbans from 1989–2000: a remote sensing approach', *Geocarto International*, **21**(1), 5–12.

Gain, P. (1998), 'Shrimp for export-symbol of destruction in Bangladesh', in Gain, P. and S. Molal (eds), *Bangladesh Environment: Facing the 21st Century*, Society for Environment and Human Development (SEHD), Dhaka, Bangladesh.

GAMS (2011), 'GAMS Distribution 24.1.3', downloaded from www.gams.com/download/.

Giri, C., Z. Zhu, L.L. Tieszen, A. Singh, S. Gillette and J.A. Kelmelis (2008), 'Mangrove forest distributions and dynamics (1975–2005) of the tsunami-affected region of Asia', *Journal of Biogeography*, **35**(3), 519–528.

GOB (2015), 'Bangladesh national portal', Government of the People's Republic of Bangladesh, www.bangladesh.gov.bd.

Gordon, D.V., T Bjørndal, D. Madan, and R.K. Talukder (2009), 'An intra-farm study of production factors and productivity for shrimp farms in Bangladesh: an index approach', *Marine Resource Economics*, **23**(4), 411–424.

Gregow, K. (1997), 'When the trees are gone. Social and environmental costs of converting mangroves into shrimp fields: a case study from Chakoria Sundarbans', UBINIG, Dhaka.

Haque, A.K.E. (2004), 'Sanitary and phyto-sanitary barriers to trade and its impact on the environment: the case of shrimp farming in Bangladesh', Trade Knowledge Network paper, International Institute for Sustainable Development, Canada.

Islam, M.S. (2003a), 'Perspectives of the coastal and marine fisheries of the Bay of Bengal, Bangladesh', *Ocean and Coastal Management*, **46**(8), 763–796.

Islam, M.S. (2003b), 'Socioeconomic impacts of alternate shrimp-shrimp-crop farming in Bangladesh', in Wahab, M.A. (ed.), *Environmental and socioeconomic impacts of shrimp farming in Bangladesh*, Bangladesh Agricultural University. Mymensingh, pp. 61–78.

Islam, M.A., M.A. Sattar and M.S. Alam (1999), 'Impact of shrimp farming on soil and water quality of some selected areas in the greater Khulna district', Research and Development Collective, Dhaka, Bangladesh.

Jahan, H. (2008), 'Socioeconomic and environmental impacts of shrimp farming: a case study in the southwest coast of Bangladesh', MS thesis, Graduate School of Asia Pacific Studies, Ritsumeikan Asia Pacific University, Japan.

Karim, M.R. (2003), 'Present status and strategies for future development of shrimp farming in Bangladesh', in Wahab, M.A. (ed.), *Environmental and Socioeconomic Impacts of Shrimp Farming in Bangladesh*, Bangladesh Agricultural University, Mymensingh, pp. 1–8.

Luenberger, D.G. (1992), 'Benefit functions and duality', *Journal of Mathematical Economics*, **21**(5), 461–481.

Macpherson, A.J., P.P. Principe and E.R. Smith (2010), 'A directional distance function approach to regional environmental-economic assessments', *Ecological Economics*, **69**(10), 1918–1925.

Murty, S., R.R. Russell and S.B. Levkoff (2012), 'On modeling pollution-generating technologies', *Journal of Environmental Economics and Management*, **64**(1), 117–135.

NACA (1995), 'Impact of shrimp farming on the environment: study 1', Network of Aquaculture Centres in Asia-Pacific, sixth meeting of the governing council (Beijing, 26–29 October 1994), GCM-6/REF 04, Bangkok.

NACA (2006), 'Evaluation of the impact of the Indian Ocean tsunami and US anti-dumping duties on the shrimp farming sector of South and South-East Asia: case studies in Vietnam, Indonesia and Bangladesh', Network of Aquaculture Centres in Asia-Pacific in collaboration with Can Tho University (Vietnam), Department of Marine Affairs and Fisheries (Indonesia) and PMTC Bangladesh Ltd.

NACA (2010), 'Shrimp price study, phase II: case studies in Vietnam, Indonesia and Bangladesh', Network of Aquaculture Centres in Asia-Pacific.

Nijera, K. (1996), 'The impact of shrimp cultivation on soils and environment in Paikgacha region, Khulna (limited to polders 20, 21, 22, 23 and 29)', Report prepared for Nijera Kori by Environment Study Centre, Dhaka, Bangladesh.

Nuruzzaman, M. (2006), 'Dynamics and diversity of shrimp farming in Bangladesh: technical aspects', in Rahman, A.A., A.H.G. Quddus, B. Pokrant and M.L. Ali (eds), *Shrimp Farming and Industry: Sustainability, Trade and Livelihoods*, University Press, Dhaka, Bangladesh.

Picazo-Tadeo, A.J., E. Reig-Martínez and F. Hernández-Sancho (2005), 'Directional distance functions and environmental regulation', *Resource and Energy Economics*, **27**(2), 131–142.

Primavera, H.J. (1994), 'Environmental and socio-economic effects of shrimp farming: the Philippine experience', *Infofish International*, **1**, 44–51.

PDO-ICZMP (2005), 'Coastal land use and indicative land zones', Working paper WP 040, Program Development Office for Integrated Coastal Zone Management Plan, Bangladesh.

Rahman, A.A., A.H.G. Quddus, B. Pokrant and M.L. Ali (2006), *Shrimp Farming and Industry: Sustainability, Trade and Livelihoods*, University Press, Dhaka, Bangladesh.

Shahid, M.A. and J. Islam (2003), 'Impact of denudation of mangrove forest due to shrimp farming on coastal environment in Bangladesh', in Wahab, M.A. (ed.),

Environmental and Socioeconomic Impacts of Shrimp Farming in Bangladesh, Bangladesh Agricultural University; Mymensingh, pp. 49–60.

Shamsuddin, S., C. Xiaoyong and M.K. Hazarika (2006), 'Evaluation of groundwater quality for irrigation in Bangladesh using geographic information system', *Journal of Hydrology and Hydromechanics*, **54**(1), 3–14.

Shephard, R.W. (1970), *Theory of Cost and Production Functions*, Princeton University Press, Princeton.

SRDI (2000, 2010), *Soil Salinity in Bangladesh*, Soil Resource Development Institute, Ministry of Agriculture, Bangladesh.

Tyteca, D. (1996), 'On the measurement of the environmental performance of farms: a literature review and a productive efficiency perspective', *Journal of Environmental Management*, **46**(3), 281–308.

Umamaheswar, L., K.O. Hattab, P. Nasurudeen and P. Selvaraj (2009), 'Should shrimp farmers pay paddy farmers? The challenges of examining salinisation externalities in south India', SANDEE working paper no. 41–09.

USAID (2006), 'A pro-poor analysis of the shrimp sector in Bangladesh', U.S. Agency for International Development, Washington DC.

Wahab, M.A., A. Bergheim and B. Braaten (2003), 'Water quality and partial mass budget in extensive shrimp ponds in Bangladesh', *Aquaculture*, **218**(1–4), 413–423.

Watanabe, M. and K. Tanaka (2007), 'Efficiency analysis of Chinese industry: a directional distance function approach', *Energy Policy*, **35**(12), 6323–6331.

APPENDIX

Linear Programming Problems for Models 2, 3 and 4

Model 2

$$\vec{D}_o(x^{k'}, y^{k'}, b^{k'}; g_y, 0) = \max \beta$$

s.t.

$$\sum_{k=1}^{K} z_k y_{km} \geq (1 + \beta) y_{k'm}, m = 1, ..., M$$

$$\sum_{k=1}^{K} z_k b_{ki} = b_{k'i}, i = 1, ..., I$$

$$\sum_{k=1}^{K} z_k x_{kn} \leq x_{k'n}, n = 1, ..., N$$

$$z_k \geq 0, k = 1, ... K$$

Model 3

$$\vec{D}_o(x^{k'}, y^{k'}, b^{k'}; 0, -g_b) = \max \beta$$

s.t.

$$\sum_{k=1}^{K} z_k y_{km} \geq y_{k'm}, m = 1, ..., M$$

$$\sum_{k=1}^{K} z_k b_{ki} = (1 - \beta) b_{k'i}, i = 1, ..., I$$

$$\sum_{k=1}^{K} z_k x_{kn} \leq x_{k'n}, n = 1, ..., N$$

$$z_k \geq 0, k = 1, ..., K$$

Model 4

$$\vec{D}_o(x^{k'}, y^{k'}; g_y) = \max \beta$$

s.t.

$$\sum_{k=1}^{K} z_k y_{km} \geq (1 + \beta) y_{k'm}, m = 1, ..., M$$

$$\sum_{k=1}^{K} z_k x_{kn} \leq x_{k'n}, n = 1, ..., N$$

$$z_k \geq 0, k = 1, ..., K$$

Table 12A.1   Efficiency of shrimp farms in different upazilas of Bangladesh

District	Sub-district	Model 1	Model 2	Model 3	Model 4
2000					
Khulna	Paikgacha	0.971	0.941	0.944	0.632
	Dacope	0.842	0.823	0.571	0.618
	Koyra	0.758	0.722	0.293	0.644
	Dumuria	0.765	0.711	0.390	0.629
	Batiaghata	0.704	0.682	0.214	0.636
	Rupsa	0.736	0.660	0.305	0.415
Bagerhat	Bagerhat sadar	0.952	0.946	0.663	0.769
	Rampal	0.964	0.961	0.728	0.774
	Mongla	0.915	0.901	0.469	0.780
	Mollahat	1.000	1.000	1.000	1.000
	Chitalmari	0.837	0.971	0.516	0.676
	Morelganj	1.000	1.000	1.000	0.783
	Kochua	0.846	0.807	0.637	0.769
Satkhira	Satkhira sadar	0.793	0.789	0.334	0.692
	Tala	0.739	0.702	0.450	0.609
	Debhata	0.847	0.825	0.512	0.651
	Asasuni	0.884	0.868	0.646	0.657
	Shyamnagar	0.882	0.862	0.564	0.667
	Kaliganj	0.886	0.867	0.610	0.667
Cox's Bazar	Chakaria	0.936	0.928	0.769	0.691
	Moheshkhali	0.943	0.936	0.780	0.685
	Cox's Bazar sadar	0.799	0.793	0.314	0.703
	Teknaf	0.782	0.781	0.302	0.667
	Ukhiya	0.816	0.822	0.418	0.655
Chittagong	Bashkhali	0.841	0.637	0.725	0.289
	Anowara	0.770	0.483	0.626	0.350
Jessore	Keshobpur	1.000	1.000	1.000	0.878
	Avaynagar	1.000	1.000	1.000	1.000
Pirojpur	Nazirpur	1.000	1.000	1.000	0.909
Patuakhali	Galachipa	1.000	1.000	1.000	0.692
	Kalapara	0.827	0.863	0.110	0.692
2010					
Khulna	Paikgacha	0.865	0.843	0.614	0.626
	Dacope	0.651	0.652	0.119	0.639
	Koyra	0.720	0.706	0.206	0.633
	Dumuria	0.801	0.763	0.390	0.625
	Batiaghata	0.656	0.626	0.127	0.615
	Rupsa	0.701	0.675	0.210	0.638

Table 12A.1   (continued)

District	Sub-district	Model 1	Model 2	Model 3	Model 4
Bagerhat	Bagerhat sadar	0.913	0.899	0.483	0.778
	Rampal	0.933	0.923	0.555	0.769
	Mongla	0.884	0.862	0.381	0.763
	Mollahat	0.850	0.831	0.567	0.784
	Chitalmari	0.899	0.876	0.613	0.824
	Morelganj	0.920	0.907	0.524	0.775
	Kochua	0.759	0.829	0.404	0.756
Satkhira	Satkhira sadar	0.844	0.841	0.362	0.739
	Tala	0.847	0.844	0.357	0.754
	Debhata	0.877	0.854	0.381	0.747
	Asasuni	0.905	0.890	0.447	0.747
	Shyamnagar	0.885	0.865	0.391	0.741
	Kaliganj	0.917	0.906	0.498	0.746
Cox's Bazar	Chakaria	0.979	0.976	0.881	0.730
	Moheshkhali	1.000	1.000	1.000	0.735
	Cox's Bazar sadar	0.852	0.848	0.269	0.762
	Teknaf	0.831	0.830	0.417	0.700
	Ukhiya	1.000	1.000	1.000	0.709
Chittagong	Bashkhali	1.000	1.000	1.000	0.538
	Anowara	1.000	1.000	1.000	0.605
Jessore	Keshobpur	1.000	1.000	1.000	0.697
	Avaynagar	1.000	1.000	1.000	0.757
Pirojpur	Nazirpur	0.624	0.532	0.415	0.480
Patuakhali	Galachipa	1.000	1.000	1.000	0.341
	Kalapara	1.000	1.000	1.000	0.523

Table 12A.2   Errors in efficiency (inefficiency) measurement by upazila

Upazila	Model 2	Model 4	M4−M2	Model 2	Model 4	M4−M2
		2000			2010	
Paikgacha	0.0593	0.3678	0.3084	0.1574	0.37404	0.2166
Dacope	0.1766	0.3818	0.2052	0.3484	0.36054	0.0121
Koyra	0.2777	0.3559	0.0782	0.2939	0.36667	0.0727
Dumuria	0.2892	0.3714	0.0822	0.2366	0.375	0.1384
Batiaghata	0.3183	0.3636	0.0453	0.3740	0.38461	0.0106
Rupsa	0.3397	0.5851	0.2454	0.3249	0.3621	0.0371
B Sadar	0.0538	0.2307	0.1769	0.1011	0.2222	0.1211
Rampal	0.0393	0.2258	0.1865	0.0766	0.2307	0.1542
Mongla	0.0989	0.2195	0.1205	0.1381	0.2368	0.0987
Mollahat	0	0	0	0.1691	0.2162	0.0471
Chitalmari	0.0285	0.3239	0.2954	0.1240	0.1765	0.0524
Morrelganj	0	0.2173	0.2174	0.0927	0.2253	0.1326
Kochua	0.1933	0.2307	0.0374	0.1708	0.2444	0.0736
S Sadar	0.2110	0.3076	0.0967	0.1585	0.2607	0.1023
Tala	0.2984	0.3913	0.0928	0.1562	0.2459	0.0897
Debhata	0.1747	0.3488	0.1741	0.1455	0.2533	0.1077
Asasuni	0.1324	0.3432	0.2108	0.1095	0.2525	0.1429
Shyamnagar	0.1383	0.3333	0.1949	0.1352	0.2592	0.1241
Kaliganj	0.1333	0.3333	0.1999	0.0944	0.2542	0.1598
Chakaria	0.0724	0.3093	0.2368	0.0235	0.2698	0.2463
Moheshkhali	0.0640	0.3148	0.2507	0	0.2655	0.2655
C sadar	0.2066	0.2973	0.0906	0.1522	0.2381	0.0858
Teknaf	0.2186	0.3333	0.1147	0.1696	0.3	0.1304
Ukhiya	0.1778	0.3454	0.1676	0	0.2912	0.2912
Bashkhali	0.3633	0.7111	0.3478	0	0.4623	0.4623
Anowara	0.5165	0.65	0.1334	0	0.3951	0.3951
Keshobpur	0	0.1225	0.1225	0	0.3028	0.3028
Avaynagar	0	0	0	0	0.2430	0.2430
Nazirpur	0	0.0909	0.0909	0.4685	0.5195	0.0510
Galachipa	0	0.3077	0.3077	0	0.6591	0.6591
Kalapara	0.13674	0.3079	0.1712	0	0.4771	0.4773

Index